Stafford County, Virginia

Court Record Book

1749–1755

Jerrilynn Eby

HERITAGE BOOKS
2016

HERITAGE BOOKS

AN IMPRINT OF HERITAGE BOOKS, INC.

Books, CDs, and more—Worldwide

For our listing of thousands of titles see our website
at
www.HeritageBooks.com

Published 2016 by
HERITAGE BOOKS, INC.
Publishing Division
5810 Ruatan Street
Berwyn Heights, Md. 20740

Heritage Books by the author:

*Land of Herrings and Persimmons: People and
Places of Upper Stafford County, Virginia*

Land of Hogs and Wildcats: People and Places of Lower Stafford County, Virginia

Laying the Hoe: A Century of Iron Manufacturing in Stafford County, Virginia

Men of Mark: Officials of Stafford County, Virginia, 1664–1991

Stafford County, Virginia Court Record Book, 1749–1755

*Stafford County, Virginia Officials, 1664–1991: Taken from the
1783 Records in the Stafford County Courthouse*

*They Called Stafford Home: The Development of
Stafford County, Virginia, from 1600 until 1865*

International Standard Book Numbers
Paperbound: 978-0-7884-5689-3
Clothbound: 978-0-7884-6453-9

Introduction

As the inevitability of war became apparent, county officials throughout Virginia were faced with the predicament of protecting vital court records. No one could conceive of the length of the conflict or its utterly devastating consequences. Gravely concerned over the possibility of invasion by enemy troops, some counties chose to move their records to Richmond, which they believed would be the best defended area of the Commonwealth. They could hardly dream that Southern forces would set fire to the capitol city as they retreated from Union troops. Many county court records sent to Richmond as a precaution were thus lost.

In March of 1862, just prior to the arrival of tens of thousands of Union soldiers on Stafford soil, the county magistrates recorded in their minutes, "The Court having maturely considered the propriety of removing the record books and papers of the County to some safer point (and having advised with the Attorney for the Commonwealth and others) are of the opinion that the said records &c. shall not be removed under any contingency from said office and further are of the opinion that the Clerk of this Court ought not to be in any wise responsible for said records &c. should he think proper to leave said County on the approach of the enemy."

In a matter of weeks Gen. Sickles' Excelsior Brigade arrived in the area and some of its members conducted one of at least two devastating raids on Stafford's courthouse and clerk's office. An article in the *New York Times* of Dec. 11, 1862 described the damage:

> "...the Judge's bench [was] a target for the 'expectorating Yankee'; the circular inclosure [sic] occupied by the jury was besmeared with mud, and valuable documents, of every description scattered about the floor and yard...In one corner of the yard stands a house of records, in which were deposited all the important deeds and papers pertaining to this section for a generation past. When our advance entered the building, they were found lying about the floor to a depth of fifteen inches or more around the door-steps and in the door-yard. It is impossible to estimate the inconvenience and losses which will be incurred by this wholesale destruction of deeds, claims, mortgages, &c."

Few records were spared and what the vandals didn't destroy or ruin, they stole. Lost at this time was the court's colonial seal, the Bible used at the court bench, an unknown quantity of early loose papers, and a number of bound volumes of court records, stolen as souvenirs. After the peace, the Stafford magistrates endeavored to retrieve missing court record books as their whereabouts became known. In 1866 and 1868 two of these were located in

Maryland and brought back. At least one other found its way to the Huntington Library in California where, at the time of this writing, it remains.

On Mar. 30, 1863 Capt. William A. Treadwell of the 4th New York Infantry Regiment stole or otherwise obtained a court order book spanning the years 1749-1755. He noted this on the cover of the book and mailed it home. An undated note on the cover records that it was at some point presented to Charles H. Duff. The book passed down through several generations until the estate of former New Jersey State Senator William Brinkerhoff presented it to the Hudson County (New Jersey) Historical Society. From this collection it passed to the Jersey City Free Public Library's New Jersey Room. Recognizing that the old Virginia volume didn't fit within the scope of their collection, in October 2011 the library turned the tattered book over to representatives of the Library of Virginia. The library conserved the document and then scanned each page to make it available to researchers. A copy was placed in the Stafford County Clerk of Court's office.

It was routine for old court records to be re-copied as they became faded or damaged; that was one of the duties of the Clerk of Court. The volume taken by Capt. Treadwell is a transcription prepared in October 1791 "in a fair and legible hand" of the court minutes of 1749 to 1755. During the years that these records were generated, the magistrates met at one of several courthouses on the south side of Potomac Creek near Belle Plain. During this period, the courthouse was burned, rebuilt, and burned again; the rebuilding and second burning and the capture of the perpetrator are recorded in the minutes. The volume is a splendid source of genealogical material as well as providing fascinating insights into slavery, indentured servants, and law and criminal justice in the mid-eighteenth century. The abstracts here presented are fully indexed as an aid to researchers.

August Court 1749
At a Court held for Stafford County
August the 7th 1749

[Page 1]

Present   JOHN MERCER   RICHARD FOOTE
               JOHN PEYTON   JAMES WAUGH

PETER DANIEL Gent. took the several oaths of a Justice & subscribed the Test, which is ordered to be certified.

THOMAS MASSEY acknowledged his deeds of Lease & Release & rect. unto JOHN WASHINGTON which are committed to record.

Deeds of Lease & Release from THOMAS STUBBLEFIELD to JOHN HOOE Gent. together with Commission for the private examination of the said Thomas's Wife, and return thereon being returned are to be recorded.

JOHN DANIEL & FRANCES his Wife acknowledged their Deed of Feoffment unto BENJAMIN TYLER and is ordered to be recorded.

Release of Dower from MARGARET WAUGH Relect of WILLIAM WAUGH decd. to MICHAEL WALLACE is admitted to record.

JOHN THOMAS acknowledges discharge of his servant MOSES WALKER.

Action of Trespass. NATHANIEL GRAY agt. BENJAMIN GREEN for £100 damage by Green's breaking & entering the close of Gray in the Parish of St. Paul's. Ordered that the surveyor of this county in company of an able Jury of Freeholders do go upon the Lands in controversy & survey and lay off the same having regard to all Patents and Evidences as shall be produced by either of the parties & if the Jury find the Deft a Trespasser they are to value the damages & to report all matters of fact.

August Court 1749

The Inspectors at BOYD'S HOLE & ACQUIA & FUTURAL HALL constable took the oath prescribed by a late Act of Assembly.

Ordered that the several Guardians, Executors, & Administrators be summoned to appear at the next Court to make up their several accounts.

DURDLEY'S will proved by the witnesses & admitted to Record & Probate granted the Exor.

Ordered that JAMES HUGHS Tiths. be added to the List.

WILLIAM WALKER Gent. his Tiths. to be added to the List.

GEORGE MASON Gent. his Tiths to be added to the List.

JOHN FITZHUGH Gent. is appointed overseer of the Road in the room of CHARLES HINSON & is ordered to keep the same in repair.

WORDEN POPE'S Deed to HUGH HORTON proved by the oath of HOWSON HOOE & is ordered to be certified.

Ordered that HUGH HORTON pay HOWSON HOOE Junr. 136 pounds of Tobacco for one days attendance to prove POPE'S deed & for coming and returning 37 miles.

Ordered that the Court of KING GEORGE be applied to by JAMES WAUGH Gent. to have a road cleared from FALMOUTH to the County Line towards Potomack & from the FREE FERRY to PEARCHES.

In the said attachments obtained by JOHN PEYTON against the Estate of WILLIAM JONES the said John produced & made oath to an account against the said William for £1.15.6. John to recover the same from William & his costs. And it appearing to the Court that there is in the hands of FOUSHEE TEBBS sub Sheriff of Prince William County the sum of £1.7.2 of the estate of the said William. He is ordered to pay the same to the said John in part of satisfaction of the above Judgt.

ROBERT BARBER in Execution at the suit of RICHARD BARNARD Gent. by consent of the said Barnard gave in the following Schedule of his Estate, vizt. 1 cow, 1 sow, 6 shoats, 1 iron pot at ROWAN'S, 1 bed & bedstead, 2 piggens and

Iron Pot about 4 pounds which I have petitioned PATRICK ROWAN for, due from EVAN PRICE Senr. 5/., from PAUL

August Court 1749

SWENY 3/. From BALDWIN DADE 4/. From FUTURAL HALL 2/. From JOSEPH GOSS 2/3, & from COLCLOUGH STRIBLING one shilling which estate is ordered to be sold and the said BARBER is discharged out of Prison.

Inspectors nominated for BOYD'S HOLE, BALDWIN DADE, THOMAS BUNBERY, WITHERS CONWAY & JOHN BUCKNER. For CAVES, THOMAS HOWCOE, WILLIAM MOUNTJOY, JOHN RIDLEHURST & THOMAS DENT. For ACQUIA, TAYLOR CHAPMAN, EDWARD WALLER, TRAVERS COOK & RICHARD HEWITT.

JAMES MAHORNER in execution at the suit of ANDREW MONROE & COMPANY by consent of the said Andrew gives in the following Schedule of his Estate, Vizt. 1 old horse, 1 old Pewter Dish, 1 old Tray, 6 pewter spoons, 1 Fishing Net, 1 old Bench, 2 old Stools, 1 old Bedstead, which Estate is ordered to be sold & the said James is discharged out of Prison.

Suit of Attachment. CHARLES WALLER Gent. agt. the Estate of ANDREW DALTON. Said Charles produced and made oath to an account against the said Andrew for 1435 pounds Crop Tobo. Said Charles to recover the same from the said Andrew & his Costs & the Sheriff having made return that he had levied the said Attachment 1 Meal Bagg. It's ordered that he sell the same to satisfie the said Charles his Judgment.

THOMAS HENAGE is appointed Constable in the room of WILLIAM ROSE.

WILLIAM ROSS, CHARLES HARDING & THOMAS HENAGE Constables took the oath prescribed by Act of Assembly.

The Inspectors of Beef, Pork, Tar, Pitch &c before appointed.

Suit on Petition. JOHN HOOE Gent. agt. WILLIAM BAXTER. Dismist no appearance.

Suit on Petition. PHILIP ALEXANDER Gent. agt. NATHANIEL GRAY is Dismist being agreed.

Suit on Petition. CHARLES HARDING agt. HENRY WIGGINTON. Judgment is granted Harding for 275 pounds of Tobo. and Costs.

August Court 1749

Suit on Petition. HUMPHREY BELL, Merchant agt. GEORGE BRENT is continued till the next Court.

Suit on Petition. AMY POWELL agt. MASON FRENCH and MARGARET his Wife and of all & singular the goods and Chattels Rights & credits of THOMAS LACY decd. Judgment granted to Amy Powell for 40 shillings of the Goods and Chattels of the said Intestate in the hands of the said Admrs.

Suit on Petition. ROBERT BARBER agt. PATRICK ROWAN. Judgment granted to Barber for £1.8.6 & Costs.

Ordered that ROBERT BARBER pay MARY JOYCE 25 pounds of Tobo. for one days attendance as an Evidence for him against PATRICK ROWAN.

Suit on Scire Facias. JOSEPH PORTER agt. THOMAS STARKE is Dismist.

Action of Trespass. ROBERT RAE agt. THOMAS STRIBLING Admr. of WILLIAM STRIBLING, decd. On defendant's motion a special Imparlance is granted him till the next Court.

Action of Trespass. JOHN RALLS agt. JAMES PHILIPS is Dismist.

Action of Trespass Assault & Battery. JAMES MAHORNER agt. DANIEL FRENCH and others, the defendant French being arrested. Judgment is granted Mahorner against him & WITHERS CONWAY his Security unless he do appear at the next Court and answer the Pltf's Action.

Action of Debt. HAYWARD TODD agt. THOMAS STUBBLEFIELD. The Deft not appearing. Judgment granted Todd against him & ALEXANDER DONIPHAN & JOSIAH FURGERSON his Securitys unless he do appear at the next Court to answer the plaintiff's action.

August Court 1749

Action of Trespass. JOHN RALLS agt. THOMAS GREEN. Judgment granted to Ralls against Green and his security GEORGE WALLER unless the said defendant do appear at the next Court & answer the Pltf's Action.

Action of Debt. DARBY REDMAN agt. ROBERT IRONS abates by the defendant's living in PRINCE WILLIAM COUNTY.

Action of Detinue. NATHANIEL OVERALL agt. GEORGE ALLEN. Judgment granted to Overall against him & WILLIAM WEST his Security unless the said defendant do appear at the next Court & answer the Pltf's Action.

Ordered that MOSES WALKER pay SYLVESTER MOSS 150 pounds of Tobacco for six days attendance as an Evidence for him against JOHN THOMAS.

Then the Court adjourned till Court in Course.
JOHN MERCER

At a Court held for Stafford County September the 8th 1749.

Present   JOHN MERCER   PHILIP ALEXANDER
                JOHN PEYTON   PETER DANIEL

Ordered that JOHN WASHINGTON'S Tithables be added to the list.

CHARLES CARTER, Esqr. one of the Admrs. of HENRY FITZHUGH, Esqr. decd. produced and made oath to an account against the said Fitzhugh's Estate which is admitted to Record.

RAWLEIGH TRAVERS Guardian to GOWRY WAUGH made oath to an account against the said Gowry which is admitted to Record.

JAMES WAUGH Gent. Guardian to RICHARD and MASON FRENCH Orphans of HUGH FRENCH decd made Oath to his accounts against the said Orphans which are admitted to Record.

The Reverend WILLIAM STUART, Clk, one of the Exors. of DAVID STUART decd. produced and made oath to an Acct. against his Estate which is admitted to Record.

PETER DANIEL Gent. Exor. of HANNAH PEARSON decd. produced an Account against her Estate which is admitted to Record. The Tobo. therein mentioned is valued at 13/ pcent.

September Court 1749

Deeds from THOMAS MASSEY to JOHN WASHINGTON with the private examination of the said Massey's Wife is admitted to Record.

RICE HOOE Guardian to FRANCIS HOOE made oath to an account against his Estate, which is admitted to Record.

The settlement of HUTCHERSON'S Estate being returned is admitted to Record.

On complaint of ANN BLACK it's ordered that the Sheriff closely confine HANNAH BAYLIS, unless she enter into Bond in £20, with two Securities in £10 each for her good behavior for a year & a day.

ISBELL HARRISON is appointed Guardian to MARGARET, SARAH & MARY HARRISON Orphans of WILLIAM HARRISON Gent. decd. having entered into Bond with THOMAS MONROE & EDWARD WALLER his Securities.

SUSANNA HARRISON Orphan of WILLIAM HARRISON Gent. decd. came into Court and made choice of ISBELL HARRISON for her Guardian.

MARY MASON brought her indenture into Court & agreed to serve her Master JACOB WILLIAMS & his Wife the time mentioned in the said Indenture.

JOSEPH SMITH Exor. of MARY QUIDLY decd. returned an Inventory of the Estate.

ALEXANDER DONIPHAN Guardian to the Orphan of WILLIAM MCCARTY decd. produced and made oath to an account against the said Orphan's Estate and the Tobo. therein mentioned is valued at 14/ pcent.

ISBELL HARRISON Admx. of WILLIAM HARRISON Gent. decd presented and made oath to an account against the decd's Estate, which is allowed and the Tobo. is valued at 13/6 pCent.

Action of Detinue. NATHANIEL OVERALL agt. GEORGE ALLEN. JOHN SANDERSON & JOHN DAGG came into Court and undertook that if the defendant should be condemned in this Action that they would pay the condemnation for him or surrender his Body to Prison and the defendant on his motion has a Special Imparlance granted him.

JOHN RALLS hath his ordinary Licence renewed.

JAMES KENNY'S Tithables ordered to be added to the List.

[Page 7 Sept. 8, 1749]

September Court 1749

GERRARD FOWKE made oath to an account against the Estate of CHANDLER FOWKE Gent. decd & against the several orphans of the said Chandler which are admitted to record.

JOB SIMS is appointed overseer of the Road from HEDGMAN'S QUARTER by Northcuts to WALLER'S MILL.

ANN GRAY Servant to EDWARD RALLS came into Court and agreed to quit her Master her Freedom dues for a discharge having one year to serve which agreement the Court approved of.

Ordered that the several Guardians that appeared at this Court rendor at the next Court Accounts according to the Act of Assembly.

Administration on the Estate of JOHN RICE is granted to ANN RICE. RAWLEIGH TRAVERS & CHARLES BRENT Securities. PETER DANIEL, WILLIAM MOUNTJOY, THOMAS MOUNTJOY & THOMAS MONROE Appraisers.

Then the Court adjourned till Court in Course.

JOHN MERCER

At a Court held for Stafford County October the 10th day 1749.

Present   PHILIP ALEXANDER   RICHARD FOOTE
               MOTT DONIPHAN   JAMES WAUGH

Ordered that the Sheriff summon Twenty five Freeholders to appear at the next Court for a Grand Jury for the Body of this County.

BENJAMIN WOODWARD is discharged from a complaint of JAMES KENNY'S.

RICHARD YOUNG & ELIZABETH his Wife (she being first privately examined & voluntarily assenting thereto) acknowledges their Deed of Feoffment with Livery & Scison & rect. thereon endorsed unto ROBERT DUELING.

The Inventory and appraisement of the Estate of JOHN RICE decd. being returned are admitted to Record.

BURDIT CLIFTON produced in Court a Writing as the last Will and Testament of SARAH MCGILL Decd. and moved that the same might be proved which was contested by PHILIP ALEXANDER Gent. who produced another writing for her last Will. Its ordered that the two wills be lodged in the hands of RICHARD FOOTE Gent. till the next Court and that a Dedimus Issue the Depositions of the witnesses concerning the said Wills.

[Page 8 Oct. 10, 1749]

October Court 1749

The Inspectors at AQUIA sold 5583 lbs Tobacco. BOYD'S HOLE 2788 lbs. Tobo. At CAVE'S 990 lbs. Tobo. and made oath to their several Accounts.

Deeds of Lease & Release & Receipt from MEREDITH EDWARDS to SAMUEL SELDEN proved by Witnesses & MARY the wife of the said Meredith being privately examined & voluntarily assented.

JAMES WAUGH Gent. Guardian to the orphans of HUGH FRENCH decd. made oath to the particulars of the said orphans Estate.

Ordered that GEORGE HINSON & MARY his Wife be summoned to appear at the next Court to answer the petition of ALEXANDER & ANDERSON DONIPHAN.

JOHN SHORT'S Ordinary License renewed.

Ordered that the Sheriff take HUGH HORTON, JOHN HORTON, WILLIAM HORTON and ANTHONY HORTON into his custody till they enter into Bond in £20 each with two Securitys each in £10 each for keeping the peace for a year & a day.

JOHN HAMILTON Gent. produced & made oath & an account against his Servant MATHEW MCENTIRE for 28 days Runaway & 180 lb. Tobo. & 10/10 expended in taking him up. Ordered that the said McEntire serve him according to Law.

MARGARET COCKLIN a servant Girl belonging to WILLIAM MOUNTJOY came into Court and agreed to serve her said Master the time that's mentioned in her indenture.

Ordered that MARGARET TRAVERS be summoned to appear at the next Court to answer the Petition of ALEXANDER DONIPHAN and others.

Ejection Firma. Thomas Turff agt. HENRY FITZHUGH Gent. for Lands and Appurtenances in the Parish of Overwharton which HENRY TYLER Gent. demised to the Pltf for a Term. It's ordered that the Surveyor go upon the Lands in Controversy & lay out the same as either party would have it, having regard to all Pattents & Evidences as shall be produced & the Sheriff is ordered to attend the survey and to remove force if any offered & the surveyor is to return the fair Platts to the Clerk's office. FRANCIS THORNTON, SAMUEL SELDEN & WILLIAM MOUNTJOY Gent. are appointed Commissioners to attend the survey.

[Page 9 Oct. 10, 1749]

October Court 1749

Administration on the Estate of JOHN HUNTER is granted WILLIAM MOUNTJOY. PETER DANIEL, JOHN MAUZY & JAMES SUDDETH Appraisers.

Suits on Attachment. HENRY TYLER agt. the Estate of THOMAS WADDLE. Tyler produced an Account against the said Waddell for £1.16.6. Tyler to receive that sum and his Costs by him in this behalf expended and the Sheriff having attached divers goods of the said Waddells. Its ordered that he sell the same and satisfie the said Tyler his Judgments.

Suit on Attachment. THOMAS WIGNETT agt. the Estate of THOMAS WADDELL. Wignet produced an Account against the said Waddell for £2.10.2. Wignett to recover that amount & his Costs and the Sheriff having fourteen shillings he is ordered to pay the same to the said Wigginton [sic] in part of satisfaction of his Judgment.

Then the Court adjourned till Court in Course.
PHILIP ALEXANDER

At a Court held for Stafford County Novr. the 14th 1749.

Present   PHILIP ALEXANDER   RICHARD FOOTE
             MOTT DONIPHAN   PETER DANIEL
             JAMES WAUGH

The Grand Jury being sworn retired & returned with their presentments. Ordered that the Offenders be summoned.

9

ROBERT a Negroe Boy belonging to GEORGE JAMES adjudged to be thirteen years of age.

LUCY a Negroe Girl belonging to GEORGE JAMES is adjudged to be thirteen years of age.

Ordered that JOANNA CAMPBELL serve her Master JOHN WASHINGTON the time she had to serve when she went from him & for 400 pounds of Tobacco & £1.11.6 expended in taking her up.

WILLIAM FITZHUGH, WILLIAM HAMPTON & BALDWIN DADE appraisers of the Estate of JOHN LAZAMBY.

[Page 10 Nov. 14, 1749]

November Court 1749

THOMAS CARVER acknowledges his Deed of Lease, Release & Receipt unto ALEXANDER DONIPHAN.

Then the Court proceeded to lay the Levy.	
To Mr. SECRETARY NELSON by Account	408
To MOSELEY BATTALEY Kings Attorney	1800
To the Clerk by Law	1250
To RACHEL SUDDETH for a survey over paid	13
To the Clerk by Account	948
To the late Sheriff by Accounts	867
To Col. NATHANIEL HARRISON in part for the COURT HOUSE	20,000
To CHARLES HARRISON Constable by Accounts	442
To BENJAMIN NEWTON for Lumber for a Bridge over MACHODICK Dams	40
To HENRY WASHINGTON'S Exor by Account	183
To WITHERS CONWAY Sub Sheriff by Accounts	720
To WILLIAM ROSS Constable by Account	294
To Capt. JAMES WAUGH Coroner by Accounts	489
To BENJAMIN STROTHER by accounts	645
To JOHN MAUZY by Accounts	675
To THOMAS HENAGE Constable by Accounts	347
To FUTERALL HALL do. by do.	395
To HUB WHITECOTTON do. by do.	251
To BUSSELL & HITE for carrying the chain for the Court house Line	75
To ANTHONY MURRAY by account	150
To JOHN BELL & HENRY DUFFIN for 2 Levies over paid BEACH	26
To 6 pCent for collecting 33,919	2035

To the Sheriff by Law	1,254
To 6 pCent on Ditto	75
	32,846
To be Levied for the Sheriff next year	556
	33,402

Credit

By Sqirel Scalps wanting		3,759
By Majr. WALKER for £4.15		678
By 1931 Tithables a 15/ per Poll		28,965
	Total	33, 402

Ordered that the Sheriff collect for each Tithable person in this County 15 lb. Tobo. to discharge the County Levy.

[Page 11 Nov. 14, 1749]

November Court 1749

Ejectment Firma. HENRY TYLER Gent. agt. HENRY FITZHUGH Gent. is continued for the survey to be finished.

JOHN ALLENTROP'S Inventory returned and admitted to Record.

THOMAS WILLIAMS a servant Boy belonging to JOHN SHORT is adjudged to be Eleven Years of Age.

TABITHA HOOE'S Release of Dower to RICE HOOE is admitted to Record.

The Inspectors at CAVES & ACQUIA took the several oaths which is ordered to be certified.

JOHN HUNTERS Inventory returned and admitted to Record.

Weights to be tried at BOYD'S HOLD by PHILIP ALEXANDER & RICHARD FOOTE Gent. At CAVES by JAMES WAUGH & PETER DANIEL Gent. At ACQUIA by JOHN PEYTON & CHARLES WALLER Gent.

STEPHEN PILCHER is appointed overseer of the Road in the room of JOHN FOLIO from WHIPSAWANSIN to KING GEORGE COUNTY.

MOSES ROWLEY is appointed Overseer of the Road in the room of JAMES WAUGH Gent. from JOHN SMITH'S to PASBYTANZY.

JOHN MERCER, PETER DANIEL & CHARLES WALLER Gent. or any two of them view the Clerk's office and report to February Court.

RICHARD FOOTE, GERRARD FOWKE, JOHN BUCKNER & BURDIT CLIFTON or any three view the place petitioned for by ALEXANDER DONIPHAN & others for a Road to TRAVIS'S LANDING & Report.

WILLIAM THORNBURY being bound over to this Court & having heard the evidences against him. It's ordered that the Sheriff take him into his custody till he enter Bond in £20 with two Securities in £10 each for his keeping the peace for a year & a day.

Then the Court adjourned till Court in Course.
PHILIP ALEXANDER

At a Court held for Stafford County December the 12th 1749.

Present	PHILIP ALEXANDER	RICHARD BERNARD
	RICHARD FOOTE	MOTT DONIPHAN
	PETER DANIEL	JAMES WAUGH

DONIPHAN &c vs TRAVIS, continued.

[Page 12 Dec. 12, 1749]

December Court 1749

CHARLES WALLER'S Will proved and admitted to Record and a Probate granted JOHN PEYTON & GEORGE WALLER two of the Exors. in the Will named. JOHN RALLS, WILLIAM MOUNTJOY, THOMAS MONROE and CHARLES BRENT Appraisers.

HOWSON HOOE'S Ordinary licence renewed.

RAWLEIGH TRAVIS'S Will proved and admitted to Record and a Probate granted the Exor The Reverd. Mr. JOHN MONCURE. PETER HEDGMAN, JAMES WAUGH, and WILLIAM MOUNTJOY Appraisers.

JAMES HANSBROUGH & LETTICE his Wife acknowledged their Deed of Lease & Release and Receipt unto PETER HANSBROUGH.

A Lease for Lives from DANIEL MCCARTY to WILLIAM BETHEL is admitted to Record.

WILLIAM BETHEL acknowledges his assignment of his Land for Lives from DANIEL MCCARTY to PETER HANSBROUGH.

Ordered that PETER DANIEL pay the Sheriff the Fraction in his hands.

Absent RICHARD BERNARD.

Ordered that JOHN HOOE, RICHARD BERNARD & HENRY FITZHUGH Gent. settle the Accounts of TOWNSHEND WASHINGTON deceased with RICHARD FOOTE Gent. & report to the next Court.

JOHN BUCKNER is appointed overseer of the Road in the room of JOHN FOLIO.

Then the Court adjourned till Court in Course.
PHILIP ALEXANDER

At a Court held for Stafford County February 13th 1749/50.

Present JOHN MERCER   PHILIP ALEXANDER
      RICHARD BERNARD MOTT DONIPHAN
      JOHN PEYTON   PETER DANIEL
Absent JOHN MERCER.

Action of Debt. ANN MASON Widow Admx. of GEORGE MASON Gent. agt. SARAH BROOKE Extx. of the last will and Testament of THOMAS BROOKE Gent. otherwise called Thomas Brooke of St. Mary's County in the Province of Maryland Gent. The Replication of this cause being argued, it's ordered that a Writ of Enquiry of damages be executed the next Court.

[Page 13 Feb. 13, 1749/50]

February Court 1749/50

Present JOHN MERCER Gent.

The Inventory and appraisements of the estate of RAWLEIGH TRAVERSE decd. is admitted to Record.

Deeds of Lease & Release and Receipt from GEORGE MASON Gent. & ANN MASON to JOHN MERCER Gent. acknowledged by the said George Mason and are admitted to Record.

A Bill of Sale from PRICILLA BOWS to her sons THOMAS and ALEXANDER HAY are admitted to record.

TAYLOR CHAPMAN'S Will proved and admitted to Record and a probate granted MARGARET one of the Exors. therein named. JOSEPH COMBS and TRAVERSE COMBS Securitys.

Ejection Ferma. SARAH CONWAY agt. MARY FOWKE. For Lands and Appurtenances in the Parish of St. Paul's in this County. Mary Fowke confessed Judgment for the Lands in dispute between them. Court ordered Sarah Conway recover of Mary her term yet to come of the Lands. Possession is awarded Conway and Fowke to put her in possession thereof She agreeing to release the rents received by her and each party to pay their own Costs.

The Sheriff is ordered to take JESSE BAILS into his Custody till he enter into Bond in £20 with two Securitys in £10 each for his keeping the peace for a year and a day.

THOMAS FITZHUGH, GEORGE JAMES & HENRY TYLER view the most convenient way for a Road from POTOMAC CHURCH to CHRISTOPHER THRELKELD'S & report.

JOHN STONE is appointed constable in the room of THOMAS HENAGE.

HASELL HARDWICK is appointed Constable in the room of WILLIAM ROSS.

JOHN LEE, HUGH ADIE, JOHN PAYTON, BENJAMIN STROTHER & BAILY WASHINGTON view the most convenient way for a Road from CHARLES HARDING'S to meet PRINCE WILLIAM ROAD by CHAPPAWAMSIC RUN.

[Page 14 Feb. 13, 1749/50]

March Court 1749/50

The Petition of HAYWARD POND against WILLIAM GREEN is Dismist.

JAMES WAUGH, PHILIP ALEXANDER and RICHARD BERNARD Gent. are ordered to be recommended to his honor the President to make choice of one for a Sheriff for this ensuing Year.

CHARLES HARDING Constable took the oath prescribed by Law.

Then the Court adjourned till Court in Course.

JOHN MERCER

At a Court held for Stafford County. March the 13th 1749/50.

Present   JOHN MERCER   RICHARD BERNARD
               MOTT DONIPHAN   PETER DANIEL
               JAMES WAUGH

THOMAS STRIBLING is appointed overseer of the Road in the room of THOMAS BUMBURY and is ordered to keep the same in repair.

Administration on the estate of THOMAS CHEESEMAN Decd. is granted GEORGE JOHNSON he having entered into Bond with MASON FRENCH & BENONI STRATTON his Securitys. WILLIAM ROGERS, BENJAMIN DERRICK, HENRY SMITH & DUNCOMB SIMPSON appraisers.

Administration on the Estate of GEORGE SIMPSON decd. is granted PETER DANIEL Gent. he having entered into Bond with WITHERS CONWAY his Security. THOMAS HAY, ALEXANDER HAY, RAWLEIGH CHINN & THOMAS MONROE Appraisers.

The overseer of the Road to the LITTLE FERRY join with some Surveyor opposite in the County of WESTMORELAND and clear MACHODIGE CREEK.

Administration on the Estate of JOHN TURNER decd. is granted SARAH TURNER she having entered into Bond with BENJAMIN DERRICK & BENONI STRATTON her Securitys. THOMAS MASSIE, WILLIAM ROGERS, MASON FRENCH & HENRY SMITH Appraisers.

WILLIAM WALKER'S Will proved and admitted to Record and a Probate granted NATHANIEL HARRISON Esqr. one of the Executors. PHILIP ALEXANDER, JOHN ALEXANDER, WILLIAM FITZHUGH & RICHARD FOOT Appraisers.

March Court 1749/50

JOHN RALLS, WHARTON RANSDALL, MICHAEL PYKE & THOMAS TURNER or any two to view the road from BRENTOWN to FALMOUTH by the PARK and POPLAR QUARTER and report what hands are most convenient & on what road the same work on now.

WILLIAM HAMPTON'S Will proved and admitted to Record and a Probate granted the Exor. No Security required.

WILLIAM MATHENY acknowledged his Lease for Lives to THOMAS MATHENY.

Deeds of Lease, Release & Receipt from JOHN LEE Gent. to JOSIAS STONE are admitted to Record.

Ordered that WILLIAM WALKER heir at Law to WILLIAM WALKER Gent. decd. & NATHANIEL HARRISON Esqr. the acting Exor. be summoned to the next Court.

CHARLES HINSON'S will proved and admitted to Record and a Probate granted the Exor. & JOSEPH HINSON Heir at Law.

ROBERT STURDY'S Will proved and admitted to Record.

ELEANOR PESTRAGE'S Will proved and admitted to Record & a Probate granted to ROBERT WASHINGTON one of the Exors. WILLIAM STUART Clerk Security.

WILLIAM BRUTON'S will proved by ISBELL DAVIS one of the witnesses.

WILLIAM BAXTER'S Will proved and admitted to Record and a probate granted to the Exor. LANGHORN DADE, CADWALLENDER DADE & HENRY DADE Appraisers.

SARAH LUCAS petitioning for her freedom. It appears to the Court by her Indenture that she is not free. Whereupon it's ordered that she serve her Master THOMAS MASSEY according to her said Indenture.

Indenture between THOMAS STRIBLING & JOHN BARRETT being acknowledged and admitted to Record.

Ordered that the Sheriff summon 24 of the most able Freeholders to appear at May Court next to be of the Grand Jury.

ALEXANDER DONIPHAN acknowledged his Deed unto ANDERSON DONIPHAN which is admitted to Record.

NATHANIEL GRAY is appointed overseer of the road from LANGHORN DADES to the LITTLE FERRY.

[Page 16 Mar. 13, 1749/50]

March Court 1749/50

Action of Trespass. BENJAMIN ROBINSON agt. THOMAS CRAFFORD. Thomas not appearing Judgment is granted the Pltf against him & JOSEPH BRAGG his Security unless the Deft do appear at the next Court & answer the Pltf's Action.

Action of Debt. ZACHRY WEBB agt. REUBEN BOYCE is Dismist.

Action of Trespass Assault and Battery. RICHARD NEWAL agt. THOMAS LACY is Dismist.

Suit on Scire Facias. JOSEPH PORTER agt. THOMAS STARK is ordered returnable to the next Court.

Suit on Petition. JOHN SILBY agt. JOHN SCOGGIN is Dismist with costs.

A Bill of Sale from JAMES PHILLIPS to JOHN RALLS Senr. being proved is admitted to Record.

Ordered that JOHN SILBY pay WILLIAM WARRELL 350 pounds of Tobacco for four days attendance as an Evidence for him agst. Scoggin & coming & returning twenty Miles four times.

Ordered that JOHN SCOGGIN pay JESSE MOSS 50 pounds of Tobo. for two days attendance as an Evidence for him at the suit of John Silby.

FRANCES DAY and ANTHONY HORTON being bound over to the Court and having heard the evidences against them. Ordered that the Sheriff take them into his Custody till they enter into Bond in £20 each, with two Securitys in £10 each for their good behavior for a year and a day.

Stafford Court.   Be it remembered that heretofore to wit on the 23d day of August in 1749 before the Justices at the Court house of the said County came

17

ANN MASON Widow, Admx. of the Goods and Chattels Rights and Credits which were of GEORGE MASON Gent. decd. at the time of his Death, by JOHN HAMILTON her Attorney and produced to the Court her certain Bill against SARAH BROOKE Widow Admx. with the will annexed of THOMAS BROOKE Gent. decd. & in a plea of Debt and pledges to prosecute to wit John Doe & Richard Roe which said Bill follows on these words to wit

[Page 17 Mar. 13, 1749/50]

March Court 1749/50

Stafford to wit   ANN MASON Widow, Admx. complains of SARAH BROOKE Widow, Admx. of THOMAS BROOKE Gent. decd., otherwise called Thomas Brooke of St. Mary's County, Maryland Gent. of a plea that Sarah render unto Ann the sum of Five thousand Pound Sterling money of Great Britain which Sarah unjustly detains &c. For that whereas the said Thomas in his Life time to wit the third day of December in 1734 at the Parish of Overwharton by his certain writing obligatory acknowledged himself to be held and firmly bound unto the said George in his lifetime in the sum of £2,000 Sterling to be paid to the said George his certain Attorney heirs Exors. Admrs. and assigns when the same shall be required. Yet the said Thomas in his lifetime and the said Deft after the death of the said Thomas although often required have not paid. Nor hath either of them paid the said five thousand pounds Sterling to the said George in his life time or to the said Pltf since the death of the said George. Administration of the estate of the said George fell to the said Ann on the last day of August in 1735 at the Parish and County aforesaid. And the said Deft after the death of the said Thomas wholly refused to pay the same and still doth refuse & unjustly detains the same to the damage of the said Ann of £50 Sterling & therefore she brings suit &c

HAMILTON for the Pltf.	Pledges	John Roe
for the Deft.		Richard Roe

[Page 18 Mar. 13, 1749/50]

March Court 1749/50

And the said Deft by ROGER DIXON her attorney came and asked the Court to hear the Writing. That the said Pltf ought not to have or maintain her Action against the said Deft. That the said Articles of agreement mentioned in the said Consideration were made the third day of December in 1734 between the aforesaid GEORGE MASON in his lifetime by the name of George Mason of Charles County in the Province of Maryland, Gent. of the one part and the said THOMAS BROOKE by the name of Thomas Brooke of St. Mary's County in the said Province of Maryland of the other part. The said George was in his

18

lifetime levied in his demense of feoffe in divers Land, Messuages Tenements, Hereditaments and slaves as well as in the said Colony of Virginia, as in the Province of Maryland. By his last will and Testament he thereby made several devises & bequests to the said GEORGE MASON party to the said Articles of agreement being his Eldest Son and heir at Law as to divers other his children by divers ventures and in the said will were contained divers bequests and devises to his sons FRANCIS and THOMAS MASON & his Daughter Sarah (the now Deft) being the Children he had by his last wife. And for as much as the Lands, Tenements, Hereditements and slaves devised to his said Sons FRANCIS and THOMAS MASON were by the will generally devised to them and their Heirs, and the said Francis and Thomas died very young and were never possessed of any of the said property, but the said GEORGE MASON has always from the death of the said George Mason his father continued the possession of the same.

[Page 19 Mar. 13, 1749/50]

March Court 1749/50

And still was possessed thereof so that divers Lawsuits, Troubles & controversies might probably happen touching the Right Title & Interest of and in the said Lands, Tenements, Hereditaments & Slaves. And whereas there was then a Treaty of Marriage had and concluded between the said THOMAS BROOKE and the said SARAH MASON, the now Deft for prevention of any suit Troubles differences touching or concerning the said premises. It was mutually covenanted and agreed upon by and between the said GEORGE MASON and the said THOMAS BROOKE and the said SARAH MASON his intended wife that all the singular the said Lands Tenements Hereditaments & Slaves by the last will and Testament of the aforesaid GEORGE MASON the Father devised severally to his said Sons FRANCIS and THOMAS brothers of the said Sarah as well in the Colony of Virginia as the Province of Maryland should be settled to the uses intents & purposes therein after mentioned. But for as much as the said Sarah was not then of the Age of twenty one years so that she was not able or capable to be a party to consent to or execute any Deed conveyance settlements according to the Intent and agreement afsd to be binding on her and her Heirs, the said Thomas Brooke & Sarah and agreed that as soon as the said Sarah should arrive at the age of twenty one years she would sign seal & execute one or more sufficient deed or Deeds of settlement or conveyance of all and singular the premises to the uses & purposes to the true intent and meaning therein after mentioned. IMPRIMIS the said GEORGE MASON for himself his Heirs Exors. & Admrs. did covenant promise and agreed & with the said THOMAS BROOKE his Heirs Exors. and Admrs. that the said George should and would anytime after the said Marriage between the said Thomas & the said Sarah should take effects & be consummated pay and deliver unto the said Thomas Brooke his Exors. & Admrs. all and every such sums of Money Goods and Chattels Comodities and other personal Estate whatsoever which the said Sarah Mason was entitled to as by the will of her Father the said George Mason decd. as by the Death of NICHOLAS MASON & ELIZABETH MASON decd. & the Death of her said Brothers FRANCIS & THOMAS MASON decd. and the said George Mason or his Heirs should and would from and immediately after

[Page 20 Mar. 13, 1749/50]

March Court 1749/50

the consummation of the said Marriage upon the request of the said THOMAS BROOKE sign seal & execute a sufficient Deed for the said Lands Tenements Hereditaments & Slaves with their Increase as well in the Colony of Virginia as the Province of Maryland which the said GEORGE MASON the Father devised to his sons FRANCIS and THOMAS. And immediately after the consummation of the said Marriage to the use of the said Thomas Brooke & Sarah his Intended wife for & during the term of their several natural lives and immediately from and after their decease to the use of the Heirs of the body of the said Sarah by the said Thomas Brooke as Lawfully begotten (& for want of such Heirs to the use of the Heirs of the body of the said Sarah by any other husband which she might happen after the death of the said Thomas Brooke to marry) and for default of Heirs of the body of the said Sarah to the use of the said GEORGE MASON & his Heirs forever. Item the said Thomas Brooke did by the said articles of agreement did convenant & promise to and with the said George Mason that the said Thomas Brooke & Sarah his intended wife in case the said Marriage should take effect

[Page 21 Mar. 13, 1749/50]

March Court 1749/50

and be consummated should and would as soon as the said Sarah should attain the age of twenty one years or within a convenient time after make sufficient deeds of conveyance to the said George Mason and his heirs all & singular the Lands Tenements Hereditaments & slaves with their Increase therein before mentioned according to the true Intent and meaning of the said Articles. Item the said George Mason did by the said Articles of agreement covenant and promise to and with the said Thomas Brooke that he the said George Mason notwithstanding the said Articles should & would consent to have a clause or provision in the Deed of Settlement to be hereafter made in pursuance of the said Articles to enable the said Thomas Brooke and Sarah his wife to exchange all or any of the Lands Tenements and Hereditaments within the Colony of Virginia for Lands & Hereditaments of equal value & equal Estate within the Province of Maryland on condition that those Lands Tenements or

20

Hereditaments so to be sold should be sold for the greatest price that could be got and the purchase money should be laid out to purchase Land Tenements or Hereditaments of Equal value & equal Estate. And the said Deft saith that he the said Thomas Brooke in his lifetime and Sarah his wife on their parts & behalfs did well & truly perform observe fulfill & keep all & singular the Covenants Articles promises conditions & agreements whatsoever mentioned in the said Articles of Agreement and this she is ready to verify wherefore she prays Judgment if the said Pltf ought to have or maintain her action afsd against her.

[Page 22 Mar. 13, 1749/50]

March Court 1749/50

And the said Deft with the leave of the Court further saith that she hath fully administered all the Goods & Chattels which were of the said THOMAS BROOKE at the time of his Death except Goods & Chattels to the value of £400 and that the said Deft hath no Goods or Chattels which were of the said Thomas at the time of his death in her hands to be administered nor has on the day of exhibiting the said Bill of the said Pltf nor at any time afterward except the said Goods & Chattels to the value of the said four hundred pounds Sterling. Wherefore the said Deft prays Judgment if the Pltf ought to have or maintain her said Action.

ROGER DIXON

And the said Pltf saith that she ought not to be precluded from maintaining her action afsd by anything before alleged by the said Deft in pledging because protesting that the said THOMAS BROOKE in his lifetime and SARAH his Wife did not on their parts & behalfs well & truly perform observe & fulfill & keep all and singular the covenants Articles conditions & agreements whatsoever mentioned in the said Articles of Agreement according to the form & effect of the condition. The said Pltf Ann saith that after the making of the Articles of Agreement, to wit on the 19th day of December in 1734 at the parish and County afsd, the intended marriage between the said Thomas & and said Sarah his wife to wit on the tenth day of January in 1738 did attain the age of twenty one years yet the said Thomas Brooke & Sarah his wife did not as soon as the said Sarah attained the age of twenty one years or within a convenient time after or at any time during the life of the said Thomas make sign seal and execute sufficient Deeds of conveyance or assurance to settle convey and assure unto the said George Mason the several Lands Tenements Hereditaments & Slaves following that is to say 2373 acres of land in the County of Prince William formerly

March Court 1749/50

called Prince William & now Fairfax in the Colony of Virginia of value of
£1180 purchased by the said George Mason the father of MADAM BRENT,
RAWLEIGH TRAVERSE, WILLIAM LAMBERT, JOHN HARPER, JOHN
SIMPSON & BRYAN FOLEY & two negroe Slaves named JENNY & KATE
of the price of £10 the children & Increase of a negroe Slave named WALKER
which said Land and the negroe Slave named Walker the said GEORGE
MASON the father devised to his said son FRANCIS MASON brother of the
said SARAH & her Heirs as also 1200 Acres of Land in the Counties of King
George & Stafford of the value of £500 purchased by the said George Mason the
father of ALEXANDER WAUGH and 320 Acres of Land in the county of
Prince William formerly Stafford & now Fairfax of the value of £160 purchased
by the said George Mason the father of MICHAEL VALENDEGHAM & 450
Acres of Land in Charles City County in the Province of Maryland of the value
of £450 purchased by the said George Mason the father of WILLIAM MOSS &
12 Negroe Slaves named BESS, MUDDY, MOSES, LEONARD, NAN,
HARRY, BEN, NICE, WILL, NELL, NAN, & BESS of the price of £280 which
slaves are the children & Increase of the said Negroe Bess, which said 1200
Acres of Land in the counties of King George & Stafford, also 320 Acres in
Fairfax, also 450 Acres in Charles County & Slaves named Bess & Muddy the
said George Mason the father by his last will & Testament devised to his son
THOMAS MASON brother of the said Sarah to the several uses Intents and
purposes in the said Articles of Agreement and to no other use intent or purpose
that is to say from & immediately after the consummation of the said Marriage
to the use of the said THOMAS BROOKE & SARAH his wife for & during
their several natural lives & immediately from & after their deaths to the use of
the Heirs of the Body of the said Sarah by the said Thomas Brooke Lawfully
begotten & for want of said Heirs to the use of the Heirs of the Body of the said
Sarah by the said Thomas Brooke or any other Husband Lawfully

March Court 1749/50

to be begotten to the use of the said George Mason and his Heirs forever. But
the said THOMAS BROOKE in his lifetime and SARAH his wife afterwards on
the 21st day of October in 1738 did sell & convey unto ZEPHANIAH WADE
and his Heirs 1140 Acres of Land with the appurtenances situate lying & being
in the County of Fairfax in the value of £570 & the said Thomas Brooke in his
lifetime and Sarah his wife afterwards to wit on the second day of May 1742 did
sell & convey to RICHARD BOGGESS & his Heirs 320 Acres of Land with the
appurtenances lying and being in the County of Fairfax of the value of £150 &

the said Thomas Brooke in his lifetime and Sarah his wife afterwards to wit on the ___ day of ___ in 1748 did likewise sell & convey to CHARLES CARTER Esqr. and his Heirs 1200 Acres of Land with the appurtenances lying and being in the Counties of King George & Stafford of the value of £500. All & every which Tracts & parcels of Land with the appurtenances thus sold and conveyed which the said George Mason the father by his last will & Testament devised to his said Sons FRANCIS & THOMAS MASON decd. & ought to have been conveyed and assured by the said Thomas Brooke & Sarah his wife unto the said George Mason the son & his Heirs.

[Page 25 Mar. 13, 1749/50]

March Court 1749/50

to the several uses Intents and purposes on the said Articles of Agreement and the said THOMAS BROOKE did not sell the said several Lands herein before mentioned for the greatest price that could have been gotten for the same nor layout the purchase money to purchase Lands Tenements or Hereditaments of Equal Value and Equal Estate within the Province of Maryland and put to the same uses & Estates in the said Articles mentioned and the said Thomas Brooke in his lifetime to wit on the last day of June 1746 did sell & dispose of the before named Negroe BESS and the before named MOSES, LEONARD, NAN & HARRY at the price of £100 which the said Thomas Brooke and SARAH his wife ought to have conveyed & assured unto the said George Mason the Son & his Heirs and the said Pltf prays Judgment together with her damages occasioned by the detaining of the said Debt.

JOHN HAMILTON for Plaintiff

Attorney for the Deft Sarah Brooke prays the Pltf

[Page 26 Mar. 13, 1749/50]

March Court 1749/50

may be barred from having or maintaining her said action against her &c.

JOHN DIXON for Deft.

It seems to the Court that the said plea afsd by her the said Pltf in manner & form afsd above in replying pleaded are Good & Sufficient in the Law to maintain the said Plts having her action afsd against the said Deft whereby the said Plt remains therein against the said Deft wherefore the said Pltf ought to recover against the said Deft her Debts afsd together with her damages but because it is not known to the Court what damages the said Plt hath sustained by reason of the several Breaches of the covenants in the said Articles of Agreements by the said Pltf. To inquire of the said Damages let a Jury come

23

before the Justices afsd at the Court house on the second Tuesday in March next. A Jury to wit CHARLES BRENT, EDWARD WALLER, THOMAS MONROE, HOWSON HOOE, HENRY SMITH, SIMON THOMAS, NICHOLAS GEORGE, JOHN FOLEY, Jr., CHARLES HARDING, PETER MAUZY, JOHN HUGHS, and GEORGE JAMES. The Jury being sworn diligently came

[Page 27 Mar. 13, 1749/50]

March Court 1749/50

to inquire what damages the said Pltf hath sustained and upon their Oath do say that the said Pltf hath sustained damages to £600. Its therefore considered that the said Pltf recover against the said Deft two thousand pounds Sterling her Debts afsd Together with her costs by her about her suit in this behalf expended of the Goods & Chattels which belonged to the said THOMAS BROOKE at the time of his Death in the hands of the said Deft to be administered. And if she hath not so much in her hands to be administered then the costs to be levied. But this Judgment except as to the Costs. It is to be discharged by the payment of £600 the damages by the Jury afsd. £400 part thereof of the Goods and Chattels of the said Thomas which the said Deft acknowledges to have in her hands to be administered & £200 the residue of the said damages of the Goods and Chattels which belonged to the said Thomas at the time of his Death which shall come to the hands of the said Deft. Then the Court adjourned till tomorrow morning 9 Oclock.

JOHN MERCER

At a Court continued and held for Stafford County 14ᵗʰ day of March 1749/50.

Present   JOHN MERCER   PHILIP ALEXANDER
                RICHARD BERNARD   RICHARD FOOTE
                MOTT DONIPHAN

The Court doth set & rate Liquors as followith   Rum 8/4 per Gallon
A quantity of Rum Punch with White Sugar 1/ & other Liquors as before rated

Present PETER DANIEL & JOHN PEYTON, Gent.
Absent J. MERCER, Gent.

Justices recommended GERRARD FOWKE, JOHN WASHINGTON Senr., THOMAS FITZHUGH, WHARTON RANSDALL and TRAVERS COOKE.

Ejection Firma. WILLIAM GOODRIGHT, Lessee of THOMAS RIDDLE agt. ENOCH BERRY is Dismist.

Action of Trespass. JOHN HUMPHREY agt. WILLIAM ELKIN. A Jury to wit HOWSON HOOE, HAYWARD TODD, GEORGE JAMES, SAMUEL THORNBURY, BENJAMIN DUNCOMB, WILLIAM GRADY, MASON FRENCH, NATHANIEL GRAY

[Page 28 Mar. 14, 1749/50]

March Court 1749/50

JOHN MAUZY, JOHN WITHERS, HENRY SMITH and WILLIAM NORTHCUT. The Jury finds for the Pltf £10. And its considered by the Court that the Pltf recover of the said Deft the said £10 & Costs.

Ordered that JOHN HUMPHREY pay JAMES WEYTON 325 pounds of Tobacco for thirteen days attendance as an evidence for him against ELKIN.

Ordered that JOHN HUMPHREY pay THOMAS WIGNALL 325 pounds of Tobacco for thirteen days attendance as an Evidence for him against ELKIN.

Ordered that JOHN HUMPHREY pay JOHN MINOR 325 pounds of Tobacco for him as an evidence against ELKIN.

Ordered that WILLIAM ELKIN pay RICHARD VINE 225 pounds of Tobacco for nine days attendance as an evidence for him at the Suit of HUMPHREY.

Ordered that WILLIAM ELKIN pay SARAH MINOR 225 pounds of Tobacco for nine days attendance as an Evidence for him at the Suit of HUMPHREY.

JAMES JEFFRIES is appointed Constable in the room of HUSBANDFOOTE WHITECOTTON.

Ordered that JOHN HUMPHREY pay JOHN HUMPHREY Junr. 319 pounds of Tobacco for seven days attendance for him to ELKIN and for coming and returning eight miles six times.

Administration on the Estate of MEREDITH EDWARDS is granted to SARAH EDWARDS. She having entered into bond with HUSBANDFOOTE WHITECOTTON her Security. SIMON THOMASON, THOMAS DENT, MATHEW GREGG & WILLIAM DENT appraisers.

Upon hearing the several depositions taken concerning the two Wills of SARAH MCGILL decd., it is the Courts opinion that the will which is not signed dated Nov. 7, 1748 is the will of the said Sarah & is ordered to be recorded.

Ejection Firma. Robert Faldo agt. JAMES WAUGH, Gent. for Lands & appurtenances in the Parish of Overwharton which JOHN WITHERS demised to the plaintiff Robert for a term &c. The Deft having pleaded not Guilty, a Jury to wit HOWSON HOOE, SAMUEL THORNBURY, WILLIAM GRAY, MASON FRENCH, HENRY SMITH, WILLIAM NORTHCUT, DANIEL HAWKINS, JOSEPH COMBS, CHARLES BRENT, and JOB SIMS.

[Page 29 Mar. 14, 1749/50]

March Court 1749/50

We find that WILLIAM WAUGH in his lifetime in the year 1747 rented a Plantation part of the Land in question to JAMES WAUGH the Deft during the term of seven years at the rent of 530 pounds of Tobacco a year. JOHN WITHERS knew of the said Incumbrance at the time of the Purchase of and Sale of the said Land. We find that the said Land was sold for less Money on account of the said Incumbrance. We find that William Waugh was seized in his demense of Fee of & in the Lands in the Declaration and being so levied by Deeds of Lease & Release conveyed the same to the Lessee of the Pltf but before the Deeds of Conveyance or the purchase. The Jury finds for the Deft.

Ordered that JAMES WAUGH pay WILLIAM HEFFERNON 50 lbs. Tobo. for two days attendance as an evidence for him at the Suit of WITHERS.

Ordered that JAMES WAUGH pay MARY MASTIN 50 lbs. Tobo. for two days attendance.

Ordered that JAMES WAUGH pay WILLIAM MATHEWS 50 lbs. Tobo. for two days attendance.

Ordered that JAMES WAUGH pay THOMAS NUGENT 68 lbs. Tobo. for two days attendance and for coming and returning 6 miles.

Ordered that JAMES WAUGH pay MARGARET BEAR 98 lbs. Tobo. for two days attendance and for coming and returning 16 miles.

Ordered that the Exors. of GILSON BERRYMAN decd. be summoned to appear at the next Court to prove his will.

Administration on the Estate of WILLIAM WASH decd. is granted to MICHAEL WALLACE. WILLIAM MATHENY, WILLIAM LUNSFORD, GARDNER BURGESS and JOHN WITHERS Appraisers.

Ordered that the Sheriff take THOMAS WILLIAMS into his Custody till he enter into Bond for his good behaviour in £20 with two Securitys in £10 each.

Then the Court adjourned till Court in Course.

JOHN MERCER

April Court 1750

At a Court held for Stafford County April the 10th 1750.

Present   PHILIP ALEXANDER   RICHARD BERNARD
                    MOTT DONIPHAN   JOHN PEYTON
                    PETER DANIEL

Administration on the Estate of LEONARD MARTIN decd. is granted to SARAH MARTIN. JAMES MCINTOSH, HENRY DADE, WILLIAM ROGERS & THOMAS MASSEY Appraisers.

Action of Debt. THOMAS TURNER Gent. agt. BENJAMIN MASSEY. The Deft Benjamin confessed Judgment unto the Pltf for 1,808 lbs of Tobacco & £23.3. The Pltf to recover this and his costs but this Judgment is to be discharged on payment of 904 pounds of Tobacco & £11.11 with Interest from June 20, 1748.

Administration with the will annexed of WILLIAM BRENTON decd. is granted to JOHN SMITH. BENNET BEASLEY, JEREMIAH SMITH Securitys. HOWSON HOOE, JOHN SHORT, JOHN ALEXANDER & WILLIAM BUNBURY Appraisers.

Inventory and appraisement of the Estate of ELENOR PESTRIDGE is admitted to record.

Inventory and appraisement of the Estate of THOMAS CHEESMAN decd. is admitted to record.

Ordered that ROBERT MASSEY, RICHARD HOOE & LANGHORN DADE divide WILLIAM BAXTER'S Estate according to his will.

Inventory and appraisement of the Estate of William Baxter decd. is admitted to record.

The order for the appraisement of the Estate of WILLIAM WALSH not being complied with it's ordered the same be renewed.

MASON FRENCH and MARGARET his wife Admrs. of THOMAS LACY decd. produced an Account against his Estate which is admitted to Record and the Tobo. valued at 14/ pCent.

The Inventory of CHARLES HINSON'S Estate is admitted to Record.

[Page 31 Apr. 10, 1750]

April Court 1750

HENRY NELSON'S Will proved & a probate granted SARAH NELSON one of the Exors. therein named. NICHOLAS GEORGE, WILLIAM KENDALL, PETER BYRAM & MASON COMBS Appraisers.

GEORGE WILLIAMS Will proved & a probate granted GEORGE WALTER & JAMES WILLIAMS two of the Exors.

JAMES WAUGH Gent. came into Court and made Oath that he is unable to attend the General Court as an Evidence for FITZHUGH against BERNARD.

Ordered that GRACE JACKSON be summoned to appear at the next Court to answer the Petition of CHARLES HARDING & CHARLES WELLS.

Ordered that JAMES FLETCHER and RACHEL his wife be summoned to the next Court to answer the petition of ROBERT SUDDOTH.

Ordered that HANCOX CARTY serve her Master WILLIAM MILLS according to Law for having a Bastard Child & that the Sheriff give her 24 lashes on her bare back well laid on.

Ordered that WILLIAM FITZHUGH Esqr. one of the Exors. of GILSON BERRYMAN be summoned to appear at the next Court to prove the said Gilson's Will.

On complaint of the Inspectors at BOYD'S HOLE WAREHOUSE it's ordered that the Admrs. of HENRY FITZHUGH Esqr. decd. build a Warehouse there forty feet by twenty, and if they refuse to build the same, then Inspectors are to agree with the work men to build one at the County's Expence.

Suit on Petition. WITHERS CONWAY agt. ROBERT COLCLOUGH, WILLIAM COLCLOUGH & SAMUEL THORNBURY Exors. of RICHARD COLCLOUGH decd. Judgment is granted the Pltf for 30 shillings by Account of the Goods & Chattels of the said Richard Colclough if so much they have.

Suit on Petition. JAMES BLAIR agt. JOHN LYLE. Judgment granted the Pltf for 830 lbs. of crop Tobo. with Costs and a Lawyer's fee.

Ordered that WITHERS CONWAY pay THOMAS STRIBLING 225 lbs. Tobo. for nine days attendance as an evidence for him to COLCLOUGH'S Exors.

Ordered that WITHERS CONWAY pay JOHN FRANKLYN 536 lbs. Tobo. for nine days attendance as an Evidence for him to COLCLOUGH'S Exors. & for coming & returning 16 miles seven times.

[Page 32 Apr. 10, 1750]

April Court 1750

Suit on Petition. DAVID CRIGE agt. JOHN HASTY. Judgment granted the Pltf for 898 lbs. crop Tobo. with Costs and a Lawyer's Fee.

Suit on Petition. RAWLEIGH TRAVERS agt. JAMES HUGHS abated by Pltf.

Suit on Petition. JOHN SHORT agt. WILLIAM ROSE. Judgment granted the Pltf for 265 lbs. Tobo. & Costs.

Suit on Petition. GEORGE BRETT agt. WILLIAM DAVIS is continued at the Pltf's Costs.

Suit on Petition. WILLIAM KENYON agt. JOHN ALLISON. Judgment is granted the Pltf for £1.16.6 with Costs and a Lawyer's fee.

Ordered that WILLIAM KENYON pay JOHN SHORT 175 lbs. Tobo. for seven days attendance as an Evidence for him against ALLISON.

Suit on Information. The Lord our King agt. PETER SIDEBOTTOM for retailing liquor without a licence. A Jury to wit WILLIAM KING, JOSEPH COMBS, WILLIAM ETHERTON, EDWARD WALLER, RICHARD HOOE, NATHANIEL GRAY, JOHN SHORT, FRANKLYN LATHAM, CHARLES WELLS, DANIEL HAWKINS, JOHN ALEXANDER & CHARLES HARDING. The Jury finds the said Peter not guilty.

Suit on Attachment obtained by PETER WIGGINGTON agt. GEORGE KNIGHT is Dismist.

Ordered that PETER SIDEBOTTOM pay THOMAS FLUMAN 561 lbs. Tobo. for eight days attendance.

Action of Trespass. ANDREW GRANT & ROBERT BROWN agt. JOHN HASTY. Judgment granted the Pltfs against Hasty & WILLIAM SEBASTIAN his Security unless the Defts do appeal at the next Court.

Action of Trespass Assault & Battery. JOHN TURNER agt. GEORGE JOHNSON is Dismist.

Action of Debt. JONATHAN FORWARD of London Merchant agt. WILLIAM KING is Dismist.

[Page 33 Apr. 10, 1750]

April Court 1750

Action of Debt. JONATHAN FORWARD of London Merchant agt. CHARLES WATTS & CARTEE WELLS, the Defts having pleaded payment the Trial thereof is referred till the next Court.

Action of Debt. JONATHAN FORWARD of London Merchant agt. RICHARD ASHBY is Dismist.

Suit on Petition. JONATHAN FORWARD of London Merchant agt. JOSEPH COOPER is Dismist.

Action of Trespass. HUGH HORTON agt. DARBY HANDLAND & RACHEL his Wife abates by the said Darby's death.

Action of Trespass Assault & Battery. ANTHONY HORTON agt. SAMUEL MCKEG. On the Deft's motion a Special Imparlance is granted him.

Action of Trespass Asault & Battery. DARBY HANDLAND agt. JOHN HORTON, HUGH HORTON & ANTHONY HORTON abates by the Pltf's death.

Action of Debt. ROBERT COLCLOUGH, WILLIAM COLCLOUGH & SAMUEL THORNBURY Exors. of RACHEL COLCLOUGH decd agt. WILLIAM CONWAY. The Deft prayed Oyer &c which is granted him.

Suit on Petition. DANIEL HAWKINS agt. JOHN TAYLOR. Judgment granted the Pltf for 107 Gallons of Cider (which the Court do rate at sixpence per Gallon) & Costs.

Present JAMES WAUGH. Absent PHILIP ALEXANDER, R. BERNARD.

Suit on Attachment obtained by PHILIP ALEXANDER Gent. against the Estate of WILLIAM ALLISON. The said Philip refusing to prosecute this suit he is non Suited & ordered to pay William damages according to Law & Costs.

Suit on Attachment obtained by JOHN ALEXANDER against the Estate of JOHN TRACY the said Alexander produced an account against the said Tracy for £3. Alexander to recover of the said Tracy the £3 and costs and the Sheriff having made return that he had attached 2 beds, Bedsteads, Cords & hides & some bed cloaths & Bolsters, 1 Iron Pott, hooks, 2 chests, 2 Boxes, 1 frying pan, some Bacon, Ham, Corn & some Meal, some Pewter, 2 Tables, 1 Bed, Iron & heaters, some Earthen wares & some other trifling things & attached in the hands of FUTURAL HALL, WILLIAM WORREL & JAMES MCCANT & summoned them as

[Page 34 Apr. 10, 1750]

April Court 1750

Garnishees who appeared & on Oath the said Hall declared that he had in his hands 23 shillings & 9 pence. The said Worrel 24 shillings & 11 pence which they are ordered to pay to the said John Alexander in part of Satisfaction of the above Judgment. Further ordered that the Sheriff sell the Goods by him attached to satisfy the said Alexander's Judgment.

Ordered that DANIEL HAWKINS pay JOHN LYNTON 125 lbs. Tobo. for five days attendance for him on TAYLOR.

Action of Trespass. JOHN PARK agt. JOSEPH CARTER. On Carter's motion a Special Imparlance is granted him till the next Court.

Suit on Petition. PHILIP ALEXANDER, Gent. agt. HENRY RENNOLDS. Judgment granted the Pltf for £5 Current Money & Costs.

Suit on Petition. JAMES HUGHS agt. SAMUEL ANGEL. Judgment granted the Pltf for 38 shillings & 6 pence by account proved and Costs.

Ordered that JAMES HUGHS pay MARY GOING 100 lbs. Tobo. for four days attendance as an Evidence against ANGEL.

Action of Trespass Assault & Battery. JOHN THOMAS agt JOSEPH WHITE being agreed is Dismist.

SARAH BREDWILL being presented by the Grand Jury for having a Bastard Child & summoned failing to appear whereupon its ordered that she pay the

31

Church Wardens of Overwharton Parish for the use of the poor 50 shillings or 500 lbs. Tobo. & Cask.

JUDITH LUNSFORD being presented by the Grand Jury for having a Bastard Child & summoned failed to appear whereupon its ordered that she pay to the Church Wardens of Overwharton Parish for the use of the poor 50 shillings or 500 lbs. Tobo. & Cask.

ELIZABETH IYCER being presented by the Grand Jury for having a Bastard Child failed to appear. Whereupon it's ordered that she pay to the Church Wardens of Overwharton Parish for the use of the poor 50 shillings or 500 lbs Tobo & Cask.

[Page 35 Apr. 10, 1750]

April Court 1750

Suit on Attachment. CATHERINE WASHINGTON agt. the Estate of CHARLES JOHNSON is Dismist.

Action of Trespass. WILLIAM FUELL agt. BAYNE SMALLWOOD. On Deft's motion a Special Imparlance is granted until the next Court.

Action of Trespass. A____ ROSE agt. MASON FRENCH & MARGARET his wife. Defts not appearing Judgment granted the Pltf in the sum sued for unless the Defts appear at the next Court.

Action upon the Case between JOHN MERCER, Gent. agt. MOSES GRIGSBY is Dismist.

Action of Debt. MOSES ROLEY agt. JAMES HUGHS. The Deft not appearing Judgment granted to Pltf for the sum sued for unless the Deft appear at the next Court.

Suit on Petition. LAWRENCE WASHINGTON, Gent. agt. JOSEPH HAWKINS is Dismist.

Suit on Petition. HENRY SMITH and LUTRELL agt. JAMES HUNTER to be tried tomorrow.

Action of Trespass. RICHARD BERNARD, Gent. agt. JOHN FRENCH. The Pltf refusing to prosecute this Suit he is nonsuited and ordered to pay the Deft damages & Costs.

Suit on Petition. MARGARET CHAPMAN & BENJAMIN STROTHER Exors. of TAYLOR CHAPMAN decd. agt. JOHN PILCHER is continued till next Court.

Suit on Scire Facias. JOHN GRAHAM agt. WILLIAM MUNDAY ordered returnable to the next Court.

Suit in Chancery. JOHN HOGG & ELEANOR his Wife agt. JAMES SAVAGE & PETER HEDGMAN, Gent. by their Attorneys alleged that the complainant John was not an Inhabitant of this Colony and therefore moved that the Complainants should give Security for their Costs. Ordered that the Complainant do give the Deft Security for their Costs at the next Court.

[Page 36 Apr. 10, 1750]

April Court 1750

Suit on Petition. HENRY SMITH & GRIFFEN JONES Securitys for the Estate of NICHOLAS SEBASTIAN agtt DANIEL MCDANIEL & THOMAS FLUMAN. Judgment is granted the Pltfs £4.13 & Costs to be discharged on payment of £2.6 with Interest from the 28th day of November 1749 till paid.

Suit on Petition. HENRY SMITH & GRIFFIN JONES Securitys for the Estate of NICHOLAS decd. agt. TIMOTHY LYONS & RICHARD and SEBASTIAN. Judgment granted the Pltfs for £2.11 & Costs to be discharged on payment of £1.5.6 with Interest from the 2d of November 1749 till paid.

Action of Trespass. MARTHA HORTON agt. WILLIAM ROSE & MARGARET his Wife. On the Deft's motion a Special Imparlance is granted them till the next Court.

Action of Trespass. GEORGE RANDOLPH agt. WILLIAM HOLBROOK & ELIZABETH his Wife. On Deft's motion a Special Imparlance is granted them till the next Court.

Action of Trespass. THOMAS & ROBERT DUNLOP agt. Rev. ROBERT ROSE. The Deft not appearing Judgment granted the Pltfs unless the Deft do appear at the next Court.

Suit on Petition. BENJAMIN DUNCOMB agt. GEORGE FRENCH. Judgment granted the Pltf 454 lbs. Tobo. & Costs.

Suit on Petition. JOHN SEMPLE agt SAMUEL MCKAY is Dismist.

Suit on Attachment obtained by JACOB JOHNSON against SAMUEL PHERSON is continued till the next Court.

Ordered that BENJAMIN DUNCOMB pay VALENTINE HUDSON 50 lbs. Tobo. for two days attendance as an evidence for him against FRENCH.

[Page 37 Apr. 10, 1750]

April Court 1750

SAMUEL SIMPSON is appointed Constable in the room of JAMES JEFFRIES.

The the Court adjourned till tomorrow 9 Oclock.
RICHARD BARNARD

At a Court Continued and held for Stafford County April 11th. 1750.

Present   PHILIP ALEXANDER   RICHARD BERNARD
               RICHARD FOOTE   MOTT DONIPHAN
               JOHN PEYTON   PETER DANIEL

GOWRY WAUGH Orphan of JOSEPH WAUGH made choice of MOTT DONIPHAN, Gent. & ALEXANDER DONIPHAN for his Guardians.

Action of Trespass. EDWARD BUSH agt. THOMAS PORTER. On the motion of the Deft a Special Imparlance is granted him till the next Court.

Action of Trespass. EDWARD BUSH agt. JOHN FITZPATRICK. On motion of the Deft a Special Imparlance is granted him till the next Court.

Action of Trespass Assault & Battery. JAMES WILLIAMS agt. JESSE BAILS. The Deft not appearing an alias Capias is ordered returnable to the next Court.

Action of Trespass. JOHN CARTER agt. JOHN WATERS. Deft not appearing Judgment granted the Pltf against him and GEORGE WALLER his Security unless the Deft do appear at the next Court.

Suit on Petition. MOSES LUNSFORD agt. WILLIAM KING Admr. of JOHN RABBLING decd. Deft having pleaded fully suit is Dismist.

Suit on Petition. JOHN JONES agt. JOHN CUBBAGE is Dismist.

Suit in Chancery. MICHAEL HALL agt. GRACE BERRY. Deft having made Oath thereto it's ordered to be certified.

April Court 1750

Suit on Petition. WILLIAM & JAMES HUNTER agt. JOHN TOBEY. Judgment granted Pltfs for £4.9.11 by Account proved with a Lawyer's fee & Costs.

Suit on Petition. VALENTINE SEVERE agt. EDWARD TEMPLEMAN is Dismist.

Suit on Petition. THOMAS TURNER, Gent. agt. CHRISTOPHER BELL is Dismist.

Suit on Petition. THOMAS TURNER, Gent. agt. PETER AIDS is Dismist.

Suit on Petition. RAWLEIGH TRAVERS agt. JAMES HUGHS abates by the Pltf's Death.

Action of Debt. CHARLES DICK agt. the honorable THOMAS LEE Esqr., CHARLES CARTER, JOHN TAYLOE, NATHANIEL HARRISON & PHILIP LEE, Esqr. Exors. of WILLIAM WALKER, Gent. decd. The Defts pray Oyer to which is granted them.

Action of Trespass. PHILIP ALEXANDER, Gent. agt. the Honble. THOMAS LEE, Esqr., CHARLES CARTER, JOHN TAYLOE, NATHANIEL HARRISON & PHILIP LEE, Esqr., Exors. of WILLIAM WALKER, Gent. On Defts motion a Special Imparlance is granted them till the next Court.

Action of Debt. JOHN CHAMPE, Gent. agt. FUTERAL HALL. Deft not appearing Judgment granted Pltf against him and WILLIAM ROSE his Security unless the Deft appear at the next Court.

Action of Trespass. FRANCIS DADE agt. BENONI STRATTON. A special Imparlance is granted Deft until the next Court.

Suit in Chancery. JENNET WILLIAMS agt. THOMAS WILLIAMS being agreed is Dismist.

Suit in Chancery. EDWARD HUMSTON agt. JOHN HUMSTON, JOHN SHORT & RICHARD BERNARD. Time is given the Defts till the next Court to answer the Complainants Bill.

Action of Trespass. PRISCILLA BOWS agt. WILLIAM BARTON. On Deft's motion an alias Capias is ordered returnable to the next Court.

[Page 39 Apr. 11, 1750]

April Court 1750

Action of Trespass Assault & Battery. WILLIAM THOMAS agt. WILLIAM BOWLING is Dismist.

Action of Detinue. JOSEPH COMBS agt. HENRY DAWSON. Deft saith that he don't detain. The Trial is referred till the next Court.

Action of Trespass. ANDREW ROSS agt. JOHN HOGG. A jury to wit NATHANIEL GRAY, CHARLES HARDING, WILLIAM KING, WILLIAM ROSS, JAMES ONEAL, THOMAS WIGNALL, JOHN MAUZY, CHARLES BRENT, JOSEPH COMBS, JOHN SHORT, HOWSON HOOE & HENRY SMITH sworn to Enquire of Damages. Jury finds for Pltf £20 Damages & his Costs.

Indictment against WILLIAM JOHNSON, THOMAS LACY, Junr., & SAMUEL KELLY is Dismist.

Action of Detinue. JOHN GRAHAM, Gent. agt. HANNAH BAYLIS. A Jury to wit BALDWIN DADE, JOSEPH COMBS, THOMAS GREEN, JOHN PEYTON, FRANKLYN LATHAM, THOMAS PRICE, ALEXANDER DONIPHAN, THOMAS HAY, JOHN THOMAS, NATHANIEL GRAY, THOMAS CRAFFORD & ANDREW KENNY. The Jury finds for Pltf the Horse in the Declaration mentioned or £5 & £3 damage. It is considered by the Court that the Pltf recover the Horse afsd or £5 as the value of the said Horse & £3 for detaining.

Action of Trespass. NATHANIEL GRAY agt. BENJAMIN DUNCOMB is continued at the Deft's costs till the next Court.

Action of Trespass. ROBERT RADISH agt. JOSEPH COMBS is continued till the next Court at the Pltf's costs.

Action of Trespass. ANDREW MUNROE, Gent. agt. JOHN JAMES. The Deft not appearing an Attachment is awarded him against the Deft's Estate for £10 & Costs, returnable to the next Court.

36

April Court 1750

Ejection Firma. Thomas Turff agt. HENRY FITZHUGH for Lands and Appurtenances in the Parish of Overwharton which HENRY TYLER, Gent. demised to the Pltf for a Term. The Survey in this Suit not being finished, it's ordered that they proceed therein & that the suit be continued untill the next Court.

Suit on Information. The Lord our King agt. ANDREW KENNY. A Jury to wit NATHANIEL GRAY, CHARLES HARDING, WILLIAM KING, WILLIAM ROSE, HENRY SMITH, JAMES ONEAL, THOMAS WIGNALL, JOHN MAUZY, CHARLES BRENT, HOWSON HOOE, JOSEPH COMBS & JOHN SHORT. Jury finds for the Deft and the Suit is Dismist.

Ejection Firma. Thomas Turff Lessee of HUGH ADIE & MARTHA his wife agt. MASON COMBS abates by the death of Martha.

Suit in Chancery. SAMUEL SELDEN, Gent. agt. DIANA WHELER, GEORGE JAMES & MARY his Wife & GEORGE JAMES the Younger (by HENRY TYLER who is appointed his Guardian). The Defts having put in their answer the Complainant hath time till the next Court to consider thereof.

Upon hearing of a Bill in Chancery brought by HUGH HORTON to prosecute certain Deeds therein mentioned is with the said Deeds ordered to be recorded.

Action of Debt. NATHANIEL GRAY agt. JOHN THOMAS. A Jury to wit GEORGE JAMES, CHARLES HARDING, WILLIAM KING, WILLIAM ROSE, HENRY SMITH, JAMES ONEAL, THOMAS WIGNALL, JOHN MAUZY, CHARLES BRENT, HOWSON HOOE, JOSEPH COMBS, & JOHN SHORT. Jury finds for Deft.

Suit on Petition. RICHARD RATLETT & HENRY SMITH agt. JAMES HUNTER. Judgment granted the Pltfs for £5 by Account with Costs & a Lawyer's Fee.

April Court 1750

Ordered that HENRY SMITH and RICHARD LUTRELL pay JOHN WRIGHT, Gent. 316 lbs. Tobo. for four days attendance as an Evidence against HUNTER & for coming & returning 36 Miles twice.

Ordered that JOHN GRAHAM pay ABRAHAM FARROW 1260 lbs. Tobo. for twelve days attendance as an Evidence for him against BAYLIS & for coming & returning 32 Miles ten times.

Ordered that JOHN GRAHAM pay JOHN BARKER 2118 lbs. of Tobo. for 18 days attendance as an Evidence for him against BAYLIS & for coming & returning 30 Miles twice, 60 Miles four times & 8 times 32 Miles.

Ordered that HANNAH BAYLIS pay JOHN HITE 50 lbs. Tobo. for two days attendance as an evidence for her at Suit of GRAHAM.

Action of Trespass. JAMES HUNTER agt. JAMES BERRY. The Deft confessed Judgment to the Pltf for £6.2.8 and Costs.

Action of Trespass. GEORGE BUCHANAN & WILLIAM HAMILTON, Exors. of the last Will & Testament of NEIL BUCHANAN, Esqr. agt. WITHERS CONWAY. The Deft confessed Judgment to the Pltfs for £7.15.9 and Costs.

Suit in Chancery. MICHAEL HALL agt. GRACE BERRY. The Deft having put in her answer the Complainant hath time to consider thereof to the next Court.

Suit in Chancery. JOHN GRAHAM agt. WALTER LUTRIDGE & others is continued for the Commission to be executed.

Suit in Chancery. THOMAS SHARPE agt. NATHANIEL GRAY & ELIZABETH his Wife is continued till the next Court to recover the Bill.

[Page 42 Apr. 11, 1750]

April Court 1750

Action of Debt. RICHARD BERNARD, Gent. agt. BENONI STRATTON. Deft for plea saith he owes nothing. The trial thereof is referred till the next Court.

Ordered the Exors. of NEIL BUCHANAN decd. pay WILLIAM HUNTER 123 lbs. Tobo. for three days attendance & for coming and returning 8 Miles twice.

Suit in Chancery. HENRY FITZHUGH, Gent. agt. SAMUEL HAYWOOD and RICHARD FOOTE, Gent. is continued till the next Court.

Action of Debt. Our Sovereign Lord the King agt. JOHN HUMPSTON, WILLIAM ROSE & JAMES BUTLER. A Jury to wit JOSEPH COMBS,

GEORGE JAMES, JOHN MAUZY, WILLIAM KING, JAMES ONEAL, THOMAS PRICE, JOHN THOMAS, JOSEPH PORTER, HASEL HARDWICK, HOWSON HOOE, THOMAS HAY, & CHARLES HARDING. The Jury finds for the Deft & this Suit is Dismist.

Action of Trespass. JOHN SHORT agt. RICHARD BERNARD, Gent. The Jury finds a promissory note from the Deft to EDWARD HUMSTON for £35 payable the 1st August 1747. The said note is not endorsed or assigned by the said Edward Humston to any person whatsoever. We find that JOHN HUMSTON has assigned the said note for the Balance thereof after a Debt of £14.7.4 due from the said John Humston to the Deft. We find that the Deft assigned to pay the balance to the Pltf. Verdict admitted to Record and to be argued the next Court.

Action of Debt. ALEXANDER CAMPBELL agt. JOHN MINOR & WOODWARD. The Defts confessed Judgment unto the Plts for £2.3.

April Court 1750

Ordered that RICHARD BERNARD, Gent. pay ANN FRANCES HOOE 275 lbs. Tobo. for eleven days attendance as an Evidence for him at the suit of SHORT.

Ordered that RICHARD BERNARD pay THOMAS PRICE 250 lbs. Tobo. for ten days attendance as an evidence for him at the Suit of SHORT.

Action of Debt. VIVION DANIEL agt. JOSEPH STONE is Dismist the Deft paying Costs.

Action of Debt. EDWARD MAXWELL & COMPANY agt. JOHN RAMY is continued at the Pltf's Costs.

Suit on the Attachment. ALEXANDER CAMPBELL agt. the Estate of JOHN DONNE is Dismist.

Suit on Scire Facias. BALDWIN DADE agt. JOHN & GERRARD ALEXANDER is Dismist.

Action of Trespass. JOHN CHAMPE, Gent. agt. CHARLES JOHNSON is Dismist.

Action of Debt. ANDREW MONROE & COMPANY agt. THOMAS ANGLESLEY. The Deft not appearing Judgment against him & the Revd.

WILLIAM STUART Clk. his Security is confirmed to the Pltfs for 1460 pounds of Tobacco in two Hogsheads of Eight hundred & fifty nett each.

Suit on Petition. THOMAS FARGUSON agt. THOMAS WOOD abates by the Pltf's Death.

Suit on Petition. HENRY TYLER, Gent. agt. FRANCIS MARTIN. Judgment granted the Pltf for 305 lbs. Tobo. & Costs.

Suit on Petition. HUMPHRY BELL agt. GEORGE BRENT is Dismist.

Action of Debt. JAMES NEILSON agt. NATHANIEL GRAY is Dismist the Deft paying Costs.

Action of Trespass. PHILIP ALEXANDER, Gent. agt. JOHN THOMAS being agreed is Dismist.

[Page 44 Apr. 11, 1750]

April Court 1750

Suit on Scire Facias. JOSEPH PORTER agt. THOMAS STARKE. The Sheriff having twice returned that the said Starke was not to be found, it's considered by the Court that the said Porter should have Execution against him for 344 lbs. Tobo. & Costs.

> Then the Court adjourned till Court in Course.
> PHILIP ALEXANDER

At a Court held for Stafford County 8th May 1750.

Present   PHILIP ALEXANDER   RICHARD FOOTE
           MOTT DONIPHAN   JOHN PEYTON

HENRY FITZHUGH, Gent. is required to take a List of the Tithables in St. Paul's Parish the insuing Year.

Mott Doniphan & John Peyton Gent. in Overwharton.

Ordered that the Church Wardens of Overwharton Parish bind SUSANNA SIMPSON to such person as they shall think proper.

The Inventory and appraisement of the Estate of LEONARD MARTIN decd. is admitted to record.

The Inventory and appraisement of the Estate of HENRY NELSON decd. is admitted to Record.

An agreement of BENJAMIN TYLER & RICHARD BROOKE being proved by the Oath of JOHN MAUZY one of the Witnesses thereto is admitted to record.

The Inventory and appraisement of the Estate of WILLIAM BRENTON decd. is admitted to Record.

The Grand Jury being sworn received their charge, retired & returning into Court with their presentments, it's ordered the Offenders be summoned.

Action of Trespass. RICHARD BERNARD, Gent. agt. JOHN FRENCH. On Deft's motion a Special Imparlance is granted him till the next Court.

[Page 45 May 8, 1750]

May Court 1750

Action of Debt. RICHARD BERNARD, Gent. agt. JOHN THOMAS. Deft confessed Judgment to the Pltf for 1715 lbs. crop Tobo. & his Costs.

Suit on Petition. JOHN CHAMP, Gent. agt. THOMAS WITHERS is Dismist.

Suit on Petition. JOHN JONES agt. JOHN CUBBAGE. Judgment granted the Pltf for eleven Shillings balance of an account with Costs & a Lawyer's fee.

Ordered that Jones pay PETER JOHNSON 154 lbs. Tobo. for one days attendance as an Evidence for him against CUBBAGE & for coming & returning 43 miles.

Action of Trespass Assault & Battery. MARY PHILIPS agt. HAYWARD TODD. On Deft's motion a Special Imparlance is granted till the next Court.

Suit on Petition. VALENTINE SEVERE agt. EDWARD TEMPLEMAN. Judgment is granted the Pltf for £1.16.3 with Costs & a Lawyer's fee.

Suit on Petition. ELIZABETH COOKE & TRAVERSE COOKE Exors. of the last Will & Testament of RAWLEIGH TRAVERS decd. agt. JAMES HUGHS. Judgment granted Pltfs for fifty shillings and Costs.

Suit on Petition. THOMAS TURNER, Gent. agt. DINAH MCCANT. Judgment granted the Pltf for 355 lbs. Tobacco by note of hand & Costs & a Lawyer's fee.

Suit on Petition. THOMAS TURNER, Gent. agt. PETER ADIE is Dismist the Deft living in WESTMORELAND.

Suit on Petition. THOMAS TURNER, Gent. agt. JOHN CLIFT. Judgment is granted the Pltf for £1.10.9 with Costs & a Lawyer's fee.

Suit on Petition. THOMAS TURNER, Gent. agt. FRANCIS DAY is Dismist the Deft living in PRINCE WILLIAM COUNTY.

Suit on Petition. THOMAS TURNER, Gent. agt. WILLIAM EATON is Dismist the Deft paying Costs.

Suit on Petition. THOMAS TURNER, Gent. agt. CHRISTOPHER BELL. Judgment granted the Pltf for 463 lbs. of Tobacco by bill with Costs & a Lawyer's fee.

Suit on Attachment obtained by PETER WIGGINTON to GEORGE KNIGHT is continued.

JOHN RALLS Junr. acknowledges his Deed of Feeoffment with livery & seison & receipt thereon endorsed unto RICHARD RALLS Senr. which is admitted to Record.

[Page 46 May 8, 1750]

May Court 1750

GRACE JACKSON Admr. of WILLIAM JACKSON decd. produced an account against his Estate which is allowed & admitted to Record & the Tobo. is valued at 14/ pCent.

Ordered that ELIZABETH COOKE & TRAVERSE COOKE Exors. of RAWLEIGH TRAVERS decd. pay THOMAS HAY 50 lbs. of Tobo. for two days attendance as an Evidence for them vs HUGHS but One to be allowed in the Bill of Costs.

Suit on Petition. CHARLES HARDING agt. ENOCH SPINKS is Dismist.

Suit on the Attachment obtained by WILLIAM ALLEN agt. JOHN TAYLOR the said Allen produced an account against said Taylor for 1100 lbs of Tobo. & Eleven Shillings & three pence ½ & one barrel of Corn whereupon its considered by the Court that the said Allen recover the same of the said Taylor & his Costs & the Sheriff having made return that he has attached 1 Cow, 1 Yearling & a calf & about 4 Barrels of Indian Corn, a pail & a Washing Tub, an

Iron Pott and old Box, an old Spinning Wheel, a Bed Stead, a pair of Cotton Cards, a point [*sic*] pott, 5 old Casks, 5 hens & Cocks & some Chickens & other Small Trifels likewise levied in the hands of JANE MASON, DANIEL HAWKINS, & GEORGE WALLER who being summoned appeared and on Oath declared the said Jane has in her hands 150 lbs. of Tobo., WILLIAM GODFREY 2/6. The other Garnishees say that they had nothing in their hands which they are ordered to pay to the said Allen in part of Satisfaction of the above Judgment & the Sheriff is ordered to sell the Goods & Chattels attached to satisfy the said Allen his Judgment.

The Inventory and appraisement of the Estate of CHARLES WALLER, Gent. decd. is admitted to Record.

CHARLES HARDING & CHARLES WELLS who became Securities for GRACE JACKSON as administrator of her decd. Husbands Estate. Petition for Counter Security & the said Grace failing to give such its ordered that THOMAS GREEN, THOMAS GOUGH, EDWARD RALLS & WILLIAM ALLEN set apart the said Grace her part of her decd. Husband's Estate & that she Deliver the residue to the petitioners.

[Page 47 May 8, 1750]

May Court 1750

The Petition brought by ROBERT SUDDUTH against JAMES FLETCHER & RACHAEL his Wife is Continued.

Suit on the Attachment obtained by the Revd. WILLIAM STUART Clk. agt. JOHN TRACY is Continued.
> Then the Court adjourned till Court in Course.
> PHILIP ALEXANDER

At a Court held for Stafford County June the 12th 1750.

Present   JOHN MERCER   PHILIP ALEXANDER
                RICHARD FOOTE   MOTT DONIPHAN
                PETER DANIEL

Ordered it be entered as a Rule of this Court that when any cause shall be continued at the Costs of either party it shall stand so continued till the Cause is again called.

Ordered that the Several Surveyors of the High Ways Rivers & creeks appointed last be continued.

ROBERT MILLION on his Motion is Levy Free.

RICHARD BERNARD Gent. made Oath to his Accounts against SURLS
LEWIS & FRANCIS DAY which is ordered to be certified.

RANDALL DAVIS is ordered to serve his Master JOHN HAMILTON, Gent.
till the first day of July next & that the said Hamilton then discharge him.

Action of Debt. PHILIP ALEXANDER, Gent. agt. WILLIAM MASON.
NATHANIEL HARRISON Esqr. undertook that if the said Deft should be
condemned in this Action that he would pay the Condemnation for him or
surrender his Body to Prison.

PETER HEDGMAN, Gent., WHARTON RANSDALL & RICHARD HEWITT
to view the Road to be showed them by JAMES SCOTT Clk. as most
convenient to meet the road appointed by Prince William Court to Acquia,
whether the same will be convenient & to whom & how the same is to run & by
whom to be cleared & all other matters necessary to the next Court.

[Page 48 June 12, 1750]

June Court 1750

Ordered that JOHN PEYTON, WILLIAM WRIGHT & HUGH ADIE do view
the most convenient way from MRS. COOKE'S through MRS. HARRISON'S
Plantation to the main road from ACQUIA to RICHLAND (and that in the near
time the said Cooke have the liberty to carry her Tobacco to the WAREHOUSE
through the said Plantation) and report to the next Court.

GILSON BERRYMANS Will proved and a Probate granted WILLIAM
FITZHUGH Esqr. & FRANCIS THORNTON, Gent. two of the Exors. therein
named. ROBERT MASSEY, LANGHORNE DADE, ROBERT HOOE &
JOHN WASHINGTON Appraisers.

A new Commission of the Peace for the County being produced, the Orders
were read and signed. Then the Court adjourned.

                                                    JOHN MERCER

A Commission of the Peace for this County being produced & read together
with Detimus for administering the Oaths FRANCIS THORNTON &
TRAVERSE COOKE, Gent. administered the Oaths to JOHN MERCER, Gent.
who subscribed the Test and administered the same to PHILIP ALEXANDER,
RICHARD FOOTE, MOTT DONIPHAN, JOHN PEYTON, PETER DANIEL,

WILLIAM FITZHUGH, Senr., FRANCIS THORNTON, GERRARD FOWKE & TRAVERSE COOKE Gent. Present—John Mercer, Philip Alexander, Richard Foote, Mott Doniphan, Francis Thornton & Garrard Fowke, Gent.

With the approbation of the Court an Indenture between SAMUEL HYDEN & GEORGE WHITE [*incomplete entry*].

WELCH'S Inventory and appraisement is admitted to Record.

PHILIP ALEXANDER, Gent. made oath to his Account against the Estate of GILSON BERRYMAN, decd. which is ordered to be certified.

Suit on Petition. JOHN PEYTON, Gent. agt. JAMES FRENSLEY is Dismist.

Suit on Petition. PHILIP ALEXANDER, Gent. agt. MASON FRENCH & MARGARET his wife, Admrs. of THOMAS LACY. Judgment granted the Pltf against them for 256 lbs. of Tobo. & Costs.

Action of Trespass. JOHN LUTHWAITE agt. PETER HEDGMAN, Gent. The Deft not appearing Judgment is granted the Pltf against him

[Page 49 June 12, 1750]

June Court 1750

& GEORGE WALLER his Security unless the Deft do appear at the next Court.

Action of Trespass. PHILIP ALEXANDER, Gent. agt. the Honorable THOMAS LEE, Esqr. & CHARLES CARTER, JOHN TAYLOE, NATHANIEL HARRISON & PHILIP LEE Esqr., Exors. of WILLIAM WALKER, Gent. On the Defts motion a Special Imparlance is granted them till the next Court.

Suit on Petition. JOHN LUTHWAITE agt. MASON FRENCH is continued till the next Court.

Suit on Petition. JOHN LUTHWAITE agt. DANIEL FRENCH is continued till the next Court.

Suit on Petition. RICHARD BERNARD, Gent. agt. MASON FRENCH & MARGARET, Admrs. of THOMAS LACY decd. is continued till the next Court.

Suit on Petition. GUSTAVUS BROWN, Esqr. agt. CHARLES HARDING is continued till the next Court at the Pltf's Costs.

Action of Debt. NATHANIEL GRAY agt. DANIEL MATHEWS is Dismist.

Action of Debt. MICHAEL WALLACE agt. JOHN PILCHER. The Deft not appearing Judgment is granted the Pltf against him & JAMES HANSBROUGH his Security unless the Deft do appear at the next Court.

Action of Trespass. WILLIAM STUART, Clk., Exor. of DAVID STUART, Clk. agt. the Honorable THOMAS LEE, Esqr., CHARLES CARTER, JOHN TAYLOE, NATHANIEL HARRISON, & PHILIP LEE, Exors. of WILLIAM WALKER, Gent, decd. On the Deft's motion a Special Imparlance is granted them till the next Court.

Suit on the Attachment obtained by ANTHONY STROTHER against JAMES HUGHS is continued.

GRACE JACKSON being presented by the Grand Jury for having a Bastard Child & summoned failing to appear its ordered that she pay to the Church Wardens of Overwharton Parish for the use of the poor fifty Shillings or 500 lbs. of Tobo. & Cask & Costs.

The Indictment found by the Grand Jury vs GREEN is Dismist.

PETER DANIEL & TRAVERSE COOKE, Gent., Feoffees of the TOWN OF MARLBOROUGH in the room of PETER HEDGMAN who refuses to act & Col. Fitzhugh who is Dead.

Present JOHN MERCER.

Then the Court adjourned till Court in Course.
JOHN MERCER

[Page 50 July 10, 1750]

July Court 1750

At a Court held for Stafford County July the 10th 1750.

| Present | RICHARD FOOTE | PETER DANIEL |
| | FRANCIS THORNTON | TRAVERSE COOKE |

HENRY FITZHUGH, Gent. took the Oath & Subscribed the Test.

A Power of Attorney to ROGER LYDON proved by one of the Witnesses thereto is ordered to be certified.

46

ROBERT STURDY'S Inventory is admitted to Record.

The Inventory of the Estate of GEORGE WILLIAMS, decd. is admitted to the Record.

MAXWELL and others their power to BURGESS & DOUGLASS is admitted to Record.

ANTHONY STROTHER made Oath to his Account against JAMES HUGHS which is ordered to be certified.

STUART and others their Power of Attorney to WRIGHT & DOUGLASS is admitted to Record.

BEATY'S Power of Attorney to BLACKBURN is admitted to Record.

The Inventory & appraisement of the Estate of GILSON BERRYMAN is admitted to Record.

SARAH BERRYMAN, Widow of GILSON BERRYMAN being returned is admitted to Record.

SARAH BERRYMAN, Widow of GILSON BERRYMAN, decd. came into Court & renounced her claim & right to the Legacy given her by her Husband's Will.

A Declaration of ELIZABETH WALLER, Widow of CHARLES WALLER, Gent., decd. being proved by the Witnesses is admitted to Record.

ROBERT BURGESS made Oath to his accounts against ANTHONY HORTON & WILLIAM DREW which is ordered to be certified.

ORSON a negroe Boy belonging to JOHN RALLS adjudged to be 10 Years of Age.

JOHN PEBBLES a Servant boy belonging to JOHN PEYTON adjudged to be 15 Years of Age.

Ordered that JOHN PEBBLES serve his Master JOHN PEYTON for 90 lbs. of Tobo. paid for taking him up when run away.

July Court 1750

JOHN HAMILTON, Gent. came into Court & discharged his Servant RANDALL DAVIS from his Service which is ordered to be Certified.

Ordered that Mr. SCOTT'S Tithables at DIPPLE, MRS. WIGGINTON'S, the Revd. MR. MONCURE'S & Ignatius's Tithables clear the Road from the said Moncure's Gate to MR. ADIE'S fence & be exempt from other Roads the said Moncure to be Overseer of the Same.

JOHN LEWIS & ALEXANDER ROSE, Gent. produced Licence to practice as attorneys, took the Oaths and Subscribed the Test.

The Inventory & appraisement of the Estate of GEORGE SIMPSON, decd. is admitted to Record.

Ordered that a Road be laid out by JOHN PEYTON, Gent. from MRS. COOKE'S through MRS. HARRISON'S Plantation doing the said Harrison as little prejudice as possible.

PETER DANIEL, Gent., Admr. of GEORGE SIMPSON, decd. produced & made Oath to an Account against the said Simpson's Estate which is admitted to Record.

Ordered that the Sheriff sell the Estate of WILLIAM LACY, decd., the same being of so small a Value that no person will administer thereon.

Ordered that a Road be cleared from ACQUIA MARSH ROAD by the PARK & POPLAR QUARTERS to WILLIAM PICKETT'S by the Tithables of MARK CANTON, THOMAS FARNHAM, THOMAS TURNER, WILLIAM SMITH, JAMES HEFFERNON, RICHARD BERRY, MICHAEL PYKE the Poplar Quarter. Michael Pyke is appointed overseer of the same.

SAMUEL THORNBURY one of the Exors. of RACHAEL COLCLOUGH decd. produced & made Oath to an account against the said Rachael's Estate which is allowed & admitted to Record & the Tobo. therein mentioned is valued at 14/ pCent.

Ordered that the Sheriff take RICHARD BROOKS, THOMAS BROOKS, & RICHARD BROOKS, Junr. into Custody till they enter into bond in £20 each & two Securitys on £10 each for keeping the peace for a Year & a day.

The Order for viewing the Road proposed by the Revd. MR. SCOTT is recorded. JOSEPH COMBS & WILLIAM WRIGHT to be put on instead of PETER HEDGMAN & RICHARD HEWITT.

[Page 52 July 10, 1750]

July Court 1750

The suit on Scire Facias. RICHARD BERNARD, Gent. agt. AGNES MCGOMERY is continued.

Action of Debt. RICHARD BERNARD, Gent agt. WILLIAM LORD. An alias capias is ordered returnable to the next Court.

Suit on Petition. RICHARD BERNARD, Gent. agt. LOVE WHITE. Judgment is granted the Pltf for 350 lbs. of Tobo. by note of hand & Costs.

Suit on Petition. RICHARD BERNARD, Gent. agt. WILLIAM BROWN is Dismist.

Suit on Petition. RICHARD BERNARD, Gent. agt. JANE CARVICE Admx. of THOMAS CARVICE, decd. Judgment granted the Pltf for 897 lbs. of Tobo. by Bill & Costs.

Suit on Petition. LYDIA PATTERSON agt. JOSEPH BRAGG. Judgment granted the Pltf for 235 lbs. of crop Tobacco by account & Costs.

Ordered that LYDIA PATTERSON pay THOMAS CRAFFORD 50 lbs. of Tobo. for two days attendance as an Evidence for her against BRAGG.

Action of Debt. JOHN HOOE, Gent. agt. WILLIAM FITZHUGH, Esqr. & FRANCIS THORNTON, Gent. acting Exors. of GILSON BERRYMAN, decd. On the Defts motion a Special Imparlance is granted them till the next Court.

Suit on Petition. JOHN HOOE, Gent. agt. WILLIAM FITZHUGH, Esqr., & FRANCIS THORNTON, Gent., Acting Exors. of GILSON BERRYMAN, decd. Judgment is granted the Pltf for 750 lbs. Tobo. by Account & Costs (when Debts of greater Dignity are paid) of the Goods & Chattels of the said Testator.

Action of Debt. THOMAS LACY, Junr. agt. WILLIAM FITZHUGH, Esqr., & FRANCIS THORNTON, Gent., Exors. of GILSON BERRYMAN, decd. On the Defts motion a Special Imparlance is granted them till the next Court.

July Court 1750

Action of Trespass. THOMAS LACY, Junr. agt. WILLIAM FITZHUGH, Esqr. & FRANCIS THORNTON, Gent. acting Exors. of GILSON BERRYMAN, decd. On the Defts motion a Special Imparlance is granted them till the next Court.

Suit on Petition. JOHN PEYTON, Gent. agt. JAMES FIRNSLY. Judgment is granted the Pltf for 189 lbs. Tobo. by note of hand & Costs.

Suit of Petition. OWIN WINKFEETS agt. CHARLES JONES is Dismist.

Suit on Petition. ANDREW JOHNSON agt. JOHN STACY is Dismist.

Suit on Petition. JOHN RALEY agt. WILLIAM DAVIS. Judgment is granted the Pltf for £3.7.6 by Account & Costs.

Ordered that JOHN RAILY pay PHILIP SHERIDAN 49 lbs. of Tobo. for one days attendance as an Evidence for him against DAVIS & for coming & returning eight Miles once.

Action of Trespass. ROBERT MASSY, Gent. agt. JACOB JOHNSON for £100 damage by means of the Deft's breaking & entering the close of the Pltf in the Parish of St. Paul's. It's ordered that the surveyor of this County go up on the Lands in Controversy & lay out the same having regard to all patents and evidences. And the Sheriff to attend the Survey & to remove force if any afforded & the Surveyor is to return three fair Platts & report to the clerk's Office in due time before the day of hearing.

Then the Court adjourned till tomorrow morning 9 Oclock.
RICHARD FOOTE

At a Court Continued & held for Stafford County July 11, 1750.

Present PHILIP ALEXANDER   RICHARD FOOTE
      JOHN PEYTON   GERRARD FOWKE

Suit on Petition. THOMAS ROSE agt. NATHANIEL GRAY.

July Court 1750

Judgment is granted the Pltf for 410 lbs. crop Tobo. by Account & with Costs & a Lawyer's Fee.

Suit on Petition. ROBERT BURGESS agt. JAMES FIRNSLY is continued.

Suit on Petition. WILLIAM BATTOE agt. JACOBUS JORDAN is Dismist the Pltf paying Costs.

Suit on Petition. ISAAC FARGUSON admr. of JOSIAH FARGUSON decd. agt. JAMES ANGEL. Judgment is granted the Pltf for £3.18.11 by Obligation with Interest from the 28th day of April 1749 till the same is paid with Costs.

Action of Trespass. THOMAS & ROBERT DUNLOP agt. ELIZABETH WALLER, GEORGE WALLER, PETER HEDGMAN, JOHN PAYTON & JOHN MAUZY, Exors. of CHARLES WALLER, decd. On the Defts motion a Special Imparlance is granted them till the next Court.

Action of Debt. ROBERT MILLIAN agt. CHARLES HARDING. On the Deft's motion a Special Imparlance is granted him till the next Court.

Suit in Chancery. JOSEPH HINSON, LAZARUS HINSON, JAMES YELTON and JUBAL his Wife, HENRY THRELKELD and MARY his Wife & GEORGE BELL & ANN his Wife agt. JAMES CRAP & JOYCE his Wife. The Complainants have time till the next Court to file their Bill.

Action of Trespass. GEORGE JOHNSON, Gent. agt. WILLIAM FITZHUGH, Esqr. & FRANCIS THORNTON, Gent. Exors. of GILSON BERRYMAN, decd. On the Defts motion a Special Imparlance is granted them till the next Court.

Action of Trespass. MICHAEL RYAN agt. WHARTON HOLLIDAY. On the Deft's motion a Special Imparlance is granted him till the next Court.

Ordered that ROBERT PHENIX who is now in Goal be set at Liberty.

July Court 1750

Ordered that JACOBUS JORDIAN pay JESSE MOSS 50 lbs. of Tobo. for two days attendance as an Evidence for him at the suit of BATTOOE.

Ordered that JACOBUS JORDIAN pay WILLIAM FOSTER 50 lbs. of Tobo. for two days attendance as an Evidence for him at Suit of BATTOOE.

Ordered that WILLIAM BATTOOE pay JOSIAS STONE 50 lbs. of Tobacco for two days attendance as an Evidence for him against JORDOIN.

Ordered that WILLIAM BATTOE pay SETH BOTTS 50 lbs. of Tobo. for two days attendance as an Evidence for him against JORDOIN.

Suit on Attachment. ROBERT BURGESS agt. the Estate of ANTHONY HORTON. The said Robert produced an Account against the said Anthony for £4.6.6 half penny. Whereupon it's considered by the Court that the said Robert recover the same & his Costs. And the Sheriff having made return that he had attached five Chair Frames, some Turners Tools, Some Pewter & other things, it's ordered that he sell the same to satisfy the said Robert his Judgment thereof and report to Court.

Suit on Attachment. ROBERT BURGESS agt. the Estate of WILLIAM DREW is continued for the Guarnishee.

Suit on Attachment. GRACE JACKSON agt. the Estate of JOHN HITE is Dismist.

Action of Trespass. WILLIAM HUNTER, Gent. agt. WILLIAM FITZHUGH, Esqr., & FRANCIS THORNTON, Gent., acting Exors. of GILSON BERRYMAN, decd. On the Defts motion a Special Imparlance is granted them till the next Court.

Action of Debt. JOHN SHORT agt. WILLIAM FITZHUGH, Esqr., & FRANCIS THORNTON, Gent. acting Exors. of GILSON BERRYMAN, decd. On the Defts motion a Special Imparlance is granted them till the next Court.

Suit in Chancery. HENRY DADE agt. NATHANIEL GRAY. Time is given the Deft to answer the Complainant's Bill.

[Page 56 July 11, 1750]

July Court 1750

Action of Debt. THOMAS VIVIAN, Gent. agt. CHARLES WELLS & BENJAMIN ROBINSON. The Defts filed their Demurer & the Pltf hath time till the next Court of Consider thereof.

Ejection Firma. Thomas Goodright agt. WILLIAM ROSE is continued to agree notes.

Action of Trespass. CHARLES HARDING agt. HANNAH BAYLIS. The Exors. to set a side the Judgment in this Suit being argued are Over Ruled & it's considered by the Court that the Pltf recover of the said Deft according to the form & effect of the Judgment.

The difference between WILLIAM MOUNTJOY & RANDALL HOLDBROOK and JENNETT his Wife concerning the processioning their Lands being argued the Court are of Opinion that the said Randall & Jennett should pay Costs. Whereupon it's considered by the Court that the said William should recover of the said Randall & Jennett his Costs by him in this behalf expended.

Suit on Petition. JAMES WAUGH, Gent. agt. PRISCILLA BOWS abates by the Pltf's Death.

Present HENRY FITZHUGH, Gent.

Suit on Scire Facias. RANDALL HOLDBROOK & JENNETT his Wife agt. PETER HEDGMAN, Gent. The said Hedgman confest Judgment to the Pltfs. Whereupon its considered by the Court that the said Randall & Jenett have Execution against the said Hedgman for five shillings or 50 pounds of Tobacco & 76 pounds of Tobacco & fifteen shillings or 150 lbs. of Tobo. & Costs of this Suit.

Suit on Attachment obtained by ANDREW ROSE agt. RANDALL HOLDBROOK & JENNETT his Wife is Dismist & the said Andrew ordered to pay Costs.

Ordered that WITHERS CONWAY declare upon Oath before some justice what Effects he hath on his hands attached for STEWART vs TRACY.

Action of Trespass Assault & Battery. INNIS BRENT agt. DANIEL HANKINS. The Deft for plea saith he is not guilty & hath

[Page 57 July 11, 1750]

July Court 1750

leave to give the special Matters in evidence. The the trial is referred till the next Court.

Action of Trespass. CHARLES HINSON & JOSEPH [*sic*] his Wife agt. JOHN PEYTON abates the Pltf JOYCE being ___.

Action of Debt. JAMES SCURLOCK agt. JAMES BALLER. The Errors to set a side the Judgment in this Suit being argued are over ruled & it's considered by the Court that the Pltf recover from the Deft in form aforesaid given.

Action of Debt. HAYWARD TODD agt. THOMAS STUBBLEFIELD. The Securitys for the Deft pleaded payment. The Trial is referred till the next Court.

Action of Trespass. JOHN RALLS agt. THOMAS GREEN is Dismist the Pltf paying Costs.

Action of Trespass Assault & Battery. JAMES MAHORNER agt. DANIEL FRENCH. The Deft for plea saith he is not guilty. The Trial is referred till the next Court.

Action of Trespass. ROBERT RAE agt. THOMAS STRIBLING Admr. of WILLIAM STRIBLING decd. The Deft pleaded that he had fully administered. The Trial is referred till the next Court.

Suit in Detinue. NATHANIEL OVERALL agt. GEORGE ALLAN. The Deft for plea Saith that he doth not Detain. The Trial is referred till the next Court.

Ejection Firma. JOHN WITHERS agt. JAMES WAUGH. The Pltf failing to prosecute his Suit on the Defts motion he is nonsuited & ordered to pay the Deft damages & Costs.

Action of Trespass. BENJAMIN ROBINSON agt. THOMAS CRAFFORD. The Deft for plea saith that he is not guilty. The Trial is referred till the next Court.

Suit on Petition. GEORGE BRETT agt. WILLIAM DAVIS is Continued at the Pltf's Costs.

Action of Trespass. ANDREW GRANT & ROBERT BROWN agt. JOHN HASTY. The Deft not appearing the Judgment

[Page 58 July 11, 1750]

July Court 1750

against him and WILLIAM SEBASTIAN his Security is confirmed and a Writ of Enquiry of damages is to be executed the next Court.

Action of Debt. JONATHAN FORWARD of London Merchant agt. CHARLES & CARTY WELLS. The Pltf is ordered to pay the Defts their Costs by them about their defence on this behalf expended.

Action of Trespass Assault & Battery. ANTHONY HORTON agt. SAMUEL MCKEG. The Pltf is ordered to pay the Deft his Costs.

Action of Debt. ROBERT COLCLOUGH, WILLIAM COLCLOUGH & SAMUEL THORNBURY Exors. of RACHAEL COLCLOUGH decd. agt. WITHERS CONWAY. The Deft pleaded payment. The Trial is referred till the next Court.

Action of Trespass. JOHN PARK agt. JOSEPH CARTER. The Deft for plea saith that he did not assume. The Trial is referred till the next Court.

Action of Trespass. WILLIAM FUEL agt. BAYNE SMALLWOOD. The Deft for plea saith he did not assume. The Trial is referred till the next Court.

Action of Trespass. ANDREW ROSE agt. MASON FRENCH and MARGARET his Wife Admrs. of THOMAS LACY, decd. is continued till the next Court.

Action of Debt. MOSES ROWLEY agt. JAMES HUGHS. The Deft not appearing the Judgment against him and GEORGE WHITE his Security is confirmed to the Pltf for £10.12.6 whereupon it's considered by the Court that the Pltf recover the same of the Deft & the said George his Costs.

Suit on Petition. LAWRENCE WASHINGTON, Gent. agt. JOSEPH HAWKINS is Dismist.

[Page 59 July 11, 1750]

July Court 1750

Suit on Petition. MARGARET CHAPMAN & BENJAMIN STROTHER Gent. Exors. of TAYLOR CHAPMAN decd. agt. JOHN PILCHER. Judgment is granted the Pltf for 300 pounds of Tobo. by Note of Hand and Costs.

Suit on Petition. MARGARET CHAPMAN & BENJAMIN STROTHER Gent., Exors. of TAYLOR CHAPMAN agt. JOHN ROBINSON. Judgment is granted the Pltf for £2.15.8 by bill & Costs.

Suit on Scire Facias. JOHN GRAHAM agt. WILLIAM MONDAY. The Sheriff having twice returned that the said William Monday was not to be found, it's considered by the Court that the said Graham have Execution against him for £17.2.3, 145 pounds of Nett. Tobo. & 15 shillings, 150 pounds of Tobacco & the Costs of this Suit.

Action of Trespass. MARTHA HORTON agt. WILLIAM ROSS & MARGARET his Wife. The Defts for plea saith that they are not guilty with leave to give the Special Matter in Evidence. The Trial is referred till the next Court.

Action of Trespass. MARTHA HORTON agt. WILLIAM ROSS. The Deft for plea saith he is not guilty with leave to give the Special Matter in Evidence. The Trial is referred till the next Court.

Action of Trespass. GEORGE RANDALL agt. WILLIAM HOLDBROOK & ELIZABETH his Wife. The Deft for plea saith they are not guilty with leave to give the Special Matter in evidence. The Trial is referred till the next Court.

In the Action upon the Case between EDWARD BUSH agt. JOHN FITZPATRICK. The Deft for plea saith he is not guilty. The Trial is referred till the next Court.

[Page 60 July 11, 1750]

July Court 1750

Action of Trespass Assault & Battery. JANE WILLIAMS agt. JESSE BAILS. The Deft for plea saith he is not guilty with leave to give the special Matter in evidence. The Trial is referred till the next Court.

Suit of Trespass. JOHN CARTER agt. JOHN WATERS is Dismist.

Action of Debt. CHARLES DICK agt. the Honorable THOMAS LEE, Esqr. & CHARLES CARTER, JOHN TAYLOE, NATHANIEL HARRISON & PHILIP LEE, Esqr., Exors. of WILLIAM WALKER, Gent., decd. The Defts prayed Oyer which is granted them.

Action of Trespass. PHILIP ALEXANDER, Gent. agt. the Honorable THOMAS LEE, Esqr. & CHARLES CARTER, JOHN TAYLOE, NATHANIEL HARRISON & PHILIP LEE, Esq., Exors. of WILLIAM WALKER, Gent., decd. The Defts for plea saith that the Testator did not assume. The Trial is referred till the next Court.

Action of Debt. JOHN CAMPBELL, Gent. agt. FRITTERAL HALL. The Deft not appearing the Judgment against him and WILLIAM ROSE his Security is Confirmed to the Pltf for £9.4.4 & his Costs. But this Judgment is to be discharged (the Costs Excepted) on payment of £4.12.2 with Interest from the second day of July 1748 till the same is paid.

Action of Trespass. FRANCIS DADE agt. BENONI STRATTON for £50 damage by means of the Deft's breaking & entering the close of the Pltf at the Parish of St. Paul's. It's ordered that the Surveyor in

[Page 61 July 11, 1750]

July Court 1750

Company of an able Jury go upon the Lands in Controversy & lay out the same as either party would have it, having regard to all Patents and Evidences as shall be produced by either of the parties & report to the next Court. And the Sheriff is to remove force if any offered and the Surveyor is to return three fair Platts & report to the Clerk's Office in due time before the day of hearing.

Suit in Chancery. JOHN HOGG & ELEANOR his Wife agt. ISAAC SAVAGE & PETER HEDGMAN, Gent. Came the parties by their attorney & the Complainants by their attorney moved that they might present their Suit & not give Security which being objected to by the Defts & the matter put to the Court they are of Opinion that the Complainants have a right to prosecute their Suit without giving Security for the Defts Costs where upon it's ordered that they proceed therein. From which order the Defts prayed an appeal to the Eleventh of the next General Court which is granted them they having entered into Bond

JOHN PEYTON & PETER DANIEL, Gent. ordered their assent to the above order to be entered.

Suit in Chancery. EDWARD HUMSTON agt. JOHN HUMSTON, JOHN SHORT & RICHARD BERNARD, Gent. further time is given the Defts till the next Court to answer the Complainant's Bill.

Action of Trespass. PRICILLA BOWS agt. WILLIAM BURTON. The Deft not appearing Judgment is granted the Pltf against him and PETER MAUZY his Security for what of the sum sued for shall [entry incomplete].

[Page 62 July 11, 1750]

July Court 1750

Action of Detinue. JOSEPH COMBS agt. HENRY DAWSON abates by the Deft's Death.

Action of Trespass. NATHANIEL GRAY agt. BENJAMIN DUNCOMB is continued.

Ejection Firma. Thomas Turff, Lessee agt. HENRY TYLER, Gent. & HENRY FITZHUGH, Gent. is continued at the Pltf's Costs.

Action of Trespass. ROBERT RADDISH agt. JOSEPH COMBS is continued at the Pltf's Costs.

Action of Debt. BENJAMIN STROTHER & JAMES WAUGH, Gent. Church Wardens of Overwharton Parish agt. DUKE DYE is Dismist.

Suit in Chancery. SAMUEL SELDEN, Gent. agt. DIANA WHEELER, GEORGE JAMES & MARY his Wife & GEORGE JAMES the Younger, Esqr., HENRY TYLER his Guardian. On the Complainant's motion a Dedimus is ordered returnable to the next Court.

Suit in Chancery. MICHAEL HALL agt. GRACE BERRY. Time is given the Complainant to reply to the Deft's answer.

Suit in Chancery. JOHN GRAHAM agt. LUTARIDGE, JAMES WAUGH, JOHN WILSON & JAMES JOHNSON abates by the Deft Waugh's Death.

Suit in Chancery. THOMAS SHARPE agt. NATHANIEL GRAY & ELIZABETH his Wife. Time is given the Defts till the next Court to answer the Complainant's Bill.

Action of Debt. RICHARD BERNARD, Gent. agt. BENONI STRATTON. A Jury to wit JOSEPH COMBS, SETH BOTTS, JOHN MAUZY, PETER WIGGINTON, CHARLES BRENT, MICHAEL RYAN, JOSIAH STONE, WILLIAM NORTHCUT, JOB SIMS, JOHN MARY, Junr., CHARLES HARDING & JAMES HANSBROUGH. Jury finds for the Pltf 3,974 pounds of

[Page 63 July 11, 1750]

July Court 1750

crop Tobacco damage one penny. And it's considered by the Court that the Pltf recover of the said Defendant the said 3,974 pounds of Tobacco (Crop) & 406 of transfer Tobacco together with the one penny damage.

RACHAEL FLETCHER late RACHAEL SEBASTIAN produced & made Oath to an account against the Estate of her late Husband ISAAC SEBASTIAN which is allowed of & admitted to Record & the Tobo. valued at 12/6 pCent.

58

Ordered that RICHARD BERNARD, Gent. pay THOMAS WASHINGTON 100 pounds of Tobacco for four days attendance as an Evidence for him vs STRATTON.

Suit in Chancery. HENRY FITZHUGH, Gent. agt. SAMUEL HAYWARD, Esqr. & RICHARD FOOTE, Gent. is continued at the Complainant's Costs.

Action of Trespass. JOHN SHORT agt. RICHARD BERNARD, Gent. is continued.

Action of Debt. ROBERT MAXWELL & CO. agt. JOHN RAMY is Dismist.

Action of Trespass. JOHN SOUTHWAITE agt. PETER HEDGMAN, Gent. On the Defts motion a Special Imparlance is granted him till the next Court.

Suit on Petition. JOHN SOUTHWAITE agt. MASON FRENCH is continued at the Pltf's costs.

Suit on Petition. JOHN SOUTHWAITE agt. DANIEL FRENCH is continued at the Pltf's Costs.

Action of Debt. PHILIP ALEXANDER, Gent. agt. WILLIAM ALLISON. The Deft pleaded payment & the Trial is referred till the next Court.

[Page 64 July 11, 1750]

July Court 1750

Suit on Petition. RICHARD BERNARD, Gent. agt. MASON FRENCH & MARGARET his wife, Admrs. of THOMAS LACY, decd. Judgment is granted the Pltf for 677 pounds of Tobacco & Costs.

Suit on Petition. GUSTAVUS BROWN, Esqr. agt. CHARLES HARDING is continued at the Pltf's Costs.

Action of Debt. MICHAEL WALLACE agt. JOHN PILCHER. The Deft not appearing the Judgment against him & JAMES HANSBROUGH his Security is confirmed to the Pltf for £11.11.6. But this Judgment is to be discharged (the Costs excepted) on payment of £5.15.9 with Interest from the 6th day of April 1747 till same is paid.

Action of Trespass. WILLIAM STUART, Clerk, Exor. of DAVID STUART, Clerk decd. agt. NATHANIEL HARRISON, Esqr. is continued.

Action of Trespass. WILLIAM STUART, Clerk, Exor. of DAVID STUART, Clerk decd. agt. the Honorable THOMAS LEE, Esqr., CHARLES CARTER, JOHN TAYLOE, NATHANIEL HARRISON & PHILIP LEE Esqr., Exors. of WILLIAM WALKER, Gent., decd. On the Defts motion further Imparlance is granted them till the next Court.

Suit on the Attachment obtained by ANTHONY STROTHER against JAMES HUGHS is Dismist the said Hughs paying Costs.

[Page 65   July 11, 1750]

July Court 1750

Action of Trespass. RICHARD BERNARD, Gent. agt. JOHN FRENCH. The Deft refusing further to defend this Suit, it's ordered that a Writ issue for a Jury to enquire of the Damages.

Action of Trespass Assault and Battery. MARY PHILIPS agt. HAYWARD TODD. The Deft for plea saith he is not guilty with leave to give the Special Matter in Evidence. The Trial is referred till the next Court.

Suit on Attachment obtained by PETER WIGGINTON against GEORGE KNIGHT. The said Peter produced a note of hand given by the said George to the said Peter for 560 pounds of Tobacco. Whereupon it's considered by the Court that the said Peter recover the same of the said George & his Costs. And the Sheriff having made return that he has attached in the hands of GEORGE WALLER who being summoned declared that he has in his hands the sum of £3.4.6. It's ordered that the Sheriff sell the same & Satisfy the said Peter his Judgment.

The Petition of ROBERT SUDDATH against JAMES FLETCHER and RACHEL his Wife is Dismist.

Suit on the Attachment obtained by WILLIAM STUART Clk. against JOHN STACY is Dismist.

Action of Trespass. THOMAS & ROBERT DUNLOPS agt. the Reverend ROBERT ROSE Clk. On the Deft's motion further Imparlance is granted him till the next Court.

Then the Court adjourned till Court in Course.

PHILIP ALEXANDER

August Court 1750

At a Court held for Stafford County August the 14th 1750.

Present   MOTT DONIPHAN   JOHN PEYTON
                      PETER DANIEL   TRAVERSE COOKE
                      FRANCIS THORNTON

A Probate of the last Will and Testament of JOHN WASHINGTON, Gent., decd. is granted LAWRENCE WASHINGTON one of the Exors. therein named who made Oath thereto & entered into Bond for his due Execution thereof.

RICHARD BERNARD, Gent. took the several oaths & Subscribed the Test.

Present RICHARD BERNARD, Gent.

Ordered that JOSEPH LANE serve his Master JOHN HOOE, Gent. for fourteen days runaway time & £1.3 & 180 pounds of Tobacco expended in taking him up.

PETER DANIEL & SARAH his Wife (she being first privately examined and voluntarily assenting thereto) acknowledged their deed of partition to ELIZABETH COOKE which on her motion is admitted to Record.

ELIZABETH COOKE acknowledged her Deed of Partition to PETER DANIEL, Gent. which is admitted to Record.

JOHN LANE came into Court & agreed to serve his Master JOHN HOOE, Gent. one Year after his time by Indenture as otherwise is expired in Case the said Hooe would have him Salivated this fall.

An Argument between TOWNSHEND DADE, JOHN WASHINGTON & TOWNSHEND WASHINGTON, Gent. was presented into Court by LAWRENCE WASHINGTON & on his motion is admitted to record.

NELL a negroe Girl belonging to PETER DANIEL adjudged to be nine Years old. LUCY nine. DINAH nine. BECK nine. JUDY nine. SUE ten.

MINGO a negro boy belonging to JAMES KENNY adjudged to be 8 years old.

JACK a negroe Boy belonging to JAMES HANSBROUGH adjudged 10 years old.

JAMES REGAN a Servant Boy belonging to EDWARD BURGESS adjudged to be twelve Years old.

[Page 67 Aug. 14, 1750]

August Court 1750

WILLIAM JOHNSON is ordered to remain in the Custody of HUGH ADIE till the next Court & that WILLIAM ALLISON have notice thereof.

JANE OSBORNE came into Court & agreed to quit her Master GEORGE ASBURY of her Freedom dues for forty shillings upon which the said Asbury agreed to set her Free.

ALEXANDER DONIPHAN is appointed Guardian to JOSEPH & TRAVERSE WAUGH Orphans of JOSEPH WAUGH decd. he having given Bond according to Law.

The Report of the viewers on PARSON SCOTT'S Road being returned is admitted to Record.

Administration of the Estate of JOHN BATEMAN decd. is granted to ANNE BATEMENT [*sic*]. WILLIAM ROGERS, HENRY DADE, JAMES MCINTOSH & GEORGE JOHNSON Appraisers.

Administration on the Estate of JOHN SKINNER decd. is granted SARAH SKINNER. JOHN THOMAS, THOMAS STRIBLING, WITHERS CONWAY & THOMAS BURNBURY Appraisers.

Action of Trespass. ROBERT MASSEY, Gent. agt. JACOB JOHNSON for £50 damages by means of the Deft's breaking & entering the Close of the Pltf at the Parish of St. Paul's. It's ordered that the Surveyor go upon the Lands in Controversy & lay off the Same as either party would have it, having regard to all Patents & Evidences as shall be provided by either of the Parties & report to the next Court.

Action of Trespass. FRANCIS DADE agt. BENONI STRATTON for £100 damages by means of the Deft's breaking & entering the Close of the Pltf at the Parish of St. Paul's. It's ordered that the Surveyor go in Company of an able Jury

August Court 1750

onto the Lands in controversy & lay off the same as either party would have it, having regard to all Patents and Evidences as shall be provided by either of the parties & report to the next Court. And the Sheriff is ordered to remove force if any offered & the Surveyor is to return three fair Platts & report to the Clerks Office in due time before the day of hearing.

A Supplementary Inventory of the Estate of RACHAEL COLCLOUGH decd. is admitted to Record.

Then the Court adjourned till tomorrow morning 9 Oclock.
RICHARD BERNARD

At a Court Continued and held for Stafford County August the 15ᵗʰ 1750.

Present	RICHARD BERNARD	RICHARD FOOTE
	MOTT DONIPHAN	JOHN PEYTON
	PETER DANIEL	GERRARD FOWKE
	TRAVERSE COOKE	

INSPECTORS NOMINATED

BALDWIN DADE, THOMAS BUNBURY, Junr., & WITHERS CONWAY for BOYD'S HOLE. WILLIAM MOUNTJOY, THOMAS MUNROE, CHARLES BRENT & THOMAS HAY for CAVE'S. EDWARD WALLER, RICHARD HEWITT, BENJAMIN STROTHER & WILLIAM WRIGHT for ACQUIA.

Suit on Petition. JOHN PEYTON agt. BENJAMIN STROTHER is Dismist.

Suit on Petition. WILLIAM WALLER, Gent. agt. WILLIAM FITZHUGH, Esqr. and FRANCIS THORNTON, Gent., acting Exors. of GILSON BERRYMAN, decd. Judgment is granted the Pltf for £2.4 & Costs of the Goods & Chattels of the said Testator.

August Court 1750

Suit on Petition. DANIEL MATHENY agt. JESSE BAILS is Dismist.

Suit on Petition. GERRARD FOWKE, Gent. agt. JOHN MINOR & MOSES ROWLEY. Judgment is granted the Pltf against them for 679 pounds of Tobo. and 79 pounds of Tobacco (& sixty three pounds of Tobo. by notes of hand & Costs).

Ordered that the Sheriff deliver to HUGH HORTON the several things in an Account by him proved and attached by ROBERT BURGESS as the Estate of ANTHONY HORTON.

Ordered that the several Guardians be summoned to appear at the next Court to make up their Accounts.

The Several Justices not yet sworn are ordered to be summoned to appear at the next Court.

WILLIAM MOUNTJOY, Admr. of JOHN HUNTER decd. produced an Account against his Estate which is admitted to Record & the crop Tobo. is Valued at 16/ pCent.

CHARLES BRENT one of the Exors. of JAMES CARTER decd. made Oath to an Account against his Estate which is admitted to Record.

TABITHA HOOE Admx. of RICE HOOE decd. produced an Account against his Estate which is ordered to be certified.

JOHN PEARSON, Exor. of ANNE PEARSON decd. produced an Account against her Estate which is admitted to Record & the Tobo. valued at 14/ pCent.

Ordered that the Sheriff agree with Workmen to build a Pillory & Stocks.

Inspectors of Beef Pork Flour &c to be continued & ALEXANDER DONIPHAN appointed in the room of RAWLEIGH TRAVERSE.

Action of Trespass. ANDREW GRANT & ROBERT BROWN agt. JOHN HASTY. The Deft came into Court & confessed Judgment unto the Pltfs for £8.19.1 ¾ and their Costs.

[Page 70 Aug. 15, 1750]

August Court 1750

Suit on Petiton. ANDREW JOHNSON agt. JOHN STACY. Judgment is granted the Pltf for £2.9 with Costs and a Lawyer's Fee. But this Judgment is to be discharged (the Costs excepted) upon payment of £1.9.6 with Interest thereon from the 25th day of March 1747 till the same is paid.

Suit on Petition. THOMAS RENOE agt. JOHN CHINN. Judgment is granted the Pltf for 450 pounds of Tobo. & Costs.

Action of Trespass. WILLIAM MATHENY agt. JOHN SIMPSON is Dismist.

Action of Trespass. ISAAC SAVAGE & PETER HEDGMAN, Gent. agt. JOHN ROBINSON. The Deft not appearing an Alias Capias is ordered returnable to the next Court.

Present PHILIP ALEXANDER, Gent.

Action of Debt. ROBERT RAE agt. WILLIAM COURTNEY is Dismist.

Action of Trespass. JOHN CUBBAGE agt. RICHARD BROOKE being agreed is Dismist.

Action of Debt. JOHN RALLS agt. JOHN GREEN & JOHN GREEN the Younger. The Defts not appearing Judgment is granted the Pltf against them & WILLIAM PATTON their Security unless the Defts do appear at the next Court.

Ordered that THOMAS RENOE pay NATHANIEL OVERALL 125 pounds of Tobacco for two days attendance as an Evidence for him against CHINN & for once coming & returning 35 Miles.

Action of Trespass. ANN SCIAS agt. RICHARD OCAIN is Dismist.

Action of Debt. JOHN WASHINGTON Exor. of WILLIAM BAXTER decd. agt. WILLIAM FITZHUGH and FRANCIS THORNTON, Gent. acting Exors. of GILSON BERRYMAN, decd. The Defts pray Oyer which is granted them.

Suit on Attachment obtained by JACOB JOHNSON agt. SAMUEL PHEARSON the said Jacob proved his account & this Suit is continued for the Garnishing.

Present PETER DANIEL

[Page 71 Aug. 15, 1750]

August Court 1750

Ordered that the Petition brought by JOHN RAILY against WILLIAM DAVIS be put on the Docket to the next Court.

Suit on Scire Facias. RICHARD BERNARD, Gent. agt. AGNES MONTGOMERY. The Sheriff having returned that the said Agnes was not to be found it's ordered that an alias Scire Facias issue returnable to the next Court.

Action of Debt. RICHARD BERNARD, Gent. agt. WILLIAM LORD. The Deft not appearing an attachment is ordered against his Estate returnable to the next Court.

Action of Debt. JOHN HOOE, Gent. agt. WILLIAM FITZHUGH, Esqr. & FRANCIS THORNTON, Gent. Acting Exors. of GILSON BERRYMAN, decd. The Defts having pleaded payment by the Testator. The Tryal is referred to the next Court.

Action of Debt. THOMAS LACY agt. WILLIAM FITZHUGH, Esqr. and FRANCIS THORNTON, Gent. Acting Exors. of GILSON BERRYMAN, decd. On the Defts motion a further Imparlance is granted them till the next Court.

Suit on Petition. ROBERT BURGESS agt. JAMES FIRNSLY is continued at the Pltf's Costs.

Action of Trespass. THOMAS & ROBERT DUNLOPS agt. ELIZABETH WALLER, EDWARD WALLER, PETER HEDGMAN, GEORGE WALLER & JOHN MAUZY, Junr., Exors. of CHARLES WALLER, Gent., decd. The Defts having pleaded that the Testator did not assume, the trial is referred till the next Court.

Action of Debt. ROBERT MILLIAN agt. CHARLES HARDING. The Deft having pleaded not guilty, the Trial is referred till the next Court.

Suit in Chancery. JOSEPH HINSON, LAZARUS HINSON, JAMES YELTON & ISBELL his Wife, HENRY THRELKELD & MARY his Wife & GEORGE BELL & ANN his Wife agt. JAMES CRAP & JOYCE his Wife. On the Defts motion further time till the next Court is given them to answer the Complainants Bill.

[Page 72 Aug. 15, 1750]

August Court 1750

Action of Trespass. GEORGE JOHNSON, Gent. agt. WILLIAM FITZHUGH, Esqr. & FRANCIS THORNTON, Gent., Acting Exors. of GILSON BERRYMAN decd. The Defts having pleaded that the Testator did not assume, the trial is referred till the next Court.

Action of Trespass. MICHAEL RYAN agt. WHARTON HOLIDAY. The Deft having pleaded not guilty, the Trial is referred till the next Court.

Suit on Attachment brought by ROBERT BURGESS against the Estate of WILLIAM DREW is continued until the next Court for the Garnishee.

Action of Trespass. WILLIAM HUNTER agt. WILLIAM FITZHUGH, Esqr. & FRANCIS THORNTON, Gent., acting Exors. of GILSON BERRYMAN decd. The Defts having pleaded that the Testator did not assume, the Trial is referred till the next Court.

Action of Debt. JOHN SHORT agt. WILLIAM FITZHUGH, Esqr. & FRANCIS THORNTON, Gent., acting Exors. of GILSON BERRYMAN decd. The Defts having pleaded payment, the Trial is referred till the next Court.

Suit in Chancery. HENRY DADE agt. NATHANIEL GRAY. The Deft having put in his answer, the Complainant hath time till the next Court to consider thereof.

Action of Debt. THOMAS VIVIEN, Gent. agt. CHARLES WELLS & BENJAMIN ROBINSON. On the Defts motion further time is given them to consider of the Demurer.

Ejection Firma. Thomas Goodright, Lessee of HAYWARD TODD agt. WILLIAM ROSE is continued to be tried upon the Facts agreed at the next Court.

[Page 73 Aug. 15, 1750]

August Court 1750

Action of Debt. HAYWARD TODD agt. THOMAS STUBBLEFIELD. Jury to wit PETER MAUZY, CHARLES BRENT, JOSEPH COMBS, ANTHONY MURRY, CHARLES HARDING, THOMAS WOOD, JACOB JOHNSON, HUGH HORTON, THOMAS PORTER, JOHN PURNELL, BENJAMIN ROBINSON & THOMAS CRAFFORD. The Jury finds for the Deft. It's considered by the Court that the Pltf take nothing by his Bill, and the Deft recover of the Pltf his Costs.

Ordered that THOMAS STUBBLEFIELD pay GEORGE MORTON, Gent. 86 pounds of Tobacco for two days attendance as an Evidence for him at the Suit of TODD & for coming & returning 12 Miles once.

Ordered that THOMAS STUBBLEFIELD pay JOHN HOOE, Gent. 50 pounds of Tobacco for two days attendance as an Evidence for him at the Suit of TODD.

Action of Trespass Assault & Battery. JAMES MAHORNER agt. DANIEL FRENCH being agreed is dismist.

Action of Trespass. ROBERT RAE agt. THOMAS STRIBLING, Admr. of WILLIAM STRIBLING, decd. is continued till the next Court.

PATRICK GRADY acknowledged his Deed of Gift to WILLIAM RANDALL.

Action of Detinue. NATHANIEL OVERALL agt. GEORGE ALLEN is continued at the Deft's Costs & to be tried at the next Court.

Action of Trespass. BENJAMIN ROBINSON agt. THOMAS CRAFFORD. A Jury to wit PETER MAUZY, CHARLES BRENT, JOSEPH COMBS, ANTHONY MURRAY, ALEXANDER DONIPHAN, THOMAS WOOD, JACOB JOHNSON, HUGH HORTON, THOMAS PORTER, JOHN DANIEL, THOMAS HAY & JOSEPH REDDISH. The Jury finds 40 Shillings damages for the Pltf & it's considered by the Court

[Page 74 Aug. 15, 1750]

August Court 1750

that the Pltf recover of the said Deft the said 40 Shillings damages and his Costs. And the Deft filed Errors in arrest of Judgment which are to be argued at the next Court.

Ordered that BENJAMIN ROBINSON pay HENRY WIGGINGTON 50 pounds of Tobacco for two days attendance as an Evidence for him vs CRAFFORD.

Ordered that BENJAMIN ROBINSON pay JEREMIAH TUNGATE 50 pounds of Tobacco for two days attendance as an Evidence for him vs CRAFFORD.

Ordered that THOMAS CRAFFORD pay MOSES LUNSFORD 50 pounds of Tobacco for two days attendance as an Evidence for him at the suit of ROBINSON.

Suit on Petition. GEORGE BRITT agt. WILLIAM DAVIS is Dismist.

Action of Debt. ROBERT COLCLOUGH, WILLIAM COLCLOUGH & SAMUEL THORNBURY, Exors. of RACHAEL COLCLOUGH decd. agt. WITHERS CONWAY is continued at the Deft's Costs.

Action of Trespass. JOHN PARKE agt. JOSEPH CARTER is continued till the next Court.

Absent PETER DANIEL

Ordered that WILLIAM WALKER & ELIZABETH his Wife be Summoned to appear at the next Court to answer the Petition of PETER MAUZY.

Present PETER DANIEL.

Action of Trespass. WILLIAM FORD agt. BANE SMALLWOOD is continued at the Deft's Costs.

Action of Trespass. ANDREW ROSE agt. MASON FRENCH & MARGARET his Wife, Admrs. of THOMAS LACY decd. is continued.

Present HENRY FITZHUGH
Absent RICHARD BERNARD, Gent.

Action of Trespass. JOHN SHORT agt. RICHARD BERNARD, Gent. The Special Verdict in this Suit being argued the Court are of Opinion that the Law is for the Pltf whereupon it's considered by the Court that the Pltf recover of the said Deft £22.12.10 and his Costs.

Present RICHARD BERNARD

Then the Court adjourned till tomorrow morning 9 Oclock.
RICHARD BERNARD

[Page 75 Aug. 16, 1750]

August Court 1750

At a Court continued and held for Stafford County August 16th 1750.

Present	PHILIP ALEXANDER	RICHARD BERNARD
	JOHN PEYTON	PETER DANIEL

Action of Trespass. GEORGE RANDALL agt. WILLIAM HOLDBROOK & ELIZABETH his Wife. A Jury to wit WILLIAM MILLS, CALVERT PORTER, FRANKLYN LATHAM, CHARLES HARDING, JOSEPH COMBS, JOHN FITZPATRICK, JOHN MAUZY, WILLIAM ROSS, JOHN PANNEL, JOHN NELSON, THOMAS PORTER & THOMAS WOOD. The Jury finds for the Pltf 1 Shilling damage and Costs.

69

Action of Trespass. MARTHA HORTON agt. WILL ROSS. A Jury to wit CALVERT PORTER, JOSEPH COMBS, JOHN FITZPATRICK, JOHN PANNALL, WILLIAM BRENTON, JOHN NELSON, THOMAS NELSON, THOMAS WOOD, NATHANIEL GRAY, WILLIAM HOLDBROOK, GEORGE RANDALL & ROBERT RADDISH. The Jury finds for the Deft & it's considered by the Court that the Pltf take nothing by her bill & the Deft recovers of the Pltf his Costs.

Action of Trespass. MARTHA HORTON agt. WILLIAM ROSS & MARGARET his Wife. A Jury to wit CALVERT PORTER, JOSEPH COMBS, JOHN FITZPATRICK, JOHN PANNALL, WILLIAM BURTON, JOHN NELSON, THOMAS NELSON, THOMAS WOOD, NATHANIEL GRAY, WILLIAM HOLDBROOK, GEORGE RANDALL & ROBERT RADDISH. The Jury finds for the Defts & it is considered by the Court that the Pltf take nothing by her Bill & the Defts recover of the Pltf their Costs.

[Page 76 Aug. 16, 1750]

August Court 1750

Action of Trespass. EDWARD BUSH agt. THOMAS PORTER. A Jury to wit NATHANIEL GRAY, JOSEPH COMBS, FRANKLYN LATHAM, WILLIAM MILLS, CHARLES HARDING, WILLIAM ROSS, JOHN MAUZY, JOHN NELSON, GEORGE RANDALL, WILLIAM BRUETON, & ROBERT RADISH. The Jury finds for the Deft & it's considered by the Court that the Pltf take nothing by his Bill & the Deft recover of the said Pltf his costs.

In the action upon the Case between EDWARD BUSH & JOHN FITZPATRICK. A Jury to wit NATHANIEL GRAY, FRANKLYN LATHAM, JOSEPH COMBS, WILLIAM MILLS, CHARLES HARDING, WILLIAM ROSS, JOHN MAUZY, JOHN NELSON, GEORGE RANDALL, WILLIAM BURTON, WILLIAM BRUETON & ROBERT RADISH. The Jury finds for the Pltf £4 and his Costs.

Action of Trespass Assault & Battery. JANE WILLIAMS agt. JESSE BAILS is continued at the Deft's Costs.

Action of Debt. CHARLES DICK agt. the Honorable THOMAS LEE, Esqr., CHARLES CARTER, JOHN TAYLOE, NATHANIEL HARRISON & PHILIP LEE, Esqr., the Exors. of WILLIAM WALKER, Gent., decd. The Defts having pleaded payment by the Testator, the Trial is referred till the next Court.

Action of Trespass. PHILIP ALEXANDER, Gent. agt. the Honorable THOMAS LEE, Esqr., CHARLES CARTER, JOHN TAYLOE, NATHANIEL

HARRISON & PHILIP LEE, Esqr., the Exors. of WILLIAM WALKER, Gent., decd. The Pltf proved his Account & his cause is continued till the next Court.

[Page 77 Aug. 16, 1750]

August Court 1750

Suit in Chancery. EDWARD HUMSTON agt. RICHARD BERNARD, Gent., JOHN SHORT & JOHN HUMSTON. On the Defts motion further time is given them to answer the Complainants Bill.

Action of Trespass. PRICILLA BOWS agt. WILLIAM BURTON. The Security for the Deft having pleaded that the Deft did not assume, the Tryal is referred till the next Court.

Action of Trespass. NATHANIEL GRAY agt. BEN DUNCOMB is continued till the next Court.

Action of Trespass. JOHN SOUTHWAITE agt. PETER HEDGMAN, Gent. On the Deft's motion a Special Imparlance is granted him till the next Court.

Suit on Petition. JOHN SOUTHWAITE agt. DANIEL FRENCH is continued till the next Court.

Suit on Petition. JOHN SOUTHWAITE agt. MASON FRENCH is continued till the next Court.

Action of Debt. PHILIP ALEXANDER, Gent. agt. WILLIAM ALLASON is dismist the Deft paying Costs.

Suit on Petition. GUSTAVUS BROWN, Esqr. agt. CHARLES HARDING is dismist.

Action of Trespass. WILLIAM STUART, Clk. Exor. of DAVID STUART Clk. agt. NATHANIEL HARRISON, Esqr. is continued till the next Court.

Action of Trespass. WILLIAM STUART Clk. agt. the Honorable THOMAS LEE, Esqr., CHARLES CARTER, JOHN TAYLOE, NATHANIEL HARRISON, & PHILIP LEE, Esqr., Exors. of WILLIAM WALKER, decd. The Defts for plea say that the Testator did not assume. The Tryal is referred till the next Court.

Present HENRY FITZHUGH, Gent.

71

Action of Trespass. RICHARD BERNARD, Gent. agt. JOHN FRENCH. The Writ for Enquiry for damages is continued till the next Court.

August Court 1750

Action of Trespass Assault & Battery. MARY PHILIPS agt. HAYWARD TODD is continued.

Action of Trespass. THOMAS and ROBERT DUNLOPS agt. ROBERT ROSE Clk. On the Deft's motion a Special Imparlance is granted him till the next Court.

Ordered that WILLIAM HOLDBROOK [*pay*] THOMAS RIDDLE 75 pounds of Tobacco for three days attendance as an Evidence for him ads RANDALL.

Ordered that GEORGE RANDALL pay MARGARET MURRY 50 pounds of Tobacco for two days attendance as an Evidence for her against HOLDBROOK.

Ordered that GEORGE RANDALL pay BEN FLETCHER 50 pounds of Tobo. for two days attendance as an Evidence for him against HOLDBROOK.

Ordered that GEORGE RANDALL pay JAMES OGLESBY 50 pounds of Tobo. for two days attendance as an Evidence for him against HOLDBROOK.

Ordered that WILLIAM HOLDBROOK pay MARY TURNER 75 pounds of Tobacco for three days attendance as an Evidence for him ads RANDALL.

Action of Trespass. ROBERT RADISH agt. JOSEPH COMBS. A Jury to wit NATHANIEL GRAY, FRANKLYN LATHAM, WILLIAM ROSS, JOHN MAUZY, GEORGE RANDALL, JOHN FITZPATRICK, WILLIAM HOLDBROOK, THOMAS WOOD, THOMAS PORTER, JOHN PANNALL, BEN SUDDOTH & WILLIAM MILLS. The Jury finds for the Pltf 100 pounds of Tobacco and 2 Barrels of Corn of the Value of twenty Seven Shillings and sixpence.

Suit in Chancery. SAMUEL SETOON, Gent. agt. DIANA WHELER, GEORGE JAMES & MARY his Wife & GEORGE JAMES the younger by HENRY TYLER his Guardian. On the Defts motion time is given them to consider of the Depons.

August Court 1750

Ordered that JAMES SUDDOTH & JAMES ONEAL be summoned to appear at the next Court to shew cause why they did not attend as an evidence for MARTHA HORTON against ROSS & Wife.

Suit in Chancery. MICHAEL HALL agt. GRACE BERRY. The Complainant having put in his Replication this Suit is set for hearing the next Court.

Suit in Chancery. THOMAS SHARPE agt. NATHANIEL GRAY. The Complainant having filed his Bill the Deft hath time till the next Court to consider thereof.

Suit in Chancery. HENRY FITZHUGH, Gent. agt. SAMUEL HAYWARD & RICHARD FOOTE, Gent. is continued till the next Court at the Complainant's Costs.

Ordered that MARTHA HORTON pay JOHN MAUZY 75 pounds of Tobacco for three days attendance as an Evidence for her against ROSS.

Ordered that MARTHA HORTON pay FRANKLYN LATHAM 75 pounds of Tobacco for three days attendance as an Evidence for her against ROSS.

Ordered that EDWARD BUSH pay [*no name given*] 75 pounds of Tobacco for three days attendance as an Evidence for him against PORTER.

Ordered that EDWARD BUSH pay JOHN PANNAL 75 pounds of Tobacco for three days attendance as an Evidence for him against PORTER.

Ordered that THOMAS PORTER pay CHARLES PORTER 75 pounds of Tobacco for three days attendance as an Evidence for him ads BUSH.

Ordered that EDWARD BUSH pay WILLIAM CAGE 160 pounds of Tobacco for two days attendance as an Evidence for him against FITZPATRICK & for coming & returning 38 Miles once.

Ordered that EDWARD BUSH pay WILLIAM MILLS 25 pounds of Tobacco for one days attendance as an Evidence for him against FITZPATRICK.

Ordered that JOHN FITZPATRICK pay JAMES ONEAL 75 pounds of Tobacco for three days attendance as an Evidence for him at suit of BUSH.

August Court 1750

Ordered that ROBERT RADISH pay JOHN NELSON 384 pounds of Tobacco for six days attendance as an Evidence for him against COMBS & for coming & returning 26 Miles three times.

Ordered that ROBERT RADISH pay JOSEPH FURR 159 pounds of Tobacco for three days attendance as an Evidence for him against COMBS & for coming & returning 28 Miles once.

Ordered that JOSEPH COMBS pay CHARLES HARDING 225 pounds of Tobacco for nine days attendance as an Evidence for him at Suit of RADISH.

Ordered that ISAAC SHEPHEARD be summoned to appear at the next Court to answer the Complaint of WILLIAM DARBY & that he bring the said Darby with him to Court & that WILLIAM ALLISON also have notice of this Order.

Then the Court adjourned till the Court in Course.
PHILIP ALEXANDER

At a Court held for Stafford County 11th Sept. 1750.

Present	JOHN MERCER	RICHARD FOOTE
	MOTT DONIPHAN	JOHN PEYTON
	FRANCIS THORNTON	

JACK, a Negro Boy belonging to NATHANIEL HARRISON, Esqr. is adjudged to be 8 years old.

JUNO, a negro Girl belonging to NATHANIEL HARRISON, Esqr. is adjudged to be 8 years old.

BEN a negro Boy belonging to JOHN ALEXANDER adjudged to be 9 years of age.

CHLOE a negro Girl belonging to JOHN ALEXANDER adjudged to be 7 years of age.

ROSE a negro Girl belonging to THOMAS BARBY adjudged to be 9 years old.

September Court 1750

DINAH a negro Girl belonging to GARDINER BURGESS adjudged to be 11 years old.

Deeds of Lease & Release from JAMES SEATON to BURDIT CLIFTON, proved by JOHN JONES, & ordered to be certified.

BATEMAN'S Inventory returned & made Oath to by Admr. & admitted to record.

ANN BATEMAN made Oath that the Balance due from her to PHEARSON is 156 pounds of Tobacco.

Ordered that BARNABY RILEY serve his Master JOHN ALEXANDER according to Law for six days runaway time, & 480 pounds of Tobacco expended in taking him up.

The Executors of CHARLES WALLER, Gent. decd. made Oath to an additional Inventory of his Estate which is admitted to Record.

ROBERT PETER made Oath to his Account against NATHANIEL GRAY which is ordered to be certified.

GEORGE a negro belonging to JOHN RALLS adjudged to be 15 years of age.

The Road by CATCHERS GATE be turned along the River Side.

JAMES KENNY acknowledged his Deed of Gift of a mullatto girl to his Son JAMES KENNY which is ordered to be recorded.

Ordered that JOHN STUART'S Tithables be added to the List.

ISABELLA HARRISON made Oath to her Accounts against the Orphans of WILL. HARRISON, Gent, decd. which were admitted to Record.

MARGARET HARRISON Orphan of WILL. HARRISON, Gent., decd. came into Court & made choice of ISABELLA HARRISON for her Guardian who is approved of by the Court having given Bond.

JAMES CROSS, a servant Boy belonging to MURDY MCOY is adjudged to be 14 years old.

WINNY a negro Girl belonging to JOHN HOOE, Junr. adjudged to be 9 years old. FRANK belonging to the said Hooe adjudged to be 12 years old.

JENNY, a negro Girl belonging to ALEXANDER JEFFRIES adjudged to be 14 years of age.

WINNY a negro Girl belonging to MATTHEW GREGG adjudged to be 9 years of age.

Administration on the Estate of JOHN GRIGSBY is granted JANE GRIGSBY. MOSES GRIGSBY & HAYWARD TODD Security. WILLIAM GRIGSBY,

[Page 82 Sept. 11, 1750]

September Court 1750

JOHN GRIGSBY, JOHN SYMPSON, & JOHN FOLEY Appraisers.

PETER HANSBROUGH acknowledges his Deeds of Lease & Release & Receipt unto JAMES HANSBROUGH which are admitted to Record.

WILLIAM ALLEN is appointed Overseer of the Road from WALLER'S MILL to the main Road & is ordered to keep the same in repair according to Law.

Present GERRARD FOWKE, Gent.

ALEXANDER DONIPHAN, Guardian to the Orphan of WILLIAM MCCARTY, decd. made Oath to his Account against the said Orphan, which is admitted to Record, & the Crop Tobacco valued at 15/ transfer at 14/; & Corn at six Shillings per Barrel.

RICE HOOE, Guardian to FRANCIS HOOE, made Oath to his Account against the said Francis, which is ordered to be recorded.

BETTY WAUGH, Widow of JAMES WAUGH, Gent., decd. came into Court & declared that she would not abide by the Provision made her by her Husband in his Will.

Licence is granted WILLIAM ALLEN to keep an Ordinary at his House giving Bond in the Office.

JAMES WAUGH'S Will proved by the Witnesses & admitted to Record.

Action of Trespass. ROBERT & THOMAS DUNLOPS agt ELIZABETH WALLER, EDWARD WALLER, PETER HEDGMAN, JOHN PEYTON,

GEORGE WALLER, & JOHN MAUZY, Exors. of CHARLES WALLER, Gent., decd. The Defts confessed Judgment to the Pltfs for 5,243 pounds crop Tobacco.

Ordered that the Sheriff summon twenty-four of the most able Freeholders to appear at the November Court next to be of the Grand Jury for the Body of this County.

Ordered that ROBERT MASSEY, Gent. be summoned to appear at November Court next to answer the Complaint of LEE MASSEY.

Action of Debt. JOHN HAMILTON, Gent. agt. MOSES ROWLEY. The Deft confessed Judgment to the Pltf for £5.8.3 ½ whereupon it's considered by the Court that the Pltf recover the same against him with Interest thereon from the fourth day of January 1749 till the same is paid together with his Costs.

[Page 83 Sept. 11, 1750]

September Court 1750

Action of Trespass. LAWRENCE WASHINGTON, Gent. agt. ISAAC FOWLER. The Deft not appearing Judgment is granted the Pltf against him & BENJAMIN STROTHER, Gent., Sheriff of this County unless the Deft do appear at the next Court and answer the Pltf's Action.

Action of Trespass. ROBERT SHEDDEN agt. PETER HEDGMAN, JOHN PEYTON, EDWARD WALLER, GEORGE WALLER, ELIZABETH WALLER, & JOHN MAUZY, Exors. of CHARLES WALLER, Gent., decd. On the Deft's motion a Special Imparlance is granted them till the next Court.

Action of Trespass Assault & Battery. HENRY NELSON agt. WILLIAM WHITSON. On the Deft's Motion a Special Imparlance is granted him till the next Court.

Action of Trespass Assault & Battery. JAMES RIDING agt. WILLIAM BYRAM is dismist, no Appearance.

Action of Trespass. ISAAC FOWLER & REBECCA his Wife agt. JOHN FLITTER is dismist, no Appearance

Action of Trespass Assault & Battery. CATHERINE WATERS agt. WILLIAM HOWARD & GRACE his Wife. On the Deft's Motion a Special Imparlance is granted them till the next Court.

Suit on Petition. LAWRENCE WASHINGTON, Gent. agt. JOSEPH HANKINS is dismist.

Suit on Petition. GUSTAVUS BROWN, Esqr. agt. CHARLES HARDING. Judgment is granted the Pltf for 50 Shillings & Costs.

Suit on Petition. ALLEN MCRAE agt. CUD. BYRAM is dismist.

Ordered that ALLEN MCRAE pay PETER BYRAM 25 Pounds Tobacco for one Days Attendance as an Evidence for him against BYRAM.

Suit on Petition. CHARLES BRENT agt. JAMES YELTON. Judgment is granted the Pltf for £1.19.6 by Note of Hand & Costs.

Action of Debt. JOHN WASHINGTON, Junr., Exor. of WILLIAM BAXTER, decd. agt. WILLIAM FITZHUGH, Esqr., & FRANCIS THORNTON, Gent., acting Exors. of GILSON BERRYMAN, decd.

[Page 84 Sept. 11, 1750]

September Court 1750

On the Defts motion a special Imparlance is granted them till the next Court.

Suit on Petition. RICHARD BERNARD, Gent., Admr. of ROBERT SOMERVILLE decd., agt. JOHN ALEXANDER is continued till the next Court at the Pltf's Costs.

Suit on Petition. JOHN RILEY agt. WILLIAM DAVIS, Exor. of MARY SMITH, decd. is continued at the Pltf's costs.

JAMES ONEAL, junr. being summoned to shew cause why he did not attend as an Evidence for MARTHA HORTON against WILLIAM ROSS & Wife appeared & having made his Excuse is discharged.

The Petition of PETER MAUZY against WILLIAM WALKER is dismist.

Action of Debt. NATHANIEL GRAY agt. JAMES MCENTOSH. The Deft came into Court & confessed Judgment to the Pltf for 1,034 pounds of Tobacco in one Cask, whereupon its considered by the Court that the Pltf recover the same against him & his Costs.

Suit of Chancery. NATHANIEL GRAY agt. JOHN THOMAS time is given the Deft till the next Court to answer the Complainant's Bill.

Suit in Chancery. RICHARD BERNARD & PHILIP ALEXANDER, Gent. Church Wardens of St. Paul's Parish agt. WILLIAM STUART Clk., Exor. of DAVID STUART, Clk., decd. is dismist.

Deeds of Lease Release & Receipt from JAMES SEATON to BURDIT CLIFTON proved by WITHERS CONWAY & certified.

Ordered that GUSTAVUS BROWN, Esqr. pay JAMES SCOTT, Clk. 97 pounds Tobacco for one Days attendance as an Evidence for him against HARDING & for coming & returning 24 Miles once.

Ordered that GUSTAVUS BROWN, Esqr. pay THOMAS MCKEY 49 pounds of Tobacco & six Pence for one Days Attendance as an Evidence for him against HARDING & for coming & returning 8 Miles once together with his Ferriages at FREDERICKSBURGH.

Then the Court adjourned till tomorrow morning 9 Oclock.
JOHN MERCER

[Page 85 Sept. 12, 1750]

September Court 1750

At a Court continued & held for Stafford County 12th Sept. 1750.

Present   JOHN MERCER   PHILIP ALEXANDER
               MOTT DONIPHAN   JOHN PEYTON

Suit on Scire Facias. RICHARD BERNARD, Gent. agt. AGNESS MONTGOMERY. The Sheriff having twice returned that the said Agness was not to be found, it's thereupon considered by the Court that the said Richard have Execution against the said Agness for £1.11 to be discharged in crop Tobacco, at 10/ pCent or Transfer at 8/4 pCent, with Interest from the second Day of March 1746 till paid & 49 pounds of Tobacco & Costs of this Suit.

Action of Debt. RICHARD BERNARD, Gent. agt. WILLIAM LORD. The Deft not appearing an Attachment is ordered against his Estate returnable to the next Court.

Action of Debt. JOHN HOOE, Gent. agt. WILLIAM FITZHUGH, Esqr. & FRANCIS THORNTON, Gent, acting Exors. of GILSON BERRYMAN, decd. is continued at the Defts Costs.

79

Action of Debt. THOMAS LACY agt. WILLIAM FITZHUGH, Esqr. & FRANCIS THORNTON, Gent., acting Exors. of GILSON BERRYMAN, decd. is continued at the Defts Costs.

Action of Trespass. THOMAS LACY agt. WILLIAM FITZHUGH, Esqr. & FRANCIS THORNTON, Gent., acting Exors. of GILSON BERRYMAN, decd. The Defts having pleaded that the Testator did not assume & they had fully administered. The Trial is referred till the next Court.

Action of Trespass. ROBERT MASSEY, Gent. agt. JACOB JOHNSON is continued till the next Court.

Suit on Petition. ROBERT BURGESS agt. JAMES FERNSLY is continued till the next Court.

Suit in Chancery. JOSEPH HINSON, LAZARUS HINSON, JAMES YELTON & ISABELLA his Wife, HENRY THRELKELD & MARY his Wife, & GEORGE BELL & ANN his Wife agt. JAMES CROP & JOYCE his Wife. Further time till the next Court is given the Defts to answer the Complainants Bill.

[Page 86 Sept. 12, 1750]

September Court 1750

Action of Trespass. GEORGE [*no last name given*], Gent. agt. WILLIAM FITZHUGH, Esqr. & FRANCIS THORNTON, Gent., acting Exors. of GILSON BERRYMAN, decd. is continued till the next Court at the Pltf's Costs.

Action of Trespass. MICHAEL RYAN agt. WHARTON HOLIDAY is continued till the next Court at the Pltf's Costs.

Suit on the Attachment brought by ROBERT BURGESS against WILLIAM DREW. It's ordered that ANN MASON, Widow the Garnishee make Oath before a Justice what Estate of the said Drew's she hath in her Hands.

Action of Trespass. WILLIAM HUNTER agt. WILLIAM FITZHUGH, Esqr. & FRANCIS THORNTON, Gent., acting Exors. of GILSON BERRYMAN, decd. is continued.

Action of Debt. JOHN SHORT agt. WILLIAM FITZHUGH, Esqr. & FRANCIS THORNTON, Gent., acting Exors. of GILSON BERRYMAN, decd. is continued at the Defts Costs.

Suit in Chancery. HENRY DADE agt. NATHANIEL GRAY. The Complainant having put in his Replication the Deft hath time till the next Court to consider thereof.

Action of Debt. THOMAS VIVION, Gent. agt. CHARLES WELLS & BENJAMIN ROBINSON. The Defts joined the Pltf's Demurer & the Tryal is referred till the next Court.

Petition of Trespass. BENJAMIN ROBINSON Pltf [*entry incomplete*] the Errors in this Suit being argued are over-ruled whereupon it's considered by the Court that the Pltf recover of the said Deft [*unnamed*] according to the Judgment.

Ejection Firma. HAYWARD TODD agt. WILLIAM ROSE is continued till the next Court.

Action of Trespass. ROBERT RAE agt. THOMAS STRIBLING, Admr. of WILLIAM STRIBLING, decd. is dismist & the Pltf ordered to pay to the Deft his Costs.

Action of Trespass Assault & Battery. INNIS BRENT agt. DANIEL HANKINS. A Jury to wit EDWARD HERNDON, GEORGE JAMES, JOHN SAUNDERSON, ANTHONY MURRY, ALEXANDER DONIPHAN, JOSIAS STONE, JOHN DOOLING, HAYWOOD TODD,

[Page 87 Sept. 12, 1750]

September Court 1750

HENRY ROBINSON, CHARLES HARDING, THOMAS CRAFFORD, & JOHN KIRK. The Jury finds for the Pltf one penny damage & one penny Costs.

Action of Debt. ROBERT COLCLOUGH, WILLIAM COLCLOUGH, & SAMUEL THORNBURY, Exors. of RACHAEL COLCLOUGH, decd. agt. WITHERS CONWAY. The Deft confessed Judgment to the Pltfs for 1,450 pounds of crop Tobacco.

Ordered that DANIEL HANKINS pay THOMAS RAILY 50 pounds of Tobacco for two days attendance as an Evidence for him at suit of BRENT.

Ordered that DANIEL HANKINS pay JOHN WALLER 50 pounds of Tobacco for two days attendance as an Evidence for him at Suit of BRENT.

Ordered that DANIEL HANKINS pay WILLIAM MOUNTJOY 25 pounds of Tobacco for one Days attendance as an evidence for him at Suit of BRENT.

Action of Trespass. JOHN PARK agt JOSEPH CARTER. By consent of the Parties the Issue in this Suit is waved & the Deft confesses Judgment to the Pltf for 1,325 pounds of crop Tobacco.

Action of Trespass. ANDREW ROSS agt. MASON FRENCH & MARGARET his Wife, Admrs. of THOMAS LACY, decd. The Dfts not appearing the Judgment against them is confirmed & a Writ of Enquiry of Damages is to be executed the next Court.

Action of Detinue. NATHANIEL OVERALL agt. GEORGE ALLEN. A Jury to wit EDWARD HERNDON, WILLIAM MOUNTJOY, THOMAS MONROE, CHARLES BRENT, JOSIAS STONE, HAYWOOD TODD, ALEXANDER DONIPHAN, GEORGE JAMES, THOMAS CRAFFORD, JOHN DOOLING, CHARLES HARDING, & HENRY ROBINSON. The Jury finds the Negro man

[Page 88 Sept. 12, 1750]

September Court 1750

mentioned in the Declaration for the Pltf or £50 to the Pltf and £8 damage for detaining the said Negro from the Pltf. It is considered by the Court that the Pltf recover of the said Deft the Negro above mentioned or £50 & £8 & his Costs.

Ordered that NATHANIEL OVERALL pay CUTH. HARRISON 125 pounds of Tobacco for two Days attendance as an Evidence for him against ALLEN, & for coming & returning 25 Miles once.

Ordered that NATHANIEL OVERALL pay WILLIAM BEARD 333 pounds of Tobacco for three Days attendance as an Evidence for him against ALLEN & for coming & returning 43 Miles.

Ordered that NATHANIEL OVERALL pay WILLIAM CURTIS 250 pounds of Tobacco for four Days attendance as an Evidence for him against ALLEN & for twice coming & returning 25 Miles.

Action of Debt. CHARLES DICK agt the Honorable THOMAS LEE, Esqr., CHARLES CARTER, JOHN TAYLOE, NATHANIEL HARRISON, & PHILIP LEE Esqr., Exors. of WILLIAM WALKER, Gent., decd. The Defts confessed Judgment to the Pltf for £85.6.4 with Interest from the 24th Day of December 1749 till the same is paid.

Action of Trespass Assault & Battery. JANE WILLIAMS agt. JESSE BAILS. A Jury to wit INNIS BRENT, THOMAS MONROE, ALEXANDER

82

DONIPHAN, THOMAS HAY, JOHN CARPENTER, BENJAMIN SUDDUTH, JOHN LINSY, JOHN SYMPSON, JOHN FOLEY, FRANKLYN LATHAM, & MOSES GRIGSBY. The Jury finds 50 Shillings for the Pltf.

[Page 89 Sept. 12, 1750]

September Court 1750

Action of Trespass. WILLIAM FUEL agt. BAYNE SMALLWOOD. A Jury to wit CHARLES BRENT, CHARLES HARDING, JOSIAS STONE, EDWARD HERNDON, JOHN KIRK, GEORGE JAMES, THOMAS CRAFFORD, JOHN DOOLING, HENRY ROBINSON, NATHANIEL OVERALL, ANTHONY MURRAY, & JAMES ONEAL. The Jury finds for the Pltf £5.7.6 damage and Costs.

Ordered that WILLIAM FUEL pay JOHN FOLEY 50 pounds of Tobacco for two Days attendance as an Evidence for him against SMALLWOOD.

Ordered that WILLIAM FUEL pay JOHN SYMPSON 50 pounds of Tobacco for two Days Attendance as an Evidence for him against SMALLWOOD.

Ordered that WILLIAM FUEL pay MOSES GRIGSBY 50 pounds of Tobacco for two Days attendance as an Evidence for him against SMALLWOOD.

Ordered that BAYNE SMALLWOOD pay JOHN HUME 50 pounds of Tobacco for two Days attendance as an Evidence for him at Suit of FUEL.

Action of Debt. ROBERT MILLION agt. CHARLES HARDING. A Jury to wit CHARLES BRENT, ANTHONY MURRAY, JOHN WALLER, HAYWOOD TODD, JOHN ROSSER, HENRY ROBINSON, THOMAS CRAFFORD, JOHN DOOLING, JAMES ONEAL, GEORGE JONES, THOMAS MOUNTJOY, & WILLIAM BURTON. By Consent of the Parties CHARLES BRENT one of the Jurors of the Jury is withdrawn & this Suit is dismist & the Pltf ordered to pay to the Deft his Costs.

Action of Trespass. PHILIP ALEXANDER, Gent. agt. the Honorable THOMAS LEE, Esqr., CHARLES CARTER, JOHN TAYLOE, NATHANIEL HARRISON, & PHILIP LEE Esqr., Exors. of WILLIAM WALKER, Gent., decd. The Defts confessed Judgment to the Pltf for £22.6.11 half penny.

September Court 1750

Action of Trespass. FRANCIS DADE agt. BENONI STRATTON abates by the Deft being dead.

Suit in Chancery. EDWARD HUMSTON agt. JOHN HUMSTON, RICHARD BERNARD & JOHN SHORT. On the Defts motion further time is granted the Defts till the next Court to answer the Complainant's Bill.

Action of Trespass. PRISCILLA BOWS agt. WILLIAM BURTON is continued at the Pltf's Costs.

Action of Trespass. NATHANIEL GRAY agt. BENJAMIN DUNCOMB is continued.

Action of Trespass. ANDREW MONROE, Gent. agt. JOHN JAMES is continued.

Absent JOHN MERCER, Gent.

Ejection Firma. Thomas Turff, Lessee of HENRY TYLER, Gent. agt. HENRY FITZHUGH, Gent. is continued at the Deft's Costs & it's agreed by the Parties that this Suit shall not abate by the Death of either Party.

Suit in Chancery. SAMUEL SELDEN, Gent. agt. DIANA WHEELER, GEORGE JAMES, & MARY his Wife, & GEORGE JAMES the Younger by HENRY TYLER his Guardian. The Depositions taken being returned this Suit is set for hearing.

Present JOHN MERCER, Gent.

Suit in Chancery. MICHAEL HALL agt. GRACE BERRY is continued

Ordered that JANE WILLIAMS pay THOMAS MOUNTJOY 25 pounds of Tobacco for one Days attendance as an Evidence for her against BAILS.

Ordered that JANE WILLIAMS pay THOMAS MOUNTJOY, Junr. 125 Pounds of Tobacco for five Days attendance as an Evidence for her against BAILS.

Suit in Chancery. RICHARD BERNARD, Gent., Admr. of THOMAS SHARP agt. NATHANIEL GRAY is continued.

Suit in Chancery. HENRY FITZHUGH, Gent. agt. SAMUEL HAYWOOD, Esqr. & RICHARD FOOTE, Gent. The Complainant having put in his Demurer the Defts have time till the next Court to consider thereof.

Ordered that JESSE BAILS pay JOHN DOOLING 50 pounds of Tobacco for two Days attendance as an evidence for him ads WILLIAMS.

Action of Trespass. JOHN SOUTHWAITE agt. PETER HEDGMAN, Gent. The Deft having put in his Plea the Pltf hath time to consider thereof till the next Court.

Suit on Petition. JOHN SOUTHWAITE agt. DANIEL FRENCH is continued.

[Page 91 Sept. 12, 1750]

September Court 1750

Action of Trespass. WILLIAM STUART, Clk., surviving Exor. of DAVID STUART, Clk., decd. agt. NATHANIEL HARRISON, Esqr. is continued

Action of Trespass. WILLIAM STUART, Clk., agt. the Honorable THOMAS LEE, Esqr., CHARLES CARTER, JOHN TAYLOE, NATHANIEL HARRISON, & PHILIP LEE Esqr., Exors. of WILLIAM WALKER, Gent., decd. The Defts confessed Judgment to the Pltf for £6.15.6 & Costs.

Action of Trespass. RICHARD BERNARD, Gent. agt. JOHN FRENCH is continued.

Action of Trespass Assault & Battery. MARY PHILIPS agt. HAYWOOD TODD is continued.

Action of Trespass. THOMAS & ROBERT DUNLOPS agt. ROBERT ROSE, Clk. The Deft having pleaded non assumpsit with Leave to give the special Matter in Evidence, the Tryal is referred till the next Court.

Action of Trespass. ISAAC SAVAGE agt. JOHN ROBINSON. The Deft not appearing Judgment is granted the Pltf against him & RICHARD BROOKE his Security unless the Deft do appear at the next Court & answer the Pltf's Action.

Action of Debt. JOHN WASHINGTON, Senr., Exor. of the last Will & Testament of HENRY WASHINGTON, decd. agt. WILLIAM FITZHUGH, Esqr. & FRANCIS THORNTON, Gent. acting Exors. of GILSON BERRYMAN, decd. The Defts prayed Oyer &c which is granted them.

Action of Debt. JOHN RALLS agt. JOHN GREEN & JOHN GREEN the Younger. The Defts confessed Judgment to the Pltf for £6.12.6 & his Costs. But this Judgment is to be discharged (the Costs excepted) on Payment of £3.6.3 with Interest from the ninth day of June 1749 till the same is paid.

Suit on Attachment obtained by JACOB JOHNSON agt. SAMUEL PHEARSON. The said Jacob produced an Account against the said Samuel for 370 pounds of Tobacco. It's therefore considered by the Court that the said Jacob recover the same of the said Samuel & his Costs.

[Page 92 Sept. 12, 1750]

September Court 1750

And the Sheriff made return that he has executed the said Attachment in the hands of ANN BATEMAN who being summoned appeared & on Oath declared that she had in her Hands 156 pounds of Tobacco which she is ordered to pay to the said Jacob in part of Satisfaction of his judgment.

PETER HEDGMAN, Gent., Guardian of WILLIAM BRENT not appearing last August Court to make up the Accounts of his said Ward's Estate & being summoned to appear this Court & make up the same from the time of his last Settlement thereof which was in August 1746, & he failing so to do, the Court proceeded to consider of the Insufficiency of his Securities, & thereupon, GERARD FOWKE & JOHN MERCER, Gent. were of Opinion that the Securities were insufficient and MOTT DONIPHAN & PHILIP ALEXANDER, Gent. were of Opinion that the said Hedgman bound with them the Security for the Estate was Sufficient & the said Hedgman not appearing it's ordered that he be attached to appear to the next Court to make up the said Accounts.

The Guardians of most of the Orphans in this County failing to appear notwithstanding they were summoned upon their Failure to appear last Court to make up their Accounts according to the Act of Assembly—The Court considering their remissness might be owing to the little Care has been generally taken thro' the country to put the Acts relating to Orphans Estates in due Execution, have agreed to order it to be a standing Rule for the future, that if any Guardian accountable to this Court for an Orphan's Estate shall fail to make up his Account yearly in August (if any Court meets in that Month) the Court will grant an Attachment against the said Guardian to compel him to appear the next Court, & if he then fails the Court will either appoint another Guardian, or order the Guardian's Bond to be sued as shall seem of most Advantage to them for their Ward's Estate. And they will in like manner order all Guardian's Bonds to be sued who do not appear the next Court according to the Act of Assembly return an Inventory of their Ward's Estate except the said Guardians for some reasonable Cause to be approved of by the Court shall allow such Guardians

86

farther Time for that Purpose. And to Prevent any Person concerned pretending Ignorance of their Duty, the Court directs that as soon as the Virginia Gazette is revived the Clerk shall send a Copy of this Order to be printed in the same, which they will be at the Expence of without any Charge to the County.

Then the Court adjourned till Court in Course.

JOHN MERCER

[Page 93 Oct. 4, 1750]

October Court 1750

At a Court held for Stafford County the 4th Octbr. 1750.

Present   PHILIP ALEXANDER   MOTT DONIPHAN
                 JOHN PEYTON   GERRARD FOWKE

Ordered that Notice be given that the County Levy is to be laid next Court.

JAMES MCENTOSH is appointed Overseer of the Road from the cross Roads to HOOE'S FERRY in the Room of BENONI STRATTON.

Ordered that JOHN GREEN be summoned to answer the Petition of HAYWOOD TODD.

On the Motion of BURDIT CLIFTON his Licence for keeping Ordinary is renewed.

LUCY a negro Girl belonging to HENRY SMITH adjudged to be nine years old.

SARAH a negro Girl belonging to WILLIAM WRIGHT adjudged to eight years old.

MOLL a negro Girl belonging to THOMAS NORMAN adjudged to be seven years old.

JOHN STUART being bound over to this Court appeared & no Person appearing against him he is discharged.

BAILY WASHINGTON is appointed Overseer of the Road from AQUIA WAREHOUSE to MR. RALL'S POST below AQUIA RUN & is ordered to keep the said Road in repair, & that his Tithables, JOHN STACY Junr., MOSES LUNSFORD, JOHN GREEN, WILLIAM PATTEN, MASON COMBS, & THOMAS HURSTS clear the same & be exempt from other Roads.

87

The Inspectors at AQUIA made Oath that they had in their Hands 3860 lbs crop Tobacco which is ordered to sold according to Law...............13/6.

TABITHA HOOE'S agt. the Estate of RICE HOOE'S Estate [sic] being proved is admitted to Record, & the Tobacco is valued to 13/ pCent & Corn at 7/ per Barrel.

JACK a Negro Boy belonging to WILLIAM GEORGE adjudged to be 12 years old.

Ordered that the King's Attorney prosecute THOMAS BATHAM, Overseer for SUSANNA BRENT, ROBERT CARTER, WILLIAM JACKSON, JAMES MCENTOSH, & DUNCOMB SYMPSON for tending Seconds.

The Attachment against PETER HEDGMAN is continued.

Action of Trespass. RICHARD BERNARD, Gent. agt. JESSE MOSS. The Deft not appearing Judgment is granted the Pltf against him & WILLIAM MOSS his Security unless the Deft appear at the next Court & answer the Pltf's Action.

Action of Trespass. FRANCIS DADE agt. THOMAS MASSEY for £100 damage by means of the Deft breaking & entering the

[Page 94 Oct. 4, 1750]

October Court 1750

Close of the Pltf at the Parish of St. Paul's. On the Deft's Motion a special Imparlance is granted him till the next Court.

Action of Trespass. CHARLES DICK agt. PHILEMON WATERS. The Deft not appearing Judgment is granted the Pltf against him & CHARLES WELLS his Security unless the Deft do appear at the next Court & answer the Pltf's Action.

Suit on Attachment obtained by HENRY PEYTON agt. EATON MEALY is continued.

Suit on Petition. THOMAS & ROBERT DUNLOPS agt. NATHANIEL GRAY is dismist.

Suit on Petition. WILLIAM HUNTER agt. ROBERT GARRET. Judgment is granted the Pltf for £2.6.7 half penny (Balance of a penal Obligation) with

Interest thereon from the 13th day of June 1749 till the same is paid with Costs & a Lawyer's Fee.

Suit on Petition. JOHN SAMPLE agt. WILLIAM SEBASTIAN. Judgment is granted the Pltf for 843 pounds of Tobacco and Costs.

The Inspectors at CAVES WAREHOUSE made Oath that they had in their Hands 2357 pounds of crop Tobacco, which is ordered to be sold according to Law............13/7

Suit on Petition. JAMES RUSSEL agt. WILLIAM GREENLEASE is continued till the next Court.

Suit on Petition. ANDREW MONROE, Gent. agt. HUGH HORTON. Judgment is granted the Pltf for 500 pounds of crop Tobacco by penal Obligation, with Interest from the 16th day of February 1746/7 till the same is paid with Costs & a Lawyer's Fee.

Suit on Petition. PHILEMON WATERS agt. MICHAEL RYAN is continued.

Suit on Petition. LAWRENCE WASHINGTON, Gent. agt. JOHN KITE is continued.

Action of Trespass. LAWRENCE WASHINGTON, Gent. agt. WILLIAM FITZHUGH, Gent. An Alias Capias is ordered returnable to the next Court.

Action of Trespass. FRANCIS THORNTON, Gent. agt. MARY KITCHEN. An Alias Capias is ordered returnable to the next Court.

JOHN RALLS on his Motion hath leave to keep Gates on the Road.

JOHN RALLS on his Motion hath his Ordinary Licence renewed.

Then the Court adjourned till the Court in Course.
PHILIP ALEXANDER

[Page 95 Nov. 13, 1750]

November Court 1750

At a Court held for Stafford County November 13th. 1750.

Present	PHILIP ALEXANDER	RICHARD BERNARD
	RICHARD FOOTE	MOTT DONIPHAN
	PETER DANIEL	

JOSEPH PARK a servant Boy belonging to RICHARD FOOTE, Gent. adjudged to be 11 years of Age.

JOHN ASH a Servant Boy, belonging to JOHN STUART, Gent. adjudged to be 11 years of Age.

JENNY a Negro Girl belonging to WILLIAM KING adjudged to be 7 years old.

VENUS a negro Girl belonging to WILLIAM KING adjudged to be 8 years old.

JACK a Negro Boy belonging to JAMES STARK adjudged to be 7 years old.

DIANA WHEELER made Oath to an Account of Cash received on Account of JOHN WHEELER decd.

Ordered that the Tithables belonging to the Estate of WILLIAM BAXTER be added to the List.

Ordered that the Tithables belonging to the Estate of WILLIAM WALKER, decd. be added to the List.

Ordered that HUB. WHITECOTTON'S Tiths. be added.

Ordered that WILLIAM JONES'S Tiths. be added.

A Bond & Security thereunto annexed acknowledged by MAXAMILLIAN ROBINSON, Gent. to JEREMIAH MURDOCK are admitted to Record.

The Grand Jury for the Body of this County being sworn, received their Charge retired, & returning into Court with their Presentments it's ordered that the several Offenders be summoned.

Ordered that the several Persons summoned to attend as Grand Jury Men & failed to appear be summoned to appear at the next Court to shew Cause why they did not attend.

The BOYDS HOLE Inspectors made Oath that they had in their Hands 1970 pounds of crop Tobacco which is ordered to be sold.

JOHN GRIGSBY'S Inventory returned & admitted to Record.

PETER HEDGMAN, Gent. Guardian to WILLIAM BRENT made Oath to his Account against as also a List of his Tenants which are ordered to be Recorded.

LEE MASSEY came into Court & made Choice of TOWNSHEND DADE Junr. for his Guardian, who is approved of having entered into Bond. And ROBERT MASSEY, Gent. came into Court & relinquished his Right as Guardian to the said Lee.

[Page 96 Nov. 13, 1750]

November Court 1750

Stafford County   Dr.

To Mr. SECRETARY NELSON by Account	234
To Mr. MOSLEY BATTELEY Kings Attorney	1800
To the Clerk by Law	1254
To do. by Account	1434
To the Sheriff by Law	1254
To WILLIAM BLACK'S Account	3305
To BURDIT CLIFTON	25
To the Sheriff for his last year's Balance	556
To CHARLES HARDING per Account	427
To HASEL HARDWICK per Account	478
To SAMUEL SYMPSON per Account	242
To JOHN STONE per Account	323
To FUTURLL HALL per Account	361
To WITHERS CONWAY	36
To MRS. FOWKE for timber for a Bridge	48
To WILLIAM PATTON for a Levy overcharged last Year	15
To GEORGE WALLER per Account	234
To Commission on 10772	647
	11419

Credit.

By the Rents at CAVES WAREHOUSE £6.10.6 sold MR. STUART for	865
By Squirrel's Scalps wanting	774
By 1904 Tiths at 6 lb. Tobacco per Poll	11424
	13,063
By a Fraction due next Year	1644
	11,419

Ordered that the Sheriff receive of every Tithable Person in this County six pounds of Tobacco for discharging the County Creditors & that he acct. for the above Fraction.

PETER DANIEL, Gent. entered his Discent in the Opinion of the Court with Regard to levying COL. HARRISON'S Tobacco for the Court House.

TAYLOR CHAPMAN'S Inventory returned & admitted to Record.

THOMAS BUNBURY, Junr., Inspector at BOYDS HOLE took the Oath prescribed by Act of Assembly which is ordered to be certified.

HENRY FITZHUGH & RICHARD FOOTE, Gent. are desired to try the w[eigh]ts at BOYD'S HOLE.

MOTT DONIPHAN & PETER DANIEL at CAVES, & JOHN PEYTON & TRAVERSE COOKE at ACQUIA.

Then the Court adjourned till tomorrow Morning 9 Oclock.

PHILIP ALEXANDER

[Page 97 Nov. 14, 1750]

November Court 1750

At a Court continued & held for Stafford County the 14th Novber. 1750.

Present	PHILIP ALEXANDER	RICHARD BERNARD
	RICHARD FOOTE	MOTT DONIPHAN
	JOHN PEYTON	PETER DANIEL

Action of Trespass. ROBERT MASSEY, Gent. agt. JACOB JOHNSON for £50 Damage by Means of the Deft's breaking & entering the Close of the Pltf at the Parish of St. Paul's. The last Order for a Survey not being complied with it's ordered that the Surveyor go upon the Lands in Controversy & lay off the same as either Party would have it, having regard to all Patents & Evidences as shall be produced by either of the Parties, & the Surveyor is to return three fair Platts & Reports to the Clerk's Office in due time before the Day of hearing.

TOM a negro Boy belonging to JOSEPH SMITH adjudged to be 12 years old.

RICHARD BERNARD, Gent. is appointed Overseer of the Road in the room of NATHANIEL GRAY.

WILLIAM MILLS is appointed Overseer of the Road in the room of JAMES ONEAL.

RICHARD FOOTE, PETER DANIEL, & JOHN PEYTON, Gent. took the Oaths in Respect to their Coroner's Commission & subscribed the Test.

Ordered that the Sheriff take DANIEL HANKINS into Custody till he enter into Bond in £10 with two Securities in £5 each for his keeping the Peace a Year & a Day.

JOHN SHORT on his Motion hath his Ordinary Licence renewed.

SKINNER'S Inventory returned & admitted to Record.

Action of Trespass. JOHN CHAMPE, Gent. agt. JOHN HASTY. On the Defts' Motion a special Imparlance is granted till the next Court.

Action of Trespass. THOMAS & ROBERT DUNLOPS agt. JAMES CROPP being agreed is dismist.

Suit on Petition. BAYNE SMALLWOOD agt. WILLIAM FUELL is continued till the next Court.

Suit on Petition. ROBERT SHEDDEN, agt. AARON GARRISON &

[Page 98 Nov. 14, 1750]

November Court 1750

BENJAMIN ROBINSON is continued.

Suit on Petition. THOMAS & ROBERT DUNLOPS agt. NATHANIEL GRAY. Judgment is granted the Pltfs for £3.12.2 farthing by Account proved & Costs.

Action of Trespass. ANTONIO MOROSINO agt. HOWSON HOOE being agreed is dismist.

Suit on Petition. HAYWOOD TODD agt. JOHN GREEN is continued.

Then the Court adjourned till Court in Course.
PHILIP ALEXANDER

At a Court held for Stafford County 21st. November 1750.

Present JOHN MERCER   MOTT DONIPHAN
     JOHN PEYTON   PETER DANIEL
     TRAVERSE COOKE

JOHN TURNER being committed to the Goal of this County by Precpt under the Hand of JOHN PEYTON, Gent. for Felony having heard the Evidence agst. him & all Matters relating to the Fact, it's the Court's Opinion that the said Turner be discharged there being no Poof that he had stolen the Goods he stands charged with.

JOHN MERCER

At a Court held for Stafford County December 11th. 1750

Present   PHILIP ALEXANDER   RICHARD BERNARD
                      MOTT DONIPHAN   PETER DANIEL
                      GERARD FOWKE

HOWSON HOOE on his Motion hath his Ordinary licence renewed.

THOMAS FITZHUGH, Gent. took the several Oaths, &subscribed the Test.

Present THOMAS FITZHUGH, Gent.

STEPHEN PILCHER is appointed Constable in the room of SAMUEL SYMPSON.

Administration on the Estate of ARCHIBALD HODGE is granted WILLIAM ROWLEY. THOMAS STRIBLING, WILLIAM BUNBURY, THOMAS BUNBURY & ROBERT MANIN Appraisers.

On Motion of WILLIAM HOWARD Licence is granted him to keep an Ordinary at his House in this County.

JOHN CHAMPE, Gent. made Oath to his Account against JOHN HASTY which is ordered to be certified.

[Page 99 Dec. 11, 1750]

December Court 1750

EDWARD BURGESS, SAMUEL THORNBURY, PETER SIDEBOTTOM, NATHANIEL GRAY, JOHN MOSS, LAWRENCE WASHINGTON, & ROBERT WASHINGTON being summoned to shew Cause why they did not attend as Grand Jurymen. Edward Burgess excused. Peter Sidebottom excused. Nathaniel Gray cont. John Moss contd. Lawrence Washington fined. Robert Washington fined.

Action of Trespass. RICHARD BERNARD, Gent., Admr. of ROBERT SOMERVILLE, decd. agt. JOHN ALEXANDER. On the Deft's Motion a special Imparlance is granted him till the next Court.

Action of Trespass. GEORGE WALLER & ELIZABETH his Wife agt. JOHN PEYTON the younger. On the Defts Motion a special Imparlance is granted him till the next Court.

Suit in Chancery. WILLIAM STUART Clk. & others agt. WILLIAM FITZHUGH, Gent. On the Deft's Motion time is given him till the next Court.

Action of Trespass Assault & Battery. JOHN CORBIN agt. WILLIAM ROSS. On the Deft's Motion a special Imparlance is granted him till the next Court.

Action of Trespass Assault & Battery. JOHN CARPENTER agt. JOHN KIRK & SARAH his Wife. On the Defts Motion a special Imparlance is granted them till the next Court.

Action of Trespass Assault & Battery. CHARLES REGAN agt. PHILIP PAYTON & WINIFRED his Wife. On the Defts Motion a special Imparlance is granted them till the next Court.

Action of Trespass Assault & Battery. DARBY OCAIN agt. STEPHEN PILCHER. On the Deft's Motion a special Imparlance is granted him till the next Court.

The Grand Jury Presentment against MARTHA HORTON is continued.

The Grand Jury Presentment against MARY PATTERSON is continued.

MARGARET BRIDWELL being presented by the Grand Jury for having a Bastard Child & summoned failed to appear, it's ordered that she pay to the Church Wardens of Overwharton Parish (for the use of the Poor of the said Parish) 50 Shillings or 500 pounds of Tobacco & Cask.

BETTY STACY being presented by the Grand jury for having a Bastard Child & summoned failed to appear it's ordered that she pay to the Church Wardens of Overwharton Parish (for the Use of the Poor of said Parish) 50 Shillings or 500

[Page 100 Dec. 11, 1750]

December Court 1750

pounds of Tobacco and Cask.

Ordered that WINIFRED RAILY be attached to answer the Grand Jury's Present. agt. her.

HENRY SUDDARD being presented by the Grand jury for swearing four Oaths & Summoned appeared & having heard his defence it's the Opinion of the Court that he be fined & thereupon ordered to pay to the Church Wardens of Overwharton Parish (for the use of the Poor of the said Parish) 20 Shillings or 200 pounds of Tobacco.

Ordered that JOHN FLITTER be attached to answer the Grant jury's Presentt.

SIMON STACY being presented by the Grand jury for swearing two Oaths & summoned...the Court is of Opinion that he be ordered to pay to the Church Wardens of Overwharton Parish 10 Shillings or 100 pounds of Tobacco.

Ordered that JOHN STACY be summoned to appear at the next Court to answer an Information exhibited against him.

Ordered that DANIEL HANKINS be summoned to answer an Information exhibited agt. him.

Ordered that WILLIAM HOWARD be summoned to answer an Information exhibited agt. him.

ROBERT SHEDDON made Oath to his Acounct. agt. GARRISON & ROBERTSON which is ordered to be certified.

MARY HYDEN, Admx. of WILLIAM HYDEN, decd. made Oath to her Account against his Estate which is admitted to record.

Action of Trespass. LAWRENCE WASHINGTON, Gent. agt. ISAAC FOWLER is dismist the Deft paying Costs.

Action of Trespass. ROBERT SHEDDEN agt. PETER HEDGMAN, JOHN PEYTON, EDWARD WALLER, ELIZABETH WALLER, GEORGE WALLER & JOHN MAUZY, Exors. of CHARLES WALLER, Gent., decd. The Defts for Plea say that the Testator did not assume. The Tryal is referred to the next Court.

Action of Trespass Assault & Battery. HENRY NELSON agt. WILLIAM WHITSON. The Deft for Plea saith that he is not guilty. The Tryal is referred till the next Court.

Action of Trespass Assault & Battery. CATHARINE WATERS agt. WILLIAM HOWARD & GRACE his Wife. The Defts for Plea say they are not guilty in Manner & Form. The Trial is referred till the next Court.

Action of Debt. JOHN WASHINGTON, Junr., Exor. of WILLIAM BAXTER, decd. agt. WILLIAM FITZHUGH, Esqr. & FRANCIS THORNTON, Gent. acting Exors. of GILSON BERRYMAN, decd. The Defts having pleaded Payment & have fully administered,

[Page 101 Dec. 11, 1750]

December Court 1750

the Tryal is referred till the next Court.

Suit on Petition. RICHARD BERNARD, Gent., Admr. of ROBERT SOMERVILLE, decd. agt. WILLIAM ALLISON is continued at the Pltf's Costs.
Present FRANCIS THORNTON, Gent.

Upon a re-hearing of the Motion between JOHN RAILY & WILLIAM DAVIS, Exors. of MARY SMITH, decd. the Court is of Opinion that the said John should recover of the said William according to the Judgment given & Costs.

EDWARD HALL acknowledges his Deed of Feoffment with Livery & Seison & Receipt thereon Indorsed unto JAMES CALK and is admitted to Record.

Ordered that JOHN RAILY pay WILLIAM SHERRIDON 86 pounds of Tobacco for two Days attendance an Evidence for him against DAVIS & for twice coming & returning 6 Miles.

Then the Court adjourned till tomorrow morning 9 Oclock.
PHILIP ALEXANDER

At a Court continued & held for Stafford County Decr. 12th. 1750.

Present   PHILIP ALEXANDER   RICHARD FOOTE
              MOTT DONIPHAN   FRANCIS THORNTON

RICHARD BERNARD, Gent. made Oath to his Answer in Chancery at the suit of HUMSTON which is ordered to be certified.

Present RICHARD BERNARD &
GERRARD FOWKE, Gent.

Suit in Chancery. NATHANIEL GRAY agt. JOHN THOMAS. The Deft on his Motion hath time till the next Court to answer the Complainants Bill.

Action of Debt. JOHN HOOE, Gent. agt. WILLIAM FITZHUGH, Esqr. & FRANCIS THORNTON, Gent., acting Exors. of GILSON BERRYMAN, decd. A Jury to wit JOHN MAUZY, WILLIAM ROSE, JOHN FITZHUGH, THOMAS STRIBLING, HAYWOOD TODD, DANIEL GRIFFIN, JOHN BELL, JAMES YELTON, MICHAEL RYAN, LAZARUS HINSON, BARNARD WILLIAMS, & CHARLES WELLS were sworn. JOHN FITZHUGH, Gent. is withdrawn & the Defts confessed Judgment to the Pltf for £170.17.4.

[Page 102 Dec. 12, 1750]

December Court 1750

But this Judgment is to be discharged of £85.8.8 with Interest from the 24th Day of November 1747 till the same is paid.

Action of Debt. RICHARD BERNARD, Gent. agt. WILLIAM LORD, is dismist.

Action of Debt. THOMAS LACY, Junr. agt. WILLIAM FITZHUGH, Esqr. & FRANCIS THORNTON, Gent., acting Exors. of GILSON BERRYMAN, decd. is continued at the Defts Costs.

Action of Trespass. ROBERT MASSEY, Gent. agt. JACOB JOHNSON is continued till the next Court.

Suit on Petition. ROBERT BURGESS agt. JAMES FRENSLEY is dismist, the Deft paying Costs.

Suit in Chancery. JOSEPH HINSON & others agt. JAMES CROPP & JOYCE his Wife. The Defts having put in their Demurer the Complainants have time to consider thereof.

Action of Trespass. GEORGE JOHNSON, Gent. agt. WILLIAM FITZHUGH, Esqr. & FRANCIS THORNTON, Gent., acting Exors. of GILSON BERRYMAN, decd. is continued.

Action of Trespass. MICHAEL RYAN agt. WHARTON HOLIDAY being agreed is dismist.

Suit on Attachment obtained by ROBERT BURGESS against the Estate of WILLIAM DREW. ANN MASON, Widow being summoned as Garnishee & failing to appear it's ordered that she be attached.

98

Action of Trespass. WILLIAM HUNTER agt. WILLIAM FITZHUGH, Esqr. & FRANCIS THORNTON, Gent., acting Exors. of GILSON BERRYMAN, decd. is continued at the Defts Costs.

Action of Debt. JOHN SHORT agt. WILLIAM FITZHUGH,

December Court 1750

Esqr. & FRANCIS THORNTON, Gent., acting Exors. of GILSON BERRYMAN, decd. is continued at the Defts Costs.

Suit in Chancery. HENRY DADE agt. NATHANIEL GRAY. The Complainant having put in his Replication the Deft hath time till the next Court to consider thereof.

Action of Debt. THOMAS VIVION, Gent. agt. CHARLES WILLS & BENJAMIN ROBINSON. The Demurer being argued is adjudged & the Plea of the said Deft & the Matters therein contained insufficient in Law to preclude the said Pltf from having & maintaining his Action aforesd. against them. Whereupon it's considered by the Court the Pltf recover of the said Deft £50 & his Costs. But this judgment is to be discharged on Payment of £24.15 with Interest from the 13th day of October 1747 till the same is paid.

Present PETER DANIEL, Gent.

Ejection Firma. Goodright Lessee of HAYWOOD TODD agt. WILLIAM ROSE is continued.

JOHN PEYTON the younger is appointed Constable in the Room of HASEL HARDWICH.

Action of Trespass. ANDREW ROSE agt. MASON FRENCH & MARGARET his Wife, Admrs. of THOMAS LACY, decd. is continued.

Action of Trespass. NATHANIEL GRAY agt. BENJAMIN DUNCOMB for £100 damage, by means of the Deft's breaking & entering the Close of the Pltf at the Parish of St. Paul's. By Consent of the Parties the Issue is waved & the Matters submitted to the Court & having heard the Arguments of the Parties by their Attorney's it is adjudged by

December Court 1750

the Court that the Lines described in the Surveyor's Platt by the Letters A, B, C, D, E F. G. H, I, K thence down the Branch to L, thence up the Creek to M, & along the Line N, O, P, Q, R, thence up the Creek to the beginning and that the Deft is a Trespasser, & it's further considered by the Court that the Pltf recover of the said Deft 40 Shillings found by the Jury on the Survey & his Costs & the Deft filed Errors in arrest of Judgment which are to be argued at the next Court.

Ordered that BENJAMIN DUNCOMB pay THOMAS STRIBLING 75 pounds of Tobacco for three Days attendance as an Evidence for him at Suit of GRAY.

Suit in Chancery. EDWARD HUMSTON agt. RICHARD BERNARD, JOHN SHORT & JOHN HUMSTON is continued for the Deft Short to put in his Answer.

Action of Trespass. PRISCILLA BOWS agt. WILLIAM BURTON is continued at the Deft's Costs.

PHILIP ALEXANDER, RICHARD BERNARD, RICHARD FOOTE & HENRY FITZHUGH, Gent. or any two of them are desired to apply to NATHANIEL HARRISON, Gent. & HUGH ADIE to give them Notice that as they have failed in their Agreement concerning building a COURT HOUSE in this County, & that great Part of the Brick Work is so insufficiently done that the Court cannot receive the same, except they agree to enter into Bond with good sufficient Security, to pull down such of the Brick Work as is insufficiently done, & rebuild the same with good & sufficient Bricks & compleat the Court House according to their former Agreement in as short a Time as can possibly & conveniently done that the Court will direct an Action to be brought against them for a Breach of their Agreement & agree with some other Person or Persons to do the same.

Ordered that the Church Wardens of St. Paul's Parish bind JOHN LACY according to Law.

Absent RICHARD FOOTE.

Suit in Chancery. HENRY FITZHUGH, Gent., agt. SAMUEL HAYWOOD, Esqr. & RICHARD FOOTE, Gent. is dismist & the Complainant ordered to pay to the Defts their Costs.

February Court 1750

Then the Court adjourned till Court in Course.
RICHARD BERNARD

At a Court held for Stafford County February 12th. 1750.

Present   JOHN MERCER   PHILIP ALEXANDER
             RICHARD FOOTE   MOTT DONIPHAN
             PETER DANIEL   GERARD FOWKE
             THOMAS FITZHUGH

Ordered that the Exors. of JAMES WAUGH, Gent. be summoned to appear at the next Court to shew Cause why they do not prove his Will.

The Inventory & appraisement of the Estate of ARCHIBALD HODGE is admitted to Record.

JOHN PEYTON being bound over to this County by Recognizance appeared & having heard the Evidences against him, it's ordered that the Sheriff take him into Custody till he enter into bond in £40 with two Securities in £25 each for his good Behavior & keeping the Peace a year & a Day. The said JOHN PEYTON, JAMES KENNY, & THOMAS SEDDON came into Court & acknowledged themselves indebted to our Sovereign Lord the King, the said Peyton in £40 & the said James & Thomas in £20 each in Case the said Peyton should not keep the Peace and be of good Behavior towards all his Majesty's liege People & especially towards MARY LUNSFORD.

Administration on the Estate of DANIEL GRIFFIN is granted to DANIEL CAMPBELL, ROBERT RAE Security. THOMAS FITZHUGH, JOHN FITZHUGH, GEORGE JAMES & HENRY TYLER Appraisers.

IGNATIUS EDWARD'S Will proved & Probate granted MARY his Widow. No Security required.

WASHINGTON & COMP. their Account proved agt. KITE ordered to be certified.

WILLIAM NEWTON acknowledged his Deeds of Lease, Release & Receipt unto JOHN STUART, Gent. is ordered to be recorded.

Ordered that PHILIP ALEXANDER, RICHARD BERNARD & RICHARD FOOTE, Gent. be recommended to his Honor the President to make Choice of for a Sheriff the ensuing year.

Deeds of Lease, Release & Receipt from WILLIAM ALLISON to JOHN SHORT

February Court 1750

proved by three of the Witnesses is admitted to Record.

Absent JOHN MERCER, Gent.

Administration on the Estate of SAMUEL KELLEY decd. is granted BETHLAND KELLEY. JOHN WASHINGTON, junr., RICHARD HOOE, ROBERT WASHINGTON, & JOHN BUCKNER Appraisers.

Ordered that MARGARET & WINIFRED SANCLAIR, Orphans of GEORGE SANCLAIR, decd. be bound out by the Church Wardens of Overwharton Parish according to Law.

ALEXANDER DONIPHAN Guardian to the Orphans of WILLIAM MCCARTY, decd. returned an Inventory of their Estate & made Oath to an Account against them which is ordered to be recorded.

Ordered that JOHN TURNER serve his Master RICHARD FRISTOE for three years runaway time & 180 pounds of Tobacco expended in taking him up.

WILLIAM MOSS is appointed Overseer of the Road in the room of RICHARD BERNARD, Gent.

PETER HEDGMAN, Gent., JOHN MAUZY & WILLIAM MOUNTJOY or any two are appointed to view the most convenient Way to turn the road that goes thro' DOOLING'S PLANTATION & report to the next Court.

Suit on Attachment obtained by RICHARD BERNARD, Gent. against the Estate of JOHN JAMES. The said Richard produced an Account against the said John for 1800 pounds of Tobacco. It's therefore considered by the Court that the said Richard recover the same of the said John & his Costs. And the Sheriff having made Return that he has attached 1 Sword, 3 Augers, 1 Drawing knife, 1 Hand Saw, 1 Adz, 2 Earthen Pots, 1 Stone Jug, a parcel old Books, 1 iron Pestle, & some other Trifles, with 2 cyder Casks & 5 Tubs & that he had also attached in the Hands of sundry Persons who being summoned appeared &

on Oath declared THOMAS EMBREY that he had in his Hands one shilling & three pence which he is ordered to pay to the said Richard in part of Satisfaction of the above Judgment. And the Sheriff is ordered to sell the Goods attached according to Law to satisfy the said Richard his judgment therewith & report to the next Court.

An Indenture between GEORGE MASON, Gent. Guardian to GEORGE MASON, junr.

[Page 107 Feb. 12, 1750]

February Court 1750

& JOSEPH SKELTON was presented & acknowledged by the said George which the Court approved of & ordered to be recorded.

Action of Trespass. THOMAS & ROBERT DUNLOPS agt. ROBERT ROSE, Clk. A Jury to wit EDWARD RALLS, WILLIAM MATTHEWS, WILLIAM MILLS, CHARLES HARDING, JOB SIMS, WILLIAM MATHENY, THOMAS MATHENY, WILLIAM NORTHCUT, JOHN ALEXANDER, THOMAS STRIBLING & RICE HOOE. The Jury finds for the Deft.

Then the Court adjourned till Court in Course.
RICHARD BERNARD

At a Court held for Stafford County March 12th. 1750.

Present PHILIP ALEXANDER   RICHARD BERNARD
     MOTT DONIPHAN   JOHN PEYTON

Administration on the Estate of BENONI STRATTON is granted ANN STRATTON she having entered into Bond according to Law. WILLIAM ROGERS, HENRY SMITH, DUNCOMB SYMPSON & MASON FRENCH are ordered to appraise the said Estate in current Money & report to the next Court.

Ordered that MARY FRAZER serve her Master JAMES SUDDUTH according to Law for having a Bastard Child & the said Mary in Court agreed to quit him her Freedom Dues for paying her Time.

Present J. MERCER, Gent.

Ordered that the Sheriff summon 24 of the most able Freeholders of this County to appear at May Court to be of the Grand Jury for the Body of this County.

103

Ordered that Liquors stand rated as before except Rum & that at 10/ per Gallon.

NATHANIEL HARRISON, Esqr. & HUGH ADIE agreed to take down the Chimney at the South End of the COURT HOUSE & to take out all the bad Bricks & finish the Court House in every other Respect with all imaginable Speed.

FRANCIS THORNTON, GERARD FOWKE, & THOMAS FITZHUGH, Gent. are recommended to his Honor the President for his Honor to make choice of for a Sheriff & the former Order on the said Thorntons Motion is set aside.

Absent JOHN MERCER, PHILIP ALEXANDER, &
RICHARD BERNARD, Gent.

[Page 108 Mar. 12, 1750]

March Court 1750

Mrs. ANNE MASON returned on Affidvt. according to Order of Court as Garnishee of WILLIAM DREW at the Suit of ROBERT BURGESS, whereupon the said Attachment as to her is dismist.

Present JOHN MERCER, Gent.

Suit on Petition. MESSRS. BUCHANAN & COCHRAN agt. RICHARD WALKER. Judgment is granted the Pltf for 276 pounds of crop Tobaco by Acct. & with Costs & a Lawyer's Fee.

Suit on Petition. MESSRS. BUCHANAN & COCHRAN agt. FUTRIL HALL. Judgment is granted the Deft for 225 pounds of Tobacco by Account, with Costs & a Lawyer's Fee.

Suit on Petition. MESSRS. BUCHANAN & COCHRAN agt. JAMES MCCANT. Judgment is granted the Pltfs for 353 pounds of crop Tobo. with Costs & a Lawyer's Fee.

JOHN FRITTER being presented by the Grand jury for swearing four Oaths & summoned failed to appear he is thereupon ordered to pay to the Church Wardens of Overwharton Parish 200 pounds of Tobacco or 20 Shillings & Costs.

Absent JOHN MERCER, Gent.

JAMES YELTON brought into Court PATRICK SMITH & claimed Service of him for runaway Time, but it appearing to the Court that he is free is discharged.

104

Then the Court adjourned till tomorrow morning 9 Oclock.

MOTT DONIPHAN

At a Court continued & held for Stafford County March 13ᵗʰ 1750.

Present RICHARD FOOTE   MOTT DONIPHAN
     JOHN PEYTON   PETER DANIEL
     GERARD FOWKE

Ejection Firma. Thomas Turff agt. HENRY FITZHUGH, Gent. for Lands & Appurtenances in the Parish of Overwharton which HENRY TYLER demised to the Pltf for a Term &c. The Court are of Opinion that the Deft is guilty of Trespass & Ejectment & that the Lines described in the Surveyor's Platt by the Letters A, B, C & the Figure 3 is the true Bounds of Peak's Pattent, & that the Lines in the said Platt described by the C, E, M, & the Figure 3 are the true Bounds of the 200 Acres given by Wilkinson for Seating & that the Law is with the Pltf. Therefore its considered by the Court that the Pltf recover of the said Deft his Form yet to come of and that the Pltf be put in possession thereof.

[Page 109 Mar. 13, 1750]

March Court 1750

And it is further considered by the Court that the Pltf recover of the said Deft the one Shilling Damages agreed on & his Costs & the Deft moved for a Non Suit, for that no Writ of Possession could be awarded the Pltf was overruled from which Judgment the Deft prayed an Appeal to the next General Court which is granted, having entered into bond with JOHN FITZHUGH, Gent., his Security for prosecuting the same with Effect.

Action of Trespass. FRANCIS DADE agt. THOMAS MASSEY for £50 damage by means of the Deft's breaking & entering the Close of the Pltf in the Parish of St. Paul's. The Deft having pleaded not guilty the Pltf joined the Issue & thereupon its ordered that the Surveyor in Company of an able jury of Freeholders go upon the Lands in Controversy & lay out the same as either Party would have it, having regard to all Patents & Evidences. They are to value the Damages & report all Matters of Fact specially to the next Court.

Ordered that HENRY FITZHUGH pay WILLIAM PEYTON 260 pounds of Tobacco for two days attendance as an Evidence for him at suit of TYLER & for twice coming & returning 35 Miles.

Ordered that HENRY TYLER pay WILLIAM PEYTON 155 pounds of Tobacco for two Days attendance as an Evidence for him against FITZHUGH & for coming & returning 35 Miles once.

Ordered that HENRY FITZHUGH pay JOHN SINCLAIR 510 pounds of Tobacco for six days attendance as an Evidence for him at Suit of TYLER & for coming & returning 40 Miles three Times.

Ordered that HENRY TYLER pay PATRICK GRADY 225 pounds of Tobo. for nine days attendance as an Evidence for him against FITZHUGH.

Then the Court adjourned till Court in Course.

RICHARD FOOTE

April Court 1751

At a Court held for Stafford County April 9th. 1751.

Present   RICHARD FOOTE   MOTT DONIPHAN
               JOHN PEYTON   GERARD FOWKE

On Motion of PETER DANIEL, Gent. its ordered that his Deed from ELIZABETH COOKE & her Deeds from him to be dated the day the same was acknowledged.

Present PETER DANIEL

THOMAS PHILIP a Servant Boy belonging to WILLIAM JOHNSON adjudged to be 14 years of Age.

In the Suit on the Attachment obtained by JOHN PEYTON & GEORGE WALLER, acting Exors. of CHARLES WALLER, Gent., decd. against the Estate of AMOS MATHENY, the said John & George produced an Obligation of the said Matheny's for £1.9.1. It's therefore considered by the Court that the said John & George recover the same of the said Amos & their Costs. And the Sheriff having returned the Attachment executed in the Hands of GEORGE WALLER, WILLIAM MATHENY, THOMAS MATHENY & MARY MATHENY the said GEORGE WALLER on Oath declares that he has in his Hands 8 Shillings which he is ordered to pay in part of Satisfaction of the above Judgment & this Suit is continued for the other Garnishees.

Suit on Petition. THOMAS & ROBERT DUNLOPS agt. JOHN RAMEY. Judgment is granted the Pltf for £2.8.7 & Costs.

Suit on Petition. RICHARD BERNARD, Gent. agt. FUTRIL HALL is dismist the Pltf paying the Deft's Costs.

Ordered that FUTRIL HALL pay JOSEPH CLIFT 75 pounds of Tobo. for three days attendance as an Evidence for him at Suit of BERNARD.

Ordered that FUTRIL HALL pay WILLIAM ROSE 75 pounds of Tobo. for three days attendance as an Evidence for him at Suit of BERNARD.

Suit on Scire Facias. RICHARD BERNARD, Gent. agt. JOHN CUBBAGE the Sheriff having returned the Scire Facias & the said John not appearing its considered by the Court that the said Richard have execution against the said John for £2.3.1 & Costs.

Suit on Petition. THOMAS & ROBERT DUNLOPS agt. ARTHUR DUAS. Judgment is granted the Pltf for £4.4 & a Lawyer's Fee.

Suit on Petition. THOMAS & ROBERT DUNLOPS agt.

[Page 111 Apr. 9, 1751]

April Court 1751

ROBERT GARRET. Judgment is granted the Pltfs for £2.14 with Costs & a Lawyer's Fee.

Suit on Petition. MOSELEY BATTALEY, Gent. agt. SAMUEL MCKEY. Judgment is granted the Pltf for £1.10 & Costs.

Suit on Petition. SETH BRYAN & RICHARD BRYAN, Exors. of the last Will & Testament of RICHARD BRYAN, decd. agt. WILLIAM KELLY. Judgment is granted the Pltfs for 480 pounds of Tobo. upon a Judgment obtained by the Testator in his lifetime against the said Deft & 59 pounds of Tobo. & 7 Shillings & sixpence Costs & a Lawyer's Fee.

Absent PETER DANIEL, Gent.

Suit on Petition. PETER DANIEL, Gent. agt. WILLIAM FOSTER. Judgment is granted the Pltf for 656 pounds of Tobacco by Account being proved & Costs.

Present PETER DANIEL, Gent.

Suit on Petition. SAMUEL HILDRUP agt. JOHN HOGG & ELEANOR his Wife. Judgment is granted the Pltf for £3.4 by a Note of hand with Costs & a Lawyer's Fee.

Suit on Petition. JOHN PEYTON, Gent. agt. THOMAS HURST. Judgment if granted the Pltf for 1000 pounds of Crop Tobacco by Note of hand & Costs.

Suit on Petition. JOHN PEYTON, Gent. agt THOMAS HURST. Judgment is granted the Pltf for £2.19.3 by Account proved & Costs.

Ordered that MARY GRACE serve her Master JOHN HUGHS according to Law for having a Bastard Child & that the said Mary failing to pay her fine or giving Security for the Same it's ordered that the Sheriff give her 25 Lashes on the bare Back well laid on.

Ordered that HENRY TYLER pay HENRY FIELD 105 pounds of Tobacco for one days attendance as an Evidence for him against FITZHUGH & for coming & returning 30 Miles once.

Ordered that HENRY FITZHUGH, Gent. pay HENRY FIELD 230 pounds of Tobacco for two days attendance as an Evidence for him at Suit of TYLER & for twice coming & returning 30 Miles.

Then the Court adjourned till Court in Course.
RICHARD FOOTE

[Page 112 May 14, 1751]

May Court 1751

At a Court held for Stafford County May 14th. 1751.

Present   RICHARD FOOTE   MOTT DONIPHAN
                JOHN PEYTON   THOMAS FITZHUGH
                PETER DANIEL

GERARD FOWKE Gent. is desired to take a List of Tithables in the lower Parish for the ensuing Year. THOMAS FITZHUGH & TRAVERSE COOKE, Gent. for the upper Parish.

The Grand Jury for the Body of this County being sworn & received their Charge, retired & returning into Court brought in these Presentments as follows We present ELIZABETH MCABOY for retailing one Pint of Punch contrary to Act of Assembly & provided by the Knowledge of two of us in the Parish of Overwharton. We also present MARY WISE for retailing one Pint of Rum

108

contrary to Act of Assembly by the Knowledge of two of us in the Parish of Overwharton. We also present FRANCIS THORNTON for profanely swearing four Oaths on the 20th of March last by the Information of RICHARD BERNARD, Gent., also for swearing one Oath at the Parish of St. Paul's the 25th of April last, also for swearing two Oaths at Overwharton Parish on the 8th day of May instant. We also present the said Thornton for stopping the Road that leads from MOSS'S FERRY to ST. PAUL'S CHURCH. We likewise present the said FRANCIS THORNTON for challenging RICHARD BERNARD, Gent. to meet and fight him with a small Sword at MONK'S RACE GROUND on the 25th of April last in St. Paul's Parish. All the above Presentments against the said Francis Thornton, Gent. is by the Information of RICHARD BERNARD, Gent. We likewise present SAMUEL SIMS for profanely swearing two Oaths at the Parish of Overwharton within two Months last past by Knowledge of two of us. We also present SAMUEL NEWBILL for profanely swearing four Oaths at Overwharton Parish within two Months last past by the Knowledge of two of us. We likewise present ANNE DILLION for having a Bastard Child in the Parish of Overwharton by the Knowledge of two of us. We also present MARY HORTON for having a Bastard Child in the Parish of Overwharton by the Knowledge of two of us. We likewise present ANN GRAY for having a Bastard Child in the Parish of Overwharton by the Knowledge of two of us.

[Page 113 May 14, 1751]

May Court 1751

We likewise present SARAH PESTRIDGE in St. Paul's Parish. We likewise present JEMIMA EDWARDS for having a Bastard Child at the Parish of Overwharton. We also present ANN HANSLEY also HAMILTON for having a Bastard Child in Overwharton Parish. We likewise present WILLIAM CASH for profanely swearing one Oath in the Parish of Overwharton on the 11th day of this Instant. We likewise present RICHARD BERNARD, Gent. for profanely swearing a great number of Oaths within this two Months last past in the Parish of St. Paul's & Overwharton by the Information of FRANCIS THORNTON, Gent. HOWSON HOOE Foreman.

Administration on the Estate of SAMUEL MCENTOSH is granted PHILIS MCENTOSH she having entered into Bond with MASON FRENCH & WILLIAM JOHNSON her Securities. WILLIAM ROGERS, GEORGE JOHNSON, HENRY SMITH & THOMAS MASSEY Appraisers.

Administration on the Estate of CASAR FRANKLYN is granted SARAH FRANKLYN she having entered into Bond with GEORGE ALLEN & FRANKLYN LATHAM her Securities. RICHARD HOOE, JOHN BUCKNER, JOHN JOHNSON & JOSEPH POWELL Appraisers.

Ordered that the Church Wardens of Overwharton Parish bind ELIZABETH TYLER & HANNAH TYLER, Orphans of HENRY TYLER, decd. according to Law.

Ordered that the Church Wardens of Overwharton Parish bind PHILEMON WATERS & RAWLEIGH WATERS according to Law.

Ordered that the Revd. JOHN MONCURE, PETER HEDGMAN, JOHN PEYTON & GEORGE BRENT, Gent. or any three of them set apart the Estate of ELIAS HORE, decd. from the Estate of WILLIAM HARRISON, decd. & then divide the said Harrison's among his Orphans & report to Court.

Ordered that the Church Wardens of Overwharton Parish bind WILLIAM MATTHEWS & SARAH MATTHEWS according to Law.

Upon hearing Petition of MICHAEL BLACK against his late Master EDWARD TEMPLEMAN it's ordered that the said Templeman pay him ten Bushels of indian Corn 30 Shillings in Money or Goods & one well fixt Musket or Fuzey or 20 Shillings Cash & Costs.

Administration on the Estate of WILLIAM JACKSON, decd. is granted ROBERT BURGESS he

[Page 114 May 14, 1751]

May Court 1751

having entered into Bond with JOHN HAMILTON Security. BENJAMIN ROBINSON, JOHN KIRK, HENRY WIGGINGTON, & JOHN RALLS junr. Appraisers.

Suit on Petition. JOHN LYNN agt. WILLIAM MOUNTJOY is dismist and the said Lynn ordered to pay to the said Mountjoy his Costs.

Then the Court adjourned till tomorrow morning 9 Oclock.
MOTT DONIPHAN

At a Court continued & held for Stafford County 15th. May 1751.

Present   MOTT DONIPHAN   JOHN PEYTON
                 PETER DANIEL   FRANCIS THORNTON

Action of Trespass Assault & Battery. HENRY NELSON agt. WILLIAM WHITSON. A Jury to wit WILLIAM ALLEN, JOHN REMY, JOSEPH

BRAGG, ELIAS HORE, WILLIAM MATHENY, THOMAS HAY, INNES
BRENT, PHILIP PEYTON, ANDREW EDWARDS, JOHN KIRK, WILLIAM
MILLS & THOMAS MATHENY. The Jury finds for the Pltf 20 Shillings
Damage & Costs.

Suit on Petition. RICHARD BERNARD, Gent. agt. WILLIAM ALLISON.
Judgment is granted the Pltf for £2 & Costs.

Ordered that WILLIAM ALLISON pay BALDWIN DADE 200 pounds of
Tobacco for eight Days attendance as an Evidence for him at Suit of
SOMERVILLE'S Admrs.

Ordered that WILLIAM ALLISON pay JOHN ALEXANDER 200 pounds of
Tobacco for eight Days attendance as an Evidence for him at Suit of
SOMERVILLE'S Admrs.

Ordered that HENRY NELSON pay EDWARD BETHELL 50 pounds of Tobo
for two Days attendance as an Evidence for him against WHITSON.

Ejection Firma. Thomas Goodright agt. WILLIAM ROSE for Land &
Appurtenances in the Parish of St. Paul's which HAYWOOD TODD demised to
the Pltf for a Term. And the Parties aforesaid by their Attorneys & by their
mutual Consent the Issue in this Suit is waved & they agreed

[Page 115 May 15, 1751]

May Court 1751

that JOSEPH KING & BENJAMIN KING were seised in their Demesne in
about 100 Acres of Land in the Parish & County aforesaid, which is the
Premises in Question according to the Deeds of Conveyance. We agree that
JOSEPH KING & BENJAMIN KING by their several Deeds the 12th day of
January 1708/9 which follow in these Words…conveyed the said Land to
SAMUEL TODD & that the said Samuel died thereof seised. We agree that the
said Samuel Todd by his last Will & Testament dated March 3, 1720/21 did
devise the said Land to his son RICHARD TODD, his Daughter MARY TODD.
We agree that the said Richard Todd by Deeds of Conveyance dated the 5th & 6th
Days of June 1732 sold his Right & Title to the said Land & Appurtenances
unto one WILLIAM HYDEN, which said William intermarried with MARY the
other Devisee, & that the said William Hyden & Mary his Wife were thereof
jointly seised. We agree that the said William Hyden and Mary his Wife sold
the said Land & Appurtes. Unto the Deft WILLIAM ROSE. We agree that the
Pltf HAYWOOD TODD is eldest Son & Heir at Law to the said RICHARD
TODD. We agree that Judgment should be entered for the Deft M.
BATTALEY Deft WILLIAM WALLER & the Matters of Law arising upon the

111

said Case being argued & by the Court here fully understood it seems to the Court that the Law is with the Pltf. Therefore it's considered by the Court that the Pltf recover of the said Deft his Term yet to come of & in the said Lands & Appurtenances and possession be awarded the Pltf to put him in Possession thereof. And it's further considered by the Court that the Pltf recover of the said Deft the one Shilling mentioned in the Said Case & his Costs. And whereas the said Lands in the said Case were never divided it's agreed by & between the said Parties that PHILIP ALEXANDER

[Page 116 May 15, 1751]

May Court 1751

RICHARD BERNARD & HOWSON HOOE Gent. divide the same & set apart to the Pltf his Part thereof & that the said Division should be binding on each of them.

Present HENRY FITZHUGH &
THOMAS FITZHUGH, Gent.

Action of Trespass. PRISCILLA BOWS agt. WILLIAM BURTON. A Jury to wit WILLIAM ALLEN, JOHN RAMEY, JOSEPH BRAGG, ELIAS HORE, WILLIAM MATHENY, NATHANIEL GRAY, INNES BRENT, PHILIP PEYTON, ANDREW EDWARDS, JOHN KIRK, WILLIAM MILLS & THOMAS MATHENY. The Jury finds for the Pltf 875 pounds of Tobacco & it's considered by the Court that the Pltf recover of the said Deft & PETER MAUZY & WITHERS CONWAY his Security the said 875 pounds of Tobacco & his Costs.

Action of Trespass. NATHANIEL GRAY agt. BENJAMIN DUNCOMB. The Judgment in this Cause being argued & overruled & it's considered by the Court that the Pltf recover of the Deft according to the Form & Effect the Judgment aforesaid.

Action of Trespass. ANDREW MONROE, Gent. agt. JOHN JAMES. Judgment is granted to the Pltf for £5.14.2 & his Costs.

Suit on Petition. JOHN SOUTHWAITE agt. DANIEL FRENCH. Judgment is granted the Pltf for 507 ½ pounds of Tobacco by Account proved & a Lawyer's Fee.

Action of Trespass. RICHARD BERNARD agt. JOHN FRENCH. It appearing by the return of the Writ of Enquiry of Damages that the same is waved by Consent of the Parties & the Damages referred to THOMAS BUNBURY,

THOMAS MASSEY, & RICHARD HOOE who have awarded ten Shillings Damages for the Pltf.

Action of Trespass. CHARLES DICK agt. PHILEMON WATERS. The Deft confessed Judgment to the

May Court 1751

Pltf for £25.11.5 & his Costs.

Action of Debt. JOHN WASHINGTON, Senr., acting Exor. of HENRY WASHINGTON, Gent., decd. agt. WILLIAM FITZHUGH, Esqr. & FRANCIS THORNTON, Gent. acting Exors. of GILSON BERRYMAN, decd. The Defts for plea say they owe nothing and have fully administered. The Tryal is referred till the next Court.

Suit on Petition. JAMES RUSSELL agt. WILLIAM GREENLEASE. The Deft confessed Judgment to the Pltf for £.1.1.6 & Costs.

Suit on Petition. LAWRENCE WASHINGTON & COMPANY agt. JOHN HITE. Judgment is granted the Pltf for £2.4 half penny by Account proved & a Lawyer's Fee.

Suit on Petition. ROBERT SHEDDON agt. AARON GARRISON & BEN ROBINSON. Judgment is granted the Pltf for £1.18.1 by Account proved & a Lawyer's Fee.

Action of Trespass. RICHARD BERNARD, Gent. agt. JOHN ALEXANDER. The Deft for Plea saith that he did not assume & hath Leave to give the special Matter in Evidence. The Tryal is referred till the next Court.

Action of Trespass. GEORGE WALLER & ELIZABETH his Wife agt. JOHN PEYTON, Junr. The Deft for Plea saith that he is not guilty. The Tryal is referred till the next Court.

Action of Trespass Assault & Battery. JOHN CORBIN agt. WILLIAM ROSS. The Deft for Plea saith he is not guilty. The Tryal is referred till the next Court.

Action of Trespass Assault & Battery. JOHN CARPENTER agt. JOHN KIRK & ELIZABETH his Wife. The Defts for Plea say they are not guilty. The Tryal is referred till the next Court.

Action of Trespass Assault & Battery. CHARLES REGAN agt. PHILIP PEYTON & WINIFRED his Wife. The Defts for plea say they are not guilty. The Trial is referred till the next Court.

Action of Trespass Assault & Battery. DARBY O'CAIN agt. STEPHEN PILCHER. The Deft for plea saith he is not guilty. The

May Court 1751

Tryal is referred till the next Court.

Suit on the Attachment obtained by THOMAS PORTER against the Estate of EDWARD BUSH is dismist & the said Porter ordered to pay the said Bush his Costs.

Suit on Information. MOSELEY BATTELEY, Gent. on the behalf of our Lord the King against WILLIAM HOWARD for retailing Liquors without Licence. The said William for Plea saith he is not guilty. The Tryal is referred till the next Court.

Action of Trespass Assault & Battery. JOHN FITZPATRICK agt. RICHARD FRISTOE & GRACE his Wife. The Defts for Plea say they are not guilty. The Tryal is referred till the next Court.

Action of Trespass Assault & Battery. JOHN FITZPATRICK agt. RICHARD FRISTOE. The Deft for Plea say he is not guilty. The Tryal is referred till the next Court.

Action of Trespass Assault & Battery. DANIEL FORD, an Infant & DAVID FORD his next Friend agt. JAMES BATTOE & WINIFRED his Wife. The Defts for Plea say they are not guilty with Leave to give the special Matter in Evidence. The Tryal is referred till the next Court.

Suit on Attachment obtained by JOHN PEYTON & GEORGE WALLER acting Exors. of CHARLES WALLER, Gent., decd. agt. DANIEL MATHENY. The said Daniel confessed Judgment to the said John & George for £2.12. It's therefore considered by the Court that the said John & George recover the same of the said Daniel & their Costs.

Suit on Petition. DANIEL MATHENY agt. BENJAMIN STROTHER & MARGARET CHAPMAN, Exors. of TAYLOR CHAPMAN, decd. is dismist & the Pltf is ordered to pay the Defts their Costs.

Ordered that DANIEL MATHENY pay JAMES ONEAL junr. 125 pounds of Tobacco for five Days attendance as an Evidence for him against CHAPMAN'S Exors.

Ordered that DANIEL MATHENY pay JOHN RAMEY 125 pounds of Tobacco for five Days attendance as an Evidence for him against CHAPMAN'S Exors.

Ordered that DANIEL MATHENY pay MARGARET MURRAY 125

[Page 119 May 15, 1751]

May Court 1751

pounds Tobacco for five Days attendance as an Evidence for him against CHAPMAN'S Exors.

Ordered that DANIEL MATHENY pay GILBERT MASON 125 pounds of Tobo. for five days attendance as an Evidence for him against CHAPMAN'S Exors.

Ordered that DANIEL MATHENY pay THOMAS SIMS 125 pounds Tobo. for five Days attendance as an Evidence for him against CHAPMAN'S Exors.

Ordered that CHAPMAN'S EXORS. pay REBECCA FOWLER 125 Pounds of Tobacco for five Days attendance as an evidence for them at Suit of MATHENY.

Ordered that CHAPMAN'S EXORS. pay THOMAS TURNER 370 pounds Tobo. for four Days attendance as an Evidence for them at Suit of MATHENY & for coming & returning 45 Miles twice.

Action of Trespass Assault & Battery. JAMES YELTON agt. ANDREW HONNY. The Deft for Plea saith he is not guilty. The Tryal is referred till the next Court.

Action of Trespass. RICHARD BERNARD, Gent. agt. JOHN SILVIA. JOHN PEYTON, Gent. undertook that if the Deft should be condemned in this Action that he would pay the Condemnation for him, or surrender his Body to Prison & upon the Deft's Motion a special Imparlance is granted him till the next Court.

Action of Trespass. JOHN MINOR agt. WILLIAM CORBIN is dismist the Deft paying half the Costs.

Suit in Detinue. ROBERT ASHBY agt. JOHN RILEY. The Deft for Plea saith that he don't detain. The Tryal is referred till the next Court.

Action of Debt. THOMAS & ROBERT DUNLOPS agt. JOHN PILCHER. Judgment is granted the Pltfs for £5.15.7 on Attachment ordered in this Suit & Costs. But this Judgment is to be discharged (the Costs excepted) on Payment of £2.17.9 half penny with Interest from the 14th day of June 1744 till the same is paid, & the Sheriff having made return that he had attached 2 old Beds, & some old Furniture, 1 iron pot & 2 pair of pot Hooks, 1 frying pan, some Pewter, 1 pail bucket & piggin, & some other Lumber &c which he is ordered to sell according to Law to satisfy the said Thomas & Robert their Judgment.

[Page 120 May 15, 1751]

May Court 1751

Action of Trespass Assault & Battery. GEORGE TOLSON agt. JOHN STACY. The Deft for Plea saith he is not guilty. The Trial is referred till the next Court.

Action of Trespass. JAMES YELTON agt. JOHN PEYTON. The Pltf failing to prosecute his Suit, he is nonsuited & ordered to pay the Deft's Damages according to Law.

Suit on Petition. GEORGE JOHNSON, Gent., agt. JOHN MINOR. Judgment is granted the Pltf against him for 800 pounds of Tobacco by penal Obligation & Costs. But this Judgment is to be discharged (the Costs excepted) on payment of 400 pounds of Tobacco with Interest from the 30th day of May 1750 till paid.

Suit on Petition. ROBERT RAE agt. JOHN CUBBAGE. Judgment is grated the Pltf for £4.11 by Note of Hand with Costs & a Lawyer's Fee.

Suit on Petition. EDWARD MUSE, agt. ROBERT EDWARDS. Judgment is granted the Pltf for 710 pounds of Tobacco by Note of Hand with Costs & a Lawyer's Fee.

Suit on Petition. ROGER LYNDON & COMPANY agt. JOHN BARKER. Judgment is granted the Pltfs for 400 pounds of crop Tobo. & Costs.

Upon the Petition of JOHN FITZPATRICK against his late Master WILLIAM MILLS it's ordered that the said Mills pay him 10 Bushels of indian corn, 30 Shillings in Money or Goods & 1 well fixt Muskett or 20 Shillings, & Costs.

Then the Court adjourned till Court in Course.
MOTT DONIPHAN

At a Court held for Stafford County 11th June 1751.

Present   JOHN MERCER   MOTT DONIPHAN
                 JOHN PEYTON   PETER DANIEL
                 TRAVERSE COOKE

WILLIAM GRIGSBY son of SARAH FLETCHER on her Motion is set Levy free, it appearing to the Court that the said Wilkinson [*sic*] is unable to labour.

Ordered that the Church Wardens of St. Paul's Parish bind HENRY SMITH GREGGS, son of BAYN GREGGS (who is run away) to such a person as they think fit, who will enter into such Indenture as the Law directs.

Action of Debt. THOMAS LACY, Junr. agt. WILLIAM FITZHUGH & FRANCIS THORNTON, Gent., acting Exors. of GILSON BERRYMAN decd. A Jury to wit HOWSON HOOE, JOHN WITHERS

[Page 121 June 11, 1751]

June Court 1751

SIMON THOMAS, CHARLES HARDING, JOHN MAUZY, FOLEY [*sic*], LAWR. SUDDUTH, JOHN BELL, WILLIAM SEBASTIAN, INNIS BRENT & ROBERT ASHBY. The Jury finds for the Pltf £6 current Money.

Action upon the Case between THOMAS LACY, Junr. agt. WILLIAM FITZHUGH & FRANCIS THORNTON, Gent., acting Exors. of GILSON BERRYMAN decd. A Jury to wit ANDREW EDWARDS, WILLIAM MATHENY, JOB SIMS, WILLIAM BYRAM, THOMAS MATHENY, WILLIAM ROSE, Junr., STEPHEN PILCHER, WILLIAM BUSSELL, PETER HANSBROUGH, WILLIAM KIRK, JOHN WATERS, & WILLIAM KING. The Jury finds for the Pltf £18 current Money & the Deft admitting the Agreet. & Services done, a new Tryal is granted them paying Costs.

Action of Debt. JOHN WASHINGTON, Junr., Exor. of WILLIAM BAXTER, decd. agt. WILLIAM FITZHUGH & FRANCIS THORNTON, Gent., acting Exors. of GILSON BERRYMAN decd. A Jury to wit HOWSON HOOE, JOHN WITHERS, SIMON THOMAS, CHARLES HARDING, CHARLES WELLS, JOHN MAUZY, Senr., JOHN FOLEY, LAWR. SUDDUTH, JOHN BELL, WILLIAM SEBASTIAN, INNES BRENT, & WILLIAM KING. By Consent of the Parties JOHN MAUZY one of the Jurors of the Jury is withdrawn & this suit is continued at the Pltf's Cost.

Action of Trespass. WILLIAM HUNTER agt. WILLIAM FITZHUGH & FRANCIS THORNTON, Gent., acting Exors. of GILSON BERRYMAN decd. The Defts confest Judgment to the Pltf for £6.2.1.

Action of Trespass. GEORGE JOHNSON Gent. agt. WILLIAM FITZHUGH & FRANCIS THORNTON, Gent., acting Exors. of

June Court 1751

GILSON BERRYMAN decd. The Defts confessed Judgment to the Pltfs for £7.10 when assessed, & Debts of greater Dignity paid.

Ordered that THOMAS LACY, junr. pay WILLIAM JOHNSON 200 pounds of Tobo. for eight days attendance as an Evidence for him against BERRYMAN'S Exors.

Action of Debt. JOHN SHORT Assignee of DAVID ROSS agt. WILLIAM FITZHUGH & FRANCIS THORNTON, Gent., acting Exors. of GILSON BERRYMAN decd. The Defts confessed Jugmt. to the Pltf for £26. But this Judgment is to be discharged (the Costs excepted) on Payment of £13 with Interest from the 13th day of October 1747 till the same is paid.

Then the Court adjourned till Court in Course.
JOHN MERCER

At a called Court for Stafford County June 17th. 1751.

Present   MOTT DONIPHAN   JOHN PEYTON
            PETER DANIEL   GERARD FOWKE
            TRAVERSE COOKE

JOHN HOLT a Convict being committed to the Goal of this County by a Metimus under the Hand of JOHN MERCER, Gent. dated the 10th Day of this Instant for Felony having heard the Evidences against him, it's the Opinion of the Court that he be sent to the General Court for a farther Tryal, & that his Confession before the Justices be sent down.

HUGH ADIE of Stafford County aged 45 years, or thereabouts being sworn & examined deposeth & saith that one of the Waist Coats JOHN HOLT the Prisoner has on & which he left in his Chest in the House where the justices

June Court 1751

of Stafford County hold Court, is his, & farther saith not.

HUGH ADIE

WILLIAM ADIE of Stafford County aged 22 years or thereabouts being sworn & examined deposeth & saith, That on Saturday the 8th of this Instant some time in the Evening he left Stafford COURT HOUSE having first locked two Chests in the House the Justices of Stafford hold Court in & then locked the Door, & upon this Deponants Returning the Monday following found the House & the Chest brake-open in one of which Chests this Deponant & his Uncle had some Cloths which he found missing & that one of the Waistcoats & the Shirt the Prisoner hath on is his & the other Waistcoat is his Uncle's, & that the Handkerchief & Hat in the said Holt's Custody is his & that the Handkerchief & Cap found on him he believes to be his & were taken out of one of the Chests which he left locked.

WILLIAM ADIE

The Examination of George Pilcher aged about 21 years of Stafford County taken before me JOHN MERCER, Gent. one of his Majesties Justices of the Peace for the said County the 10th day of June 1751 touching divers Felonies with which JOHN HOLT stands charged. The said GEORGE PILCHER being examined deposeth & saith That being informed that a white Man who was suspected to be runaway was seen about MR. WAUGH'S Plantation he went this Morning in Pursuit of him & meeting the said JOHN HOLT told him he believed he was a Runaway which the said Holt confessed, & that he belonged to MOSES GRIGSBY & the said John Holt confessed to him likewise that he had stolen the Cloaths he had on & about him to wit two Jacketts, a Shirt, a Hat, a Cap & three linen Handkerchiefs out of a Chest in the old House where the Justices of Stafford sit & hold Court by straining the Lid of it open & added that he had done worse, upon which this Deponent told him he supposed he had burnt the COURT HOUSE which at first the said JOHN HOLT denied but afterward acknowledged that thereupon this Deponent took him up & brought him before me & further saith not.

GEORGE PILCHER
the mark

The Examination of JOHN HOLT Runaway Sert. man belonging as he said to MOSES GRIGSBY of Stafford County taken before me JOHN MERCER, Gent. this 11th day of June 1751

June Court 1751

This Examinant saith he ran away from his Master's house last Thursday Morning & lurked about the Plantation of GOWRY WAUGH till last Saturday Night when he went to Stafford Courthouse which he entered after pulling down a Board nailed over some Planks by which means he crept into the House where Court sits that after sleeping there some time he pulled the Lid of a Chest which he found there locked but strained it so as to get it open, & took out of the said Chest two Jacketts, a Shirt a Hat a Cap & three linen Handkerchiefs all which he had on & about him when taken up & brought before me. That afterwards he went about the time of the Moon's rising to the new building erecting there for a Court House of the said County and carried some Fire with him which he found in the old House with which he set Fire to some Planks standing in a Corner of the new Court House by which the Roof & wooden Work of the said new Court House was burnt down & destroyed that afterwards he went and lurked about the said GOWRY WAUGH'S Plantation till this morning when he was there taken up by George Pilcher and brought before me. He said that no other Person was with him or persuaded him thereto. But what he did was by the Instigation of the Devil.

JOHN HOLT

Taken before me at Stafford County this 10th day of June 1751.

JOHN MERCER

Memorandum. The Prisoner upon Tryal denied his Confession but the Court ordered that the same should be sent down among other Papers.

HUGH ADIE, WILLIAM ADIE & GEORGE PILCHER severally acknowledged themselves to be indebted to our Lord the King in the Sum of £10 Case they fail to give their Attendance at the next General Court at the Court House in WILLIAMSBURGH on the 6th Day thereof to give Evidence against JOHN HOLT prisoner at the Bar & do not depart thence without Leave of the said Court then this Recognizance to be void.

MOTT DONIPHAN

At a Court held for Stafford County July 9th. 1751.

Present   JOHN MERCER   MOTT DONIPHAN
              JOHN PEYTON   PETER DANIEL
              FRANCIS THORNTON

July Court 1751

A new Commission of the Peace for this County being produced & read together with a Didimus for administering the Oaths, PETER DANIEL & FRANCIS THORNTON, Gent. administered the several Oaths to JOHN MERCER & MOTT DONIPHAN who subscribed the Test & then administered the said Oaths to the said PETER DANIEL, FRANCIS THORNTON, & JOHN PEYTON who also subscribed the Test.

Present the above Justices

The Order for appraising PETER MAUZY'S Estate is ordered to be revived the action not being complied with.

PHILIP ALEXANDER, Gent. produced a Commission from his Honor the President to be Sheriff of the County was sworn accordingly.

GEORGE WALLER & WITHERS CONWAY sworn under Sheriffs.

PHILIP ALEXANDER, JOHN ALEXANDER, & JOHN WASHINGTON, Gent. acknowledged their Bond to our Lord the King which is ordered to be recorded.

The Sheriff is ordered to agree with some Person to repair the Prison & report to the next Court.

Ordered that the Vestries of Overwharton & St. Paul's Parish divide their Parishes into so many Precincts as to them shall seem convenient for processioning every particular Person's Land & to appoint the particular Times between the last of September & the last of March next ensuing when such processioning shall be made in every Precinct & to appoint two intelligent honest Freeholders of every Precinct to see such processioning performed according to the Directions of the Act of Assembly.

Then the Court adjourned till tomorrow morning 9 Oclock.

JOHN MERCER

At a Court held for Stafford County August 13th. 1751.

Present	MOTT DONIPHAN	JOHN PEYTON
	PETER DANIEL	FRANCIS THORNTON

LONDON a Negro Boy belonging to WILLIAM ETHERINGTON adjudged to be 11 years of Age.

DAVY a Negro Boy belonging to WILLIAM ETHERINGTON adjudged to be 10 years of Age.

The Commission of the Peace for the County being read RICHARD BARNARD, HENRY FITZHUGH, GERARD FOWKE, & THOMAS FITZHUGH, Gent. pursuant thereto took the several Oaths & subscribed the Test & abjuration Oath which is ordered to be certified.

Present the above Justices

Ordered that FRANCIS THORNTON, GERARD FOWKE, & THOMAS FITZHUGH, Gent. be recommended to his Honor the President for his Honor to make Choice of

[Page 126 Aug. 13, 1751]

August Court 1751

for a Sheriff for the ensuing Year.

Inspectors nominated.

BALDWIN DADE, THOMAS BUNBURY, Junr., WITHERS CONWAY, & JOHN HOOE for BOYD'S HOLE. WILLIAM MOUNTJOY, THOMAS MONROE, THOMAS HAY, & INNIS BRENT for CAVES. EDWARD WALLER, RICHARD HEWITT, BEN STROTHER, & ELIAS HORE for AQUIA.

On Complaint of WILLIAM HOWARD it's ordered that the King's Attorney Indict EDWARD RALLS, ANTHONY HORTON, ALEXANDER BAXTER, & JOHN FOY for a Riot.

Then the Court adjourned till tomorrow morning 9 Oclock.
JOHN MERCER

At a Court continued & held for Stafford County August 14th. 1751.

Present	JOHN MERCER	RICHARD BARNARD
	MOTT DONIPHAN	JOHN PEYTON
	PETER DANIEL	FRANCIS THORNTON
	THOMAS FITZHUGH	

122

Action of Trespass. THOMAS LACY, Junr. agt. WILLIAM FITZHUGH & FRANCIS THORNTON, Gent., acting Exors. of GILSON BERRYMAN decd. A Jury to wit JOHN WITHERS, BENJAMIN ROBINSON, JOHN BELL, JOSHUA KENDALL, HENRY DAWSON, ROBERT ASHBY, JOHN CARPENTER, WILLIAM ROSS, WILLIAM MILLS, CHARLES HARDING, JOHN KIRK, & WILLIAM KING. The Jury finds for the Pltf £17.3.7 half penny.

Action of Debt. JOHN WASHINGTON, Exor. of WILLIAM BAXTER, decd. agt. WILLIAM FITZHUGH & FRANCIS THORNTON, Gent., acting Exors. of GILSON BERRYMAN decd. The Defts confessed Judgment to the Pltf for £137.1.2. But this Judgment is to be discharged (the Costs excepted) on payment of £63.6.10 with Interest from this day till paid.

August Court 1751

Action of Trespass. WILLIAM STUART, Clk., Exor. of DAVID STUART, Clk. agt. NATHANIEL HARRISON, Esqr. A Jury to wit ANDREW EDWARDS, JOHN BUCKNER, NICHOLAS SAVIN, JOB SIMS, SOLOMON WAUGH, THOMAS PRICE, THOMAS LACY, FRANKLYN LATHAM, JOHN WEATHERS, LAZARUS HINSON, RICHARD FRISTOE, & WILLIAM BYRAM. The Jury finds for the Deft.

Ordered that the King's Attorney prosecute WILLIAM WATERS & WILLIAM EDWARDS for tending Seconds by Information of CHARLES HARDING, Constable.

Ordered that NATHANIEL HARRISON, Esqr. pay JOHN FITZHUGH 75 pounds Tobo. for three days attendance as an Evidence for him at Suit of STUART.

GEORGE CROSBY is appointed Guardian to URIEL CROSBY, Orphan of GEORGE CROSBY, decd. having given his bond according to Law.

Absent JOHN MONCURE

Action of Trespass. ROBERT MASSEY, Gent. agt. JACOB JOHNSON for £100 damage by means of the Deft's breaking & entering the close of the Pltf at the Parish of St. Paul. Jury to wit ANDREW EDWARDS, FRANKLYN LATHAM, JOB SIMS, SOLOMON WAUGH, BENJAMIN ROBINSON, ROBERT ASHBY, WILLIAM ROSS, WILLIAM MILLS, CHARLES HARDING, HAYWOOD TODD, JOHN MATHERS, & LAZARUS HINSON. The Jury finds for the Pltf the back Line from A to B to be the true Line &

twenty Shillings damage & the Deft filed Errors in arrest of Judgment which are to be argued the next Court.

Present JOHN MERCER

Action of Trespass. DAVID ROSS, Merchant agt. JOHN NIXON. GEORGE MASON, Gent. undertook that if the said Deft should be condemned in this Action that he would pay the Condemnation for him, or surrender his Body to Prison whereupon at the Deft's Motion a special Imparlance is granted him till the next Court.

The Depons of URSULA SIMS & THEODOCIA CONYERS being produced and

August Court 1751

sworn thereto upon their further Examination in Court together with the Deposition of JENNET HOLDBROOK are ordered to be recorded & a Probate granted HENRY DAWSON of the Nuncupative Will of HANNAH BAYLIS to which the said Depositions relate upon his giving Security.

Ordered that HENRY DAWSON pay URSULA SIMS 100 pounds of Tobacco for four days attendance to prove the Nuncupative Will of HANNAH BAYLIS, decd.

Ordered that HENRY DAWSON pay JENNET HOLDBROOK 100 pounds of Tobacco for four days attendance to prove the Nuncupative Will of HANNAH BAYLIS, decd.

Ordered that HENRY DAWSON pay THEODOCIA CONYERS 100 pounds of Tobo. for four days attendance to prove the Nuncupative Will of HANNAH BAYLIS, decd.

Then the Court adjourned till tomorrow morning 9 Oclock.
JOHN MERCER

At a Court held for Stafford County Sepr. 10th. 1751.

Present MOTT DONIPHAN JOHN PEYTON
      PETER DANIEL   GERARD FOWKE
      THOMAS FITZHUGH

HARRY a negro Boy belonging to CARTY WELLS adjudged to be 8 years old.

The King's Attorney is ordered to prosecute GEORGE RANDALL, JOHN BELL, FRANKLYN LATHAM, GEORGE BELL, ELIZABETH HINSON & JAMES STUART for tending Seconds of Tobo. by information of JOHN PAYTON, Constable.

The King's Attorney is ordered to prosecute WILLIAM HOWARD for tending Seconds of Tobo.

HENRY DAWSON who proved the Nuncupative Will of HANNAH BAYLIS, decd. at the last Court was directed to give Security at this Court & failing to give such Security on Motion of JOHN FOUSHEE, Gent. Administration on the Estate of the said Hannah is granted him, he having entered into Bond according to Law. GEORGE WALLER, WILLIAM ALLEN, JOHN PEYTON, & EDWARD WALLER Appraisers.

JOHN SHORT is appointed Overseer & Director for bringing on Shore Ballast at BOYD'S HOLE. EDWARD WALLER for AQUIA & WILLIAM MOSS for MACHOTIQUE.

Then the Court adjourned till tomorrow morning 9 Oclock.

RICHARD BARNARD

[Page 129 Sept. 11, 1751]

September Court 1751

At a Court continued & held for Stafford County Sepr. 11th. 1751.

Present   RICHARD BARNARD   JOHN PEYTON
                       PETER DANIEL   FRANCIS THORNTON
                       THOMAS FITZHUGH

Ordered that the Sheriff summon 24 of the most able Freeholders of this County to appear at November Court for a Grand Jury for the Body of this County.

Administration on the Estate of CATHARINE WATERS, decd. is granted JOHN PEYTON, Gent. he having entered into Bond according to Law. BENJAMIN ROBINSON, JOHN KIRK, JOHN CARPENTER, & BENJAMIN TOLSON Appraisers.

Action of Trespass. JOHN PEYTON & GEORGE WALLER, acting Exors. of CHARLES WALLER, Gent., decd. agt. JACOB AMBROSE DEKAYSOR. The Deft not appearing judgment is granted the Pltfs against him & GEORGE

BRENT his security unless the said Deft appear at the next Court & answer the Pltf's Action.

Absent RICHARD BARNARD

Action of Trespass. RICHARD BARNARD, Gent., Admr. of all & singular the Goods & Chattels, Rights & Credits of ROBERT SOMERVILLE, decd. agt. JOHN ALEXANDER. A Jury to wit FRANKLYN LATHAM, ROBERT ASHBY, THOMAS PRICE, WILLIAM MILLS, BENJAMIN ROBINSON, STEPHEN PILCHER, JAMES YELTON, JOHN WEATHERS, JOHN WITHERS, JOHN BELL, RICHARD FRISTOE, junr., & CHARLES HARDING. The Jury finds for the Pltf £6 & Costs.

Present RICHARD BARNARD

Action of Trespass. ROBERT SHEDDON, Merchant agt. JOHN PEYTON & GEORGE WALLER, acting Exors. of CHARLES WALLER, Gent., decd. The Defts confessed judgment to the Pltf for £5.4.

[Page 130 Sept. 11, 1751]

September Court 1751

Ordered that RICHARD BARNARD, Gent. pay PHILIP ALEXANDER, Gent. 120 pounds of Tobacco for five days attendance as an Evidence for him against JOHN ALEXANDER.

Action of Trespass Assault & Battery. CHARLES REGAN agt. PHILIP PEYTON and WINIFRED his wife. A Jury to wit JOHN MAUZY, JAMES ONEAL, RAWLEIGH CHINN, WILLIAM MATTHEWS, THOMAS SEDDON, ANDREW EDWARDS, THOMAS WOOD, WILLIAM BURTON, MOSES ROWLEY, GARDNER BURGESS, THOMAS HAY, & THOMAS CRAWFORD. The Jury finds for the Pltf one penny.

Ordered that JOHN ALEXANDER pay NICHOLAS SAVIN 100 pounds of Tobo. for four days attendance as an Evidence for him at the Suit of BARNARD.

Ordered that JOHN ALEXANDER pay MARGARET SMITH 100 pounds of Tobo. for four days attendance as an Evidence for him at the Suit of BARNARD.

Ordered that JOHN ALEXANDER pay WILLIAM KELLEY 75 pounds of Tobo. for three days attendance as an Evidence for him at Suit of BARNARD.

Ordered that CHARLES REGAN pay MARY LUNSFORD 175 pounds of Tobo. for seven days attendance as an Evidence for him against PEYTON & Wife.

Ordered that CHARLES REGAN pay HANNAH PEYTON 247 pounds of Tobo. for seven days attendance as an Evidence for him against PEYTON & Wife & for coming & returning six Miles four Times.

Action of Trespass Assault & Battery. JOHN CARPENTER agt. JOHN KIRK & SARAH his Wife. A Jury to wit JOHN MAUZY, JAMES ONEAL, RAWLEIGH CHINN, WILLIAM MATTHEWS, THOMAS SEDDON, ANDREW EDWARDS, BENJAMIN ROBINSON, WILLIAM BURTON, MOSES RAWLEIGH, GARDNER BURGESS, THOMAS HAY, & THOMAS CRAWFORD. The Jury finds for the Pltf 40 Shillings.

Ordered that JOHN CARPENTER pay LYDIA PATTERSON 175 pounds of Tobo. for seven Days attendance as an Evidence for him against KIRK & Wife.

[Page 131 Sept. 11, 1751]

September Court 1751

Ordered that JOHN CARPENTER pay WILLIAM PATTERSON 175 pounds of Tobo. for seven days attendance as an Evidence for him against KIRK & Wife.

Ordered that JOHN CARPENTER pay THOMAS WOOD 175 pounds of Tobo. for seven days attendance as an Evidence for him against KIRK & Wife.

Ejection Firma. Robert Faldo agt. Richard Aldo for Land & Appurtenances at the Parish of Overwharton which JOHN FOUSHEE, Gent. demised to the Pltf for a Term &c. It appearing by the Return of the Sheriff that he had delivered a Copy of the said Declaration with the Endorsment to HENRY DAWSON, Tenant in Possession of the Premises upon the said Land & he not appearing, it's ordered that unless the said Tenant do appear at the next Court & confess Lease, Entry & Ouster or Judgment shall be given for the Pltf to put him in Possession thereof.

Action of Trespass. ROBERT BROWN & ANDREW GRANT agt. JOSEPH WATERS. The Deft not appearing Judgment is granted the Pltf against him & WILLIAM SEBASTIAN his Security unless the Deft do appear at the next Court.

Suit on Petition. HENRY STUDDART agt. ELIZABETH HACKNEY. Judgment is granted the Pltf for £2.10 & Costs.

Suit on Petition. JOHN PEYTON agt. SAMUEL BROWN. Judgment is granted the Pltf for £1.15 & Costs.

Suit on Petition. PHILEMON WATERS agt. THOMAS SEDDON is dismist & the Pltf ordered to pay to the Deft his Costs.

Ordered that THOMAS SEDDON pay JOHN PEYTON 125 pounds of Tobo. for five days attendance as an Evidence for him at Suit of WATERS.

Ordered that PHILEMON WATERS pay ABRAHAM FARROW 137 pounds of Tobo. for two days attendance & for coming & returning 29 Miles once.

Ordered that PHILEMON WATERS pay HENRY NORMAN 134 pounds of Tobo. for two days attendance as an Evidence for him against SEDDON & for coming & returning 28 Miles once.

Then the Court adjourned till tomorrow morning 9 Oclock.

RICHARD BARNARD

[Page 132 Sept. 12, 1751]

September Court 1751

At a Court continued & held for Stafford County Sepr. 12th. 1751.

Present	RICHARD BARNARD	MOTT DONIPHAN
	JOHN PEYTON	PETER DANIEL
	FRANCIS THORNTON	GERARD FOWKE
	THOMAS FITZHUGH	

Action of Trespass Assault & Battery. JOHN FITZPATRICK agt. RICHARD FRISTOE, Junr. A Jury to wit JOHN MAUZY, FRANKLYN LATHAM, STEPHEN PILCHER, WILLIAM BUSSELL, JOHN WITHERS, JOHN WEATHERS, HENRY DAWSON, ALEXANDER DONIPHAN, THOMAS PRICE, JOHN CORBIN, CHARLES JONES, & JAMES YELTON. The Jury finds for the Pltf ten Shillings damage.

Action of Trespass Assault & Battery. JOHN FITZPATRICK agt. RICHARD FRISTOE & GRACE his Wife. The Jury finds for the Pltf 40 Shillings damage.

FRANCIS THORNTON, Gent. being presented by the Grand jury for swearing & summoned appeared & being heard the Court are of the Opinion that the said Francis should pay to the Church Wardens of St. Paul's Parish 25 Shillings or 250 pounds Tobacco for the use of the poor of the said Parish, & ten Shillings, or 100 pounds of Tobacco to the Church Wardens of Overwharton Parish for the use of the poor of that Parish, & Costs.

SAMUEL SIMS being presented by the Grand jury for swearing two Oaths, & summoned failed to appear whereupon it's ordered that he pay to the Church Wardens of Overwharton Parish ten Shillings, or 100 pounds of Tobo. & Costs.

SAMUEL NUBIL being presented by the Grand jury for swearing four Oaths and summoned failed to appear whereupon it's ordered that he pay to the Church Wardens of Overwharton Parish 20 Shillings or 200 pounds of Tobacco & Costs.

[Page 133 Sept. 12, 1751]

September Court 1751

ANN DILLON being presented to the Grand jury for having a Bastard Child & summoned failed to appear whereupon it's ordered that she pay to the Church Wardens of Overwharton Parish for the use of the Poor 50 Shillings or 500 pounds of Tobacco with Cask & Costs.

MARY HORTON being presented to the Grand jury for having a Bastard Child & summoned failed to appear whereupon it's ordered that she pay to the Church Wardens of Overwharton Parish 50 Shillings or 500 pounds Tobacco & Cask & Costs.

ANN GRAY being presented to the Grand jury for having a Bastard Child & summoned failed to appear whereupon it's ordered that she pay to the Church Wardens of Overwharton Parish 50 Shillings or 500 pounds Tobacco & Cask & Costs.

SARAH PESTRIDGE being presented to the Grand jury for having a Bastard Child & summoned failed to appear whereupon it's ordered that she pay to the Church Wardens of Overwharton Parish 50 Shillings or 500 pounds Tobacco & Cask & Costs.

JEMIMA EDWARDS being presented to the Grand jury for having a Bastard Child & summoned failed to appear whereupon it's ordered that she pay to the Church Wardens of Overwharton Parish 50 Shillings or 500 pounds Tobacco & Cask & Costs.

WILLIAM CASH being presented to the Grand jury for swearing one Oath failed to appear. It's ordered that he pay to the Church Wardens of Overwharton Parish five Shillings or 50 pounds of Tobacco & Costs.

RICHARD BARNARD, Gent. being presented by the Grand jury for swearing & being heard the Court are of Opinion that he should pay to the Church Wardens of Overwharton Parish ten Shillings or 100 pounds of Tobacco, and to the Church Wardens of St. Paul's Parish ten Shillings or 100 pounds of Tobacco & Costs.

Suit on Petition. PHILEMON WATERS agt. ARTHUR DUWES. Judgment is granted the Pltf for 290 pounds of Tobacco by Note of hand with Costs & a Lawyer's Fee.

Action of Debt. JONATHAN SYDENHAM & THOMAS HODSON, Merchants in London agt. DANIEL HANKINS. The Deft not appearing the Judgment against him & GEORGE WALLER his Security is confirmed

[Page 134 Sept. 12, 1751]

September Court 1751

for £14 current Money. The Pltf agrees to stay Execution three Months.

Ordered that JOHN FITZPATRICK pay CHARLES HARDING 200 pounds of Tobo. for eight days attendance as an Evidence against FRISTOE & Wife.

Ordered that JOHN FITZPATRICK pay JOHN KIRK 200 pounds of Tobo. for eight days attendance as an Evidence against FRISTOE & Wife.

Ordered that RICHARD FRISTOE pay SARAH ELLIS 125 pounds of Tobacco for five Days attendance as an Evidence for him at Suit of FITZPATRICK.

Ordered that RICHARD FRISTOE pay JOHN MATTHEWS 150 pounds of Tobacco for six days attendance as an Evidence for him at Suit of FITZPATRICK.

Ordered that RICHARD FRISTOE pay ROBERT FRISTOE 200 pounds of Tobacco for eight days attendance as an Evidence for him at Suit of FITZPATRICK.

Action of Trespass Assault & Battery. JOHN CORBIN agt. WILLIAM ROSS. A Jury to wit JOHN MAUZY, ALEXANDER DONIPHAN, WILLIAM BUSSELL, JOHN WITHERS, HENRY DAWSON, THOMAS PRICE, CHARLES JONES, HAYWOOD TODD, ANDREW EDWARDS, JOHN WEATHERS, GARDNER BURGESS, & JOHN BELL. The Jury finds 40 Shillings for the Pltf & Costs.

Action of Trespass, Assault & Battery. JAMES YELTON agt. ANDREW KENNY. The Jury finds for the Pltf 40 Shillings damage & Costs.

[Page 135 Sept. 12, 1751]

September Court 1751

Suit on Petition. BAYNE SMALLWOOD, Gent. agt. WILLIAM FUELL is dismist & the Pltf ordered to pay the said Deft his Costs.

Ordered that JAMES YELTON pay THOMAS BELL 245 pounds of Tobacco for eight Days attendance as an Evidence for him against KENNY & for coming & returning five Miles three Times.

Ordered that JAMES YELTON pay LAZARUS HINSON 200 pounds of Tobo. for eight Days attendance as an Evidence for him against KENNY.

Ordered that JOHN CORBIN pay WILLIAM CORBIN 175 pounds of Tobacco for seven days attendance as an Evidence for him against ROSS.

Ordered that JOHN CORBIN pay RAWLEY LUNSFORD 175 pounds of Tobacco for seven days attendance as an Evidence for him against ROSS.

Ordered that BAYNE SMALLWOOD pay JOHN LINSY 125 pounds of Tobacco for five days attendance as an Evidence for him against FUELL.

Ordered that BAYNE SMALLWOOD pay CHARLES HARDING 75 pounds of Tobacco for three days attendance as an Evidence for him against FUELL.

Ordered that WILLIAM FUELL pay MOSES ROWLEY 25 pounds of Tobacco for one days attendance as an Evidence for him at Suit of SMALLWOOD.

Ordered that WILLIAM FUELL pay WILLIAM BURTON 200 pounds of Tobacco for eight days attendance as an Evidence for him at Suit of SMALLWOOD.

Ordered that WILLIAM FUELL pay HAYWOOD TODD 200 pounds of Tobacco for eight days attendance as an evidence for him at Suit of SMALLWOOD.

Action of Trespass Assault & Battery. DARBY O'CAIN agt. STEPHEN PILCHER. A Jury to wit ALEXANDER DONIPHAN, JOHN MAUZY, WILLIAM BUSSELL, THOMAS CRAFFORD, CHARLES JONES, GARDNER BURGESS, JOHN CORBIN, JOHN WITHERS, FRANCIS

BROOKE, HENRY DAWSON, THOMAS PRICE, & ANDREW EDWARDS.
The Jury finds for the Pltf 40 Shillings damage & his costs.

[Page 136 Sept. 12, 1751]

September Court 1751

Action of Debt. JONATHAN SYDENHAM & THOMAS HODSON,
Merchants in London agt. MARK HENTON. The Deft not appearing an
Attachment is awarded the Pltfs against his Estate for £16 & Costs returnable to
the next Court.

Action of Trespass. DAVID ROSS, Merchant agt. JOHN NIXON. The Deft
not appearing the Judgment against him is confirmed & a Writ of Enquiry of
Damages is to be executed the next Court.

Action of Debt. ANDREW COCHRANE & COMPANY agt. ADAM
STEPHEN. The Deft prayed Oyer &c which is granted him.

Action of Debt. ANDREW COCHRANE & COMPANY agt. WILLIAM
SWEATNIM. The Deft not appearing Judgment is granted the Pltf against him
& WITHERS CONWAY his Security unless the Deft do appear at the next
Court & answer the Pltf's Action.

Suit on Petition. JOHN PEYTON, Gent. & GEORGE WALLER acting Exor. of
CHARLES WALLER, Gent. decd. agt. JOHN GRANT. Judgment is granted
the Pltfs for £4.14.9 half penny & Costs.

Suit on Information brought on behalf of the Lord the King against WILLIAM
HOWARD for retailing Liquors without Licence. The Jury finds the Deft guilty
& the said William is ordered to pay to our Lord the King 2,000 pounds of
Tobacco & the said William being whipt he is discharged from this Judgment.

Ordered that JOHN PEYTON pay STEPHEN PILCHER 200 pounds of
Tobacco for eight days attendance as an Evidence for him at Suit of WALLER.

Ordered that DARBY O'CAIN pay JOHN WEATHERS 150 pounds of Tobo.
for six days attendance as an Evidence for him against PILCHER.

Ordered that DARBY O'CAIN pay JOHN INGLISH 175 pounds of Tobacco for
seven days attendance as an Evidence for him against PILCHER.

Ordered that DARBY O'CAIN pay JOHN BELL 175 pounds of Tobacco

September Court 1751

for seven days attendance as an Evidence for him against PILCHER.

Suit on Petition. JOHN PEYTON, Gent. agt. SAMUEL ANGELL is continued at the Defts Costs.

Absent JOHN PEYTON

Suit on Petition. JOHN PEYTON, Gent. agt. ROBERT ASHBY. Judgment is granted the Pltf for 305 pounds of Tobacco & Costs.

Suit on Petition. JOHN PEYTON, Gent. agt. JOSEPH COOPER. Judgment is granted the Pltf for 915 pounds of crop Tobacco & Costs.

Suit on Petiton. RICHARD BARNARD, Gent. agt. SARAH SKINNER, Admx. of JOHN SKINNER, decd. Judgment is granted the Pltf for 759 pounds of Tobacco.

Suit on Petition. RICHARD BARNARD, Gent. agt. JOHN CHRISTY. Judgment is granted the Pltf for 916 pounds of crop Tobacco & Costs.

Action of Debt. CHARLES ASHTON, Gent. agt. WILLIAM FITZHUGH & FRANCIS THORNTON, Gent., acting Exors. of GILSON BERRYMAN decd. The Defts confessed Judgment to the Pltf for £1,000 current Money of Virginia. But this Judgment is to be discharged (the Costs excepted) on Payment of £500 like money with Interest thereon from the 27th day of November 1746 till the same is paid.

Suit on Petition. JOHN PELTER & JUDITH his Wife agt. JOSHUA KENDALL. Judgment is granted the Pltfs for £2.10 & Costs.

Ordered that JOHN PELTER & JUDITH his Wife pay RACHAEL LUNSFORD 125 pounds of Tobacco for five days attendance as an Evidence for them against KENDALL.

Ordered that JOHN PELTER & JUDITH his Wife pay ELIZABETH DENT 125 pounds of Tobo. for five days attendance as an evidence for them against KENDALL.

September Court 1751

Ordered that JOHN PELTER & JUDITH his Wife pay ELIZABETH MOORE 150 pounds Tobacco for six days attendance as an Evidence for them against KENDALL.

Suit on Petition. ELIZABETH COOKE & TRAVERSE COOKE, Exors. of the last Will & Testament of RAWLEIGH TRAVERSE, decd. agt. WILLIAM BRUIN. Judgment is granted the Pltfs for £1.9 & Costs.

Suit on Petition. THOMAS HURST agt. WILLIAM HOWARD is continued at the Pltf's Costs.

Suit on Petition. ALEXANDER & DANIEL CAMPBELL agt. HUSBANDFOOTE WHITECOTTON. Judgment is granted the Pltfs for £3.16.1 with Costs & a Lawyer's Fee.

Suit on Petition. JAMES HUGHS agt. MOSES ROWLEY. Judgment is granted the Pltf for 450 pounds of Tobacco & Costs.

Suit on Petition. FRANCIS DAY agt. JOHN WITHERS is dismist and the Pltf ordered to pay to the Deft his Costs.

Ordered that FRANCIS DAY pay WILLIAM OSBORNE 150 pounds of Tobacco for six Days attendance as an Evidence for him against WITHERS.

Ordered that JOHN WITHERS pay WILLIAM MATTHEWS 125 pounds of Tobo. for five Days attendance as an Evidence for him at Suit of DAY.

Action of Trespass. ANDREW ROSE agt. THOMAS JACKSON. The Deft not appearing Judgment is granted the Pltf against him & GEORGE RANDALL his Security unless the Deft appear at the next Court.

Action of Trespass. JAMES RICHEE, Merchant agt. NATHANIEL HARRISON, Exor. of WILLIAM WALKER Gent. decd. The Deft by his Attorney confessed Judgment to the Pltf for £38.8.2 three farthings.

Suit on Petition. JOHN SUTHERLAND agt. ISAAC FOWLER is continued at the Pltf's Costs.

Suit on Petition. JOHN HAMILTON, Gent. agt. SAMUEL ANGELL. Judgment is granted the Pltf for 30 Shillings & Costs.

September Court 1751

Ordered that JOHN COOPER pay YELVERTON PEYTON 75 pounds of Tobacco for three Days attendance as an Evidence for him against ANGELL.

Suit on Petition. SALLY RAPIER agt. HENRY HURST is dismist & the Pltf ordered to pay the Deft his Costs.

Action of Trespass. LAWRENCE WASHINGTON & COMPANY agt. ANDREW EDWARDS & BETTY his Wife, Admrs. of JAMES WAUGH, Gent. decd. On the Pltf's Motion an Alias Capias is ordered returnable to the next Court.

Ordered that the Attachment against the several Guardians be continued till the next Court.

Ordered that HENRY STUDDARD pay WILLIAM HOWARD 175 pounds of Tobacco for seven days attendance as an Evidence for him against HACKNEY.

Ordered that HENRY STUDDARD pay WILLIAM BYRAM 150 pounds of Tobacco for six days attendance as an Evidence for him against HACKNEY.

Suit in Chancery. CHARLES WELLS & BENJAMIN ROBINSON agt. THOMAS VIVION & PETER DANIEL, Gent. having filed their Replication the Complainants have Time till the next Court to consider thereof.

Suit in Chancery. SAMUEL SELDON Gent. agt. DIANA WHEELER, GEORGE JAMES & MARY his Wife & GEORGE JAMES the younger by HENRY PEYTON his Guardian is set for hearing at the next Court.

Suit on Petition. PHILEMON WATERS agt. MICHAEL RYAN. Judgment is granted the Pltf for 400 pounds of Tobacco with Costs & a Lawyer's Fee.

Action of Trespass. LAWRENCE WASHINGTON & COMPANY agt. WILLIAM FITZHUGH. The Deft for Plea saith that he did not assume & hath Leave to give the special Matter in Evidence. The Tryal is referred till the next Court.

September Court 1751

Action of Trespass. JOHN CHAMPE, Gent. agt. JOHN HASTY. The Deft for Plea saith that he did not assume. The Tryal is referred till the next Court.

Action of Trespass. RICHARD BROOKE agt. NATHANIEL HARRISON, Esqr., acting Exor. of WILLIAM WALKER, Gent. decd. The Deft for Plea saith that the Testator did not assume. The Tryal is referred till the next Court.

In the Indictment brought by MOSLEY BATTALEY, Gent., Attorney for our Lord the King agt. JOHN STACY. The said Stacy for plea saith he is not guilty & the Tryal is referred till the next Court.

WINIFRED RILEY being presented by the Grand jury for having a bastard Child failed to appear whereup it's ordered that she pay to the Church Wardens of Overwharton Parish (for the use of the Poor of the said Parish) 50 Shillings or 500 pounds of Tobacco & Cask & Costs.

Action of Trespass. JOHN PEYTON, Gent. & GEORGE WALLER acting Exors. of CHARLES WALLER, Gent., decd. agt. RAWLEIGH CHINN. The judgment of April Court last against him & BENJAMIN STROTHER Sheriff of the said County is continued & a Writ of Enquiry of Damages is to be executed the next Court.

Action of Trespass. RICHARD BARNARD, Gent. agt. JOHN SILVA. The Deft for Plea saith he did not assume. The Tryal is referred till the next Court.

Action of Trespass. THOMAS & ROBERT DUNLOPS agt. JAMES FRENSLEY. The Sheriff for the Deft for Plea saith that the Deft did not assume. The Trial is referred till the next Court.

Action of Trespass. HORATIO DADE agt. WILLIAM FITZHUGH, Esqr. & FRANCIS THORNTON, Gent., acting Exors. of GILSON BERRYMAN, decd. The Defts for Plea saith that the Testator

October Court 1751

did assume & fully administered. The Tryal is referred till the next Court.

Then the Court adjourned till Court in Course.

RICHARD BARNARD

At a Court held for Stafford County Octor. 8th. 1751.

A Commission of Oyer & Terminer & Dedimus for the Tryal of COFFEE, a negro Man belonging to RICHARD BARNARD, Gent. for Felony being produced & read. RICHARD FOOTE Gent. having first taken the several Oaths & subscribed the Test administered the said Oaths to MOTT DONIPHAN, JOHN PEYTON, PETER DANIEL, HENRY FITZHUGH & THOMAS FITZHUGH, Gent. who likewise subscrited the Test & Abjuration Oath.

Present the above Justices.

COFFEE a Negro Man Slave belonging to RICHARD BARNARD, Gent. being committed to the Goal of this County for Felonies, Burglary & being indicted for the same & the Evidences against him being examined, the Court are of Opinion that the said COFFEE is not Guilty of the Felony & Burglary & it's ordered that he be discharged & that the Sheriff convey him to his said Master.

RICHARD FOOTE

At a Court held for Stafford County Octor. 8th. 1751.

Present	MOTT DONIPHAN	JOHN PEYTON
	PETER DANIEL	HENRY FITZHUGH
	THOMAS FITZHUGH	

Ordered that JOHN ALEXANDER pay RICHARD FOOTE, Gent. 125 pounds of Tobacco for five days attendance as an Evidence for him at Suit of BARNARD.

RICHARD FOOTE, Gent. took the several Oaths in Respect of his Coroner's Commission.

On Petition of TRAVERSE COOKE ordered that WILLIAM WRIGHT & NATHANIEL SMITH

[Page 142 Oct. 8, 1751]

October Court 1751

& HUGH ADIE view the most convenient Way for a Road from the said Cooke's to the main Road & Report.

JOHN STACY, junr., RICHARD FRISTOE, junr., ROBERT ASHBY, Junr., & THOMAS ASHBY being bound over to this Court by Recognizance appeared & having heard the Evidences against them the Court are of Opinion that each of them enter into Bond of £20 with two Securities of £10 each for their good Behavior & keeping the Peace a Year & a Day. BENJAMIN ROBINSON & HENRY WIGGINGTON acknowleged themselves Securities for the said John Stacy & Richard Fristoe. CHARLES HARDING & JOHN CARPENTER for the said Robert Ashby. RICHARD FRISTOE, Senr. & THOMAS CRAFFORD for Thomas Ashby.

Then the Court adjourned till tomorrow morning 9 Oclock.
MOTT DONIPHAN

At a Court continued & held for Stafford County 9th. October 1751.

Present MOTT DONIPHAN   JOHN PEYTON
     HENRY FITZHUGH   THOMAS FITZHUGH

WILLIAM ALLEN on his Motion hath his Ordinary Licence renewed.

Action of Detinue. THOMAS ASHBY agt. JOHN RILEY. A Jury to wit ALEXANDER DONIPHAN, JOHN MAUZY, JOHN PEYTON, CHARLES HARDING, WILLIAM WILLS, JOB SIMS, HENRY DAWSON, WILLIAM BUSSELL, JOHN FOLEY, WILLIAM ALLEN, WILLIAM KENDALL, & HUSBANDFOOTE WHITECOTTON. The Jury finds for the Pltf £8 damage & Costs. And the Deft filed Errors in arrest of Judgment which are to be argued at the next Court.

Ordered that THOMAS ASHBY pay THOMAS CRAFFORD 200 pounds of Tobacco for eight days attendance as an Evidence for him against RILEY.

Ordered that THOMAS ASHBY pay AARON GARRISON 250 pounds of Tobacco for ten days Attendance as an Evidence for him against RILEY.

[Page 143 Oct. 9, 1751]

October Court 1751

Ordered that THOMAS ASHBY pay JOHN CARPENTER 250 pounds of Tobacco for ten days attendance as an Evidence for him against RILEY.

Ordered that THOMAS ASHBY pay DAVID ASHBY 1015 pounds of Tobacco for seven days attendance as an Evidence for him against RILEY & for coming & returning 70 Miles four Times.

Ordered that THOMAS ASHBY pay HENRY WIGGINGTON 250 pounds of Tobacco for ten days attendance as an Evidence for him against RILEY.

Ordered that JOHN RILEY pay ROBERT ASHBY, Senr. 250 pounds of Tobacco for ten days attendance as an Evidence for him at Suit of ASHBY.

RICHARD PARKER, Gent. intending to practice as an Attorney at Law is ordered to be certified that he is a Person of Honesty, Probity & good Demeanor.

Ordered that THOMAS ASHBY pay BENJAMIN ROBINSON 225 pounds of Tobacco for nine days attendance as an evidence for him against RILEY.

Ordered that JOHN RILEY pay JOHN FITZPATRICK 200 pounds of Tobacco for eight days attendance as an evidence for him at Suit of ASHBY.

Action of Trespass. RICHARD BROOKE agt. NATHANIEL HARRISON, Esqr., acting Exor. of WILLIAM WALKER, Gent, decd. A Jury to wit ALEXANDER DONIPHAN, HENRY DAWSON, WILLIAM KENDALL, junr., WILLIAM BUSSELL, JOHN MAUZY, Junr., JOHN FOLEY, Senr., CHARLES HARDING, JOHN PEYTON, Junr., HUSBANDFOOTE WHITECOTTON, WILLIAM MILLS, JOB SIMS & WILLIAM ALLEN. The Jury finds for the Pltf £88.2.9. The Deft filed Errors in arrest of Judgment which are to be argued at the next Court.

Action of Trespass. JOHN CHAMPE, Gent. agt. JOHN HASTY.

[Page 144 Oct. 9, 1751]

October Court 1751

The Jury finds for the Pltf 1,350 pounds of crop Tobacco & Costs.

Action of Trespass. JOHN PEYTON & GEORGE WALLER, acting Exors. of CHARLES WALLER, Gent., decd. agt. JOHN BAYLIS. The Deft confessed Judgment to the Pltfs for £5.18.1. Whereupon it's considered by the Court that the Pltfs recover the same against him & their Costs.

Upon the Motion of BURDIT CLIFTON & JAMES SEATON it's ordered that RICHARD FOOTE, JOHN BUCKNER & JOHN WASHINGTON, Junr. divide the Estate of JAMES SEATON, decd. among this Children & report.

Action of Trespass Assault & Battery. GEORGE TOLSON agt. JOHN STACY. A Jury to wit ALEXANDER DONIPHAN, HENRY DAWSON, WILLIAM

KENDALL, WILLIAM BUSSELL, JOHN MAUZY, JOHN FOLEY, CHARLES HARDING, JOHN PEYTON, HUSBANDFOOTE WHITECOTTON, WILLIAM MILLS, JOB SIMS & WILLIAM ALLEN. The Jury finds for the Pltf £5 & his Costs.

Ordered that GEORGE TOLSON pay NICHOLAS RILEY 250 pounds of Tobacco for ten days attendance as an evidence for him against STACY.

Suit in Chancery. NATHANIEL GRAY agt. JOHN THOMAS is continued till the next Court.

Suit in Chancery. HENRY DADE agt. NATHANIEL GRAY is continued till the next Court.

Suit in Chancery. CHARLES WELLS & BENJAMIN ROBINSON agt. THOMAS VIVION & PETER DANIEL, Gent. A Dedimus is ordered returnable to the next Court.

[Page 145 Oct. 9, 1751]

October Court 1751

Action of Trespass. ANDREW ROSE, Merchant agt. MASON FRENCH & MARGARET his wife, Admrs. of THOMAS LACY, decd. is continued till the next Court.

Suit in Chancery. EDWARD HUMSTON agt. RICHARD BARNARD, Gent. & others is continued till the next Court at the Pltf's Costs.

Present GERARD FOWKE, Gent.

Suit in Chancery. SAMUEL SELDON, Gent. agt. DIANA WHEELER, GEORGE JAMES & MARY his Wife, & GEORGE JAMES the Younger by HENRY TYLER his Guardian. Upon hearing of the Bill & Answer it's ordered that the several Depositions taken in this Suit be recorded & that each party pay their own Costs.

Suit in Chancery. JOSEPH HINSON, LAZARUS HINSON, JAMES YELTON & ISBELL his Wife, HENRY THRELKELD & MARY his Wife, GEORGE BELL & ANN his Wife agt. JAMES CROP & JOYCE his Wife, Exors. of CHARLES HINSON, decd. The Demurer in this Suit being argued is adjudged good whereupon it's decreed, ordered that this Suit be dismist & that each Party pay their own Costs.

140

JAMES HANSBROUGH is appointed Guardian to MASON FRENCH, Orphan of HUGH FRENCH, decd.

Ordered that GEORGE PURVIS & MARY his wife be summoned to appear at the next Court to answer the Petition of HUSBANDFOOTE WHITECOTTON.

Ordered that ISAAC FOWLER pay MARY TURNER 50 pounds of Tobacco for two days attendance as an Evidence for him at Suit of SUTHERLAND.

Then the Court adjourned till tomorrow morning 9 Oclock.
MOTT DONIPHAN

At a Court held for Stafford County November 12th 1751.

Present   MOTT DONIPHAN   JOHN PEYTON
               PETER DANIEL   FRANCIS THORNTON
               THOMAS FITZHUGH

The Grand jury being impannelled & sworn received their Charge & retired, & returning into Court with their Presentments it's ordered that the Offenders be summoned to answer the same.

[Page 146 Nov. 12, 1751]

November Court 1751

WILLIAM HEDGMAN, Gent. Assistant to JOHN MAUZY, Gent., Surveyor of this County acknowledged his Bond & took the several Oaths.

ALEXANDER SCOTT, orphan of WILLIAM SCOTT, decd. came into Court & made Choice of PHILIP ALEXANDER & JOHN SHORT, Gentlemen for his Guardians.

Then the Court proceeded to lay the Levy.

Stafford County   Dr.   Pounds of Tobacco

To Mr. SECRETARY NELSON by Account	189
To MOSLEY BATTALEY King's Attorney	2000
To the Clerk by Law	1254
To do. by Account	1370
To the Sheriff by Law	1254
To JOHN BLACK by Account	945
To JAMES HANSBROUGH by ditto	626

141

To JOHN SAUNDERSON for Stocks	500
To EDWARD GROVES for Guarding the Prison on Barnard's Negro	880
To JOHN MINOR for guarding the Prison on HOLT	25
To ditto on GRAY	351
To HENRY SUDDUTH for guarding GRAY in Prison 8 days	200
To ANTHONY LATHAM for ditto 8 days	200
To JOHN MONROE for ditto one day	25
To GEORGE HINSON for ditto one day	25
To JAMES HUGHS for ditto	500
To JOHN PEYTON, Coroner by Account	120
To RICHARD FOOTE, Coroner	165
To GEORGE WALLER per Account	1471
To THOMAS MONROE by do.	1025
To WITHERS CONWAY by ditto	1752
To JOHN STONE, Constable	361
To STEPHEN PILCHER do.	230
To JOHN PEYTON, Constable	527
To JAMES WAUGH'S Admrs.	416
To CHARLES HARDING by Account	716
To NATHANIEL HARRISON, Esqr. & HUGH ADIE to be kept	
in the Sheriff's Hands till the Court House is finished	20,000
& received	37,120
To 6 pCent on 37,120	2,227
	39,347

By 1890 Tithables with a Fraction of 343 to be accounted
For at the laying the next Levy or 21 per Poll   39, 347

[Page 147 Nov. 12, 1751]

November Court 1751

Ordered that the Sheriff collect 21 pounds of Tobacco for each Tithable in this County for their County Levy.

Ordered that WILLIAM KELLY & PHILIS his Wife be summoned to answer the Petition of MASON FRENCH & WILLIAM JOHNSON.

THOMAS WHITEHOUSE a servant Boy belonging to ANN ALLENTHORP adjudged to be 13 Years of Age.

Ordered that EDWARD RALLS, ALEXANDER BAXTER & THOMAS FOY be attached to appear to the next Court to answer an Indictment exhibited against them.

Then the Court adjourned till tomorrow morning 9 Oclock.

MOTT DONIPHAN

At a Court continued & held for Stafford County Novemr. 13th. 1751.

Present   RICHARD BARNARD   JOHN PEYTON
                     PETER DANIEL   FRANCIS THORNTON
                     GERARD FOWKE

Ordered that the Sheriff pay WILLIAM HOWARD 49 pounds of Tobacco out of the Fraction in his Hands.

Ordered that HENRY FITZHUGH, ROBERT MASSEY & JOHN WASHINGTON, Junr., Gent. or any two of them allott, assign, & set apart to SARAH the Widow of GILSON BERRYMAN decd. her part of the said Gilson's Estate.

Action of Trespass. FRANCIS DADE, Gent. agt. THOMAS MASSEY for £100 damage by means of the Deft's breaking & entering the Close of the Pltf in the Parish of St. Paul's it's ordered that the Surveyor of this County in Company of an able Jury of Freeholders go upon the Lands in Controversy & lay off the same as either Party would have it, & as the said Jury shall think fit having regard to all Patents & Evidences as shall be produced by either of the Parties & the Sheriff is ordered to attend the Survey to remove Force if any offered & the Surveyor is to return three fair Platts & Reports to the Clerk's Office in due time before the Day of hearing.

Ordered that HUGH LOFTIS serve his Master ROBERT MANIN nine Days & £2.5.6 and 180 pounds of Tobacco expended in taking him up. Tobacco for Money 12/6 pCent.

[Page 148 Nov. 13, 1751]

November Court 1751

MARGARET YOUNG came into Court and agreed to serve her Master WILLIAM THORNBURY two years to cure her of the Disorder she now labours under which the Court approves of.

Ordered that the Church Wardens of Overwharton Parish bind SARAH the Daughter of JOHN ROBINSON to WILLIAM MILLS according to Law.

SAMUEL EARLE, Heir at Law to HANNAH BAILIS, prayed Administration with the Nuncupative Will annexed of the said Hannah. HENRY DAWSON to whom the Estate of the said Hannah was devised failing to give such Security & the Administration granted. JOHN FOUSHEE, Gent. be revoked upon the said Earle's giving Security at the next Court.

Ordered that the Persons who appraised the Estate of THOMAS DENT decd. divide & set apart to CAIN WITHERS his part of WILLIAM CAVE'S Estate in right of his Wife ELIZABETH.

Suit on Scire Facias. NATHANIEL GRAY agt. WILLIAM KELLY & PHILIS his Wife, Admrs. of JAMES MCINTOSH decd. The Sheriff having made Return that he had executed the said Scire facias & the said William & Philis failing to appear it's considered by the Court that the said Nathaniel have Execution against them for 1,035 pounds of Tobo. in one Cask, 85 pounds of Tobacco & 15 Shillings, or 150 pounds of Tobacco of the Goods & Chattels of the said James in their hands.

Suit on Petition. MARY PONTON agt. MICHAEL RYAN. Judgment is granted the Pltf for 25 Shillings & one penny & Costs.

Ordered that MARY PONTON pay WILLIAM MILLS 75 pounds of Tobacco for three Days attendance as an Evidence for her against RYAN.

Suit on Petition. ROBERT LYNDON agt. ALEXANDER SYMPSON. Judgment is granted the Pltf for 218 pounds of Tobacco & Costs.

Suit on Information. Our Lord the King against ELIZABETH MCABOY for retailing liquors without Licence. The said Elizabeth for Plea saith she is not Guilty & the Tryal is referred till the next Court.

Suit on Petition. WILLIAM KENDALL agt. BENJAMIN MCCULLOUGH. Judgment is granted the Pltf for 300 pounds of Tobacco & Costs.

[Page 149 Nov. 13, 1751]

November Court 1751

Suit on Information. Our Lord the King agt. MARY WISE for retailing Liquors without Licence, an Attachment is ordered against her Body returnable to the next Court.

Suit on Information. Our Lord the King agt. FRANKLYN LATHAM for tending Seconds of Tobo. The said Franklyn for Plea saith that he is not guilty & the Tryal is referred till the next Court.

Action of Detinue. JOHN FOUSHEE, Gent. Admr. of HANNAH BAYLIS, decd. agt. HENRY DAWSON. SAMUEL EARL, SIMON THOMASIN, GEORGE RANDALL, & WILLIAM HOWARD undertook that if the Deft should be condemned in this Action they would pay the Condemnation for him or surrender his Body to Prison, and on motion of the said Deft a special Imparlance is granted him till the next Court.

Action of Trespass. ISAAC FOWLER & REBEKAH his Wife agt. FRANCIS DAY. The Deft not appearing Judgment is granted the Pltf against him & PHILIP ALEXANDER, Gent. Sheriff of this County unless the Deft do appear at the next Court & answer the Pltf's Action.

Suit of Debt. BENJAMIN STROTHER & JOHN LEE, Gent. Church Wardens of Overwharton Parish agt. MARTHA HORTON. The Deft not appearing Judgment is granted the Pltfs against her & EDWARD RALLS her Security unless the Deft do appear at the next Court & answer the Pltf's Action.

Action of Debt. MOSLEY BATTALEY, Gent. agt. MOSES ROWLEY. WITHERS CONWAY undertook that if the Deft should be condemned in this Action he would pay the Condemnation for him, or surrender his Body to Prison & the Deft on his Motion had a special Imparlance granted him till the next Court.

Action of Trespass Assault & Battery. MARY STRINGFELLOW agt. WILLIAM DEARING & ELIZABETH his Wife is dismist the Defts paying Costs.

Action of Trespass. JOHN STONE agt. ROBERT MANIN. The Pltf not appearing the Deft is non-suited.

[Page 150 Nov. 13, 1751]

November Court 1751

Suit in Chancery. JENNETT ROWLEY agt. MOSES ROWLEY. The Deft not having put in his Answer an Attachment is ordered agsint him returnable to the next Court.

Suit on Petition. PHILIP ALEXANDER, Gent. agt. THOMAS SKINNER. Judgment is granted the Pltf for £2.5.4 & Costs.

Action of Trespass Assault & Battery. JOHN HONEY agt. CHARLES & BENJAMIN PORTER is dismist the Defts paying Costs.

145

Action of Trespass. GEORGE SPICER agt. ABRAHAM FLETCHER. The Deft not appearing Judgment is granted the Pltf against him & ABRAHAM GARDNER his Security unless the Deft do appear at the next Court.

Action of Trespass. PHILIP SHERIDAN agt. JAMES GRIGSBY. The Deft not appearing Judgment is granted the Pltf against him & PHILIP ALEXANDER, Gent. Sheriff of this County unless the Deft do appear at the next Court.

Suit on Petition. ANDREW EDWARDS & BETTY his Wife, Admrs. of JAMES WAUGH, Gent., decd. agt. JOHN PEYTON & GEORGE WALLER acting Exors. of CHARLES WALLER, Gent., decd. is continued at the Pltf's Costs.

Suit on Petition. GEORGE KNIGHT agt. WILLIAM HOWARD is dismist & the Pltf ordered to pay to the Deft his Costs.

Then the Court adjourned till tomorrow morning 9 Oclock.
RICHARD BARNARD

At a Court continued & held for Stafford County the 14th November 1751.

Present RICHARD BARNARD JOHN PEYTON
     PETER DANIEL   GERARD FOWKE

Suit in Chancery. CHARLES WELLS & BENJAMIN ROBINSON agt. THOMAS VIVION & PETER DANIEL, Gent. is continued till the next Court to consider the Depositions.

[Page 151 Nov. 14, 1751]

November Court 1751

Suit in Chancery. EDWARD HUMSTON agt. RICHARD BARNARD, JOHN SHORT, & JOHN HUMSTON is continued till the next Court for the Pltf to put in his Replication.

Action of Trespass. JOHN LEWTHWAITE agt. PETER HEDGMAN, Gent. Further time is given the Pltf till the next Court to put in his Replication.

Administration on the Estate of JOHN TOBY is granted JOHN TOBY, Junr. he having entered into Bond with WILLIAM HOWARD & GEORGE RANDALL his Securities. JOSEPH CARTER, THOMAS NORMAN, JEREMIAH STARK, & JOHN CARTER Appraisers.

146

Action of Debt. JOHN WASHINGTON, Exor. of the last Will & Testament of HENRY WASHINGTON, Gent. decd. agt. WILLIAM FITZHUGH, Esqr. & FRANCIS THORNTON, Gent. acting Exors. of GILSON BERRYMAN, decd. A Jury to wit FRANKLYN LATHAM, RICHARD RANDALL, SAMUEL MITCHELL, JOHN TOBY, MOSES LUNSFORD, JOHN ENGLISH, ANDREW KENNY, FRANCIS BROOKS, JOHN THOMAS, GEORGE RANDALL, GEORGE CROSBY, & HENRY SUDDUTH. The Jury finds for the Pltf £27.17.5 half penny. It's considered by the Court that the Pltf recover the same with lawful Interest thereon from the 30th day of June 1748 till the same is paid.

Action of Trespass. LAWRENCE WASHINGTON & COMPANY agt. WILLIAM FITZHUGH, Gent. The Deft confessed Judgment to the Pltf for £10.13.

Action of Trespass. GEORGE WALLER & ELIZABETH his Wife agt. JOHN PEYTON the Younger is dismist the Deft paying Costs.

Action of Detinue. THOMAS ASHBY agt. JOHN RILEY is continued till the next Court at the Pltf's Costs.

Action of Debt. HORATIO DADE agt. WILLIAM FITZHUGH, Esqr. & FRANCIS THORNTON, Gent. acting Exors. of GILSON BERRYMAN, decd. A Jury to wit FRANKLYN LATHAM, RICHARD RANDALL, SAMUEL MITCHELL, JOHN TOBY, MOSES LUNSFORD, JOHN ENGLISH,

[Page 152 Nov. 14, 1751]

November Court 1751

ANDREW KENNY, FRANCIS BROOKS, JOHN THOMAS, GEORGE RANDALL, GEORGE CROSBY & HENRY SUDDUTH. The Jury finds for the Pltf £29.16.6 half penny.

Action of Trespass. ANDREW GRANT & ROBERT BROWN agt. JOSEPH WATERS is dismist the Deft paying Costs.

Action of Trespass. JOSEPH BURGESS & ELIZABETH his Wife agt. WILLIAM SCAPLEHORN. The Deft for Plea saith he is not guilty & hath Leave to give the special Matter in Evidence. The Tryal is referred till the next Court.

Ordered that the Sheriff take ANDREW KENNY into his Custody till he enter into Bond in £20 with two Securities in £10 each for his good Behavior a Year & a Day he being a noted Gamester & an idle Person.

Action of Debt. JOHNTHAN SYDENHAM & THOMAS HODSON agt. MARK HENTON. The Deft not appearing an Attachment is ordered against his Estate & upon the Return thereof Judgment is granted the Pltf for £16 current Money. And the Sheriff having made return thereon that he had attached one Sword, two feather Beds & furniture, one Cow & Calf, one Trunk, one Chest, a parcel of pewter, & nine Rooms of Tobacco hanging it's ordered that he sell the same & satisfy the Pltfs their Judgment.

Action of Trespass. JOHN FOUSHEE, Gent. agt. SAMUEL EARL. The Deft for plea saith that he is not guilty. The Tryal thereof is referred till the next Court.

Action of Detinue. JOHN FOUSHEE, Gent. agt. SAMUEL EARL. The Deft for Plea saith he don't detain. The Tryal thereof is referred till the next Court.

[Page 153 Nov. 14, 1751]

November Court 1751

Ejection Firma. Robert Faldo agt. Richard Aldo for Land and Appurtenances in the Parish of Overwharton which JOHN FOUSHEE, Gent. demised to the Pltf for a Term &c, SAMUEL EARL being admitted Deft in the Room of the said Aldo pleaded not guilty & confessed Lease entry & ouster, and agreed to insist only on the Title at Tryal which Issue the Pltf joined & the Tryal thereof is referred till the next Court.

Action of Trespass. DAVID ROSS, Merchant agt. JOHN NIXON. A Jury to wit FRANKLYN LATHAM, RICHARD RANDALL, SAMUEL MITCHELL, JOHN TOBY, MOSES LUNSFORD, JOHN ENGLISH, FRANCIS BROOKS, JOHN THOMAS, GEORGE RANDALL, GEORGE CROSBY, ANTHONY LATHAM, & CHARLES HARDING. The Jury finds for the Pltf one penny damage & the Pltf being solemnly called came not whereupon on Motion of the Deft he is non-suited & ordered to pay the said Deft damages according to Law & Costs.

Action of Debt. ANDREW COCHRAN & COMPANY agt. WILLIAM SWEATNIM. The Deft not appearing the Judgment against him & WITHERS CONWAY his Security is confirmed to the Pltf for £9.13 & Costs, but this Judgment is to be discharged (the Costs excepted) on payment of £4.16.6 with lawful Interest thereon from the 19th day of February 1750 till the same is paid & the said Withers as Security for the said Deft prayed an Attachment against his Estate which is granted him.

148

Suit on Petition. THOMAS HURST agt. WILLIAM HOWARD. Judgment is granted the Pltf for 250 pounds of Tobacco & Costs.

Ordered that THOMAS HURST pay MOSES LUNSFORD 150 pounds of Tobacco for six days attendance as an Evidence for him against HOWARD.

Ordered that THOMAS HURST pay LUCY BREDWILL 125 pounds of Tobacco for five days Attendance as an Evidence for him against HOWARD.

Ordered that THOMAS HURST pay RACHAEL LUNSFORD 150 pounds of Tobacco for five days Attendance as an Evidence for him against HOWARD.

[Page 154 Nov. 14, 1751]

November Court 1751

Action of Trespass. JOHN THOMAS agt. WILLIAM SCAPLEHORN. The Deft for plea saith he is not guilty. The Tryal is referred till the next Court.

Action of Trespass. JOHN PEYTON the younger agt. JAMES YELTON. The Deft for plea saith that he is not guilty. The Tryal is referred till the next Court.

Action of Debt. ANDREW EDWARDS & BETTY his Wife, Admrs. of JAMES WAUGH, Gent., decd. agt. RAWLEIGH CHINN. The Deft having pleaded payment the Tryal is referred till the next Court.

Action of Trespass. ANDREW ROSS agt. THOMAS JACKSON is dismist the Deft paying Costs.

Action of Trespass. MICHAEL HARPER agt. FRANKLYN LATHAM. The Deft for plea saith he is not guilty. The Tryal is referred till the next Court.

Suit on Petition. JOHN SUTHERLAND agt. JAMES YELTON is continued at the Pltf's Costs.

Suit on Petition. JOHN COOPER agt. SAMUEL ANGELL. Judgment is granted the Pltf for £5 with Costs & a Lawyer's Fee.

Suit on Petition. JAMES NEILSON agt. NATHANIEL GRAY. Judgment is granted the Pltf for a Hogshead of Tobacco about 890 nett with Costs & a Lawyer's Fee.

Suit on Petition. DANIEL CAMPBELL agt. FRANCIS MARTIN & SAMUEL BROWN is continued at the Pltf's Costs.

Then the Court adjourned till Court in Course
RICHARD BARNARD

At a Court held for Stafford County February 11th. 1752.

Present   MOTT DONIPHAN   JOHN PEYTON
       PETER DANIEL   HENRY FITZHUGH
       THOMAS FITZHUGH

PHILIP ALEXANDER, Gent. Sheriff of this County came into Court and protested against the PRISON as being insufficient whereupon it's ordered that he agree with Workmen to repair the same.

HOWSON HOOE on his Motion hath his Ordinary Licence renewed.

[Page 155 Feb. 11, 1752]

February Court 1752

WILLIAM BARNARD, Gent. produced a Licence under the Hands & Seals of PEYTON RANDOLPH Esqr., JAMES POWER, & GEORGE WYTHE, Gent. to practice as an Attorney having taken the several Oaths & subscribed the Test & abjuration Oath is ordered to be certified.

Action of Trespass. FRANCIS DADE agt. THOMAS MASSEY for £100 Damage by Means of the Deft's breaking & entering the Close of the Pltf at the Parish of St. Paul's. The several Orderes for a Survey in this Suit not being complied with, it's again ordered that the Surveyor of the said County in Company of an able Jury of Freeholders go upon the Lands in controversy & lay off the same as either Party would have it, having regard to all Patents & Evidences as shall be produced by either of the Parties & if the Jury should find the Deft a Trespasser they are to value the damages & report all Matters of Fact to the next Court.

Ordered that TRAVERSE COOKE have a Bridle Way from his House to MR. MONCURE'S Road that leads to ACQUIA thro' WILLIAM BUTLER'S & JOHN MONTGOMERY'S Cornfields & thro' an old Field of MRS. WIGGINGTON'S in & near the old Road.

Ordered that a bridle Way be cleared from JOSEPH & MARY CARTER'S to ACQUIA WAREHOUSE.

Ordered that MARY PONTON pay JANE WILLIAMS 75 pounds of Tobacco for three days attendance as an Evidence for her against RYAN.

150

Ordered that the Church Wardens of Overwharton Parish bind SUSANNA SYMPSON & WILLIAM WHEELER according to Law.

Ordered that the Church Wardens of St. Paul's Parish bind ROBERT NORMAN, ISAAC JOY & ANNE JOY according to Law.

THOMAS FLETCHER & JOHN MINGOS being bound over unto this Court by Recognizance appeared & no Evidence appearing against them they are discharged.

HUSBANDFOOTE WHITECOTTON is appointed Constable in the room of STEPHEN PILCLHER.

[Page 156 Feb. 11, 1752]

February Court 1752

On Petition of CAIN WITHERS Licence is granted him to keep an Ordinary at the late Dwelling House of THOMAS DENT, decd.

Action of Trespass. WILLIAM MOUNTJOY agt. GEORGE GHENT. ANDREW EDWARDS who was Bail for the Deft appearing brough him into Court & delivered him up in discharge of himself which is ordered to be certified.

Ordered that WILLIAM DARBY serve his Master JAMES YELTON for 18 Days runaway Time & 360 pounds of Tobacco expended in taking him up.

Ordered that TADIE WHEELER serve his Mistress ELIZABETH MCABOY according to Law for five days runaway Time & 90 pounds of Tobo. in taking him up.

Then the Court adjourned till Court in Course.
MOTT DONIPHAN

At a Court held for Stafford County for the Proof of public Claims Prositions [*sic*] & Grievances February 11th. 1752.

Present   RICHARD BARNARD   MOTT DONIPHAN
               JOHN PEYTON   PETER DANIEL
               HENRY FITZHUGH

SYLVESTER MOSS produced a Certificate under the Hand of JOHN PEYTON, Gent. for taking up a negro Boy named PHILL belonging to JOHN BALLENTINE of Prince William County which is ordered to be certified to the Assembly & it's adjudged by the Court to be above ten Miles from his Master's.

SYLVESTER MOSS produced a certificate under the Hand of JOHN PEYTON, Gent. for taking up a Servant Man named JOHN ANDERSON belonging to EDWARD RANDALL of Westmoreland County which is ordered to be certified to the Assembly & it's adjudged by the Court to be above five Miles from his Master's.

SYLVESTER MOSS, Assignee of JOHN MURPHY produced a certificate under the Hand of JOHN PEYTON, Gent. for taking up a Servant Man named WILLIAM BUTLER belonging to SNODALL HORTON of this County which is to be certified to the Assembly & it's adjudged by the Court to be above five Miles from his Master's.

WILLIAM DYE produced a Certificate under the Hand of GERARD FOWKE, Gent. for taking up a Servant Man named WILLIAM TUFTS who would not declare his Master's Name and made

[Page 157 Feb. 11, 1752]

February Court 1752

Oath thereto and that the said Servant made his Escape by breaking the County Goal which is ordered to be certified to the Assembly.

WILLIAM JONES & THOMAS FLETCHER produced a Certificate under the Hand of HENRY FITZHUGH, Gent. for taking up MICHAEL STORM a Servant belonging to MOSES GRIGSBY of this County which is ordered to be certified to the Assembly & it's adjudged by the Court to be above ten Miles from his Master's.

WILLIAM CORBIN produced a Certificate under the Hand of PETER DANIEL, Gent. for taking up a Negro Fellow named TOM belonging to JAMES MAXWELL of Culpeper County which is ordered to be certified to the Assembly & it's adjudged by the Court to be above twenty Miles from his Master's.

JOHN CANADY produced a Certificate under the Hand of MOTT DONIPHAN, Gent. for taking up WILLIAM DARBY a Servant belonging to JAMES YELTON of this County which is ordered to be certified to the Assembly & it's adjudged by the Court to be above five Miles from his Master's.

GEORGE PILCHER produced a Certificate under the Hand of JOHN MERCER, Gent. for taking JOHN HOLT a Servant Man belonging to MOSES GRIGSBY of this County which is ordered to be certified to the Assembly & it's adjudged by this Court to be above five Miles from his Master's.

A Petition of TOWNSHEND DADE, Gent. for a Ferry over POTOMACK RIVER to upper CEDAR POINT in the Province of Maryland being read is ordered to be certified to the Assembly.

It's ordered to be certified to the Assembly by this Court that they are willing that this Court day be altered from the second Tuesday to the second Monday in every Month.

MOTT DONIPHAN

At a Court held for Stafford County March 8th. 1752.

Present   MOTT DONIPHAN   JOHN PEYTON
               PETER DANIEL   GERARD FOWKE
               THOMAS FITZHUGH

BURDITT CLIFTON on his Motion hath his Ordinary Licence renewed.

Suit on Petition. MICHAEL WALLACE agt. GEORGE PURVIS & MARY his Wife, Admrs. of

[Page 158 Mar. 8, 1752]

March Court 1752

MEREDITH EDWARDS, decd. Judgment is granted the Pltf for 560 pounds of Tobacco & Costs.

GOWRY WAUGH came into Court & discharged MOTT DONIPHAN, Gent. & ALEXANDER DONIPHAN his Guardians acknowledging that upon his coming of Age his Guardians have delivered up the Whole Estate in their Hands to which he had any Claim & settled & adjusted all Accounts relaing to the same or the profits thereof.

Administration on the Estate of TOBIAS HYCHE is granted ROBERT GARRETT he having entered into Bond. THOMAS GOUGH, BENJAMIN ROBINSON, WILLIAM ETHERINGTON, & WILLIAM BYRAM Appraisers.

Ordered that Liquors stand rated as before except Rum & that at 10/ per Gallon instead of 8/ & rum Punch with white Sugar at 15 d. per Quart instead of 12 d.

Action of Trespass. THOMAS & ROBERT DUNLOPS agt. JAMES FERNSLEY. BENJAMIN STROTHER, Gent., late Sheriff of this County as bail for the said Deft agreed to wave the Issue & confess Judgment to the Pltfs for £10.7.9 half penny & Costs and the Pltfs agree to stay Execution three Months.

Administration on the Estate of HANNAH BAYLIS decd. is granted SAMUEL EARL, Gent. he having entered into Bond with JOB SIMS & WILLIAM PICKETT his Securities. WILLIAM ALLEN, EDWARD WALLER, EDWARD RALLS & JOHN MASON Appraisers.

In the Suit on Attachment obtained by WILLIAM PICKET against the Estate of MARK HENTON by consent of the Parties all matters in difference between them are referred to the Determination of ANDREW ROSS, ROBERT RAE & DANIEL CAMPBELL & their Award to be made the Judgment of the Court.

Suit on Information. Our Sovereign Lord the King agt. MARY WISE. The said Mary for Plea saith she is not guilty. The Tryall thereof is referred till the next Court.

The same against WILLIAM WATERS.

The same against JAMES STEWARD.

The same against WILLIAM EDWARDS.

The same against ELIZABETH HINSON.

The same against GEORGE BELL.

The same against JOHN BELL.

The same against WILLIAM HOWARD.

The same against GEORGE RANDALL.

March Court 1752

Action of Trespass. FRANKLYN LATHAM agt. WILLIAM HARPER. The Deft for plea saith he is not guilty in manner & form. The Tryal is referred till the next Court.

Action of Trespass Assault & Battery. JOHN STACY agt. HENRY DAWSON. The Deft for plea saith he is not guilty. The Tryal is referred till the next Court.

Action of Trespass. WILLIAM BYRAM agt. JOHN STACY is dismist the Deft paying Costs.

Action of Trespass. ISAAC FOWLER & REBECCA his Wife agt. FRANCIS DAY is dismist the Deft paying Costs.

Action of Debt. BENJAMIN STROTHER & PETER DANIEL, Gent., Church Wardens of Overwharton Parish agt. MARTHA HORTON. The Deft not appearing judgment against her & EDWARD RALLS her Security is confirmed for 50 Shillings or 500 pounds of Tobacco & Cask.

Action of Trespass. JAMES MARSHALL, Merchant agt. WILLIAM FITZHUGH, Esqr. & FRANCIS THORNTON, Gent. acting Exors. of GILSON BERRYMAN, decd. The Defts for Plea saith that the Testator did not assume & that they have fully administered. The Tryal is referred till the next Court.

Action of Trespass. FRANCIS THORNTON, Gent. agt. JOHN LEEWRIGHT & MARY his Wife. The Defts for Plea saith that they are not guilty. The Tryal is referred till the next Court.

Action of Trespass Assault & Battery. WILLIAM WARREL agt. JESSE MOSS & BENJAMIN DUNCOMB. The Defts for Plea say they are not guilty. The Tryal is referred till the next Court.

Action of Trespass. WILLIAM FITZHUGH, Esqr. & FRANCIS THORNTON, Gent. acting Exors. of GILSON BERRYMAN, decd. agt. WILLIAM KELLY & PHILIS his Wife, Admrs. of JAMES MCINTOSH. The Defts for Plea say that the Intestate did not assume. The Tryal is referred till the next Court.

Suit in Chancery. JENNET FOWLEY agt. MOSES ROWLEY. The Deft not appearing an Attachment is ordered against him returnable to the next Court.

Action of Trespass. PHILIP ALEXANDER, Gent. agt. WILLIAM FITZHUGH, Esqr. & FRANCIS THORNTON, Gent. acting Exors. of GILSON

BERRYMAN, decd. The Defts for Plea say that the Testator did not assume & that they have fully administered. The Pltf joined (*entry incomplete*).

[Page 160 Mar. 8, 1752]

April Court 1752

Action of Trespass. JOHN SAUNDERSON agt. THOMAS SEDDON. The Deft having put in his Plea, the Pltf hath time to consider thereof till the next Court.

Action of Trespass Assault & Battery. WILLIAM SCAPLEHORN agt. CLEMENT SACHEVERAL. The Deft not appearing the Judgment against him & WITHERS CONWAY his Security is confirmed & a Writ of Enquiry of Damages is to be executed the next Court.

Action of Trespass. JOB WINGLEY agt. NATHANIEL HARRISON, acting Exor. of WILLIAM WALKER, Gent. decd. The Deft for Plea saith that the Testator did not assume & that he has fully administered. The Tryal is referred till the next Court.

The the Court adjourned till tomorrow morning 9 Oclock.

MOTT DONIPHAN

At a Court held for Stafford County 14th. April 1752.

Present   RICHARD BARNARD   MOTT DONIPHAN
               JOHN PEYTON   FRANCIS THORNTON
               THOMAS FITZHUGH

On Complaint of DANIEL CHAMBERS it's ordered that the Sheriff take SAMUEL BURTON into his Custody till he enter into Bond for his Appearance at the next Court.

Ordered that the Church Wardens of Overwharton Parish bind JOHN GRINNAN, MILLY GRINNAN & DANIEL GRINAN & SARAH GRINAN according to Law.

Upon Attachment obtained by BENJAMIN CLIFT who was Security for JANE CARRICOE'S due Administration on her Husband's Estate it's ordered that the Sheriff sell such of the Estate as is attached & what Money arises by such to deliver to the said Benjamin for his Indemnification.

Action of Detinue. URIEL CROSBY by GEORGE CROSBY his Guardian agt. EDWARD RALLS. By consent of the Parties all Matters in Difference between them are referred to the determination of the Revd. JOHN MONCURE & JOHN PEYTON, Gent. & their award is to be made the Judgment of the Court, & it's ordered that a Dedimus issue to examine the Witnesses before them.

Suit on Petition. MICHAEL WALLACE agt. ISAAC FOWLER. Judgment is granted the Pltf for 295 pounds of Tobo. & Costs.

Ordered that ISAAC FOWLER pay FRANCIS DAY 75 pounds of Tobacco for three days attendance as an Evidence for him at suit of WALLACE.

On Petition of WILLIAM ELLIOTT for his Freedom, it's the Opinion of the Court

April Court 1752

that the said Elliott is free, whereupon it's ordered that he be discharged from PHILIP ALEXANDER, Gent. who for some time hath detained him as a servant by Purchase from one GEORGE CLARK, Merchant in the Province of Maryland.

Upon Petition of THOMAS PAIRIMAIN late Servant to BENONI STRATTON, decd. against JOHN ADDISON & ANN his Wife, Admrs. of the said Stratton. Ordered that the said John & Ann pay the said Thomas ten bushels of Corn, 30 Shillings in Money or Goods, one well fixt Musket or Fuzy, & 20 Shillings Cash & Costs.

Action of Trespass. JAMES MARSHALL agt. WILLIAM FITZHUGH, Esqr. & FRANCIS THORNTON, Gent. acting Exors. of GILSON BERRYMAN, decd. The Defts confessed Judgment to the Pltf for £21.4.9 three Farthings.

Administration on the Estate of WILLIAM BRUIN is granted JAMES SUDDUTH he having entered into Bond. THOMAS HAY, WILLIAM MILLS, LAWRENCE SUDDUTH & JOHN WEATHERS Appraisers.

JOHN PEYTON the Younger being indicted & a Bill found against him by the Grand jury for an Assault & Battery on MARY LUNSFORD pleaded not guilty. A Jury to wit EDWARD RALLS, JOB SIMS, ROBERT DOOLIN, JAMES GIVENS, FRANCIS BROOKS, MICHAEL HARPER, EDWARD BEHTELL, THOMAS JORDAN, WILLIAM MOSS, JOHN LEWRIGHT, WILLIAM BYRAM & JOHN LEWRIGHT were sworn to try the Issue joined & retired.

Action of Trespass Assault & Battery. JOHN FITZPATRICK agt. ROBERT ASHBY. The Deft not appearing Judgment is granted the Pltf against him & his Security.

April Court 1752

Action of Trespass Assault & Battery. CHARLES BENSON agt. JOHN INGLISH being agreed is dismist.

Action of Trespass. JOHN HONEY agt. THOMAS PORTER being agreed is dismist.

Action of Trespass Assault & Battery. WILLIAM MOSS agt. ENOCH HENSLY being agreed is dismist.

Suit on Scire facias. WILLIAM WALLER, Gent. agt. WILLIAM FITZHUGH, Esqr. & FRANCIS THORNTON, Gent. acting Exors. of GILSON BERRYMAN, decd. The Sheriff having returned the Scire facias executed & the said William & Francis failing to appear it's considered by the Court that the said William have Execution for 45 Shillings & 59 pounds of Tobacco.

Suit on Petition. RICHARD BARNARD, Gent. agt. JAMES MAHORNER. Judgment is granted the Pltf for 860 pounds of Tobacco in one Cask, with Interest from the first Day of April 1749 till paid & Costs.

Suit on Petition. JOHN GREGG agt. SAMUEL ANGEL. Judgment is granted the Pltf for £2.15 & Costs.

In the Suit on Attachment obtained by JOHN PEYTON, Gent. against the Estate of ROBERT HATTON the said John produced a Note of Hand of the said Robert for £2.15.5. It's therefore considered by the Court that the said John recover the same of the said Robert & his Costs. And the Sheriff having made return that he had attached one drugget Coat, one pair of Yarn Stockings, two pair of old Breaches, two old Shirts, one old Hat, Linen to make a Shirt, two Caps & one Handkerchief who is ordered to sell the same to satisfy the said Peyton his Judgment.

The Suit on Attachment obtained by LYDIA PATTISON against the Estate of JAMES MINGOS is dismist.

The Petition brough by WILLIAM JOHNSON & MASON FRENCH against WILLIAM KELLY & PHILLIS his Wife, Admrs. of JAMES MCINTOSH, decd. is dismist.

Suit on Petition. JOSEPH COMBS agt. EDWARD SEBASTIAN. Judgment is granted the Pltf for £3.4.6 & Costs.

April Court 1752

Action of Trespass Assault & Battery. GEORGE GHENT agt. JAMES HUGHS. An Alias Capias is ordered returnable to the next Court.

Action of Trespass. ANTHONY STROTHER agt. JOHN NORRAY & MARY his Wife is dismist.

Suit on Petition. ALLEN MARIE agt. SAMUEL ANGELL is continued at the Deft's Costs.

Suit on Petition. BENJAMIN STROTHER, Gent. agt. SAMUEL BREDWELL. Judgment is granted the Pltf for £2.10 & Costs.

Action of Debt. RICHARD BARNARD, Gent. agt. WILLIAM LORD. The Deft confessed Judgment to the Pltf for 5,702 pounds of Tobacco with lawful Interest thereon from the 15th day of May 1746 till paid.

ALICE DOGAL being presented by the Grand jury for having a Bastard Child & summoned failing to appear it's ordered that she pay the Church Wardens of Overwharton Parish 50 Shillings or 500 pounds of Tobacco with Cask & Costs.

Action of Debt. JOHN CORBIN, Esqr. agt. NATHANIEL HARRISON, Esqr., acting Exor. of WILLIAM WALKER, Gent., decd. An Alias Capias is ordered returnable to the next Court.

Action of Debt. VALENTINE PEYTON agt. JOSEPH SEBASTIAN, junr. The Deft confessed Judgment to the Pltf for £6.9.

Action of Trespass. ANTHONY STROTHER agt. DUKE WHALEBONE being agreed is dismist.

Action of Trespass. WILLIAM HOWARD agt. EDWARD RALLS is dismist the Deft paying Costs.

Ordered that WILLIAM WALKER be summoned to answer the Petition of WILLIAM MOUNTJOY.

Then the Court adjourned till tomorrow morning 9 Oclock.

RICHARD BARNARD

At a Court continued & held for Stafford County April 15th. 1752.

Present   RICHARD BARNARD   MOTT DONIPHAN
                JOHN PEYTON   PETER DANIEL
                FRANCIS THORNTON   THOMAS FITZHUGH

[Page 164 Apr. 15, 1752]

April Court 1752

WILLIAM BLACK on his Motion hath his Ordinary Licence renewed.

The Jury sworn yesterday against JOHN PEYTON the Younger brought in their verdict as Guilty, which Verdict is admitted to Record & the Court assesses one Shilling damage. It's therefore considered by the Court that the said Peyton pay to our Lord the King the said one Shilling & Costs.

Suit on Petition. ANDREW EDWARDS & BETTY his Wife Admrs. of JAMES WAUGH, Gent., decd. agt. JOHN PEYTON, Gent. & GEORGE WALLER, acting Exors. of CHARLES WALLER, Gent., decd. Judgment is granted the Pltfs for £4.10 & an half penny.

Action of Trespass. JOHN FINIGHAN agt. DANIEL & JOHN MATHISS. A Plurias Capias is ordered returnable to the next Court.

Suit on Petition. JOHN PEYTON, Gent. agt. JOHN BAILS. The Deft confessed Judgment to the Pltf for £4.6.1 half penny & Costs.

Suit on Petition. SAMUEL SIMS agt. JOB SIMS is dismist & the Pltf ordered to pay to the said Deft his Costs.

Ordered that JOB SIMS pay WILLIAM NORTHCUT 100 pounds of Tobacco for four days attendance as an Evidence for him at Suit of SAMUEL SIMS.

Ordered that JOB SIMS pay ROBERT DEULIN 100 pounds of Tobacco for four days attendance as an Evidence for him at Suit of SAMUEL SIMS.

Action of Trespass. JOHN PEYTON the Younger agt. JAMES YELTON. A Jury to wit HENRY DAUWSON, CHARLES HARDING, DANIEL CHAMBERS, JAMES ONEAL, WILLIAM ROSE, ANDREW EDWARDS, FRANKLYN LATHAM, JOHN SILVIA, SAMUEL MITCHEL, GEORGE

160

ALLEN, WILLIAM JORDAN, & THOMAS HAY. The Jury finds for the Pltf £10 & Costs.

April Court 1752

Ordered that JAMES YELTON pay MARY LUNSFORD 25 pounds of Tobacco for one days attendance as an Evidence for him at Suit of PEYTON.

Ordered that JOHN PEYTON the Younger pay JAMES HUGHS 100 pounds of Tobacco for four days attendance as an Evidence for him against YELTON.

Ordered that JOHN PEYTON the younger pay FRANCIS MASTIN 75 pounds of Tobacco for three days attendance as an Evidence for him against YELTON.

Absent RICHARD BARNARD & JOHN PEYTON, Gent.

Action of Trespass. RICHARD BARNARD, Gent. agt. JOHN SILVIA. By Consent of the Parties the Issue to be try'd by a Jury is waved & all Matters in Difference between them are referred to the Determination of FRANCIS THORNTON, JOHN PEYTON, & NATHANIEL GRAY, Gent. & their award is to be made the Judgment of the Court.

Present R. BARNARD & JOHN PEYTON

Action of Detinue. JOHN FOUSHEE, Gent. agt. SAMUEL EARL, Gent. A Jury to wit DANIEL CHAMBERS, JAMES ONEAL, JOHN BELL, ANDREW EDWARDS, FRANKLYN LATHAM, JOHN SILVIA, SAMUEL MITCHEL, WILLIAM JORDAN, THOMAS HAY, GEORGE SPICER, JACOB JOHNSON, & GEORGE ALLEN. The Jury finds for the Pltf the said Negroes in the declaration mentioned of the Price of £360 damage for detaining the Negroes. It's considered by the Court that the Pltf recover of the Deft the Negroes aforesaid of the Price aforesaid of £360, the Value of them & £18 for detaining the said Negroes. The Deft filed Errors in arrest of Judgment which are to be argued at the next Court.

Ordered that JOHN SILVIA pay BALDWIN DADE 100 pounds of Tobacco for four days attendance as an Evidence for him at the Suit of BARNARD.

Action of Trespass. JOHN PEYTON & GEORGE WALLER, acting Exors. of CHARLES WALLER, Gent. decd. agt. RAWLEIGH CHINN. A Jury to wit EDWARD RALLS, JOHN GREGG, JOB SIMS, MICHAEL HARPER, EDWARD BETHEL, ROBERT DUELIN, WILLIAM NORTHCUT, ROBERT

ASHBY, HENRY DAWSON, CHARLES HARDING & FRANCIS BROOKS. The Jury finds for the Pltf £3.1 damage

April Court 1752

& their Costs.

Action of Debt. MARY FOWKE agt. ANDREW EDWARDS & BETTY his Wife, Admrs. of JAMES WAUGH, Gent. decd. The Deft for Plea say they owe nothing & have fully administered. The Tryal is referred till the next Court.

Action of Detinue. THOMAS ASHBY agt. JOHN RILEY is continued at the Pltf's Costs.

Action of Trespass. JOHN PEYTON & GEORGE WALLER acting Exors. of CHARLES WALLER, Gent., decd. agt. JACOB AMBROSE DEKEZOR. The Deft for Plea saith that he did not assume. The Tryal is referred till the next Court.

Suit on Petition. JOHN PEYTON agt. SAMUEL ANGEL. Judgment is granted the Pltf for 615 pounds of Tobacco & seven Shillings & two pence Costs.

Suit on Petition. MOTT & ALEXANDER DONIPHAN Guardians to GOWRY WAUGH agt. JOHN SMITH. Judgment is granted the Pltf for 530 pounds of Tobacco and Costs.

Action of Debt. TRAVERSE COOKE agt. RAWLEIGH CHINN. The Deft confessed Judgment to the Pltf for £5.8 & a half penny & 802 pounds of Tobacco & his Costs.

Ordered that MOTT & ALEXANDER DONIPHAN pay THOMAS HAY 100 pounds of Tobacco for four days attendance as an Evidence for them against SMITH.

Action of Debt. ANDREW EDWARDS & BETTY his Wife, Admrs. of JAMES WAUGH, Gent., decd. agt. RAWLEIGH CHINN. The Deft confessed Judgment for £8.6.1 with lawful Interest thereon from the 8th day of August 1749 till paid.

Action of Trespass. JOHN FOUSHEE, Gent. agt. SAMUEL EARL, Gent. A Jury to wit EDWARD RALLS, JOB SIMS, MICHAEL HARPER,

April Court 1752

EDWARD BETHEL, ROBERT DUELIN, WILLIAM NORTHCUT, JAMES GWIN, FRANCIS BROOKS, JOHN LEWRIGHT, WILLIAM BYRAM, WILLIAM MOSS, & THOMAS JURDIN were sworn to try the Issue joined and retired.

Then the Court adjourned till 9 Oclock tomorrow morning.

RICHARD BARNARD

At a Court continued & held for Stafford County April 16th. 1752.

Present   RICHARD BERNARD   MOTT DONIPHAN
                  JOHN PEYTON   PETER DANIEL

Action of Trespass. RICHARD FRISTOE agt. JOHN KIRK & SARAH his Wife. The Deft for plea say they are not guilty. The Tryal is referred till the next Court.

Action of Trespass. LAWRENCE WASHINGTON & COMPANY agt. ANDREW EDWARDS & BETTY his Wife, Admrs. of JAMES WAUGH, Gent., decd. The Defts for plea say that the Testator did not assume. The Trial is referred till the next Court.

Action of Trespass. RICHARD BROOKE agt. NATHANIEL HARRISON, Esqr., acting Exor. of WILLIAM WALKER, Gent., decd. The Errors in this Suit being waved by the Deft it's considered by the Court that the Pltf recover of the Deft according to the Form & Effects of the Judgment aforesaid.

Action of Debt. HUGH MITCHEL agt. WILLIAM DAVIS. The Deft having put in his Plea the Pltf hath time to consider thereof till the next Court.

Action of Debt. MOSELEY BATTALEY, Assignee of WILLIAM ROWLEY agt. MOSES ROWLEY. The Deft having pleaded payment the Tryal is referred till the next Court.

Action of Trespass Assault & Battery. WILLIAM MARRIOLL agt. JESSE MOSS & BENJAMIN DUNCOMB being agreed is dismist.

Suit on Information brought in behalf of our Sovereign Lord the King agt. WILLIAM EDWARDS for tending seconds of Tobacco, and the said William having pleaded not guilty. a Jury therupon to wit, JACOB JOHNSON,

THOMAS WEATHERS, ANTHONY LATHAM, HENRY DAWSON, FRANKLYN LATHAM, JAMES ONEAL, JOHN BELL, SASFIELD NOXALL, JOHN PEYTON, STEPHEN MUMFORD, JOHN LEACH & JAMES ONEAL, Junr. The Jury brought in their Verdict in these Words "Guilty four Tithables, John Peyton foreman." It's considered by the Court that the said William pay to our Lord the King 2,000 pounds of Tobacco & Costs of this Suit.

[Page 168 Apr. 16, 1752]

April Court 1752

Suit on Information. Our Lord the King agt. WILLIAM WATERS the said William having pleaded not Guilty. The Jury finds the Deft not Guilty.

Suit on Information. Our Lord the King agt. GEORGE BELL, the said George having pleaded not Guilty a Jury...finds the Deft not Guilty.

Suit on Information. Our Lord the King agt. JOHN BELL, the said John having pleaded not guilty. A Jury finds the Deft not Guilty.

Suit on Information. Our Lord the King agt. ELIZABETH HINSON, the said Elizabeth having pleaded not guilty. A Jury finds the Deft not Guilty.

Suit on Information. Our Lord the King agt. FRANKLYN LATHAM, the said Franklyn having pleaded Not Guilty. A Jury finds the Deft not Guilty.

[Page 169 Apr. 16, 1752]

April Court 1752

Suit on Information. Our Lord the King agt. JAMES STUART, the said James having pleaded not guilty. A Jury thereupon to wit JACOB JOHNSON, JAMES ONEAL, THOMAS WEATHERS, CHARLES HARDING, HENRY DAWSON, JAMES FERNSLEY, JAMES ONEAL, junr., SASFIELD NOXALL, JOHN LEECH, ANDREW EDWARDS, NICHOLAS RILEY, & WILLIAM MUMFORD who finds the Deft not Guilty.

Suit on Information. Our Lord the King agt. GEORGE RANDALL, the said George having pleaded not guilty. The Jury finds the Deft not Guilty.

Ordered that the Sheriff attach MOSES ROWLEY & ANNE HANSLEY to appear at the next Court to give Security for their good Behavior.

Action of Trespass. JOHN SAUNDERSON agt. THOMAS SEDDON. The Pltf put in his Replication & the Deft hath time to consider thereof till the next Court.

Action of Trespass Assault & Battery. ELIZABETH MCABOY agt. THOMAS JURDIN. The Deft for plea saith he is not guilty. The Trial is referred till the next Court.

Action of Trespass Assault & Battery. WILLIAM SCAPLEHORN agt. CLEMENT SACHAVAREL. The Deft not appearing Judgment is granted the Pltf & a Writ of Enquiry of damages is to be executed the next Court.

Action of Trespass. GEORGE SPICER agt. ABRAM FLETCHER. The Deft for plea saith he is not guilty & hath leave to give the special Matter in Evidence. The Tryal is referred till the next Court.

Action of Trespass. JANE WILLIAMS agt. DARBY KELLY is dismist.

[Page 170 Apr. 16, 1752]

April Court 1752

Action of Trespass. PHILIP SHERIDEN agt. JAMES GRIGSBY being agreed is dismist.

Action of Trespass Assault & Battery. WILLIAM WARRELL agt. BENJAMIN DUNCOMB being agreed is dismist.

Action of Trespass. JOHN FOUSHEE, Gent. agt. SAMUEL EARL, Gent. The Jury sworn yesterday returning into Court found for the Pltf £30 damage.

Ejection Firma. Robert Faldo, Lessee of JOHN FOUSHEE, Gent. agt. SAMUEL EARLE is continued by consent of the Parties. A Dedimus is to be issued returnable to the next Court.

Action of Trespass. WILLIAM FITZHUGH, Esqr. & FRANCIS THORNTON, Gent. acting Exors. of GILSON BERRYMAN, decd. agt. JAMES KELLY & PHILLIS his Wife, Admrs. of JAMES MCINTOSH, decd. A Jury to wit EDWARD RALLS, JOB SIMS, ROBERT DUELIN, JAMES GWYN, FRANCIS BROOKS, MICHAEL HARPER, EDWARD BETHEL, THOMAS JURDIN, WILLIAM MOSS, JOHN LERIGHT, WILLIAM BYRAM, & WILLIAM NORTHCUT. The Jury finds for the Pltf £9.13.3 damage.

Action of Trespass. MICHAEL HARPER agt. FRANKLYN LATHAM. A Jury to wit EDWARD RALLS, JOB SIMS, ROBERT DEULIN, FRANCIS

BROOKS, THOMAS JURDIN, WILLIAM MOSS, JOHN LEWRIGHT, WILLIAM BYRAM, GEORGE BELL, JOHN BELL, GEORGE ALLEN, & EDWARD BETHEL. The Jury finds for the Pltf 40 Shillings damage & Costs.

[Page 171 Apr. 16, 1752]

April Court 1752

Ordered that MICHAEL HARPER pay EDWARD BETHEL 125 pounds of Tobacco for five days attendance as an Evidence for him against LATHAM.

Ordered that MICHAEL HARPER pay BENJAMIN ASBURY 90 pounds of Tobacco for three days attendance as an evidence for him against LATHAM & for coming & returning five Miles once.

Ordered that MICHAEL HARPER pay THOMAS SMITH 125 pounds of Tobacco for five days attendance as an Evidence for him against LATHAM.

Action of Trespass. FRANKLYN LATHAM agt. MICHAEL HARPER. A Jury to wit EDWARD RALLS, JOB SIMS, ROBERT DEULIN, FRANCIS BROOKS, THOMAS JURDIN, WILLIAM MOSS, JOHN LEWRIGHT, WILLIAM BYRAM, GEORGE BELL, JOHN BELL, GEORGE ALLEN, & EDWARD BETHEL. The Jury finds for the Pltf £3 damage & Costs.

Ordered that FRANKLYN LATHAM pay JUDITH BUMLEY 171 pounds of Tobacco for three days attendance as an Evidence for him at Suit of HARPER and for coming & returning 32 Miles.

Ordered that FRANKLYN LATHAM pay HENRY WOOD 171 pounds of Tobacco for three days attendance as an Evidence for him at Suit of HARPER and for coming & returning 32 Miles.

Ordered that FRANKLYN LATHAM pay WILLIAM BRUMLEY 171 pounds of Tobacco for three days attendance as an Evidence for him at Suit of HARPER and for coming & returning 32 Miles once.

Ordered that FRANKLYN LATHAM pay JAMES ONEAL 75 pounds of Tobacco for three days attendance as an Evidence for him against HARPER.

Ordered that FRANKLYN LATHAM pay JAMES ONEAL, junr. 75 pounds of Tobacco for three days attendance as an Evidence for him against HARPER.

Ordered that FRANKLYN LATHAM pay JOHN ONEAL 75 pounds of Tobacco for three days attendance as an Evidence for him against HARPER.

Action of Trespass Assault & Battery. JOHN STACY agt. HENRY DAWSON.
A Jury to wit EDWARD RALLS, JOB SIMS, ROBERT DEULIN, FRANCIS
BROOKS, THOMAS JURDIN, WILLIAM MOSS, JOHN LEWRIGHT,
WILLIAM BYRAM, GEORGE BELL, JOHN BELL, GEORGE ALLEN, &
EDWARD BETHEL. The Jury finds for the Deft. It's considered by the Court
that the Pltf take nothing by his Bill & that the Deft recover

[Page 172 Apr. 16, 1752]

May Court 1752

of the Pltf his Costs.

Ordered that JOHN STACY pay WILLIAM BYRAM 75 pounds of Tobacco for
three days attendance as an Evidence for him against DAWSON.

Ordered that HENRY DAWSON pay NICHOLAS RILEY 75 pounds of
Tobacco for three days attendance as an Evidence for him at Suit of STACY.

Then the Court adjourned till Court in Course.
RICHARD BERNARD

At a Court held for Stafford County May 12th. 1752.

Present   MOTT DONIPHAN   JOHN PEYTON
                    HENRY FITZHUGH   FRANCIS THORNTON
                    THOMAS FITZHUGH

JOHN STUART Gent. having moved this Court for a Mill on MENESENS
RUN being one of the Branches of MACOTIQUE DAMS it's thereupon ordered
that the Sheriff summon 12 good & lawful Men of his Bailiwick who being
summoned & sworn are well & truly to enquire whether building a Mill on the
Place proposed by the said Stuart may or will effect the adjacent Lands of any
Person & if it should to value the damages & report to the next Court.

JOHN COLEMAN a servant boy belonging to WILLIAM KENDALL adjudged
to be 11 years old.

Ordered that JOHN PEYTON Constable be summoned to appear at the next
Court to answer the complaint of THOMAS FITZHUGH, Gent.

Ordered that HUGH KING serve his Master ROBERT HEDGES according to
Law for fifty days runaway time & 90 pounds of Tobacco expended in taking
him up.

JOHN FINIGHAN being bound over to this Court by recognizance appeared & having heard the Evidences against him it's ordered that the Sheriff take him into his Custody till he enter into Bond in £20 with two Securities in £10 each for his good Behavoir & keeping the Peace a Year & a day.

RICHARD BROOKS, MARY BROOKS, THOMAS BROOKS, RICHARD BROOKS, junr., HANNAH BROOKS, MARY BROOKS, & JOHN WILSON being bound over to this Court by Recognizance appeared & having heard the Evidences against them it's ordered that the Sheriff take them into his custody till they & each of them enter into Bond in £20 with two Securities in £10 each for their good behavior & keeping the Peace a year & a day.

Action of Trespass. JAMES YELTON agt. JOHN PEYTON the younger is dismist the Pltf paying Costs.

ALEXANDER DONIPHAN & MICHAEL PIKE acknowledged themselves indebted to our Sovereign Lord the King in the Sum of £10 each to

[Page 173 May 12, 1752]

May Court 1752

be levied on their Goods & Chattels Lands & Tenements upon Condition that RICHARD BROOKS, MARY BROOKS, THOMAS BROOKS, RICHARD BROOKS, junr., HANNAH BROOKS, MARY BROOKS, & JOHN WILSON keep the peace towards SARAH PEYTON & all his Majesty's liege People a year & a day.

> Present PETER DANIEL &
> RICHARD BARNARD, Gent.

Action of Trespass. JOHN LEWTHWAITE agt. PETER HEDGMAN, Gent. The Pltf having filed his Demurer the Deft hath time to consider thereof till the next Court.

Action of Trespass. PHILIP ALEXANDER, Gent. agt. WILLIAM FITZHUGH, Esqr. & FRANCIS THORNTON, Gent. acting Exors. of GILSON BERRYMAN, decd. The Defts for Plea say that the Testator did not assume & that they have fully administered. The Tryal is referred till the next Court.

Action of Trespass. JOSEPH BURGESS & ELIZABETH his Wife agt. WILLIAM SCAPLIN is dismist the Deft paying Costs.

Action of Debt. ANTHONY STROTHER agt. JOSEPH BRAGG. The Deft not appearing an Attachment is awarded the Pltf against the Deft's estate for £14 & Costs returnable to the next Court.

Action of Trespass. MARY WISE agt. THOMAS MOUNTJOY is dismist the Deft paying Costs.

Action of Trespass Assault & Battery. MARY WISE agt. THOMAS MOUNTJOY & ELIZABETH his Wife is dismist the Defts paying Costs.

Suit on Petition. WILLIAM CUNNINGHAM agt. ANDREW EDWARDS is continued at the Deft's Costs.

Action of Trespass. NATHANIEL HARRISON, Esqr. & LUCY his Wife & CHARLES & LANDON CARTER, Esqrs. Admrs. of HENRY FITZHUGH, Gent. decd. agt. WILLIAM SCAPLEHORN is dismist.

Action of Trespass. WEATHERS CONWAY agt. WILLIAM FITZHUGH, Gent. being agreed is dismist.

Action of Debt. THOMAS CUMMINS agt. NATHANIEL GRAY. Judgment is granted the Pltf against him & WITHERS CONWAY his Security unless the Pltf [*sic*] do appear at the next Court & answer the Pltf's Action.

Action of Debt. PETER RUST, Gent. agt. JEREMIAH CARTER. An Alias Capias is ordered returnable to the next Court.

Absent R. BERNARD, Gent.

Action of Trespass. FRANCIS THORNTON, Gent. agt. JOHN LEWRIGHT & MARY his Wife. A Jury to wit JOHN SHORT, WILLIAM PICKET, WILLIAM KING, EDWARD BURGESS, JOHN SYMPSON, HAYWOOD TODD, GARDNER BURGESS, CHARLES WELLS, JOHN WEATHERS, MOSES LUNSFORD, WILLIAM HORTON, & ROBERT DUELIN

[Page 174 May 12, 1752]

May Court 1752

were sworn & went out to consult on their Verdict.

ALLEN MACRAE Merchant made Oath to his Accout against SAMUEL ANGEL which is ordered to be certified.

Then the Court adjourned till tomorrow morning 9 Oclock.
RICHARD BERNARD

At a Court held for Stafford County 13th. May 1752.

Present   RICHARD BERNARD   PETER DANIEL
               HENRY FITZHUGH   THOMAS FITZHUGH

In the Suit on Attachment obtained by WILLIAM PICKET against the Estate of
MARK KENTON, the Referrees to whom the Matters in Difference were
referred having reported that there was due to the said Pickett from the said
Kenton seven Shillings & eight Pence. It's thereupon considered by the Court
that the said William recover the same of the said Mark & his Costs.

Ordered that the Execution against WILLIAM EDWARDS at suit of the King
upon a Judgment obtained against him on an Information for tending Seconds of
Tobo. be stayed till August next for the Court to advise therein.

On Motion of BENJAMIN STROTHER late Sheriff of this County an
attachment is awarded him against the Estate of JAMES FRENSLEY.
Judgment being passed agasint the said James & him as Sheriff for taking
Insufficient Bail at the suit of THOMAS & ROBERT DUNLOPS for £10.7.9
half penny & Costs.

In the Suit on Attachement obtained by THOMAS WASHINGTON against the
Estate of RANDALL DAVIS the said Thomas produced an Account against the
said Randall for £2.18.11 three farthings. It's considered by the Court that the
said Robert recover the same of the said Randall & his Costs & the Sheriff
having returned that he had executed the said attachment in the Hands of
HENRY TYLER & ANDREW KENNY who declared the said Tyler that he had
in his Hands twelve Shillings & six pence & the said Andrew twelve Shillings &
six pence which they are ordered to pay to the said Thomas in part of
Satisfaction of the above Judgment.

Present FRANCIS THORNTON &
GERARD FOWKE, Gent.

Action of Trespass. JOHN THOMAS agt. WILLIAM SCAPLEHORN. A Jury
to wit ROBERT WASHINGTON, ANDREW EDWARDS, JOB SIMS,

May Court 1752

JOHN LEWRIGHT, GEORGE ALLEN, LAZARUS HINSON, JOHN PEYTON, JACOB JOHNSON, BENJAMIN DUNCOMB, WILLIAM MOSS, WILLIAM BRUMLEY & ANDREW BEATY. The Jury finds for the Pltf forty Shillings damage & Costs.

Action of Trespass Assault & Battery. JOHN FITZPATRICK agt. THOMAS ASHBY. The Deft for plea saith he is not guilty. The Pltf Tryal is referred till the next Court.

Action of Trespass Assault & Battery. JOHN FITZPATRICK agt. ROBERT ASHBY is dismist the Deft paying Costs.

Action of Trespass Assault & Battery. JOHN FITZPATRICK agt. RICHARD FRISTOE, Junr. The Deft for plea saith he is not guilty. The Tryal is referred till the next Court.

Action of Trespass Assault & Battery. WILLIAM BLACK agt. JOB SIMS. The Deft for plea saith he is not guilty. The Tryal is referred till the next Court.

Action of Trespass Assault & Battery. ANDREW KENNY & ANN his Wife agt. JOB SIMS is dismist the Pltfs paying Costs.

Action of Trespass Assault & Battery. JOB SIMS agt. ANDREW KENNY is dismist the Deft paying Costs.

Action of Trespass. JAMES GRAY agt. NATHANIEL HARRISON, Esqr. acting Exor. of WILLIAM WALKER Gent., decd. The Deft by his Attorney confessed Judgment to the Pltf for £8.14.

Action of Trespass. DAVID ROSS agt. JOHN NIXON. The Deft for plea saith that he did not assume. The Tryal is referred till the next Court. JOHN HAMILTON, Gent. entered himself Security for Pltf's Costs.

May Court 1752

Action of Trespass Assault & Battery. GEORGE GHENT agt. SAMUEL NUBIL. The Deft for plea saith that he is not guilty. The Tryal is referred till the next Court.

Action of Trespass Assault & Battery. JAMES HUGHS agt. GEORGE GHENT. The Deft for plea saith that he is not guilty. The Tryal is referred till the next Court.

Suit in Chancery. EDWARD PAYNE & ANN HOLLAND his Wife agt. RANDALL HOLDBROOK & JENNET his Wife is continued at the Complainant's Costs.

Suit on Petition. ALLEN MACRAE agt. SAMUEL ANGEL is continued at the Deft's Costs.

Upon the Grand jury's presentment against RANDALL HOLDBROOK & JENNET his Wife it's ordered that a new summons issue returnable to the next Court.

Suit on Petition. ALEXANDER & DANIEL CAMPBELL agt. CHARLES HOPKINS. Judgment is granted the Pltf for £1.16.10 & Costs.

Suit on Petition. ANDREW COCHRAN & COMPANY agt. JOHN HAMILTON, Gent. Judgment is granted the Pltfs for £3.8.10 with Costs & a Lawyer's Fee.

Action of Trespass. WILLIAM GALE, Merchant agt. WILLIAM FITZHUGH, Esqr. & FRANCIS THORNTON, Gent. acting Exors. of GILSON BERRYMAN, decd. The Defts for plea say that the Testator did not assume & they have fully administered. The Tryal is referred till the next Court.

Action of Debt. JOHN CORBIN, Esqr. agt. NATHANIEL HARRISON, Esqr. acting Exor. of WILLIAM WALKER Gent., decd. The Deft by his Attorney confessed Judgment to the Pltf for £800.16. But this Judgment is to be discharged (the Costs excepted) on Payment of £400.8 with Interest thereon from the 15th day of October 1748 till the same is paid.

Action of Trespass. JOHN SAUNDERSON agt. WILLIAM HORTON. The Deft for plea saith he is not guilty. The Tryal is referred till the next Court.

Action of Trespass. JOHN FINIGAN agt. DAVID & JOHN MATHISS is dismist.

May Court 1752

Suit in Chancery. WILLIAM STUART Minister of St. Paul's Parish & the Churchwardens of the said Parish agt. WILLIAM FITZHUGH, Gent. further time is given the Complainants to consider the Deft's Answer.

Action of Trespass. ANDREW BEATY agt. HOWSON HOOE. The Deft for plea saith he is not guilty. The Tryal is referred till the next Court.

Action of Trespass. ANDREW ROSE agt. MASON FRENCH & MARGARET his Wife, Admrs. of THOMAS LACY, decd. A Jury to wit ROBERT WASHINGTON, ANDREW EDWARDS, JOB SIMS, JOHN LEWRIGHT, GEORGE ALLEN, LAZARUS HINSON, JOHN PEYTON, JACOB JOHNSON, BENJAMIN DUNCOMB, WILLIAM MOSS, WILLIAM BRUMLEY & ANDREW BEATY. The Jury finds for the Pltf £8.5.5 damage.

Suit in Chancery. EDWARD HUMSTON agt. RICHARD BERNARD, JOHN SHORT & JOHN HUMSTON. The Complainant having put in his Replication to the Deft's Answer time is given them till the next Court to consider thereof & a Dedimus is ordered for taking Depositions in this Suit.

Action of Trespass. ROBERT MASSEY agt. JACOB JOHNSON is continued at the Pltf's Costs.

Ejection Firma. Robert Faldo agt. SAMUEL EARL, Gent. for Lands & Appurtenances in the Parish of Overwharton which JOHN FOUSHEE, Gent. demised to the Pltf for a Term &c. A Jury to wit GEORGE ALLEN, JOHN LEWRIGHT, WILLIAM MOSS, BENJAMIN DUNCOMB, ROBERT WASHINGTON, LAZARUS HINSON, JOHN PEYTON, JOB SIMS, ABRAHAM FLETCHER, JOSEPH POWEL, FRANKLYN LATHAM & WILLIAM MURPHEY. The Jury finds for the Pltf one Shilling damage & his Costs.

May Court 1752

And the Deft filed Errors in arrest of Judgment which are to be argued the next Court.

ELIZABETH BURGESS being brought before the Court for stealing a Woman's Cloak belonging to ELIZABETH KITCHEN out of the House of JOHN HAMILTON, Gent. it's ordered that the Sheriff take her into his Custody till she enter into Bond in £10 with two Securities in £5 each for her personal Appearance at the next Grand jury Court for this County.

WILLIAM WILLIAMS & ELIZABETH KITCHEN came into Court & acknowledged themselves indebted to our Lord the King each in the Sum of £5 in case they or either of them fail to appear at the next Grand jury Court for this County to give Evidence against ELIZABETH BURGESS.

Action of Debt. MARY FOWKE agt. ANDREW EDWARDS & BETTY his Wife, Admrs. of JAMES WAUGH, Gent., decd. The Defts confessed Judgment to the Pltf for £100. But this Judgment is to be discharged (the Costs excepted) on payment of £50 with Interest from the 21st day of May 1748 till the same is paid.

Action of Trespass. FRANCIS THORNTON, Gent. agt. JOHN LEWRIGHT & MARY his Wife. The Jury sworn yesterday in this Suit returning into Court & not having agreed in their Verdice by consent of the Parties ROBERT DUELING, one of the Jurors is withdrawn & the Defts agreed to pay the Pltf all the Costs of a Suit brought by him against the Deft Mary while sole & all the Costs he hath & is to be out in his suit & moreover to pay to the said Pltf two hogsheads of Tobo. in two casks of 950 nett one this Summer & the other the next, whereupon the Pltf agreed that this suit should be dismist.

Ordered that FRANCIS THORNTON, Gent. pay WITHERS CONWAY 125 pounds of Tobacco for five days attendance as an Evidence for him against LEWRIGHT & Wife.

Ordered that FRANCIS THORNTON, Gent. pay BENJAMIN DUNCOMB 50 pounds of Tobacco for two days attendance as an Evidence for him against LEWRIGHT & Wife.

Ordered that FRANCIS THORNTON, Gent. pay FUTRALL HALL 50 pounds of Tobacco

[Page 179 May 13, 1752]

June Court 1752

for two days attendance as an Evidence for him against LEWRIGHT & Wife.

Ordered that FRANCIS THORNTON, Gent. pay GEORGE ALLEN 125 pounds of Tobacco for five days attendance as an Evidence for him against LEWRIGHT & Wife.

Ordered that FRANCIS THORNTON, Gent. pay CALOHILL MINNIS 50 pounds of Tobacco for two days attendance as an Evidence for him against LEWRIGHT & Wife.

Ordered that FRANCIS THORNTON, Gent. pay MAXIMILLIAN WHITING 125 pounds of Tobacco for five days attendance as an Evidence for him against LEWRIGHT & Wife.

Ordered that JOHN LEWRIGHT & MARY his Wife pay WILLIAM MOSS 125 pounds of Tobacco for five days attendance as an Evidence for them at suit of THORNTON.

Ordered that JOHN LEWRIGHT & MARY his Wife pay NATHANIEL JONES 215 pounds of Tobacco for five days attendance as an Evidence for them at suit of THORNTON and for coming & returning 15 Miles twice.

Ordered that JOHN LEWRIGHT & MARY his Wife pay THOMAS WALKER 50 pounds of Tobacco for two days attendance as an Evidence for them at suit of THORNTON.

Then the Court adjourned till Court in Course.
RICHARD BERNARD

At a Court held for Stafford County June 9th. 1752.

Present	JOHN MERCER	MOTT DONIPHAN
	JOHN PEYTON	PETER DANIEL
	FRANCIS THORNTON	GERARD FOWKE

A new Commission for the Peace for the County being produced & read together with a Dedimus for administering the Oaths, Mott Doniphan & Peter Daniel, Gent. administered the several Oaths to John Mercer, Gent. who subscribed the Test & abjuration Oath and then the said Mercer administered the Oaths to the others.

Present the above Justices

Action of Debt. ANTHONY STROTHER agt. JOSEPH BRAGG. The Deft confessed Judgment to the Pltf for £10 current Money it's ordered that the Pltf recover the same and his costs. But this Judgment is to be discharged on Payment of £8.3.8 with Interest thereon from the 19th day of October 1750 till the same is paid.

RICHARD BARNARD, Gent. being asked in Court to swear in the Commission of the Peace refused.

175

[Page 180 June 9, 1752]

June Court 1752

ALEXANDER ROSE, Gent. is assigned by the Court Attorney for ROBERT alias TUBBY belonging to PETER DANIEL, Gent. to enquired into the Alligations of his Petition in respect of his Freedon.

By Consent of Peter Daniel, Gent.

A Dedimus is ordered to take the depositions of Witnesses on behalf of Robert alias Tubby.

The Petition of JOHN STUART, Gent. for a Mill on MENESANS RUN upon the return of the Jury's Report is rejected.

Present JOHN MERCER, Gent.

Ordered that NATHANIEL HARRISON, Esqr. & LUCY his Wife, Admrs. of HENRY FITZHUGH, Esqr., decd. pay JOHN HUME 25 pounds of Tobacco for one days attendance as an Evidence for them against SCAPLIN.

Ordered that NATHANIEL HARRISON, Esqr. & LUCY his Wife, Admrs. of HENRY FITZHUGH, Esqr., decd. pay JOSEPH GOSS 25 pounds of Tobacco for one days attendance as an Evidence for them against SCAPLIN.

Ordered that FRANCIS THORNTON, Gent. pay CATHERINE ALLEN 25 pounds of Tobacco for one day's attendance as an Evidence for him against LEWRIGHT and Wife.

Ordered that ROSE LYNAUGH serve her Master PETER ROUT according to Law for having a Bastard Child & the said Rose failing to give Security for her fine the Sheriff is ordered to give her 25 Lashes on the bare Back well laid on.

Ordered that the Sheriff take JOB SIMS into his Custody till he entered into Bond in £10 with two Securities of £5 each for his good behavior a year & a day.

Action of Trespass. PHILIP ALEXANDER, Gent. agt. WILLIAM FITZHUGH, Esqr. & FRANCIS THORNTON, Gent. acting Exors. of GILSON BERRYMAN, decd. A Jury to wit EDWARD RALLS [*no other names listed*]. The jury finds for the Pltf the whole Amount £29.17.9 farthing.

Absent JOHN MERCER

Action of Detinue. JOHN FOUSHEE, Gent. agt. SAMUEL EARL, Gent. The Errors in arrest of Judgment in this Cause being argued are over ruled, whereupon it's considered by the Court that the Pltf recover of the said Deft according to the Form & Effect of the Judgment aforesaid. The Deft appealed the judgment to be heard at the next General Court.

[Page 181 June 9, 1752]

July Court 1752

Ordered that the Church Wardens of Overwharton Parish bind CATHERINE'S Child now in Possession of THOMAS WEATHERS to the said Weathers according to Law.

Then the Court adjourned till Court in Course.
MOTT DONIPHAN

At a Court held for Stafford County 14th. July 1753.

Present   JOHN MERCER   MOTT DONIPHAN
                PETER DANIEL   FRANCIS THORNTON

HENRY FITZHUGH & WILLIAM FITZHUGH, Gent. took the several Oaths, & subscribed the Test & abjuration Oath.

Present Henry & William Fitzhugh, Gent.

THOMAS ROGERS, Gent. produced a Licence under the hands & Seals of PEYTON RANDOLPH, Esqr., JAMES POWERS, & GEORGE WYTHE, Gent. to practice as an Attorney.

GERARD FOWKE Gent. produced a Commission from under the Hand of the Honbl. ROBERT DINWIDDIE, Esqr. to be Sheriff of this County.

On Petition of JEOFFERY BOX a Servant Boy belonging to EDWARD RALLS it appearing to the Court that the said Edward stripped & whipped the said Jeoffry contrary to the act of Assembly whereupon it's ordered that the said Ralls pay the said Jeoffry 40 Shillings according to Law.

It appearing to the Court that JEOFFRY BOX an Orphan Child belonging to EDWARD RALLS who purchased him from his Brother JOHN RALLS to whom he was bound by the Church Wardens of Overwharton Parish has been most barbarously & inhumanly used by his said Master is thereupon discharged

177

& the said Jeoffry acknowledges his Indenture with ADAM PAVEY which is ordered to be recorded.

HARRY a negro Boy belonging to JOHN GREGG adjudged by the Court to be eight years of Age.

CHARLES a negro boy belonging to JOHN GREGG adjudged to be 15 years of Age.

Ordered that WILLIAM KELLY serve his Master WILLIAM KENDALL for two days runaway time & 180 pounds of Tobo. expended in taking him up.

Suit on Petition. JOHN SUTHERLAND agt. JAMES YELTON. Judgment is granted the Pltf for £2.1.9 with Costs & a Lawyer's Fee.

Suit on Petition. ALEXANDER & DANIEL CAMPBELLS agt.

July Court 1752

SAMUEL BROWN & FRANCIS MARTIN. Judgment is granted the Pltfs for £2.7.4 half penny with Costs & a Lawyer's Fee.

Action of Trespass. JOB WIGLEY agt. NATHANIEL HARRISON, Esqr., acting Exor. of WILLIAM WALKER, Gent., decd. The Deft for plea saith that the Testator did not assume. The Tryal is referred till the next Court.

Absent MERCER, Gent.

Action of Trespass. GEORGE SPICER agt. ABRAM FLETCHER. A Jury to wit THOMAS NORMAN, WILLIAM WRIGHT, HUSBANDFOOTE WHITECOTTON, CHARLES WELLS, JOHN SAUNDERSON, JOHN GREEN, CHARLES HARDING, BENJAMIN ROBINSON, JOHN WITHERS, THOMAS WOOD, JOHN PEYTON, & ANDREW EDWARDS. The Jury finds for the Pltf one penny damage.

In the Action upon the Cause between JOHN FOUSHEE agt. SAMUEL EARL, the special Verdict in this Suit being argued, is adjudged imperfect whereupon a new jury is ordered.

Ordered that GEORGE SPICER pay EDWARD HAMPTION 50 pounds of Tobacco for two days attendance as an Evidence for him against FLETCHER.

Ordered that GEORGE SPICER pay JOHN HOOE 50 pounds of Tobacco for two days attendance as an Evidence for him against FLETCHER.

Ordered that ABRAHAM FLETCHER pay BENJAMIN MASSEY 75 pounds of Tobacco for three days attendance as an Evidence for him at Suit of SPICER.

Ordered that ABRAM FLETCHER pay ISAAC ROSE 125 pounds of Tobo. for five days attendance as an Evidence for him at the Suit of SPICER.

Ordered that JOHN BRYAN serve his Master DARBY OCAIN for two days runaway time & 180 pounds of Tobacco & two Shillings & six pence expended in taking him up.

Then the Court adjourned till tomorrow morning 9 Oclock.
MOTT DONIPHAN

[Page 183 July 15, 1752]

July Court 1752

At a Court continued & held for Stafford County July 15th. 1752.

Present   MOTT DONIPHAN   PETER DANIEL
       JOHN PEYTON   FRANCIS THORNTON
       WILLIAM FITZHUGH

Ejection Firma. Robert Faldo agt. SAMUEL EARL for Lands & Appurtenances in the Parish of Overwharton which JOHN FOUSHEE, Gent. demised to the Pltf for Term. The Errors in this Cause being argued are overruled whereupon it's considered by the Court that the Pltf recover his &c. according to the Form & Effect of the Judgment aforesaid.

Present JOHN MERCER, Gent.

Action of Trespass. FRANKLYN LATHAM agt. MICHAEL HARPER. The Errors in this Cause being argued are overruled.

Action of Trespass. MICHAEL HARPER agt. FRANKLYN LATHAM. The Errors in this Cause being argued are overruled.

Action of Detinue. JOSEPH PORTER agt. JOHN RILEY is dismist the Deft paying Costs.

Action of Trespass Assault & Battery. ELIZABETH MCABOY agt. JOB SIMS. The Deft for Plea saith he is not guilty & hath leave to give the special Matter in Evidence. The Tryal is referred till the next Court.

Suit on Petition. ANDREW EDWARDS & BETTY his Wife, Admrs. of JAMES WAUGH, decd. agt. THOMAS FREEMAN, Admr. of HENRY REYNOLDS, decd. Judgment is granted the Pltfs for £5.

Action of Debt. THOMAS CUNNING agt. NATHANIEL GRAY. The Deft not appearing the Judgment against him & WITHERS CONWAY his Security is confirmed to the Pltf for £20.5

[Page 184 July 15, 1752]

July Court 1752

and the said WITHERS prayed an Attachment which is granted him.

Action of Trespass Assault & Battery. JOHN FITZPATRICK agt. THOMAS ASHBY. A Jury to wit HENRY DAWSON, JOB SIMS, WILLIAM ALLEN, JAMES HANSBROUGH, MICHAEL RYAN, JOHN STONE, JOHN LEACH, JOHN SMITH, HOWSON HOOE, PETER MURPHY, WILLIAM TRAVERSE & JOHN SAUNDERSON. The Jury finds for the Pltf 40 Shillings damage & his Costs.

Action of Trespass Assault & Battery. JOHN FITZPATRICK agt. RICHARD FRISTOE, the Younger. A Jury to wit WILLIAM LAMPTON, GEORGE WHITE, ROGER HILL, WILLIAM WALKER, ROBERT ENGLISH, PHILEMON WATERS, DAVID WAUGH, ANDREW KENNY, JOHN THOMAS, ALEXANDER DONIPHAN, RICHARD PILCHER, & FRANKLYN LATHAM. The Jury finds for the Pltf for 50 Shillings damage & his Costs.

JOHN MERCER, JOHN PEYTON & PETER DANIEL are appointed to view the Clerk's Office & Surveyor's Book & report.

Ordered that JOHN FITZPATRICK pay THOMAS WOOD 182 pounds of Tobacco for two days attendance as an Evidence for him against FRISTOE & for coming & returning 44 Miles once.

Ordered that JOHN FITZPATRICK pay PHILEMON WATERS 125 pounds of Tobacco for two days attendance as an Evidence for him against ASHBY & for coming & returning 25 Miles once.

Ordered that JOHN FITZPATRICK pay JAMES WHALEY 188 pounds of Tobacco for two days Attendance for him as an Evidence for

July Court 1752

him against ASHBY & for coming & returning 46 Miles once.

Action of Trespass Assault & Battery. WILLIAM BLACK agt. JOB SIMS. A Jury to wit WILLIAM LAMPTON, GEORGE WHITE, ROGER HILL, WILLIAM WALKER, ROBERT ENGLISH, DAVID WAUGH, JOHN THOMAS, ALEXANDER DONIPHAN, RICHARD PILCHER, CHARLES HARDING, WILLIAM MILLS, & MICHAEL HARPER. The Jury finds for the Deft & it's considered by the Court that the Pltf take nothing by his Bill & the Deft go home & that he recover of the Pltf his Costs.

Present HENRY FITZHUGH, Gent.

Ordered that WILLIAM BLACK pay ANDREW KENNY 50 pounds of Tobacco for two days Attendance as an Evidence for him against JOB SIMS.

Ordered that WILLIAM BLACK pay ANN KENNY 50 pounds of Tobacco for two days attendance as an Evidence for him against JOB SIMS.

Ordered that JOB SIMS pay WILLIAM MASON 50 pounds of Tobacco for two days Attendance as an Evidence for him at Suit of WILLIAM BLACK.

In the Action upon the Case between DAVID ROSS agt. JOHN NIXON, the Pltf failing to prosecute his Suit the Deft is non-suited and ordered to pay the Deft his Costs.

Action of Trespass Assault & Battery. GEORGE GHENT agt. SAMUEL NUBILL. The Pltf failing to give Security for the Costs this suit is dismist & the Pltf ordered to pay the Deft his Costs.

Action of Trespass Assault & Battery. GEORGE GHENT agt. JAMES HUGHS. The Pltf failing to give Security for the Costs this suit is dismist & the Pltf ordered to pay the Deft his Costs.

Action of Trespass. ANDREW BEATTY agt. HOWSON HOOE is dismist each Party paying their own Costs.

Ordered that ANDREW BEATTY pay MICHAEL RYAN 50 pounds Tobacco for two days attendance as an Evidence for him against HOOE.

Action of Trespass. JOHN SAUNDERSON

July Court 1752

agt. WILLIAM HORTON. A Jury to wit ROBERT ENGLISH, WILLIAM
MASON, JAMES HANSBROUGH, PETER HANSBROUGH, EDWARD
RALLS, JOHN STONE, JOB SIMS, WILLIAM LAMPTON, CHARLES
HARDING, & ALEXANDER DONIPHAN. The Jury finds for the Pltf £12
damage and his Costs.

Action of Detinue. URIEL CROSBY by GEORGE CROSBY his Guardian agt.
EDWARD RALLS. All Matters in difference between them being by consent
referred to the determination of the Reverend JOHN MONCURE Clk. & JOHN
PEYTON, Gent. and that their award should be the judgment of the Court, that
there is due to the said George Crosby as Guardian of the said Uriel £44.6.2
current Money and Costs.

Action of Debt. RICHARD BERNARD, Gent. agt. THOMAS FREEMAN,
Exor. of HENRY RENNOLDS decd. The Deft not appearing Judgment is
granted to the Pltf against him unless the Deft do appear at the next Court &
answer the Pltf's Action.

Action of Trespass. JAMES STUART agt. JAMES CROP. The Pltf failing to
prosecute his Suit the Deft is nonsuited & the Pltf is ordered to pay the Deft's
damages & Costs.

Ordered that JOHN SAUNDERSON pay JOSEPH COMBS 75 pounds of
Tobacco for three days attendance as an Evidence for him against HORTON.

Ordered that JOHN SAUNDERSON pay THOMAS ASHBY 75 pounds of
Tobacco for three days attendance as an evidence for him against HORTON.

Ordered that the Sheriff restore to ELIZABETH KITCHEN her Goods in his
Custody stolen by ELIZABETH BURGESS.

Suit on Petition. MICHAEL WALLACE agt. CUTHBERT BYRAM.
Judgment is granted the Pltf for 525 pounds of Tobacco with Costs & a
Lawyer's Fee.

Ordered that MICHAEL WALLACE pay BENJAMIN STROTHER 75 pounds
of Tobacco for three days attendance as an Evidence for him against BYRAM.

In the Detinue between THOMAS ASHBY agt. JOHN RILEY the Errors

[Page 187 July 15, 1752]

August Court 1752

in this Suit being argued is adjudged good & the Jury's Verdict is set aside & a new Jury ordered.

Suit on Petition. DANIEL NEAL, Exor. of the last Will & Testament of PRESLEY NEAL, decd. agt. WILLIAM NASH. Judgment is granted the Pltf for 380 pounds of crop Tobacco & a Lawyer's Fee & Costs.

Then the Court adjourned till Court in Course.
JOHN MERCER

At a Court held for Stafford County 11th. August 1752.

Present   JOHN MERCER   MOTT DONIPHAN
           PETER DANIEL   FRANCIS THORNTON

CHLOE a negro Girl belonging to JOHN MERCER, Gent. adjudged to be 12 years old.

SERAPHINA a negro Girl belonging to JOHN MERCER, Gent. adjudged to be 12 years old.

SYLVIA a negro Girl belonging to JOHN MERCER, Gent. adjudged to be 12 years old.

DORINDA a negro Girl belonginbg to JOHN MERCER, Gent. adjudged to be 15 years old.

ESSEX a negro boy belonging to JOHN MERCER, Gent. adjudged to be 15 years old.

TOM a negro Boy belonging to JOSEPH COMBS adjudged to be 6 years of Age.

CATE a negro Girl belonging to ELIZABETH PARANDINE adjudged to be 8 years old.

MOTT a negro Girl belonging to ELIZABETH PARANDINE adjudged to be 7 years old.

DICK a negro boy belonging to GEORGE JEFFERICE adjudged to be 9 years old.

ANGELAH a negro Girl belonging to JOSEPH JEFFERICE adjudged to be 12 years old.

VALENTINE a negro boy belonging to JOHN RALLS Senr. adjudged to be 10 years old.

ROSE a negro Girl belonging to JOHN RALLS Senr. adjudged to be 10 years old.

LUCY a negro Girl belonging to JACOB WILLIAMS adjudged to be 9 years old.

Present HENRY FITZHUGH, Gent.

The several Nominations for Inspectors continued except at Aquia & WILLIAM WRIGHT to be put in instead of ELIAS HORE.

The Inspectors of Beef, Pork, Flower &c continued.

CHLOE a negro girl belonging to JOHN SHORT adjudged to be 11 years old.

Ordered that FRANCIS NEIGHING serve his Master WILLIAM PATTEN for thirty days runaway time & £10.1 in taking him up.

CHLOE a negro Girl belonging to CARTY WELLS adjudged to be 8 years old.

JOHN NORRIS who intermarried with the Widow of JOHN TURNER came into Court & agreed to give WILLIAM TURNER two years schooling & to maintain the said William during his Minority he having the Negroe's Work for his Maintenance if the negro lives so long which agreement the Court approved of.

PEG a negro Girl belonging to BENJAMIN ROBINSON adjudged to be 8 years old.

SUDA a negro Girl belonging to BENJAMIN ROBINSON adjudged to be 8 years old.

August Court 1752

Ordered the Reverend JOHN MONCURE be recommended to his Honor the Governor as a fit Person to be added to the Commission of the Peace & to be put the last on the Quorum & that THOMAS FITZHUGH be recommended to be added & to be put in the Race he was formerly in.

Ordered that the Sheriff pay NATHANIEL HARRISON, Esqr. & HUGH ADIE the Tobacco in his Hands levied for finishing the Court House.

Then the Court adjourned till tomorrow morning 9 Oclock.
JOHN MERCER

At a Court continued and held for Stafford County 12th. August 1752.

Present   JOHN MERCER   MOTT DONIPHAN
            PETER DANIEL   FRANCIS THORNTON

Suit on Petition. JOHN NELSON agt. ISAAC ROSE is dismist the Deft paying Costs.

Suit on Petition. DAVID ROSS agt. EDWARD TEMPLEMAN. Judgment is granted the Pltf for £5.15 & Costs & a Lawyer's Fee to be discharged on payment of £2.17.6 with Interest thereon from the second day of July 1750 till paid.

Action of Trespass. ANDREW COCHRANE & COMPANY agt. JAMES GREEN. The Deft confessed Judgment to the Pltf for 1,119 pounds of Tobacco, that the Deft to pay half the Pltf's Costs.

Suit on Scire Facias. RICHARD BERNARD, Gent. agt. JOHN CUBBAGE. The Sheriff having returned the scire facias executed & the said John failing to appear it's considered by the Court that the said Richard have execution against the said John for £2.3.1 & 86 pounds of Tobacco & the Costs of this Suit.

Ejection Firma. Thomas Turff & Timothy Twigg for Lands & Appurtenances in the Parish of St. Paul's which HAYWOOD TODD demised to the Pltf for a Term. It appearing by the Return of the Sheriff that ALEXANDER GRANT'S tenement in Possession of the Premises hath been duly served with a Copy of the Declaration & he not appearing it's ordered that unless the said Alexander do appear at the next Court as a Deft in this Cause Judgment will be given against him & his Majesty's Writ of Habere facias possession

August Court 1752

awarded the Plft & put him in Possession thereof.

Suit on Petition. MICHAEL RYAN agt. ALEXANDER DONIPHAN.
Judgment is granted the Pltf for 830 pounds of Tobacco & Costs.

Suit on Petition. MICHAEL RYAN agt. PETER MURPHY & ELIZABETH his
Wife. Judgment is granted the Pltf for 400 pounds of Tobacco & Costs.

Suit on Petition. SAMUEL HILDROP agt. BARNABAS WILLIAMS.
Judgment is granted the Pltf for £2.17.6 with Costs & a Lawyer's Fee.

Suit on Petition. ALLEN MCRAE agt. ARTHUR DUAS. Judgment is granted
the Pltf for 298 pounds of Tobacco with Costs & a Lawyer's Fee.

BEN a negro Boy belonging to JOHN MAUZY, junr. adjudged to be ten years
old.

WILL a negro Boy belonging to JOHN MAUZY, junr. adjudged to be nine
years old.

Suit on Petition. BENJAMIN TYLER agt. RICHARD BROOX is dismist the
Deft paying Costs.

Action of Trespass. BENJAMIN TYLER agt. THOMAS TURNHAM is dismist
the Pltf paying Costs.

Action of Trespass Assault & Battery. JAMES HUGHS agt. GEORGE
GHENT. A Jury to wit HENRY DAWSON, CHARLES HARDING, THOMAS
CRAFFORD, LAZARUS HINSON, JAMES ONEAL, ROBERT ENGLISH,
JOHN CARPENTER, NICHOLAS RALEY, BENJAMIN ROBINSON, JOHN
KIRK, JOHN FITZPATRICK, & THOMAS MATHENY. The Jury finds for
the Pltf £10 damage & his Costs.

Suit on Petition. MICHAEL RYAN agt. JAMES HANSBROUGH is dismist &
the Pltf ordered to pay the Deft his Costs.

Action of Detinue. THOMAS ASHBY agt. JOHN RAILLEY. A Jury to wit
JOHN MAUZY senr., SOLOMON WAUGH, RICHARD RANDALL,
WILLIAM FOSTER, WILLIAM POWEL, PETER MURPHY, JAMES
ONEAL, ROBERT ENGLISH, ANDREW EDWARDS, LAZARUS HINSON,

186

GEORGE WHITE, & ROBERT GARRARD. The Jury finds for the Pltf the Mare mentioned in the declaration to the Value of 40 Shillings

[Page 190 Aug. 12, 1752]

August Court 1752

and £8 damage & find that the Deft don't detain the Colt in the Declaration mentioned.

Action of Trespass. MICHAEL RYAN agt. MARY PONTON. A Jury to wit THOMAS CRAWFORD, JOSEPH JEFFERIE, FRANCIS BROOX, JOHN CARPENTER, JAMES WAYTON, JAMES HANSBROUGH, BENJAMIN ROBINSON, HENRY WIGGINTON, NICHOLAS RALEY, JOHN MAUZY, ALEXANDER DONIPHAN, & JEREMIAH WEATHERLY. The Jury finds for the Deft and the Pltf to pay the Deft his Costs.

Ordered that THOMAS ASHBY pay BENJAMIN ROBINSON 50 pounds of Tobacco for two days Attendance as an Evidence for him against RILEY [*sic*].

Ordered that THOMAS ASHBY pay NICHOLAS RILEY 50 pounds of Tobacco for two days Attendance as an Evidence for him against RILEY [*sic*].

Ordered that THOMAS ASHBY pay HENRY WIGGINGTON 50 pounds of Tobacco for two days Attendance as an Evidence for him against RILEY [*sic*].

Action of Debt. JOHN LEE & BENJAMIN STROTHER, Gent. Church Wardens of Overwharton Parish agt. JAMES YELTON. A Jury to wit JOHN MAUZY, Senr., RICHARD RANDALL, SOLOMON WAUGH, WILLIAM FOSTER, WILLIAM POWEL, PETER MURPHY, JAMES ONEAL, ROBERT ENGLISH, GEORGE WHITE, ROBERT GARRARD, ANDREW EDWARDS, & CHARLES HARDING. The Jury finds for the Pltfs 50 Shillings & their Costs.

Ordered that THOMAS ASHBY pay AARON GARRISON 50 pounds of Tobacco for two days Attendance as an Evidence for him against RILEY [*sic*].

Ordered that MARY PONTON pay WHARTON HOLIDAY 50 pounds of Tobacco for two days attendance as an Evidince for her at Suit of RYAN.

Ordered that MARY PONTON pay ELIZABETH HOLLIDAY 50 pounds of Tobacco for two days attendance as an Evidince for her at Suit of RYAN.

Ordered that MARY PONTON pay JANE WILLIAMS 50 pounds of Tobacco for two days attendance as an Evidince for her at Suit of RYAN.

October Court 1752

At a Court held for Stafford County October 10th. 1752.

Present JOHN PEYTON   PETER DANIEL
      HENRY FITZHUGH   FRANCIS THORNTON

A new Commission of the Peace for this County together with a Dedimus for administering the Oaths being produced & read Henry Fitzhugh & Francis Thornton, Gent. administered the said Oaths to John Peyton, Gent. who subscribed the Test & abjuration Oath & then administered the said Oaths to the said Henry Fitzhugh and Francis Thornton, Peter Daniel & JOHN STUART, Gent. who subscribed the test & abjuration Oath.

Present the Justices above named.

FRANK, a negro Girl belonging to JOHN THORNBURY adjudged to be 8 years old.

NED a negro Boy belonging to JOHN THORNBURY adjudged to be 10 years old.

CHLOE a negro Girl belonging to HOWSON HOOE adjudged to be 9 years old.

Ordered that the Sheriff summon 24 of the most able Freeholders of this County to be of the Grand jury for the Body of the County.

BOYD'S HOLE Inspectors sold 3,079 pounds of crop Tobo at 13 Shillings & 4 Pence pCent.

CAVES Inspectors sold 1,966 pounds of crop Tobacco at 13 Shillings & 6 pence pCent.

ACQUIA Inspectors sold 3,771 pounds of crop Tobacco at 13 Shillings & 6 Pence pCent.

WAKEFIELD a negro Boy belonging to NATHANIEL HARRISON Esqr. is adjudted to be 12 years old.

STAFFORD a negro Boy belonging to NATHANIEL HARRISON, Esqr. adjudged to be 12 years old.

LONDON a negro Boy belonging to NATHANIEL HARRISON, Esqr. adjudged to be 12 years old.

HAMPSHIRE a negro Boy belonging to NATHANIEL HARRISON, Esqr. adjudged to be 11 years old.

BRAUGHTON a negro Boy belonging to NATHANIEL HARRISON, Esqr. adjudged to be 12 years old.

BRANDON a negro Boy belonging to NATHANIEL HARRISON, Esqr. adjudged to be 13 years old.

SCIPIO a negro Boy belonging to THOMAS IRSONROE adjudged to be 10 years old.

DICK a negro Boy belonging to SAMUEL BREDWELL adjudged to be 10 years old.

PHILLIS a negro Girl belonging to SAMUEL BREDWELL adjudged to be 11 years old.

CHARLES a negro boy belonging to EVAN PEYTON adjudged to be 10 years old.

CUPID a negro boy belonging to MARGARET BARBEE adjudged to be 9 years old.

SAMPSON a negro Boy belonging to WILLIAM MATTHEWS junr. adjudged to be 11 years old.

LUCY a negro Girl belonging to WILLIAM MATTHEWS, junr. adjudged to be 10 years old.

MOTT DONIPHAN, Gent. took the several Oaths & subscribed the Test & abjuration Oath.

Present MOTT DONIPHAN Gent.

Licence is granted JOHN THOMAS to keep an Ordinary at BOYD'S HOLE he

October Court 1752

having complied with what the Law in such Cases require.

Licence is granted JOHN LEEWRIGHT to keep an Ordinary at the cross roads.

SYLVESTER MOSS is appointed Overseer of the Road in the Room of CHARLES WELLS.

> Then the Court adjourned till tomorrow morning 9 Oclock.
> MOTT DONIPHAN

At a Court continued & held for Stafford County 11th October 1752.

Present MOTT DONIPHAN   PETER DANIEL
     HENRY FITZHUGH   JOHN STUART

Action of Trespass. JOHN FOUSHEE, Gent. agt. SAMUEL EARL. A Jury to wit JOHN PEYTON, THOMAS BELL, JOHN FITZPATRICK, WILLIAM FOSTER, THOMAS CRAFFORD, ROBERT ENGLISH, THOMAS WASHINGTON, JOHN SILVY, THOMAS MATHENY, BAILY WASHINGTON, ROBERT GARRARD, & WILLIAM WALKER. The Pltf offered the Will of JOHN BAILEY decd. & a Deed from John Bailey to the Pltf as Evidence in this Cause to which Evidence the Deft offered a Demurrer for Cause shewn that the Action was brought for a Legacy whereas the same was only recoverable in a Court of equity which was overruled. The Jury finds for the Deft and the Pltf filed Errors in arrest of Judgment which are to be argued at the next Court.

Action of Trespass Assault & Battery. ELIZABETH MCABOY agt. JOB SIMS. A Jury to wit ANDREW EDWARDS, SOLOMON WAUGH, JOHN WITHERS, WILLIAM JORDAN, JOHN BELL, THOMAS HAY, ALEXANDER DONIPHAN, RICE HOOE, CHARLES CARTER, ROGER HILL, JOHN ENGLISH, & TRAVERSE COOKE. The Jury finds for the Pltf 40 Shillings damage & her Costs.

ANDREW EDWARDS is appointed Guardian to RACHAEL FRENCH Orphan of HUGH FRENCH, decd. & hath entered into Bond according to Law.

Ordered that ELIZABETH MCABOY pay WILLIAM NORTHCUT 100 pounds of Tobacco for four days attendance as an Evidence for her against SIMS.

November Court 1752

Ordered that ELIZABETH MCABOY pay HESTER PARSONS 100 pounds of Tobacco for four days attendance as an Evidence for her against SIMS.

Ordered that ELIZABETH MCABOY pay ANN GRAY 125 pounds of Tobacco for five days attendance as an Evidence for her against SIMS.

Ordered that ELIZABETH MCABOY pay CONSTANT NORTHCUT 125 pounds of Tobacco for five days attendance as an Evidence for her against SIMS.

Ordered that ELIZABETH MCABOY pay ELIZABETH PHILLIPS 125 pounds of Tobacco for five days attendance as an Evidence for her against SIMS.

Ordered that JOB SIMS pay MARY WISE 125 pounds of Tobacco for five days attendance as an Evidence for him at Suit of MCABOY.

Ordered that JOHN FOUSHEE pay GEORGE WALLER 125 pounds of Tobacco for five days attendance as an Evidence for him against EARL.

Ordered that HUGH BOWEN serve his Master JOHN PEYTON for three days runaway time & £1.4 expended in taking him up & Costs.

Ordered that JAMES PEPPLES serve his Master JOHN PEYTON for three days runaway time & £14. expended in taking him up & Costs.

FRANKLYN LATHAM is appointed Overseer of the Road in the Room of WILLIAM MILLS.

Then the Court adjourned till Court in Course.
MOTT DONIPHAN

At a Court held for Stafford County 14th November 1752.

Present   MOTT DONIPHAN   JOHN PEYTON
                PETER DANIEL   HENRY FITZHUGH
                FRANCIS THORNTON

The Grand jury for the body of this County to wit TRAVERSE COOKE, WILLIAM MILLS, JAMES ONEAL, JOHN GRAVAT, RICHARD FRISTOE, BEN DUMCOMB, BENJAMIN ROBINSON, THOMAS PRICE, GEORGE

WALLER, THOMAS GOUGH, WILLIAM HORTON, THOMAS SEDDON, JOHN WALLER, THOMAS NORMAN, DAVID WAUGH, CHARLES WELLS, & JOB SIMS received their Charge and retired & after some time returned into Court with these presentments. WILLIAM JONES for retailing three quarts of Cyder at the Parish of St. Paul's by the Information of JOHN THOMAS. Whereupon the said William Jones is to be summoned to appear at the next Court to answer the Presentment.

Then the Court proceeded to lay the Levy.

[Page 194 Nov. 14, 1752]

November Court 1752

Stafford County...Dr.

To Mr. Secretary NELSON by Account	738
To Mr. MOSELAY BATTALEY King's Attorney	2000
To the Clerk by Law	1254
To ditto by Account	1450
To PETER DANIEL Coroner by Account	120
To CHARLES HARDING Constable	472
To MATTHEW GREGG for Timber for a Bridge	60
To JACOB JOHNSON Constable	353
To JOHN STONE Constable	353
To HUSBANDFOOTE WHITECOTTON	292
To RICHARD FOOTE Coroner by Account	449
To the Sheriff by Law	1254
To WITHERS CONWAY by Account	276
To JAMES HANSBROUGH by ditto	690
To HUGH ADIE allowed him by Act of Assembly	14,900
To Coll. NATHANIEL HARRISON for a Chimney to the Court House	1440
To ditto for the loss he sustained in burning the COURT HOUSE	3000
To MARY FOWKE for Timber for a Bridge	34
To WILLIAM BLACK by Account	1076
To GEORGE WALLER by Account	<u>141</u>
	29,952
To 6 pCent on 29,952	<u>1795</u>
	31,747

Cr.

By the late Sheriff	343
By 1914 Tithables a 17 p Poll with a Fraction in	32,090

192

Ordered that the Sheriff collect 17 pounds of Tobacco for each Tithable in this County the ensuing Year.

ISAAC KNIGHT an Evidence for our Lord the King against GEORGE CARTER, Junr. failing to appear it's ordered that his Bond be sued & that the said George Carter, JAMES CARTER, & JOHN CARTER be discharged from their Recognizance.

Then the Court adjourned till tomorrow morning 9 Oclock.

MOTT DONIPHAN

[Page 195 Nov. 15, 1752]

November Court 1752

At a Court continued & held for Stafford County 15th November 1752.

Present   MOTT DONIPHAN   PETER DANIEL
             HENRY FITZHUGH   FRANCIS THORNTON

On Petition of WILLIAM GARRARD leave is given him to build on the COURT HOUSE Lot of this County to keep a Ordinary.

Present JOHN PEYTON, Gent.

Suit on Petition. RICHARD RANDALL agt. JOHN PEYTON. Judgment is granted the Pltf for 250 pounds of Tobacco & Costs.

In the Suit on Attachment obtained by JOHN PEYTON, Gent. against the Estate of JAMES MINGOS the said Peyton produced a Note of Hand for 600 pounds of crop Tobacco & an Account of the said Mingos for £3.2.7 current Money. It's considered by the Court that the said Peyton recover the same of the said Mingos & his Costs. The the Sheriff having made return that he had attached one Gun it's thereupon ordered that he sell the same to satisfy the said John his Judgment.

Action of Debt. CAIN WITHERS agt. BARNABAS WILLIAMS. The Deft not appearing judgment is granted the Pltf against him & JOHN HAMILTON & GEORGE WATERS his Securities unless the Deft do appear at the next Court & answer the Pltf's Action.

Action of Trespass. HARRY PIPER agt. JEREMIAH CARTER. An Alias Capias is ordered against the Deft returnable to the next Court.

Action of Debt. HARRY PIPER Assignee of RICHARD JACKSON agt. JEREMIAH CARTER an Alias Capias is ordered returnable to the next Court.

Action of Debt. SAMUEL COURTNEY agt. JEREMIAH CARTER. The Deft not appearing an Attachment is awarded him against the Deft's Estate for 1500 pounds of Tobacco & Costs.

Action of Trespass. BARNABAS WILLIAMS agt. CAIN WITHERS is dismist the Pltf paying the Deft his Costs.

Action of Detinue. BARNABAS WILLIAMS agt. CAIN WITHERS is dismist the Pltf paying the Deft his Costs.

[Page 196 Nov. 15, 1752]

November Court 1752

Action of Trespass. JAMES HEFFERNON and ELEANOR his Wife agt. RICHARD BROOX & MARY his Wife. Deft paying Costs.

Suit on Petition. WITHERS CONWAY agt. RAWLEY CHINN is dismist the Deft paying Costs.

Suit on Petition. ANDREW EDWARDS & BETTY his Wife Admrs. of JAMES WAUGH, decd. agt. RICHARD PILCHER is dismist the Deft paying Costs.

Suit on Petition. THOMAS HORNBUCKLE agt. BENJAMIN CLARY. Judgment is granted the Pltf for £2.5 by Account proved & Costs.

Suit on Petition. JOHN ADDISON & ANN his Wife Admrs. of BENONI STRATTON, decd. agt. ALEXANDER MURPHY & NATHANIEL PRICE. Judgment is granted the Pltfs for £4.8 & Costs.

Action of Debt. JOHN ADDISON & ANN his Wife Admrs. of BENONI STRATTON, decd. agt. THOMAS PAIRMAIN & BENJAMIN DERRICK. The Defts confessed Judgment to the Pltfs for £5.10.6, but his Judgment is to be discharged on payment of £2.15.3 with Interest thereon from the 20th day of March 1751 till paid.

Suit on Petition. WILLIAM DAVIS agt. WILLIAM FITZHUGH, Esqr. & FRANCIS THORNTON, Gent. acting Exors. of GILSON BERRYMAN, decd. is continued till the next Court at the Pltf's Costs.

194

Ordered that THOMAS HORNBUCKLE pay WILLIAM HORNBUCKLE 150 pounds of Tobacco for six days attendance as an Evidence for him against CLARY.

Suit on Petition. MARGARET REYNOLDS agt. PETER MURPHY is dismist the Deft paying Costs.

Suit on Petition. THOMAS BELL agt. ANDREW KENNY. Judgment is confessed to the Pltf for 40 Shillings & Costs.

Suit on Petition. WILLIAM MOUNTJOY agt. ANDREW KENNY.

[Page 197 Nov. 15, 1752]

November Court 1752

Judgment is confessed to the Pltf for £2.2.3 & Costs.

Suit on Petition. ELIZABETH LATIMORE agt. JOSEPH COMBS is dismist the Pltf paying the Deft's Costs.

Suit on Petition. TRAVERSE COOKE agt. WILLIAM FOSTER. Judgment is granted the Pltf for 400 pounds of Tobacco by Account proved & Costs.

Suit on Scire Facias. JOHN HOOE, Gent. agt. WILLIAM FITZHUGH, Esqr. & FRANCIS THORNTON, Gent. acting Exors. of GILSON BERRYMAN. The said William & Francis having pleaded payment the Trial is referred till the next Court.

Suit on Scire Facias. GEORGE JOHNSON agt. WILLIAM FITZHUGH, Esqr. & FRANCIS THORNTON, Gent. acting Exors. of GILSON BERRYMAN. An alias scire fascias is ordered against them returnable to the next Court.

Ordered that THOMAS HORNBUCKLE pay WILLIAM FOSTER 175 pounds of Tobacco for seven days attendance as an evidence for him against CLARY.

Upon a Bill in Chancery exhibited by GERARD FOWKE, JOHN WASHINGTON & JOHN ALEXANDER against DAVID GALLAWAY Merchant it's ordered that a dedimus Issue to take the Deposition of JOHN ROGERS.

Present JOHN STUART, Gent.

195

Action of Debt. ROBERT ENGLISH agt. MORNING RICHARDS. The Deft not appearing Judgment is granted against him & GEORGE BRENT his Security unless the Deft do appear at the next Court & answer the Pltf's Action.

Action of Debt. MICHAEL WALLACE agt. ROBERT GARRARD. The Deft not appearing Judgment is granted the Pltf against him unless the Deft do appear at the next Court & answer the Pltf's Action.

Action of Trespass. ROBERT & EDWARD MAXWELL agt. WILLIAM HORTON is dismist the Pltf paying Costs.

Ejection Firma. JOHN LEEWRIGHT agt. James Thrustout for Lands & Appurtenances in the Parish of Overwharton which MAXAMILLIAN ROBINSON, Gent. demised to the Pltf for a Term &c. JOHN RALLS, Senr. is admitted Deft in the Room of the said Thrustout & prayed an Imparlance till the next Court which is granted him.

Suit on Attachment. THOMAS MATHENY agt. the Estate of DANIEL MATHENY. The said Thomas produced an Account against the said Daniel

November Court 1752

for £17.11 & 347 pounds of Tobo. & his Costs. And the Sheriff having made return that he has attached four Hogsheads of Tobo. in AQUIA WAREHOUSE it's thereupon ordered that he sell the same and satisfy the said Thomas his Judgment.

Ejection Firma. John Seekwright agt. James Thrustout for Lands & Appurtenances in the Parish of Overwharton which JANE ORR, MARGARET ORR, JOHN SMITH & WILLIAM GREENLEES demised to the Pltf for a Term &c. It appearing by the motion of the Sheriff that WILLIAM GREENLEES Tenant in possession of the Premises hath been duly served with a Copy of the Declaration & Indorsement & he not appearing it's ordered that the said William do appear at the next Court or Judgment shall be granted the Pltf.

Ordered that JOHN ENGLISH pay HUSBANDFOOTE WHITECOTTON 125 pounds of Tobo. for five days attendance as an Evidence for him against WITHERS.

Suit on Petition. JOHN MCCULLOUGH agt. WILLIAM DAVIS. A dedimus is ordered to take the Depositions of the Witnesses returnable to the next Court.

Suit on Petition. PATRICK ROWAN agt. JOHN THOMAS. Judgment is granted the Pltf for £3.9.9 half penny & Costs.

Suit on Petition. WILLIAM KELLY & PHILLIS his Wife agt. JOHN HOLLAND & WILLIAM SCAPLIN. Judgment is granted the Pltf for £3 on penal Obligation & Costs.

Action of Trespass. ROBERT & EDWARD MAXWELL agt. FRANCIS PAYNE is dismist the Deft paying Costs.

Action of Trespass. ROBERT & EDWARD MAXWELL agt. JAMES HURST is dismist the Deft paying Costs.

Action of Trespass. ROBERT & EDWARD MAXWELL agt CUTHBERT BYRAM. The Deft not appearing, Judgment is granted

[Page 199 Nov. 15, 1752]

November Court 1752

the Deft against him & PETER BYRAM his Security unless the Deft do appear at the next Court & answer the Pltf's Action.

Action of Trespass. WILLIAM HOWARD agt. RICHARD HEWITT. The Deft not appearing Judgment is granted the Pltf against him & ROBERT FRISTOE his Security unless the Deft do appear at the next Court & answer the Pltf's Action.

Action of Trespass. WILLIAM HOWARD agt. ELIZABETH HARRIS. The Deft not appearing Judgment is granted the Pltf against her & FRANCIS BROOKS her Security unless the Deft do appear at the next Court & answer the Pltf's Action.

Action of Trespass Assault & Battery. FRANCIS BROOX agt. DARBY OCAIN. The Deft not appearing Judgment is granted the Pltf against him & THOMAS CRAFFORD his Security unless the Deft do appear at the next Court & answer the Pltf's Action.

Ejection Firma. Thomas Turff agt. Timothy Twigg for Lands & Appurtenances in the Parish of Overwharton which HENRY TYLER demised to the Pltf for a Term &c. HENRY FITZHUGH, Esqr. being admitted Defendant in the Room of the said Timothy Twigg prayed an Imparlance till the next Court which is granted him.

197

Action of Debt. EDWARD CONNER agt. DARBY OCAIN. The Deft not appearing Judgment is granted the Pltf against him & BENJAMIN STROTHER his Security the Deft do appear at the next Court & answer the Pltf's Action.

Action of Debt. GEORGE BUCHANAN & WILLIAM HAMILTON agt. RAWLEIGH CHINN. The Deft not appearing Judgment is granted the Pltfs & LAURANCE SUDDERTH his Security unless the Deft do appear at the next Court & answer the Pltf's Action.

Action of Debt. EDWARD MUSE agt. JEREMIAH CARTER. An alias Capias is ordered returnable to the next Court.

Suit in Chancery. JOHN BAYLIS agt. JOHN FOUSHEE, Gent. is dismist & the Complainant ordered to pay the Deft his Costs.

[Page 200 Nov. 15, 1752]

November Court 1752

The Petition of the Church Wardens of Overwharton Parish against PATRICK REDMAN is dismist & they ordered to pay the said REDMAN his Costs.

Ordered that the Church Wardens of Overwharton Parish pay WHARTON HOLIDAY 75 pounds of Tobacco for three days attendance as an Evidence for them against PATRICK REDMAN.

Ordered that the Churchwardens of Overwharton Parish pay ELIZABETH HOLIDAY 75 pounds of Tobacco for three days attendance asn an evidence for them against PATRICK REDMAN.

Ordered that the Church wardens of Overwharton Parish pay ANN RICE 75 pounds of Tobacco for three days attendance as an evidence for them against REDMAN.

Ordered that PATRICK REDMAN pay THOMAS FOXWORTHY & SARAH his Wife each 75 pounds of Tobacco for three days attendance as an Evidence for him at Suit of the Church Wardens of Overwharton Parish.

Upon Complaint of THOMAS FITZHUGH, Gent. against JOHN PEYTON, Constable for not receiving Runaways sent him it's ordered that he be fined 30 Shillings for the use of our Lord the King & Costs.

Ordered that PATRICK REDMAN pay ANN POWEL 100 pounds of Tobacco for four days attendance as an Evidence for him at Suit of the Church Wardens of Overwharton Parish.

Action of Trespass. WILLIAM ALLISON agt. THOMAS PAIRMAIN. Judgment is confessed by the Deft to the Pltf for £5.4.7 half penny & his Costs.

Action of Debt. WILLIAM CUNNINGHAM agt. SOLOMON WAUGH. DAVID WAUGH came into Court and undertook that if the Deft should be condemned in this Action he would pay the Condemnation for him or surrender his the Deft's Body to Prison, & the Deft prayed Oyer &c. which is granted him.

Suit on Petition. WILLIAM ALLISON agt. GEORGE ELLIOTT. Judgment is confessed by the Deft to the Pltf for £2.14.9 half penny with Costs & a Lawyer's Fee.

Suit on Petition. WILLIAM HARRISON agt. BURKET PRATT is dismist the Deft paying Costs.

Ejection Firma. Thomas Turff agt. Timothy Twigg for Lands & Appurtenances in the Parish of Overwharton which JOHN MAUZY demised to the Pltf for a Term &c. It appearing by the return of the Sheriff that WILLIAM ETHERINGTON Tenant in Possession of the Premises being duly served with a Copy of the said declaration & he not appearing it's ordered that unless he

[Page 201 Nov. 15, 1752]

December Court 1752

do appear at the next Court or Judgment shall be granted the Pltf.

Ejection Firma. Thomas Turff & Timothy Twigg for Lands & Appurtenances in the Parish of Overwharton which HENRY FITZHUGH Esqr. demised to the Pltf for a Term &c. THOMAS SEDDON being admitted Deft in the Room of the said Timothy Twigg pleaded not guilty & confessed Lease, Entry, & Ouster & agreed to insist only on the Title at Tryal, which Issue the Pltf joined & the Tryal is referred till the next Court.

Action of Trespass. ROBERT & EDWARD MAXWELL agt. PETER STACY is dismist the Deft paying Costs.

Suit on Petition. JOSEPH DUNAWAY agt. JAMES YELTON. Judgment is granted the Pltf for 333 pounds of Tobacco by Account proved & Costs.

Suit on Petition. CHARLES HARDING agt. ROBERT BURGESS. By Consent of the Parties all Matters of Difference between them are referred to the determination of the Reverend JOHN MONCURE & JOHN PEYTON, Gent. & their Award to be made the Judgment of the Court.

Ordered that JOSEPH DUNAWAY pay SAMUEL ANGEL 50 pounds ot Tobacco for two days attendance as an Evidence for him against YELTON.

Ordered that the Inspectors at CAVES sell the old Scale Beam belonging to that Warehouse & Account for the Sale thereof at the laying of the next Levy.

Then the Court adjourned till Court in Course.

MOTT DONIPHAN

At a Court held for Stafford County 12th of Decr. 1752.

Present   JOHN PEYTON   PETER DANIEL
               FRANCIS THORNTON   JOHN STUART

A new Commission of the Peace for this County being produced & read together with a dedimus for administering the Oaths FRANCIS THORNTON, Gentleman & JOHN STUART administered the several Oaths to JOHN MERCER, Gent. who subscribed the Test & abjuration Oath & then administered the said Oaths to the said Francis Thornton, John Stuart, John Peyton, & Peter Daniel who

[Page 202 Dec. 12, 1752]

December Court 1752

subscribed the Test & abjuration Oath.

Present the above Justices.

GLASGOW a Negro Boy belonging to WILLIAM CUNNINGHAM, Merchant adjudged to be 11 years old.

Suit on Petition. CHARLES HARDING agt. ROBERT BURGESS. The Refferrees having reported that there was a balance due from the Deft to the Pltf of 217 pounds of transfer Tobacco it's considered by the Court that the Pltf recover the same from the Deft & Costs.

Absent PETER DANIEL, Gent.

HANNAH a negro Girl belonging to JAMES JEFFERICE adjudged to be ten years old.

200

Orderd that BENJAMIN STROTHER, Gent. be recommended to his Honor the Governor as a fit Person to be added to the Commission of the Peace for this County.

SAMUEL EARL Admr. of HANNAH BAYLIS decd. offered his Account against the said Bailis Estate with his Vouchers which the Court ordered to be lodged with the Clerk to be considered of.

Ordered that the Sheriff summon JAMES CARTER, GEORGE CARTER, GEORGE CARTER the Younger, ISAAC KNIGHT, ROBERT WHITLEY, JOHN PORTER, JOSEPH PORTER, & NATHANIEL SMITH to shew Cause why an Information should not be filed against them for certain Libels supposed to be ___ by them & to answer other Matters as shall be objected against them on behalf of our Lord the King.

Ordered that DANIEL SHEHON serve his Master JOHN MERCER, Gent. for 16 days runaway Time & 26 Shillings expended in taking him up.

Action of Trespass. ELIZABETH MCABOY agt. JOHN WALLER by consent of the Parties all Matters in difference between them are referred to the determination of JOHN PEYTON & TRAVERSE COOKE, Gent. & their award to be made the Judgment of the Court.

Then the Court adjourned till Court in Course.
JOHN MERCER

At a Court continued & held for Stafford County the 15th. Decemr. 1752.

Present JOHN MERCER   JOHN PEYTON
      FRANCIS THORNTON WILLIAM FITZHUGH
      THOMAS FITZHUGH JOHN STUART

MOTT DONIPHAN took the several Oaths of a Justice and subscribed the abjuration Oath.

Present MOTT DONIPHAN

Ejection Firma. Timothy Turff Lessee of HENRY FITZHUGH Gent. agt. THOMAS SEDDON. A dedimus to take the Depositions of the Witnesses returnable to this Court.

December Court 1752

Suit on Petition. WILLIAM MILLS agt. PETER MURPHY. Judgment is granted the Pltf for £4.6.3 & Costs.

Suit on Information brought on behalf of our Sovereign Lord the King agt. ELIZABETH MCABOY for retailing Liquors without Licence. A Jury to wit ROBERT [*no last name given*], GEORGE BELL, JOHN WEATHERS, ANDREW EDWARDS, ROBERT ENGLISH, GEORGE RANKINS, JOHN INGLISH, PETER MURPHY, MICHAEL RYAN, MERREMON TILLER, LAURANCE SUDDOTH, & BENJAMIN SELMAN. The Jury finds the Deft guilty. The Court being of Opinion that the Act of Assembly upon which this Information was brought is repealed it's thereupon considered by the Court that the said Elizabeth go home & that the suit be dismist.

Suit on Petition. WILLIAM HUNTER agt. RAWLEIGH CHINN. Judgment is granted the Pltf for £2.17.7 with Costs & a Lawyer's Fee.

Suit on Attachment obtained by SAMUEL WHITSON agt. the Estate of THOMAS SHARP, the said Samuel produced an Account against the said Thomas for £3.19.5. It's considered by the Court that the said Samuel recover the same of the said Thomas & his Costs. JOHN PEYTON, Gent. who being summoned appeared & on Oath declared that he had in his Hands one Shilling & three pence of the Estate of the said Thomas which he is ordered to pay the said Samuel in part of satisfaction of his Judgment.

Suit on Attachment obtained by JOHN PEYTON, Gent. agt. the Estate of JOSEPH BRAGG. The said John produced an Account against the said Joseph for £20.17.3 & 418 pounds of crop Tobacco. It's considered by the Court that the said John recover the same of the said Joseph & his Costs. The Sheriff having returned the said attachment executed on Tobacco hanging & in the hands of ROBERT FRISTOE who on Oath declared that he had 1000 pounds of crop Tobacco of the Estate of Joseph Bragg in his Hands which he is ordered to pay to the said Peyton in part satisfaction of this Judgment & the Sheriff is ordered to sell the Tobacco hanging to satisfy the said Judgment.

Upon the Indictment preferred against EDWARD RALLS, ALEXANDER BAXTER and

December Court 1752

JOHN FOY who pleaded not guilty. A Jury to wit ROBERT GARRARD, GEORGE BELL, JOHN WITHERS, ANDREW EDWARDS, ROBERT ENGLISH, GEORGE RANKINS, JOHN ENGLISH, PETER MURPHY, MICHAEL RYAN, MERRYMAN TILLER, LAWRENCE SUDDUTH & BENJAMIN SELMAN. The Jury find EDWARD RALLS, ANTHONY HORTON, ALEXANDER BAXTER, and JOHN FOY guilty. It is adjudged by the Court that the said Ralls be fined £10 for the use of our Lord the King & that they pay the Costs.

Ordered that the Sheriff take EDWARD RALLS, ALEXANDER BAXTER & JOHN FOY into his Custody till they enter into bond in £100 Each with two securities each in £50 for their good Behavior & keeping the Peace a Year & a day.

On Motion of THOMAS SPALDING his Petition in Relation of his Ear being bit off is admitted to record.

Suit on Petition. THOMAS FICKLIN agt. JOHN JAMES. Judgment is granted the Pltf for £2.19.8 with Costs & a Lawyer's Fee.

Suit on Petition. ROBERT WALKER agt. JOHN ALEXANDER. By Consent of both parties all Matters in difference between them are referred to the determination of WILLIAM FITZHUGH & ROBERT MASSEY Gent. & their award to be made the Judgment of the Court, & it's further agreed by & between the said Parties that if either of them do meet the last Saturday in this Month at BOYD'S HOLE the Arbitrators are to proceed.

Ordered that JOHN ALEXANDER pay ROBERT STRIBLING 25 pounds of Tobacco for one days attendance for him as an Evidence at suit of WALKER.

Administration on the Estate of RICHARD WHITMILL is granted ANDREW KENNY he having entered into bond with RICHARD RANDALL & PETER MURPHY his Securities. WILLIAM GERRARD, JOHN FITZHUGH, GOWRY WAUGH & HENRY TYLER Appraisers.

Then the Court adjourned till Court in Course.
JOHN MERCER

February Court 1753

At a Court held by a Commission of Oyer & Terminer for Stafford County 13th. Febry. 1753.

A Commission of Oyer & Terminer for the Tryal of BOB a negro Man Slave belonging to BURKETT PRATT together with a Dedimus for administering the Oaths. FRANCIS THORNTON & THOMAS FITZHUGH Gent. pursuant to the said dedimus administered the Oaths to JOHN MERCER, Gent. who administered the said Oaths to the said FRANCIS THORNTON, THOMAS FITZHUGH, MOTT DONIPHAN, JOHN PEYTON, HENRY FITZHUGH, WILLIAM FITZHUGH & JOHN STUART, Gent. who subscribed the Test & abjuration Oath.

BOB a negro Man Slave belonging to BURKET PRATT was committed to the Jail of this County by a Mitimus under the hand of JOHN STUART, Gent. one of his Majesty's Justices was led to the Bar in Custody of the Sheriff & thereupon MOSLEY BATTALEY, Gent. Deputy attorney of our Lord the King brought into Court an Indictment against the said Bob. On 18th day of February in the twenty sixth year of the Reign of our Sovereign Lord George the second Mosley Battaley came before the Justices of Stafford County with letters bearing date at Williamsburg the thirtieth day of January last past & giveth the Court to understand & be informed that Bob a negro man Slave belonging to BURKETT PRATT on the 19th day of January in the night of the same day with force & arms did feloniously & burglarily break & enter the Mansion House of ELIZABETH BUCKNER Widow at the Parish of Saint Paul's with an intent feloniously & burglarily to take steal & carry away the Goods & Chattels of the said Elizabeth Buckner being in the House that is to say 11 pieces of Pork of the Value of 16 Shillings, & 20 Gallons of Cyder of the Value of 14 Shillings being in the same House against the Peace of our said Lord the King. Wherefore Mosley Battaley prays that the said Slave Bob may be arraigned & tryed for the said Felony & Burglary & may thereof be convicted & Judgment may pass against him & Execution thereupon awarded. And thereupon

February Court 1753

the said BOB was publickly arraigned & pleaded that he was not guilty & put himself upon the Court. The Witnesses were examined in open Court who being fully heard the said Court do adjudge that the said Bob is guilty of the Felony & Burglary. Therefore it is considered that the said Bob be hanged by the Neck untill he is dead, & the Sheriff is ordered to make Execution of the said Bob on Tuesday the 27th instant. And the said Bob is valued by the Court to £50.

JOHN MERCER

At a Court held for Stafford County 13th. February 1753.

Present   JOHN MERCER   MOTT DONIPHAN
                JOHN PEYTON   PETER DANIEL
                FRANCIS THORNTON   WILLIAM FITZHUGH
                JOHN STUART

HENRY FITZHUGH took the several Oaths & subscribed the Test and abjuration Oath.

Present HENRY FITZHUGH, Gent.

On Motion of WILLIAM ALLEN his Ordinary Licence is renewed.

An Award between STUART and BERRY acknowledged by the Arbitrators is admitted.

Present THOMAS FITZHUGH, Gent.

CHARLES HARDING & SAMUEL MITCHEL Constables took the Oath prescribed in respect to killing Deer ordered to be certified.

Then the Court adjourned for an hour.

Ordered that BAILY WASHINGTON, Gent. be recommended to his Honor the Governor as a fit Person to be added to the Commission of the Peace for this County.

LIMBRICK a negro Boy belonging to ANN MASON adjudged to be 12 years old.

Absent FRANCIS THORNTON, WILLIAM FITZHUGH, THOMAS FITZHUGH.

Ordered that THOMAS PINKER serve his Master ADAM STEPHEN one year for striking him.

Then the Court adjourned till tomorrow morning 9 Oclock.

JOHN MERCER

At a Court continued & held for Stafford County 14th of February 1753.

205

Present   JOHN MERCER   MOTT DONIPHAN
                 PETER DANIEL   HENRY FITZHUGH

[Page 207 Feb. 14, 1753]

February Court 1753

Ordered that the Sheriff of RICHMOND pay HUGH ADIE 3,920 pounds of Tobacco levied by the Publick in part for Criminals in Stafford County.

Ordered that the Sheriff of MIDDLESEX pay HUGH ADIE 1,005 pounds of Tobacco levied by the public in part for Criminals in Stafford County.

Ordered that the Sheriff of WESTMORELAND pay HUGH ADIE 2,386 pounds of Tobacco in part for Criminals in Stafford County.

Ordered that MARGARET CORNWALL serve her Master JOHN FOLEY, Senr. for seven days runaway time & £2.1.6 expended in taking her up.

Present JOHN PEYTON, Gent.

Ordered that MARGARET CORNWALL serve her Master JOHN FOLEY. Senr. according to Law for having a bastard Child & further that she serve her said Master one Year for striking her Mistress.

Ordered that the Sheriff attach GEORGE CARTER & JAMES CARTER to appear at the next Court to answer the Complaint of ROBERT EDWARDS.

Present WILLIAM FITZHUGH & JOHN STUART, Gent.

Ordered that the Sheriff take JOSEPH PORTER into his Custody till he enter into Bond of £40 with two Securities in £20 each for his good Behavoir & keeping the Peace a Year & a day. The said Joseph Porter, TRAVERSE COOKE, & WILLIAM CARTER came into Court & acknowledged themselved indebted to our Lord the King for £20 to be levied of their Goods & Chattels, Lands & Tenaments in case the said JOSEPH PORTER should be of good behavior & keep the Peace a year & a day.

Ordered that the King's Attorney prosecute GEORGE CARTER, GEORGE CARTER, the Younger, and JAMES CARTER for Libels & other Misdemeanors.

Ordered that the Sheriff take ROBERT WHYTLY, JOHN PORTER, NATHANIEL SMITH, GEORGE CARTER, GEORGE CARTER the younger,

& JAMES CARTER into his Custody till they enter into Bond in £50 each with two Securities in £25 each for their good behavior a year & a day.

[Page 208 Feb. 14, 1753]

March Court 1753

Action of Debt. CAIN WITHERS agt. BARNABAS WILLIAMS. ALEXANDER DONIPHAN came into Court & undertook that if the said Deft should be condemned in this Action he would pay the Condemnation for him or surrender his body to prison and the Deft prayed Oyer &c which is granted him.

Then the Court adjourned till Court in Course.

At a called Court held for Stafford County 24th February 1753.

Present   MOTT DONIPHAN   JOHN PEYTON
                PETER DANIEL   THOMAS FITZHUGH

DUKE WHALEBONE being committed to the Joal of this County by a Mittimus under the hand of JOHN PEYTON, Gent. for felony having heard the Evidences against him & all matters relating to the facts, it's the Court's Opinion that the said Whalebone be discharged.

                            MOTT DONIPHAN

At a Court held for Stafford County March 19th. 1753.

Present   MOTT DONIPHAN   JOHN PEYTON
                PETER DANIEL   FRANCIS THORNTON
                THOMAS FITZHUGH   JOHN STUART

JOHN MURDOCK, Gent. having petitioned for an Acre of Land on Cannons Run to set a Water Mill upon it's thereupon ordered that the Sheriff summon twelve good and lawful Men to meet upon the land petitioned for and examine the Land petitioned for, and the Land adjacent thereto on both sides of the said Run which may be effected or laid under Water by building such Mill together with Timber & other Conveniences thereon & shall report the same with the true value of the Acre and of the damages of the Party holding the same.

March Court 1753

Ordered that HENRY POOLEY serve his Master HENRY FITZHUGH for 85 days runaway time & 180 pounds of Tobacco expended in taking him up.

LUKE POWELL an insolvent debtor under Execution at the Suit of ALEXANDER & DANIEL CAMPBELLS produced a Schedule of his Estate amounting to 20 shillings in the Hands of ADAM STEPHEN whereupon the said Powell is discharged.

Ordered that PETER CRANN serve his Mistress ANN MASON for five days runaway time & five Shillings & nine pence & 180 pounds of Tobo. expended in taking him up.

Ordered that the Sheriff summon 24 of the most able freeholders of this County to appear at May Court next to be of the Grand jury for the Body of this County.

Suit on Petition. WILLIAM CAMPBELL agt. ANDREW EDWARDS. Judgment is confessed by the Deft to the Pltf for £3.5.4 half penny with Costs & a Lawyer's Fee.

Ordered that the Church Wardens of Overwharton Parish bind JOSEPH JAMES & MARGARET PATTISON according to Law.

On Complaint of WILLIAM ROSS Senr. it's ordered that his Servant FRANCIS BOLLING serve him one year for striking him.

Ordered that Liquors stand rated as they were last year.

Action of Debt. GEORGE YOUNG agt. JAMES FERNSLY. JOHN HAMILTON Attorney for the Pltf is ordered to pay the Deft his Costs.

Action of Debt. GEORGE YOUNG, Assignee of TALBOT RESTIN agt. JAMES FRENSLEY is dismist & JOHN HAMILTON Attorney for the Pltf is ordered to pay the Deft his Costs.

Suit on Petition. MARY CHAMBERS agt. SAMUEL ANGEL. Judgment is granted the Pltf for £2.10.4 with Costs & a Lawyer's Fee.

Absent PETER DANIEL

Ejection Firma. Solomon Saveall agt. Simpleton Spendall for Lands & Appurtenances in the Parish of St. Paul's which BURDIT CLIFTON demised to the Pltf for a Term &c. THOMAS VIVION, Gent. being admitted Deft in the Room of the said Spendall prayed an Imparlance till the next Court which is granted.

Action of Debt. JOHN BIORN [*sic*] agt. PETER MURPHY is dismist the Deft paying Costs.

[Page 210 Mar. 19, 1753]

April Court 1753

Action of Trespass Assault & Battery. JOHN ADDISON agt. WILLIAM THOMAS. An alias capias is ordered returnable to the next Court.

Action of Trespass. JAMES ONEAL agt. MICHAEL HARPER is dismist the Deft paying Costs.

Action of Debt. JOHN ENGLISH agt. ANDREW KENNY is dismist the Deft paying Costs.

Action of Debt. ANDREW COCHRANE & COMPANY agt. RAWLEIGH CHINN. Judgment is confessed by the Deft to the Pltf for £16.5.8 & Costs.

Action of Trespass Assault & Battery. WILLIAM SMITH agt. MICHAEL DEHALL is dismist the Deft paying Costs.

Action of Trespass. JAMES YELTON agt. MARGARET LATHAM is dismist the Deft paying Costs.

Present PETER DANIEL

Suit on Petition. JOHN SAUNDERSON agt. WILLIAM HORTON. Judgment is granted the Pltf for £4.13.2 half penny & 29 pounds of Tobacco & Costs.

Ordered that JOHN SAUNDERSON pay JOHN RALLS, Senr. 75 pounds of Tobacco for three days attendance as an Evidence for him against HORTON.

Then the Court adjourned till Court in Course.
MOTT DONIPHAN

At a Court held for Stafford County 10th of April 1753.

Present   MOTT DONIPHAN   JOHN PEYTON
                 PETER DANIEL   HENRY FITZHUGH

WILL a negro boy belonging to JOHN PEYTON, Gent. is adjudged to be ten years old.

PETER a negro boy belonging to JOHN PEYTON, Gent. adjudged to be 8 years old.

TITUS a negro boy belonging to JOHN PEYTON, Gent. adjudged to be 8 years old.

Ordered that JANE THOMPSON serve her Master THOMAS SMITH according to Law for having a bastard Child.

Ordered that JAMIMA MILLS serve her Master WILLIAM MILLS for 14 days runaway time & £1 & 180 pounds of Tobacco expended in taking her up.

Ordered that the Church Wardens of St. Paul's Parish bind JOHN & ALEXANDER CARRICOS & SARAH KELLY according to Law.

[Page 211 Apr. 10, 1753]

April Court 1753

Ordered that WILLIAM COVE serve his Master DARBY OCAIN for six days runaway time & 160 pounds of Tobo. expended in taking him up.

Administration on the Estate of WILLIAM KIRK is granted MARY EAVES she having entered into Bond, PETER WIGGINTON & GEORGE BUSH her Securities.

Then the Court adjourned till Court in Course.
MOTT DONIPHAN

At a called Court held for Stafford County 11th April 1753.

Present   MOTT DONIPHAN   JOHN PEYTON
                 PETER DANIEL   HENRY FITZHUGH

GEORGE CARTER being committed to the Goal of this County by a mittimus under the hand of John Peyton, Gent. for felony & burglary & the Evidences against him not appearing he is again ordered into the Sheriff's Custody without Bail till Thursday sev'night which day is appointed for his further Tryal.
MOTT DONIPHAN

At a called Court held for Stafford County 19th. April 1753.

Present   MOTT DONIPHAN   JOHN PEYTON
                    PETER DANIEL   HENRY FITZHUGH
                    FRANCIS THORNTON   WILLIAM FITZHUGH

GEORGE CARTER being again brought before the Court for Felony & Burglary & having heard the Evidences against him the Court are of Opinion that the said George is not guilty & he is discharged.

                                      MOTT DONIPHAN

At a Court held for Stafford County 8th May 1753.

Present   JOHN MERCER   MOTT DONIPHAN
                    PETER DANIEL   HENRY FITZHUGH
                    FRANCIS THORNTON   WILLIAM FITZHUGH

Ordered that JOSEPH NEALE serve his Master JOHN FITZHUGH, Gent. for six days runaway time & £6.15.

JANE RIGBY came into Court & refused to take upon her the Burthen of the Execution of the last Will of her decd. Husband ALEXANDER RIGBY & renounced all benefit & advantage which she might claim by such last Will, whereupon it's ordered that THOMAS ROLLINGS of WESTMORELAND COUNTY & MARY his Wife who is the Heir at Law to the said decd. be summoned to appear at the next Court to inform the Court whether they will take Administration with the Will annexed.

[Page 212 May 8, 1753]

May Court 1753

The Grand jury to wit HORATIO DADE, ROBERT WASHINGTON, EDWARD BURGESS, BENJAMIN ROBINSON, JOHN GRAVET, JOHN GREEN, JOHN GORDON, JOHN KIRK, BENJAMIN DERRICK, WILLIAM KING, SIMON THOMAS, DUNCAM SIMPSON, JOHN SMITH, WILLIAM SWETMAN, JOHN RALLS, & ROBERT ASHBY returned into Court with the following Presentments. We present WILLIAM HOWARD for retailing Liquors without Licence for one Quart of Rum. We also present WILLIAM SCAPLIN of the Parish of St. Paul's for retailing Cyder contrary to Law for three Quarts & one Pint of Cyder. We also present MARY PINVEST of Overwharton Parish for bearing a base born Child by the Information of the Churchwardens of the said Parish.

Ordered that the several Offenders be summoned to answer the said Presentments.

RACHAEL a negro Girl belonging to WILLIAM [*no last name given*] adjudged to be ten years old.

Present JOHN MERCER

Ordered that the Churchwardens of Overwharton Parish bind FRANCIS YEOFFRY he being an Orphan left in this County by his Mother & is likely to become a Parish Charge.

RICHARD FOOTE, Gent. & WILLIAM FOOTE being summoned as Garnishees upon an Attachment obtained by ALEXANDER BROWN against the Estate of SOLOMON HARDWICK the said Richard declared he has in his Hands 19 Shillings & the said William 16 Shillings which they are ordered to pay to the said Alexander in part Satisfaction of his debt.

Then the Court adjourned till tomorrow morning 9 Oclock.
JOHN MERCER

At a Court held by a Commission of Oyer & Terminer for Stafford County the 8th May 1753.

A Commission of Oyer & Terminer for the Tryal of JOE a negro Man slave belonging to GERARD FOWKE, Gent.

[Page 213 May 8, 1753]

May Court 1753

Joe was committed to the Gaol of this County and was led to the Bar in Custody of the Sheriff & thereupon MOSLEY BATTALEY, Gent. deputy Attorney of our Sovereign Lord the King brought into Court an Indictment against the said Joe. Be it remembered that one Joe on the 21st day of April in the Parish of St. Paul's did feloniously steal, take & carry away out of the dwelling house of ISAAC ROSE in the Parish aforesaid one Gun of the Value of £3 current Money the Property of WILLIAM FITZHUGH, Gent. Wherefore the said Mosley Battaley prays that the said Joe may be arraigned & tryed for the said Felony & Burglary & may be thereof convicted & Judgment may pass against him & execution be thereupon awarded. And thereupon the said Joe was publickly arraigned & pleaded not Guilty & for Tryal thereof put himself upon the Court. The said Court do adjudge that the said Joe is guilty of the said Felony. It's

212

ordered that the said Joe be burnt in his right Hand which was done by the Gaoler in open Court & it's further ordered that the said Joe have one of his Ears nailed to the Pillory & stand there one Quarter of an Hour & then his Ear to be cut off.

JOHN MERCER

[Page 214 May 9, 1753]

May Court 1753

At a Court continued & held for Stafford County 9th May 1753.

Present MOTT DONIPHAN   JOHN PEYTON
      PETER DANIEL   HENRY FITZHUGH
      FRANCIS THORNTON WILLIAM FITZHUGH

HANNAH a negro Girl belonging to JOHN ALEXANDER adjudged to be 12 Years old.

Suit on Petition. THOMAS WASHINGTON agt. JOHN JAMES. Judgment is granted the Pltf for £3.10.11 farthing by Account with Costs.

Action of Trespass. PATRICK BOGLE & COMPANY agt. JOHN KITCHEN. The Deft not appearing Judgment is granted the Pltf against him & WILLIAM SWETMAN his Security unless the Deft do appear at the next Court & answer the Pltf's Action.

Action of Trespass. PATRICK BOGLE & COMPANY agt. BENJAMIN MCCULLOUGH. The Deft not appearing Judgment is granted the Pltf against him & EDWARD WALLER his Security unless the Deft do appear at the next Court & answer the Pltf's Action.

Action of Debt. NICHOLAS SAVIN agt. JOSEPH GOSS & JOHN THOMAS. The Defts confessed Judgment to the Pltf for £15.7.2 & Costs. But this Judgment is to be discharged on payment of £7.13.1 with Interest thereon from the 7th day of December 1751 till the same is paid.

Action of Debt. WILLIAM ROWLEY agt. JOHN JAMES. The Deft not appearing Judegment is granted the Pltf againt him & ROGER HILL & MARY MURRY his the Deft do appear at the next Court & answer the Pltf's Action.

Action of Trespass. GOWRY WAUGH agt. RAWLEIGH CHINN. The Deft not appearing Judgment is granted the Pltf against him & SOLOMON WAUGH his Security unless the Deft do appear at the next Court & answer the Pltf's Action.

Action of Debt. BENJAMIN STROTHER & WILLIAM MOUNTJOY
Churchwardens of Overwharton Parish agt. HENRY HURST. The Deft not
appearing

[Page 215 May 9, 1753]

May Court 1753

on Motion of the Pltfs an attachment is ordered against the Deft's Estate for 50
Shillings current money or 500 pounds of Tobacco & Costs returnable to the
next Court.

Suit on Attachment obtained by PETER HEDGMAN, Gent. against the Estate
of ROBERT PHILLIPS the said Peter produced an Account against the said
Robert for 307 pounds of Tobacco. It's considered by the Court that the said
Peter recover the same from the said Robert & his Costs.

Suit on Petition. WILLIAM BAILY agt. JEREMIAH CARTER. Judgment is
granted the Pltf for £2.4.2 half penny by note of hand with Costs & a Lawyer's
Fee.

Action of Trespass. ANTHONY STROTHER agt. BENJAMIN SELLMAN.
The Deft not appearing Judgment is granted the Pltf against him and ROBERT
ENGLISH, THOMAS WITHERS, & WILLIAM GARRARD his Securities
unless the Deft do appear at the next Court & answer the Pltf's Action.

Action of Trespass Assault & Battery. JOHN FITZPATRICK agt. JOB SIMS.
The Deft not appearing Judgment is granted the Pltf against him & WILLIAM
GARRARD his Security unless the Deft do appear at the next Court & answer
the Pltf's Action.

Action of Debt. WILLIAM CUNNINGHAM & COMPANY agt. WILLIAM
ROSS, Senr. The Deft confessed Judgment to the Pltf for £25.5.4. It's
considered by the Court that the Pltf recover the same & his Costs. But this
Judgment is to be discharged on payment of £12.16.8 with Interest thereon from
the 9th day of December 1751 till the same is paid.

Action of Trespass. PATRICK BOGLE & COMPANY agt. JAMES
CONNELL. The Deft not appearing Judgment is granted the Pltf against him &
THOMAS MADDOX his Security unless the Deft do appear at

May Court 1753

the next Court & answer the Pltf's Action.

Action of Trespass. JAMES CONNELL agt. EDWARD CONNER. The Pltf failing to prosecute his Action on the Deft, he is nonsuited. The Pltf is ordered to pay the Deft's damage & Costs.

Suit on the Attachment obtained by ALEXANDER BROWN against the Estate of BENNET ROSE is continued for the Garnishee.

Suit on the Attachment obtained by WITHERS CONWAY against the Estate of THOMAS LACY is continued for the Garnishee.

Suit on the Attachment obtained by ALEXANDER BROWN against the Estate of THOMAS LACY is continued for the Garnishee.

Suit on Attachment obtained by BENJAMIN MASSEY against the Estate of JOHN DUNBAR. The said Benjamin produced an account against the said John for £4.5 & an half penny. It's considered by the Court that the said Pltf recover the same of the said Deft & his Costs. And the Sheriff having returned the said Attachment executed in the hands of JOHN HOOE, HOWSON HOOE, GEORGE ELLIOTT, & JOHN THOMAS who declared the said John Hooe had in his Hands 551 pounds of Tobacco & three Hogsheads & one Bushel of ears of Corn, the said Howson Hooe one Meal Bag, the said George Elliott a Saddle & Coat which the Sheriff is ordered to sell according to Law & pay out of the said Sale of the said Corn & Tobacco to the said John Hooe £3.11 & to the said Georg Elliott 16 Shillings & one Penny half penny & the residue he is ordered to pay to the said Benjamin in satisfaction of the above Judgment.

CHARLES HARDING being summoned as a Garnishee upon an Attachment obtained by ROBERT DULIN against JOHN TRAPP and declared that he had in his hands of the said Trapp's Estate three Shillings & three Pence which he is ordered to pay to the said Duling.

Absent JOHN PEYTON

Suit on Petition. JOHN PEYTON, Gent. agt. ROBERT EDWARDS. Judgment is granted the Pltf for £2.2.3 by Account & Costs.

Suit on Petition. JOHN PEYTON Gent. agt. ROBERT EDWARDS. Judgment is granted the Pltf for £2.2.3 by Account & Costs.

Suit on Petition. JOHN PEYTON, Gent. agt. WILLIAM KNIGHT. Judgment is granted the Pltf for £3.4.8 half penny by Account & Costs.

Suit on Petition. JOHN PEYTON, Gent. agt. JEREMIAH CARTER. Judgment is granted the Pltf for £1.6.8 half penny by Account & Costs.

May Court 1753

Present JOHN PETYON, Gent.

Suit on Petition. WILLIAM FOSTER agt. CHARLES HOPKINS. Judgment is granted the Pltf for 300 pounds of Tobacco by Account & Costs.

Ordered that WILLIAM FOSTER pay SAMUEL WHITSON 100 pounds of Tobacco for four days Attendance as an Evidence for him against HOPKINS.

Action of Debt. JOHN PEYTON, Gent. agt. RANDOLL JOHNSON. The Deft confessed Judgment to the Pltf for £14.18.4. It's considered by the Court that the Pltf recover the same of the Deft & his Costs.

Action of Debt. ROBERT PETER agt. JOHN THOMAS. The Deft confessed Judgment to the Pltf for £29.3.6. But this Judgment is to be discharged (the Costs excepted) on payment of £14.11.9 with Interest thereon from the 6th day of January 1753 till the same is paid.

Action of Debt. JOHN PEYTON, Gent. Assignee of HENRY STUDDARD agt. JEREMIAH CARTER. The Deft not appearing an Attachment is ordered against the Deft's Estate for £10 & Costs returnable to the next Court.

Action of Trespass Assault & Battery. JAMES YELTON agt. JOHN PEYTON, Junr. The Deft for plea saith he is not guilty. The Trial thereof is referred till the next Court.

Action of Debt. GEORGE MASON, Esqr. agt. RANDALL JOHNSON. The Deft not appearing Judgment is gratned the Pltf against him & JOHN RALLS junr. & MOSES LUNSFORD his Securities unless the Deft do appear at the next Court & answer the Pltf's Action.

Action of Debt. WILLIAM CUNNINGHAME & COMPANY agt. LEONARD ALVEY & ELIAS ASHBY. The Defts not appearing Judgment is granted the Pltf unless the Defts do appear at the next Court & answer the Pltf's Action.

Ordered that PRESLEY COX pay WILLIAM MOUNTJOY 100 pounds of Tobacco for four days attendance as an Evidence for him against WITHERS.

Ordered That PRESLEY COX pay GEORGE WHITECOTTON 100 pounds of Tobacco for four days attendance as an Evidence for him against WITHERS.

THOMAS LACY being bound over to this Court & tho solemnly called failed to appear it's therefore ordered that his Recognizance be sued.

[Page 218 May 9, 1753]

May Court 1753

Action of Detinue. JOHN PEYTON, Gent. agt. JEREMIAH CARTER. TRAVERSE COOKE & CHARLES BRENT came into Court & undertook that if the said Deft should be condemned in this suit he would pay the Condemnation or render his Body to Prison or that they would do it for him, & the Deft prayed an Imparlance till the next Court which is granted him.

Action of Debt. ROBERT DREGHORN agt. JEREMIAH CARTER. TRAVERSE COOKE & CHARLES BRENT came into Court & undertook that if the said Deft should be condemned in this suit he would pay the Condemnation or render his Body to Prison or that they would do it for him, & the Deft prayed an Imparlance till the next Court which is granted him.

Action of Debt. WILLIAM HUNTER agt. JOHN HAMILTON. The Deft not appearing Judgment is granted the Pltf against him & GOWRY WAUGH, CAIN WITHERS, HENRY TYLER & WILLIAM GARRARD his Securities unless the Deft do appear at the next Court & answer the Pltf's Action.

Action of Debt. JACOB WILLIAMS agt. WILLIAM SCAPLIN. The Deft not appearing Judgment is granted the Pltf against him & JOHN OLIVER his Security unless the Deft do appear at the next Court & answer the Pltf's Action.

Action of Trespass. ALEXANDER BROWN agt. JEREMIAH WEATHERLY is dismist the Deft paying Costs.

Suit on Petition. JOHN PEYTON, Gent. agt. ARTHUR DENT. Judgment is granted the Pltf for 712 pounds of crop Tobacco by Bill & Costs.

Ordered that THOMAS SHARP pay ISAAC BASNEL 135 pounds of Tobo. for three days attendance as an Evidence for him against WHITSON & for coming & returning 20 Miles once.

In the Suit on Attachment obtained by ALEXANDER BROWN against the Estate of SOLOMON HARDWICK, the said Alexander produced an Account against the said Solomon for £9.5.7 farthing. It's therefore considered by the Court that the said Alexander recover the same of the said Solomon and his Costs & the Sheriff having made return that he had attached one feather bed & furniture, one Cattail bed & furniture, two iron Pots & hooks, one ladle & firetongs, a parsol of Taylor's Tools, a parcel of pewter, a parcel of bottles, a parcel of teaware, two Chests, one small Kettle, one frying Pan, three Chairs, a parcel of earthen Ware, two Candlesticks, one narrow Ax, & two Wedges, one Cow & Calf, & several other Trifles & in the hands of RICHARD FOOTE, BALDWYN DADE, RICE HOOE, & JACOB WILLIAMS. It's therefore ordered by the Court that the Sheriff

[Page 219 May 9, 1753]

May Court 1753

sell the said Goods & satisfy the Said Alexander his Judgment.

In the Suit on Attachment obtained by JOHN ALEXANDER against the Estate of SOLOMON HARDWICK the said John produced an Account against the said Solomon for £3.18. It's therefore considered by the Court that the said John recover the same of the said Solomon & his Costs. The Sheriff having made return that he had attached one feather bed & furniture, one Cattail bed & furniture, two iron Pots & hooks, one ladle & firetongs, a parsol of Taylor's Tools, a parcel of pewter, a parcel of bottles, a parcel of teaware, two Chests, one small Kettle, one frying Pan, three Chairs, a parcel of earthen Ware, two Candlesticks, one narrow Ax, & two Wedges, one Cow & Calf, & several other Trifles & in the hands of JACOB WILLIAMS, WILLIAM DAVIS, WILLIAM JONES, Senr., WILLIAM JONES, Junr., ANDREW HUNT, JOHN BROWN, WILLIAM LONG, ALEXANDER HARDIE, & WILLIAM SCAPLIN. It's therefore ordered that the Sheriff sell the said Goods & satisfy the said John his Judgment. And the said Jacob Williams, William Davis, William Jones, Senr., William Jones, Junr., Andrew Hunt, John Brown, William Long, Alexander Hardie, & William Scaplin not appearing it's ordered that unless they do appear at the next Court & declare what of the Estate of the said Solomon they have in their Hands that Judgment will be given against them for what shall appear due to the said John upon the above Judgment.

The Petition of GEORGE WALLER, WILLIAM ALLEN, WILLIAM MOUNTJOY, PETER HEDGMAN, THOMAS HAY, AMOS MATHENY, THOMAS MATHENY, JAMES MATHENY, JOHN MASON, JOHN WALLER, RALPH HUGHS, JESSE BAILS, & THOMAS MONROE agt. ELIZABETH MCABOY is dismist & the Petitioners ordered to pay the said Elizabeth her Costs & a Lawyer's Fee.

Ordered that ELIZABETH MCABOY pay ROBERT DULING 25 pounds of Tobacco for three days attendance as an Evidence for her at Suit of GEORGE WALLER & others.

Upon the Petition of MARGARET SMITH, it's the Opinion of the Court that the said Margaret is free whereupon it's ordered that ROBERT ASHBY (the elder) to whom the said Margaret was bound pay to the said Margaret her freedom dues & Costs & that he be discharged from the dues mentioned in her Indenture.

Ordered that the Churchwardents of Saint Paul's Parish bind JOHN TOMENS son of THOMAS TOMENS, decd.,

[Page 220 May 9, 1753]

May Court 1753

it appearing to the Court that the Mother of the Child is incapable of maintaining him.

Then the Court adjourned till tomorrow morning 9 Oclock.
JOHN MERCER

At a Court continued & held for Stafford County May 10th. 1753.

Present   JOHN MERCER   MOTT DONIPHAN
               PETER DANIEL   FRANCIS THORNTON

Suit on Petition. Messrs. BUCHANAN & COCHRANE agt. WILLIAM MOSS. Judgment is granted to the Pltfs for 416 pounds of Tobacco & 16 Shillings by Account with Costs & a Lawyer's Fee.

Action of Debt. ALEXANDER & DANIEL CAMPBELLS agt. JOHN LEECH is dismist the Deft paying Costs.

Action of Debt. Messrs. BUCHANAN & COCHRANE agt. JAMES GREEN. The Deft confessed Judgment 2,146 pounds of crop Tobacco & Costs. But this Judgment is to be discharged on Payment of 870 pounds of Tobacco with Interest thereon from the 27th day of June 1752 till the same is paid.

Suit on Petition. Messrs. BUCHANAN & COCHRANE agt. JOHN LEEWRIGHT. Judgment is granted the Pltfs for 500 poounds of Tobacco with Costs & a Lawyer's Fee.

Suit on Petition. WILLIAM RAWLEY agt WILLIAM POTES. Judgment is granted the Pltf for 330 pounds of Tobacco with Costs & a Lawyer's Fee.

Suit on Petition. WILLIAM ROWLEY agt. TIMOTHY LINES. Judgment is granted the Pltf for 511 pounds of Tobacco with Costs & a Lawyer's Fee.

Suit on Petition. JOHN PEYTON, Gent. agt. PHILIP SULLIVANT. Judgment is granted the Pltf for £2.18 by Note of hand & Costs.

Suit on Petition. WILLIAM STRIBLING agt. THOMAS EMBREY. Judgment is granted the Pltf for £2.10 & Costs.

Suit on Petition. MOSLEY BATTALEY. Gent. agt. THOMAS LACY. Judgment is granted the Pltf for 35 Shillings by Acount & Costs.

Present JOHN PEYTON, Gent.

Ordered that JOHN WALKER serve his Master JOHN THOMAS for eight days runaway Time & £1.10.6 expended in taking him up & Costs.

Present FRANCIS THORNTON
absent JOHN MERCER, Gent.

Action of Detinue. JOHN FOUSHEE, Gent. agt. SAMUEL EARL

[Page 221 May 10, 1753]

May Court 1753

A Jury to wit RICE HOOE, JOHN ALEXANDER, GOWRY WAUGH, WILLIAM MOUNTJOY, HAYWOOD TODD, HUSBANDFOOTE WHITECOTTON, GEORGE WHYTHE, THOMAS STRIBLING, WILLIAM STRIBLING, JOHN THOMAS, & JOHN CARTER. The Jury finds that JOHN BAILES in the Will mentioned died seized & possessed of negro GEORGE of the Price of £20, also negro JUDE of the Price of £15, also negro COFFEE of the price of £30 being three of the Negros in the declaration mentioned. And the Will stated In the Name of GOD amen &c we find a Bill of Sale from JOHN BAYLIS nephew & devisee of the said Testator to the Pltf JOHN FOUSHEE. We also find that HANNAH BAYLIS possessed herself of the said Slaves & died so possessed intestate & without Issue. We also find that the Deft SAMUEL EARL took out Administration on the Estate of the said HANNAH BAYLIS. We find that the Pltf Foushee demanded the said Slaves of the said Earl and that the said Earl refused to deliver them. We also find that the said Foushee was never possessed of the said Slaves. We find for the Pltf the negros above mentioned or the Price above mentioned and £10 damage & this Suit is continued till the next Court for the Matters of Law arising to be argued.

Ordered that JOHN FOUSHEE, Gent. pay GEORGE WALLER 125 pounds of Tobacco for five days attendance as an Evidence for him against EARL.

Suit on Petition. JOHN HONEY agt. JAMES RIDINGS. Judgment is granted the Pltf for 500 pounds of Tobacco by Account & Costs.

Ordered that JAMES RIDINGS pay SAMUEL EARLE 75 pounds of Tobacco for three days attendance as an Evidence for him at Suit of HONEY.

Ordered that JAMES RIDINGS pay MARY WALLER 75 pounds of Tobacco for three days attendance as an Evidence for him at Suit of HONEY.

Present JOHN MERCER, THOMAS FITZHUGH Gent.

Suit on Petition. Messrs. BUCHANAN & COCHRANE agt. THOMAS FLEEMAN. Judgment is granted the Pltf for 420 pounds of tobo. & Costs upon the following Certificate, "Westmoreland. At a Court held for the said County the twenty eighth day of July 1752 DAVID CRAIG Merchant produced into Court his Book, and made Oath that the several Ballances due on the several Accounts contained in the said book are justly owing to Messrs. Buchanan & Cochrane Merchants in Glasgow. Test GEORGE LEE."

Absent JOHN MERCER & FRANCIS THORNTON

FRANCIS THORNTON Gent. in open Court acknowledged that the Summons in the Words following (to wit) "GEORGE the second by the grace of God of Great Britain

[Page 222 May 10, 1753]

June Court 1753

France and Ireland…To the Sheriff of Stafford County Greeting. We command you to Summon JOHN MERCER to appear before a Council in WILLIAMSBURGH on Wednesday immediately after the next Court of Oyer & Terminer to answer a Complaint exhibited by FRANCIS THORNTON, WILLIAM FITZHUGH, & JOHN STUART, Justices of the Peace for the County aforesaid against the said JOHN MERCER, Judge of the said Court, concerning the said Mercer's Behavior as a Justice & that you make due return hereof to the Council Office. Witness ROBERT DINWIDDIE, Esqr. our Lieut. Governor at WILLIAMSBURGH the 16th day of April in the 26th year of our Reign."

was filled up by him the said FRANCIS THORNTON & by him delivered to the Sheriff of this County to be executed on the said JOHN MERCER last night after the Courts breaking up. The aforesaid Mercer complained to this Court, that the aforesaid Writ was executed on him in a public Manner & that it was an Insult offered the Court which being just to the Court they are of Opinion that the same is not look'd upon as such by them & on Motion of the said Thornton it's ordered to be entered, that the said Thornton in Court declared that the Clark of the Council gave him the Summons blank & asked him whether the Same should be served on the said Mercer in WILLIAMSBURGH or whether he would take it up & serve him with it in Stafford.

Present JOHN MERCER

At a Court held for Stafford County 12th. June 1753.

Present   JOHN MERCER   MOTT DONIPHAN
             JOHN PEYTON   THOMAS FITZHUGH

MARGARET WASHINGTON one of the Executors of the last Will & Testament of JOHN WASHINGTON, decd. qualified an an Exor. which is ordered to be certified.

BEN a negro boy belonging to JOHN FRENCH is adjudged to be 13 years of Age.

Ordered that JAMES CRAP, Junr. be summoned to appear at the next Court to answer the Petition of ROSE CONNER.

LONDON a negro Boy belonging to JOHN PEYTON, Gent. adjudged to be 9 years old.

JACK a negro Boy belonging to JOHN PEYTON, Gent. adjudged to be 9 years old.

WINNY a negro Girl belonging to JOHN PEYTON, Gent. adjudged to be 9 years old.

Administration on the Estate of WILLIAM WORLEY is granted THOMAS BUNBURY, Junr. he having given Bond. WILLIAM BUNBURY, THOMAS STRIBLING, JOEL STRIBLING & JOHN FRENCH Appraisers.

THOMAS LACY, JACOB JOHNSON & JOHN THOMAS came into Court & acknowledged themselves indebted to our Lord the King, the said Thomas Lacy in the Sum of £40 & the said Johnson & Thomas in the Sum of £20 each for the said Lacy's good behavior & keeping the Peace a Twelve Month & a day.

Then the Court adjourned till Court in Course.

JOHN MERCER

[Page 223 July 12, 1753]

July Court 1753

At a Court of Oyer & Terminer for Stafford County 12th. June 1753.

A Commission of Oyer & Terminer for the Tryal of JOE a negro man Slave belonging to GERARD FOWKE, Gent. together for a Dedimus for administration of the Oaths. JOE a negro Man Slave belonging to GERARD FOWKE, Gent. who was committed to the Goal of this County by a Mitimus under the hand of WILLIAM FITZHUGH, Gent., one of his Majesties Justices of the Peace for this County was led to the Bar in Custody of the Sheriff & thereupon MOSELY BATTALEY, Gent. Deputy Attorney of our Sovereign Lord the King brought into Court an Indictment against the said Joe. Be it remembered that on the 12th day of June the said Mosly Battaley gives the Court here to understand & be informed that Joe on the 19th day of May in 1753 between the Hours of ten & twelve in the night at the Parish of Saint Paul's with force & Arms did feloniously & burglarily break & enter the House of JOSEPH DOWDY, planter & thence did steal take & carry away sundry Goods & Chattels to the Value of twenty Shillings, that is to say one new brown Linen Bagg of the Value of six Shillings, one pair of Women's Pumps to the Value of five Shillings, one brown linen Petticoat of the Value of seven Shillings & one linen Apron of the Value of two Shillings, & other Enormities to the said JOSEPH DOWDY & the said Joe was publickly arraigned & pleaded that he was not guilty & for Trial put himself upon the Court. The Witnesses were examined in open Court as well as the said facts what he could alledge in his defense. The said Court do adjudge that the said Joe is not guilty of the Felony & Burglary. Thereupon it's ordered that he be discharged.

JOHN MERCER

At a Court held for Stafford County July the 10th. 1753.

Present   JOHN MERCER   MOTT DONIPHAN
                    PETER DANIEL   HENRY FITZHUGH

Suit on Petition. CHRISTIAN YOUNG agt. JOSEPH COMBS is dismist the Deft paying Costs.

Suit on Petiton. CHARLES DICK, Gent. agt. JAMES YELTON.

July Court 1753

Judgment is granted the Pltf for £1.9.3 half penny with Costs & a Lawyer's Fee.

Suit on Petition. PHILIP ALEXANDER, Gent. agt. JOHN THOMAS. Judgment is granted the Pltf for £3.6.6 & Costs.

Suit on Petition. WILLIAM ROWLEY, Gent. agt. RIDGINAL BOLAND. Judgment is granted the Pltf for 395 pounds of Tobacco with Costs & a Lawyer's Fee.

Suit on Petition. WILLIAM ROWLEY, Gent. agt. WILLIAM SCAPLIN & JOHN STONE. Judgment is granted the Pltf for 881 pounds of Tobacco with Costs & a Lawyer's Fee. But this Judgment is to be discharged (the Costs excepted) on Payment of 316 pounds of Tobacco with Interest from the 25th day of March 1751 till the same is paid.

Suit on Petition. JOHN PEYTON, Gent. agt. DANIEL DUNAWAY. Judgment is granted the Pltf for 302 pounds of Tobacco & Costs.

Present WILLIAM FITZHUGH, FRANCIS THORNTON, Gent.

Suit on Petition. JOHN PEYTON, Gent. agt. CHARLES HOPKINS. Judgment is granted the Pltf for 806 pounds of crop Tobacco & Costs.

Suit on Petition. WILLIAM BLACK agt. ARTHUR DUAS. Judgment is granted the Pltf for 400 pounds of Tobacco & Costs.

Suit on Petition. JOSEPH BLACK agt. JOHN WHITCUM. Judgment is granted the Pltf for £1.15 & one farthing & Costs.

Suit on Petition. JOHN ENGLISH agt. ANDREW KENNY & PETER MURPHY. Judgment is granted the Pltf for £4.6 & Costs.

Ordered that the Church Wardens of St. Paul's Parish bind THOMAS DUNCOMB son of JOHN DUNCOMB according to Law.

A Letter enclosed to the Clerk of this Court directed to Mr. JOHN MERCER from NATHANIEL WALTHOE which was delivered by FRANCIS THORNTON, Gent. in Court & read & then delivered to the said Mercer at his request whereupon the said Thornton moved that the same might be recorded which being objected to by the said Mercer, who put to the Court who were divided.

Ordered that JAMES HANSBROUGH be summoned to appear at the next Court to answer the Complaint of MASON FRENCH.

Action of Trespass. SAMUEL BREDWELL agt. CHARLES HARDING. The Deft not appearing Judgment is granted the Pltf against him & BENJAMIN STROTHER his Security

[Page 225 July 10, 1753]

July Court 1753

unless the Deft do appear at the next Court and answer the Pltf's Action.

Action of Debt. JOHN KNOX agt. THOMAS RIDDLE. The Deft not appearing Judgment is granted the Pltf against him & GEORGE RANDALL his Security unless the Deft do appear at the next Court & answer the Pltf's Action.

Ejection Firma. Thomas Trueman agt. Benjamin Bedright for Lands & Appurtenances in the Parish of Overwharton which JOHN ROUT demised to the Pltf for a Term &c. It appearing by the return of the Sheriff that JOSEPH MAUZY Tenant in Possession of the Premises hath been duly served with a Copy of the Declaration, & he not appearing it's ordered that unless he the said Tenant or those under whom he claims do appear at the next Court to be held for this County, Judgment will be granted the Pltf against him.

The Suit on Attachment obtained by WILLIAM BLACK against the Estate of RAWLEIGH CHINN, Junr. is dismist & the said Rawleigh is ordered to pay the said William his Costs.

Action of Debt. WILLIAM YOUNG agt. JOHN THOMAS is dismist the Pltf paying Costs.

Action of Debt. JOHN GRAHAM, Gent. agt. HENRY WIGGINTON & ANN PORTER. The Defts not appearing Judgment is granted the Pltf against them & THOMAS PORTER, ABRAHAM BREDWELL, & WILLIAM GARRARD, their Securities unless the Defts do appear at the next Court & answer the Pltf's Action.

Action of Debt. WILLIAM BLACK agt. SAMUEL WHITCOM & JOSEPH CARTER. BENJAMIN STROTHER came into Court & undertook that if the Deft Whitom should be condemned in this Action he would pay the Condemnation for him or render his Body to Prison whereupon on Motion of the said Whitcom a special Imparlance is granted him and an alias capias ordered against the said Carter returnable to the next Court.

Action of Trespass. DAVID MCQUALTY agt. ELIZABETH MCABOY is dismist & the Deft ordered to pay her Costs.

Action of Detinue. DAVID MCQUALTY agt. ELIZABETH MCABOY. The Deft for Plea saith she don't detain. The Tryal is referred till the next Court.

Action of Debt. ALEXANDER & DANIEL CAMPBELLS agt. FRANCIS MARTIN. The Deft confessed Judgment to the Pltfs for £15.12.5 & Costs. But this Judgment is to be discharged on payment of £7.16.8 three farthings with Interest thereon from the 16th day of June 1752 till the same is paid.

[Page 226 July 10, 1753]

July Court 1753

Action of Trespass. DARBY OCAIN agt. ISAAC BREDWELL. The Deft not appearing Judgment is granted the Pltf against him & ABRAHAM BREDWELL his Security unless the Deft do appear at the next Court & answer the Pltf's Action.

Suit on Petition. CATHERINE WATERS agt. JOSEPH CARTER. Judgment is granted the Pltf for £3.1 & Costs.

Ordered that MARGARET WATERS pay WILLIAM CASH 55 pounds of Tobacco for one days attendance as an Evidence for her against CARTER & for coming & returning ten Miles once.

Action of Trespass. WILLIAM GALE, Merchant agt. WILLIAM FITZHUGH & FRANCIS THORNTON, Gent. acting Exors. of GILSON BERRYMAN, decd. A Jury to wit TRAVERSE COOKE, JOHN CARTER, BENJAMIN ROBINSON, ANDREW EDWARDS, WILLIAM ADIE, EDWARD HAMPTON, GARDNER BURGESS, WILLIAM ETHERINGTON, ROBERT GARRAT, WILLIAM HORTON, JOB SIMS, & GEORGE PILCHER. The Jury finds for the Pltf £17.4.4 half penny.

Suit on Petition. EDWARD MUSE agt. JOHN RAMY. Judgment is granted the Pltf for 302 pounds of Tobacco with Costs & a Lawyer's Fee.

Ordered that EDWARD MUSE pay ROBERT EDWARDS 25 pounds of Tobacco for one days attendance as an Evidence for him against RAMY.

Suit of Scire Facias. JOHN HOOE, Gent. agt. WILLIAM FITZHUGH & FRANCIS THORNTON Gent. acting Exors. of GILSON BERRYMAN, decd. The said William and Francis confessed Judgment to the said John for 750 pounds of Tobacco & 59 pounds of Tobacco & the Costs of this Suit.

Suit on Scire Facias. BENJAMIN STROTHER & JOHN LEEWRIGHT Church

[Page 227 July 10, 1753]

August Court 1753

Wardens of Overwharton Parish agt. JOHN FLITTER. The Sheriff having returned the said Scire facias executed & the said Flitter being called & failing to appear it's considered by the Court that the said Benjamin & John have Execution against the said Flitter for 20 Shillings & Costs.

MARY DUAS being presented by the Grand jury for having a Bastard Child & failing to appear it's ordered that she pay the Church Wardens of Overwharton Parish (for the use of the Poor of the said Parish) 50 Shillings or 500 pounds of Tobacco & Costs.

Licence is granted MOSES LUNSFORD to keep an Ordinary at his House in this County.

Action of Trespass Assault & Battery. MOSES GRIGSBY agt. DANIEL CHAMBERS. A dedimus is ordered returnable to the next Court.

Ordered that WILLIAM HOWARD, WILLIAM JONES, & WILLIAM SCAPLIN be summoned to appear at the next Court to answer the several Informations exhibited against them.

Action of Trespass. JOB WIGLY agt. NATHANIEL HARRISON, Esqr., acting Exor. of WILLIAM WALKER, decd. The Deft confessed Judgment to the Pltf for £34.9 & Costs.

The Court adjourned till Court in Course.
JOHN MERCER

At a Court held for Stafford County 14th August 1753.

Present   JOHN MERCER   MOTT DONIPHAN
                  PETER DANIEL   THOMAS FITZHUGH

Ordered that GERARD FOWKE, FRANCIS THORNTON, & THOMAS FITZHUGH, Gent. be recommended to his Honor the Governor for his Honor to make Choice of a Sheriff for the ensuing Year.

Present JOHN STUART, WILLIAM FITZHUGH

Inspectors recommended—For BOYD'S HOLE, BALDWIN DADE, THOMAS BUNBURY, Junr., WITHERS CONWAY & ROBERT YATES.
For CAVE'S THOMAS MONROE, THOMAS HAY, INNIS BRENT & WILLIAM GARRARD.
For AQUIA EDWARD WALLER, RICHARD HEWITT, BENJAMIN STROTHER, & WILLIAM WRIGHT.

Inspectors of Beef, Pork, Tar &c continued.

JOHN RATLET a servant Boy belonging to JAMES ONEAL adjudged to be 15 years old.

Ordered that the Sheriff sell the Estate of LYDIA PATTISON according to Law, the same being so small a Value that no Person will administer thereon.

Absent THOMAS FITZHUGH, WILLIAM FITZHUGH

[Page 228 Aug. 14, 1753]

September Court 1753

Ordered that the Sheriff take MOSES LUNSFORD into his custody till he enter into bond of £40 with two Securities of £20 each for his good Behavior a year & a day.

Ordered that the Sheriff pay JAMES HANSBROUGH the Fraction in his Hands.

Then the Court adjourned till Court in Course.
JOHN MERCER

At a Court held for Stafford County 11th September 1753.

Present	JOHN MERCER	JOHN PEYTON
	HENRY FITZHUGH	THOMAS FITZHUGH

DANIEL a negro boy belonging to JOHN TYLER adjudged to be 12 years old.

228

Ordered that the Sheriff summon 24 of the most able Freeholders of this County to appear at Novr. Court next to be of the Grand jury for the Body of this County.

JUGG a negro Girl belonging to SARAH WHITECOTTON adjudged to be 12 years old.

GRAY a negro boy belonging to WILLIAM GARRARD adjudged to be 12 years old.

SYLVIA a negro Girl belonging to WILLIAM GARRARD adjudged to be 11 years old.

SARAH PESTRIDGE having entered into Bond a probate is granted her, of the last Will & Testament of BENJAMIN DUNCOMB, decd. being appointed whole & sole Exex. thereof.

ALEXANDER HARDIE being bound over to this Court by a Mittimus under the Hand of WILLIAM FITZHUGH, Gent. & no evidence appearing against him is discharged.

Ordered that ISBELL FRAZIER serve her Master MICHAEL BLACK for twenty days runaway time & 90 pounds of Tobacco expended in taking her up.

Suit in Chancery. THOMAS PRICE & SARAH his Wife agt. ELIZABETH BUCKNER, Execux. of the last Will & Testament of JOHN BUCKNER, decd. By Consent of the Parties a dedimus is ordered returnable to his Court.

Then the Court adjourned till tomorrow morning 9 Oclock.

JOHN MERCER

At a Court continued & held for Stafford County 12th. September 1753.

Present	JOHN MERCER	JOHN PEYTON
	HENRY FITZHUGH	THOMAS FITZHUGH

Suit on Petition. MARGARET FRENCH agt. JOHN HOLLAND & JOHN THOMAS. Judgment is granted the Pltf for £3.12 & Costs. But this Judgment is to be discharged on Payment

September Court 1753

of £1.18 with Interest thereon from the 7th day of November 1752 till the same is paid.

Suit on Petition. THOMAS & ROBERT DUNLOPS agt. SNODALL HORTON, junr. Judgment is granted the Pltfs for £2.3.8 with Costs & a Lawyer's Fee.

Suit on Petition. WILLIAM BLACK agt. JOSEPH WINLOCK. Judgment is granted the Pltf for 35 Shillings & 5 Pence half penny & Costs.

Action of Debt. WILLIAM BLACK agt. WILLIAM BUSSELL. The Deft confessed Judgment to the Pltf for £6 & Costs. But this Judgment is to be discharged on Payment of £3 with Interest from the 13th day of August 1752 till the same is paid.

Action of Debt. WILLIAM BLACK agt. MERRIMOND TILLER. The Deft not appearing Judgment is granted the Pltf against him & GERARD FOWKE, Gent. Sheriff unless the Deft do appear at the next Court & answer the Pltf's Action.

Ordered that JOHN LEEWRIGHT pay ANDREW MCKENNAN 50 pounds of Tobacco for two days attendance as an Evidence for him against JOHNSON.

Present MOTT DONIPHAN Gent.

Suit on Petition. ROBERT WALKER agt. JOHN ALEXANDER. Judgment is granted the Pltf for £3.9.9 & Costs.

Ordered that JOHN ALEXANDER pay THOMAS STRIBLING 175 pounds of Tobacco for eleven days attendance as an evidence for him at Suit of WALKER.

Ordered that JOHN ALEXANDER pay ALEXANDER HARDY 325 pounds of Tobacco for 13 days attendance as an evidence for him at Suit of WALKER.

JOE a negro Boy belonging to DIANA SIMPSON adjudged to be 11 years old.

Action of Trespass. ROBERT & EDWARD MAXWELLS agt. SAMUEL WHITSON. The Deft not appearing Judgment is granted the Pltfs against him & BENJAMIN STROTHER, Gent. his Security unless the Deft do appear at the next Court & answer the Pltf's Action.

Action of Trespass. ROBERT & THOMAS DUNLOPS agt. WILLIAM HORTON. BENJAMIN ROBINSON undertook that if the Deft should be condemned in this Action he the said Robinson would pay

[Page 230 Sept. 12, 1753]

September Court 1753

the Condemnation for him or surrender his Body to Prison whereupon the Deft prayed a special Imparlance which is granted him till the next Court.

Action of Trespass. WILLIAM MOUNTJOY agt. GEORGE GHENT. A Jury to wit EDWARD BETHEL, JEREMIAH WEATHERLY, GEORGE BELL, SAMUEL EARLE, EDWARD PILCHER, WILLIAM NORTHCUT, ALIAS ASHBY, JOHN RALLS, junr., WILLIAM ETHERINGTON, WILLIAM PICKETT, JAMES GWYNN & ROBERT GARRETT. The Jury finds for the Pltf 1,157 pounds of Tobacco & Costs. The Deft filed Errors in Arrest of Judgment, which are to be argued the next Court.

Action of Debt. SAMUEL COURTNEY agt. JEREMIAH CARTER. The Deft not appearing an Attachment ordered in this Suit. Judgment is granted to the Pltf for 1,500 pounds of Tobacco & Costs. But this Judgment is to be discharged on payment of 750 pounds of Tobacco with Interest from the 16th day of June 1750 till the same is paid & the Sheriff having made return that he had attached Tobacco hanging ordered that he sell the same according to Law to satisfy the said Judgment.

Action of Debt. JOHN WEATHERS agt. MOURNING RICHARDS. JOHN PEYTON, Gent. came into Court & undertook that if the Deft should be condemned in this Action that he would pay the Condemnation for him or surrender his Body to Prison.

Ordered that WILLIAM MOUNTJOY pay JACOB HOLSCLAW 303 pounds of Tobacco for three days attendance as an evidence for him againt GHENT & for coming & returning 38 Miles twice.

Ordered that WILLIAM MOUNTJOY pay JOHN SOWELL 303 pounds of Tobacco for three days attendance as an evidence for him againt GHENT & for coming & returning 38 Miles twice.

Ordered that WILLIAM MOUNTJOY pay JAMES ONEAL 75 pounds of Tobacco for three days attendance as an evidence for him againt GHENT.

September Court 1753

Ordered that WILLIAM MOUNTJOY pay SAMUEL ANGEL 75 pounds of Tobacco for three days attendance as an Evidenvce for him against GHENT.

The above Orders of attendance are not to be allowed in the Bill of Costs.

Ejection Firma. Thomas Turff agt. Timothy Twigg for Lands & Appurtenances in the Parish of St. Paul's which Haywood Todd demised to the Pltf for a Term &c. JOHN SHORT being admitted Deft in the Room of the said Timothy pleaded the general Issue confest Lease, Entry & Ouster & insisted only on the Title at Tryal, & the Tryal thereof is referred till the next Court.

Action of Trespass Assault & Battery. JAMES YELTON agt. JOHN PEYTON. A Jury to wit EDWARD BETHEL, JEREMIAH WEATHERLY, WILLIAM NORTHCUT, ELIAS ASHBY, JOHN RALLS, junr., WILLIAM ETHERINGTON, WILLIAM PICKET, JAMES QUINN, ROBERT GARRETT, ROBERT ENGLISH, WILLIAM LUNSFORD, & ROBERT ASHBY, junr. The Jury finds for the Pltf one Shilling damage & one Shilling Costs.

Ordered that JAMES YELTON pay ANDREW KENNY 100 pounds of Tobacco for four days attendance as an Evidence for him against PEYTON.

Ordered that JAMES YELTON pay ELIZABETH MCABOY 125 pounds of Tobacco for five days attendance as an Evidence for him against PEYTON.

Ordered that JAMES YELTON pay MARY WISE 125 pounds of Tobacco for five days attendance as an Evidence for him against PEYTON.

Ordered that JOHN PEYTON pay EDWARD PILCHER 125 pounds of Tobacco for five days attendance as an Evidence for him against YELTON.

Present JOHN STUART, Gent.

Action of Trespass. JOHN CHAMP, Esqr. agt. SOLOMON WAUGH. GOWRY WAUGH came into Court & undertook that if the Deft should be condemned in this Action that he would pay the Condemnation for him or surrender his Body to Prison & the Deft for plea saith he did not assume. The Tryal is referred till the next Court.

Absent JOHN PEYTON, Gent.

September Court 1753

Action of Trespass. JOHN PEYTON, Gent. and GEORGE WALLER, acting Exor. of CHARLES WALLER, Gent. decd. agt. JACOB AMBROSE DEKEYSER. A Jury to wit EDWARD BETHELL, JEREMIAH WEATHERLY, WILLIAM NORTHCUT, ELIAS ASHBY, WILLIAM ETHERINGTON, WILLIAM PICKETT, JAMES GWINN, ROBERT GARRETT, ROBERT ENGLISH, WILLIAM LUNSFORD, ROBERT ASHBY, Junr., & WILLIAM BUSSELL. The Jury finds for the Pltf £6.9.3 half penny & Costs.

Action of Trespass. JOHN LEWTHWAITE agt. PETER HEDGMAN, Gent. By Consent of the Parties all Matters in difference between them are referred to the determination of JOHN CHAMP & THOMAS TURNER, Esqr. & their award to be made the Judgment of this Court.

Suit on Petition. RICHARD BARNARD, Gent. agt. JOHN THOMAS. Judgment is granted the Pltf for 793 pounds of Tobacco & Costs.

Absent MOTT DONIPHAN

Suit on Petition. PRISCILLA BOWS agt. GEORGE WHITE. Judgment is granted the Pltf for 1,000 pounds of Tobacco & Costs.

Present MOTT DONIPHAN

JOHN FOUSHEE, Gent. came into Court & upon Oath declared that he had no Effects of JOHN BAYLIS in his Hands which is ordered to be certified.

Suit on Petition. JEREMIAH WEATHERLY agt. RICHARD BARNARD & JOHN WASHINGTON, Gent., Exors. of the last Will & Testament of JOHN WASHINGTON, decd. Judgment is granted the Pltf for £3.5 of the Goods and Chattels of the said Testator in the Hands of the said Exors.

Ordered that PRISCILLA BOWS pay WHARTON HOLIDAY 125 pounds of Tobacco for five days attendance as an Evidence for her against WHITE.

September Court 1753

Ordered that PRISCILLA BOWS pay ELIZABETH HOLLIDAY 125 pounds of Tobacco for five days attendance as an Evidence for her against WHITE.

Ordered that PRISCILLA BOWS pay WILLIAM TODD 625 pounds of Tobacco for 25 days attendance as an Evidence for her against WHITE.

Ordered that GEORGE WHITE pay JAMES HUGHS 225 pounds of Tobacco for nine days attendance as an Evidence for him at Suit of BOWS.

Ordered that JEREMIAH WEATHERLY pay JOHN LEEWRIGHT 400 pounds of Tobacco for 16 days attendance as an evidence for him against WASHINGTON'S Exors.

Ordered that the Exors. of JOHN WASHINGTON pay WILLIAM WARD 200 pounds of Tobacco for eight days attendance as an Evidence for them at Suit of WEATHERLY.

Ordered that the Exors. of JOHN WASHINGTON pay JOHN STRANGE 375 pounds of Tobacco for four days attendance as an Evidence for them at Suit of WEATHERLY and for coming & returning ____ [*miles not given*] Miles three times.

> Then the Court adjourned till tomorrow morning 9 Oclock.
> JOHN MERCER

At a Court continued & held for Stafford County 13th September 1753.

Present   JOHN MERCER   JOHN PEYTON
                HENRY FITZHUGH   THOMAS FITZHUGH

Suit on Petition. GEORGE WHITE agt. DANIEL CHAMBERS. Judgment is granted the Pltf for £3.11.7 half penny & Costs.

Ordered that DANIEL CHAMBERS pay JAMES RAYNES 375 pounds of Tobacco for 15 days attendance as an Evidence for him at Suit of WHITE.

Ordered that DANIEL CHAMBERS pay HENRY JONES 375 pounds of Tobacco for 15 days attendance as an Evidence for him at Suit of WHITE.

Ordered that GEORGE WHITE pay JOHN GRINAN 420 pounds of Tobacco for 17 days attendance as an evidence for him against CHAMBERS.

Ordered that DANIEL CHAMBERS pay ELENOR GRINAN 450 pounds of Tobacco for 18 days attendance as an Evidence for him at Suit of WHITE.

> Present MOTT DONIPHAN, Gent.

234

Suit on Petition. ROBERT SUDDUTH agt. ALEXANDER BROWN. Judgment is granted the Pltf for £4.19 with Costs & a Lawyer's Fee.

Ordered that ROBERT SUDDUTH pay ORIGINAL ROE 225 pounds of Tobacco for three days attendance as an Evidence for him against BROWN & for coming & returning 25 Miles.

[Page 234 Sept. 13, 1753]

September Court 1753

Ordered that ROBERT SUDDUTH pay NATHANIEL JONES 106 pounds of Tobacco for five days attendance as an Evidence for him against BROWN & for coming & returning 15 Miles three times.

Ordered that ALEXANDER BROWN pay THOMAS BUNBURY, Senr. 125 pounds of Tobacco for five days attendance as an Evidence for him at Suit of SUDDUTH.

Ordered that ALEXANDER BROWN pay THOMAS BUNBURY 125 pounds of Tobacco for five days attendance as an Evidence for him at Suit of SUDDUTH.

Ordered that ALEXANDER BROWN pay ANDREW HUNT 125 pounds of Tobacco for five days attendance as an Evidence for him at Suit of SUDDUTH.

Ordered that ALEXANDER BROWN pay JOHN ALEXANDER 125 pounds of Tobacco for five days attendance as an Evidence for him at Suit of SUDDUTH.

Suit on Petition. WILLIAM PICKETT agt. WILLIAM MATHENY. Judgment is granted the Pltf for £2.3 & Costs.

Ordered that WILLIAM PICKETT pay JOHN WOOD 220 pounds of Tobacco for four days attendance as an Evidence for him against MATHENY & for coming & returning 20 Miles once.

Ordered that WILLIAM PICKETT pay RICHARD COLE 208 pounds of Tobacco for four days attendance as an Evidence for him against MATHENY & for coming & returning 18 Miles once.

Ordered that WILLIAM MATHENY pay SAMUEL SIMS 100 pounds of Tobacco for four days attendance as an Evidence for him at Suit of PICKETT.

Suit on Petition. JOHN ENGLISH agt. CAIN WITHERS. Judgment is granted the Pltf for 880 pounds of Tobacco & Costs.

235

Ordered that JAMES RUSSELL pay EDWARD MUSE 170 pounds of Tobacco for two days attendance as an Evidence for him against HAMILTON & for coming & returning 40 Miles once.

Suit on Petition. JOHN GRAHAM, Gent. agt. MARY CARTER. Judgment is granted the Pltf for £3.1.10 half penny with Costs & a Lawyer's Fee.

Ordered that JOHN GRAHAME pay SIMON LUTTRELL 220 pounds of Tobacco for four days attendance as an Evidence for him against CARTER & for coming & returning 20 Miles twice.

Ordered that JUSTICE BRYAN pay JOHN BELL 450 pounds of Tobacco for 15 days attendance as an evidence for him against OCAIN.

[Page 235 Sept. 13, 1753]

September Court 1753

Action of Trespass. JOHN LEECH agt. JOHN HAMILTON. The Deft for Plea saith he did not assume & hath leave to give the special Matter in Evidence. The Tryal is referred till the next Court.

Action of Trespass. RICHARD BERNARD, Gent. agt. WILLIAM ROSE. The Deft having filed his plea the Pltf hath Time till the next Court to consider thereof.

Action of Trespass. WILLIAM PICKET agt. MARK CANTON. The Deft having filed his plea the Pltf hath Time till the next Court to consider thereof.

Action of Trespass Assault & Battery. JOHN RILEY agt. THOMAS CRAFFORD. The Pltf failing to prosecute his Suit is nonsuited & ordered to pay the Deft damages according to Law & Costs.

Suit on Petition. JOHN PEYTON agt. JAMES YELTON. Judgment is granted the Pltf for £3.6.6 & 40 pounds of Tobacco & Costs.

Ordered that JOHN PEYTON pay ELIZABETH KETCHING 225 pounds of Tobacco for nine days attendance as an Evidence for him against YELTON.

Action of Trespass. JOHN FOUSHEE, Gent. agt. SAMUEL EARLE. The Pltf refusing to appear to argue the Errors in this Cause it's thereupon considered by the Court that the Deft recover of the Pltf according to the Form & Effect of the Judgment aforesaid.

236

JOHN RAMY undertook in Court to pay for JAMES YELTON 43 Shillings at the laying of the next Levy it being for a Fine due to the Church wardens of Overwharton Parish.

Action of Trespass. JAMES RIDINGS agt. JOHN HONEY. The Pltf failing to prosecute his Suit he is nonsuited & ordered to pay the Deft's damages.

Action of Trespass. MASON COMBS agt. SAMUEL EARLE, Admr. of HANNAH BAYLIS decd. The Deft for plea saith that the Intestate did not assume & that he hath fully administered. The Tryal is referred till the next Court.

> Then the Court adjourned till Court in Course.
> JOHN MERCER

At a Court held for Stafford County October 9th. 1753.

Present   MOTT DONIPHAN   JOHN PEYTON
              HENRY FITZHUGH   WILLIAM FITZHUGH

[Page 236 Oct. 9, 1753]

October Court 1753

VENUS a negro Girl belonging to GEORGE HARDING adjudged to be 12 years old.

LEWIS a negro Boy belonging to WILLIAM HORTON adjudged to be 12 years old.

MILLY a negro Girl belonging to JOHN HORTON adjudged to be 13 years old.

JOHN STUART, Gent. made Oath to an Account against servant ISABELL MOORE for 26 days runaway time & £2.1.8 expended in taking her up ordered that she serve for the same according to Law. The Cash to be discharged in Tobacco at 13/ pCent.

WILLIAM STUART, Clerk is appointed Guardian to JANE & SEGISMOND MASSEY, Orphans of SIGISMOND MASSEY, decd. & entered into Bond with JOHN STUART his Security.

ISABELL MOORE servant to JOHN STUART, Gent. confessed in Court that she had five years to serve the 17th day of July 1752 which on the Motion of the said Stuart is ordered to be certified.

237

JOHN HOOE, LAWRENCE WASHINGTON, & JOHN WASHINGTON, Gent. are desired to set apart to HORATIO DADE & MARY his Wife late Widow of SEGISMOND MASSEY decd. their Part of the said Massey's Estate.

The Inspectors at BOYD'S HOLE sold 2587 pounds of Tobacco at ten Shillings & eight pence pCent. At AQUIA 6762 lbs. of Tobacco for ten Shillings & nine pence pCent. At CAVES 956 pounds of Tobo. at eleven Shillings & one penny pCent.

SAPHO a negro Girl belonging to Doctor MICHAEL WALLACE adjudged to be ten years old.

MIRANDA a negro Girl belonging to MICHAEL WALLACE adjudged to be ten years old.

POMPY a negro boy belonging to MICHAEL WALLACE adjudged to be twelve years old.

Absent JOHN PEYTON, Gent.

Administration on the Estate of JOHN LINTON decd. is granted JOHN PEYTON, Gent. he having entered into Bond according to Law.

Present JOHN PEYTON, Gent.

Ordered that the Church wardens of Overwharton Parish bind SARAH CUNNINGHAM according to Law.

In the Suit on Attachment obtained by ANN MASON widow against the Estate of RANDOLPH JOHNSON for £8.12 due her for Rent, it's therefore considered by the Court that the said Ann recover the same of the said Randolph & her Costs. And the Sheriff having returned the said Attachment executed in the Hands of WILLIAM KING, on Tobacco hanging on the Fence, on Tobacco moved off the Premises by SAMUEL ANGEL, & on the Balance that was in the Hands of the said Ann & the said William declared that he had no Estate

[Page 237 Oct. 9, 1753]

October Court 1753

of the said Randolph's in his Hands, and the Sheriff is ordered to sell the Tobacco attached to satisfy the said Ann her judgment.

Then the Court adjourned till Court in Course.

MOTT DONIPHAN

At a Court held for Stafford County for the Proof of public Claims, Propositions & Greivances, October 29th. 1753.

Present   MOTT DONIPHAN   JOHN PEYTON
                   PETER DANIEL   THOMAS FITZHUGH
                   WILLIAM FITZHUGH

DANIEL CHAMBERS of this County produced a certificate under the Hand of MOTT DONIPHAN, Gent. for taking up WILL a runaway negro Man Slave belonging to JOHN TAYLOE of RICHMOND COUNTY & it's adjudged by the Court to be above ten Miles from his Masters.

JOHN HOLLAND of said County produced a certificate under the Hand of WILLIAM FITZHUGH, Gent. for taking up DICK a runaway negro boy belonging to JOSEPH SMITH of WESTMORELAND COUNTY & it's adjudged to be above ten Miles from his Masters.

JOHN EATON produced a Certificate under the Hand of WILLIAM FITZHUGH, Gent. for taking up a runaway Servant Woman named MARY WILLIAMSON belonging to JOHN ROSE of KING GEORGE COUNTY & it's adjudged to be above five Miles from her Masters.

WILLIAM GARRARD produced a Certificate under the Hand of MOTT DONIPHAN, Gent. for taking up SAM a negro Man Slave belonging to SAMPSON DEMOVELL of NORTHUMBERLAND COUNTY and it's adjudged to be above ten miles from his Masters.

JOHN SMITH produced a Certificate from under the Hand of MOTT DONIPHAN for taking up a runaway servant man named JOHN SMITH belonging to RICHARD COBB of NORTHUMBERLAND COUNTY

[Page 238 Oct. 29, 1753]

November Court 1753

& it's adjudged to be above ten Miles from his Masters.

MOTT DONIPHAN

At a Court held for Stafford County 13th. November 1753.

Present   MOTT DONIPHAN   JOHN PEYTON

PETER DANIEL   FRANCIS THORNTON
WILLIAM FITZHUGH

WILLIAM MILLS produced an Account against his Servant JAMIMA
SCULCROFT for two days runaway Time & 180 pounds of Tobacco expended
in taking her up ordered that she serve her said Master for the same according to
Law.

Then the Court proceeded to lay the Levy.

To Mr. SECRETARY NELSON by Account	480
To Mr. MOSELY BATTALEY Kings Attorney	2000
To the Sheriff by Law	1254
To the Clerk by Law	1254
To ditto by Account	4080
To Mr. JOHN PEYTON by Account	1260
To WITHERS CONWAY by Account	2744
To ANDREW EDWARDS by Account	1000
To WILLIAM GARRARD by Account	4455
To WILLIAM NORTHCUT by Account	350
To JOHN STONE Constable by Account	365
To JACOB JOHNSON Constable by Account	451
To GEORGE RINGLES by do.	252
To SAMUEL MITCHELL do.	406
To ROBERT ENGLISH for guarding the Prison on	880
CARTER & PRATT'S negro	
To WILLIAM CORBIN for do.	710
To JOSEPH WHITE for do. on Carter	360
To ANDREW KENNY for do.	360
To CHARLES HARDING Constable p. Account	492
	23159
To 6 pCt. on 23159	1390
	24549

Cr.

By HENRY TYLER for Cash in CAVES Inspector's Hands	3383
By Mr. PEYTON for a Scale Beam	200
	3583

240

December Court 1753

Dr.	24549
Cr.	3583
	20,966

By 1961 Tithables at 11 lb. Tobacco per Tithe   20,966
  & a Fraction of 505 in the Sheriff's Hands

Ordered that JANE ELLIOTT serve her Master JACOB WILLIAMS according to Law for having a Bastard Child.

Then the Court adjourned till Court in Course.
MOTT DONIPHAN

At a Court held for Stafford County 11th. December 1753.

Present   JOHN MERCER   MOTT DONIPHAN
            JOHN PEYTON   HENRY FITZHUGH

Ordered that JOSIAS BARNS serve his Master JOHN STUART, Gent. for two days runaway time & 180 pounds of Tobacco expended in taking him up.

Present FRANCIS THORNTON & WILLIAM FITZHUGH, Gent.

Suit on Petition. CHARLES STUART & COMPANY agt. FRANCIS BROOKS. Judgment is granted the Pltf for £4.19 with Costs & a Lawyer's Fee.

Suit on Petition. WALTER JAMESON agt. JEREMIAH CARTER. Judgment is granted the Pltf for £2.10.6 with Costs & a Lawyer's Fee.

Suit on Petition. WILLIAM ALLEN agt. WILLIAM SWETMAN. Judgment is granted the Pltf for £2.7.4 with Costs.

Suit on Petition. THOMAS ALLISON agt. RICHARD SIMS is dismist the Deft paying Costs & a Lawyer's Fee.

Suit on Petition. THOMAS BENNETT, jurn. agt. JEREMIAH CARTER. Judgment is granted the Pltf for 372 pounds of Tobacco & 18 Shillings 10 pence with costs & a Lawyer's Fee.

Suit on Petition. JOHN RALLS agt. WILLIAM COPEN. Judgment is granted the Pltf for £4.14.1 farthing & Costs.

Suit on Petition. JOHN BAILIE agt. FUTRIL HALL is dismist the Pltf paying Costs.

Absent JOHN MERCER, Gent.

Suit on Petition. JOHN MERCER, Gent. agt. ROBERT ASHBY. Judgment is granted the Pltf for 59 pounds of Tobacco & £3.9.4 half penny & Costs.

Suit on Petition. JOHN MERCER, Gent. agt. WILLIAM COPEN. Judgment is granted the Pltf for £2.1 & Costs.

[Page 240 Dec. 11, 1753]

December Court 1753

Suit on Petition. BARTRAM EWELL Gent. agt. RANDALL JOHNSON. Judgment is granted to the Pltf for £4.4.7 half penny with Costs & a Lawyer's Fee.

Suit on Petition. BARTRAM EWELL, Gent. agt. WILLIAM POTTER. Judgment is granted the Pltf for £2.7.11 three farthings with Costs & a Lawyer's Fee.

Ordered that BARTRAM EWELL pay WILLIAM CARR 415 pounds of Tobacco for seven days attendance as an Evidence for him against WILLIAM POTTER & for coming & returning 20 Miles four times.

Action of Debt. THOMAS & ROBERT DUNLOPS agt. AMOS & WILLIAM MATHENY. The Defts not appearing Judgment is granted the Pltfs against them & THOMAS MATHENY their Security unless the Defts do appear at the next Court & answer the Pltf's Action.

Action of Debt. THOMAS & ROBERT DUNLOPS agt. JAMES MATHENY. The Deft not appearing Judgment is granted the Pltfs against him & ROBERT DULIN his Security unless the Deft do appear at the next Court & answer the Pltf's Action.

Action of Debt. THOMAS & ROBERT DUNLOPS agt. WILLIAM MATHENY. The Deft not appearing Judgment is granted the Pltfs against him & THOMAS MATHENY his Security unless the Deft do appear at the next Court & answer the Pltf's Action.

Action of Debt. THOMAS & ROBERT DUNLOPS agt. JOB SIMS. The Deft not appearing Judgment is granted the Pltfs against him & GERARD FOWKE, Gent. his Security unless the Deft do appear at the next Court & answer the Pltf's Action.

Action of Trespass. THOMAS & ROBERT DUNLOPS agt. JAMES YELTON. The Deft confessed Judgment to the Pltfs for £2.19.7 half penny & Costs.

Action of Debt. THOMAS & ROBERT DUNLOPS agt. RICHARD BROOKS. The Deft not appearing an Attachment is granted him against the Deft's estate for £14.4.8 half penny with Interest from the first day of January

December Court 1753

1753 till paid & the Costs.

Action of Debt. THOMAS & ROBERT DUNLOPS agt. RICHARD BROOKS. BENJAMIN ROBINSON, EDWARD BETHEL, & GEORGE RANDALL came into Court & undertook that if the Deft should be condemned in this Action that they would pay the Condemnation for him or surrender his Body to Prison, whereupon the Pltf hath a special Imparlance granted him till the next Court.

Action of Debt. CHARLES STUART & COMPANY agt. SNODALL HORTON, Junr. The Deft not appearing, Judgment is granted the Pltf against him & WILLIAM HORTON his Security unless the Deft appear at the next Court and answer the Pltf's Action.

Action of Debt. WILLIAM BLACK agt. RAWLEIGH CHINN, JAMES CHINN and JOSEPH CHINN. The Defts not appearing, Judgment is granted the Pltf against them & CAIN WITHERS their Security unless the Deft appear at the next Court and answer the Pltf's Action.

Action of Debt. WILLIAM BLACK agt. RAWLEIGH CHINN, Senr. The Deft failing to give Special Bail was committed to the Sheriff's Custody & in Custody confessed Judgment to the Pltf for £9.7.4 & Costs. But this Judgment is to be discharged (the Costs excepted) on Payment of £4.13.8 with Interest from the first day of October 1749 till the same is paid.

Action of Debt. WILLIAM BLACK agt. RAWLEIGH CHINN, Senr. The Deft failing to give Special Bail was committed to the Sheriff's Custody & in Custody confessed Judgment to the Pltf for £22.15.7 half penny & Costs. But this Judgment is to be discharged the Costs excepted on Payment of £11.7.9 farthing with Interest from the first day of June 1752 till the same is paid.

WILLIAM WATSON came into Court and agreed to serve his Master PETER ROUT two Years after his time by Indenture is expired in Consideration thereof the said Rout doth oblige himself to teach the said Watson the Trade of a Weaver.

[Page 242 Mar. 12, 1754]

March Court 1754

which agreement the Court approved of.

Ordered that WILLIAM COLE serve his Master DARBY OCAIN for three days runaway time & 90 pounds of Tobacco expended in taking him up.

Then the Court adjoured till tomorrow moring 9 Oclock.

JOHN MERCER

At a Court held for Stafford County 12th. March 1754.

Present   MOTT DONIPHAN   JOHN PEYTON
                  PETER DANIEL   THOMAS FITZHUGH
                  JOHN STUART

PETER a negro Boy belonging to MOTT DONIPHAN is adjudged to be 13 years old.

RICHARD FRISTOE on his Petition is set Levy free.

Ordered that the Sheriff summon 24 of the most able Freeholders of this County to appear at May Court to be of the Grand jury for the Body of this County.

Present JOHN MERCER & HENRY FITZHUGH, Gent.

Administration on the Estate of JOHN SMITH is granted CATHARINE SMITH she having entered into Bond with JAMES HANSBROUGH & DAVID ARCHIBALD her Securities. THOMAS SEDDON, WILLIAM MATHEWS, CHARLES BENSON, & JOHN GRANT Appraisers.

Present FRANCIS THORNTON, WILLIAM FITZHUGH, Gent.

GEORGE WHITECOTTON took the several Oaths & subscribed the Test and abjuration & is admitted under Sheriff of this County.

244

Ordered that GEORGE WALLER & JOB SIMS be added to the Appraisers of HANNAH BAYLIS decd.

Absent JOHN STUART & WILLIAM FITZHUGH

Administration on the Estate of THOMAS LACY decd. is granted ALEXANDER DUGLASS he having entered into bond with NATHANIEL PRICE & WILLIAM YOUNG his Securities. ROBERT YATES, HENRY SMITH & JACOB JOHNSON Appraisers.

Absent FRANCIS THORNTON, HENRY FITZHUGH

Administration on the Estate of JOHN OGLE is granted JOHN BROWN he having entered into bond with JACOB WILLIAMS & WILLIAM DAVIS his Securities. THOMAS BUNBURY, THOMAS BUNBURY, Junr., & JOHN ALEXANDER Appraisers.

BENJAMIN ASHBY on his Petition is set Levy free.

Present HENRY FITZHUGH

Action of Trespass. WILLIAM ROWLEY, Gent. agt. RAWLEIGH CHINN, Junr. & JAMES CHINN. The Defts confessed Judgment to the Pltf for £19.0.6 three farthings

[Page 243 Mar. 12, 1754]

March Court 1754

& Costs.

Action of Debt. WILLIAM BLACK agt. JOHN INGLISH. The Deft not appearing Judgment is granted the Pltfs against him & ROBERT INGLISH his Security unless the Deft do appear at the next Court & answer the Pltf's Action.

Action of Debt. WILLIAM YOUNG agt. JOHN THOMAS. The Deft not appearing Judgment is granted the Pltfs against him & WITHERS CONWAY his Security unless the Deft do appear at the next Court & answer the Pltf's Action.

Action of Debt. JOHN CLARK, agt. DARBY OCAIN. The Deft not appearing Judgment is granted the Pltfs against him & RICHARD OCAIN his Security unless the Deft do appear at the next Court & answer the Pltf's Action.

Action of Debt. MARGARET FRENCH, Admx. of MASON FRENCH decd. agt. OSWOULD CHRISTMOND & ALEXANDER DOUGLASS. The Defts confessed Judgment to the Pltf for £8 & Costs.

Action of Debt. CHARLES CARTER, Esqr. agt. JOHN THOMAS. The Deft confessed Judgment to the Pltf for £19.12 & Costs.

Suit on Petition. ALLEN MCRAE agt. JOHN CHINN. Judgment is granted the Pltf for 481 pounds of Tobacco with Costs & a Lawyer's Fee.

Suit on Petition. Messrs. DUNMORE & COMPANY agt. WILLIAM EATON. Judgment is granted the Pltf against him for 460 lbs. of crop Tobacco with Costs & a Lawyer's Fee. But this Judgment is to be discharged on payment of 230 lbs. of like Tobacco with Interest from the third day of May 1750 till paid.

Suit on Petition. Reverd. DAVID STUART, Clerk agt. JOHN GRIGSBY. Judgment is granted the Pltf for 25 Shillings & Costs.

Suit on Petition. MICHAEL WALLACE agt. JAMES YELTON.

March Court 1754

Judgment is granted the Pltf for £3.18 & Costs. But this Judgment is to be discharged on payment of £1.19 with Interest thereon from the 11th day of May 1752 till the same is paid.

Suit on Petition. MARY ELKIN Admrx. of RICHARD ELKIN agt. WILLIAM TODD & RICHARD BRIAN. Judgment is granted the Pltf for £2.3 with Interest thereon from the 13th day of December 1751 till the same is paid with Costs & a Lawyer's Fee.

Suit on Petition. ALLEN MCRAE agt. SAMUEL ANGEL. Judgment is granted the Pltf for £4.6.3 with Costs & a Lawyer's Fee.

Ordered that ALLEN MCRAE pay WILLIAM CARR 340 pounds to Tobo. for four days attendance as an Evidence for him against ANGEL & for coming & returning 20 Miles four times.

Suit on Petition. MOSELY BATTALEY Gent. agt. FRANCIS DADE. Judgment is granted the Pltf for £4.6.8 & Costs.

Suit on Petition. EDWARD & ROBERT MAXWELLS & COMPANY agt. JOHN GREEN, junr. Judgment is granted the Pltfs for £4.12 & an half penny & Costs.

Suit on Petition. EDWARD & ROBERT MAXWELLS & COMPANY agt. WILLIAM FOSTER. Judgment is granted the Pltfs for £1.18.9 & Costs.

Suit on Petition. EDWARD & ROBERT MAXWELLS & COMPANY agt. JOHN NUMA. Judgment is granted the Pltfs for £1.11.11 & Costs.

Suit on Petition. EDWARD & ROBERT MAXWELLS & COMPANY agt. ARTHUR DENT. Judgment is granted the Pltfs for 885 pounds of Tobacco & Costs.

Suit on Petition. THOMAS TURNER, EDWARD DISON, JOHN TAYLOE, & THOMAS JETT, Exors. of the last Will & Testament of HARRY TURNER decd. agt. N_____. Judgment is granted the Pltfs for £4.15 three farthings with Costs & a Lawyer's Fee.

Suit on Petition. SAMUEL EARLE Gent. agt. WILLIAM FOSTER. Judgment is granted the Pltf for £4.19 & Costs.

Action of Trespass. WILLIAM ROWLEY, Gent. agt. RAWLEIGH CHINN, Senr. The Deft confessed Judgment to the Pltf for £7.13 & one farthing & Costs.

Suit on Petition. SUSANNA TURLAND, Exex. of the last Will & Testament of WILLIAM TURLAND decd. agt. PETER MURPHY. Judgment is granted the Pltf for £3.1.9 with Costs & a Lawyer's Fee.

Then the Court adjourned till tomorrow morning 9 Oclock.
JOHN MERCER

[Page 245 Mar. 13, 1753]

March Court 1754

At a Court continued & held for Stafford County 13th. March 1754.

Present	JOHN MERCER	MOTT DONIPHAN
	JOHN PEYTON	PETER DANIEL
	HENRY FITZHUGH	THOMAS FITZHUGH
	JOHN STUART	

Action of Trespass. EDWARD & ROBERT MAXWELLS & COMPANY agt. WILLIAM KANADY is dismist the Deft paying Costs.

Action of Trespass Assault & Battery. MARY YOUNG agt. GEORGE BUSSELL. The Pltf failing to prosecute she is nonsuited & ordered to pay the Deft's damages according to Law & Costs.

Action of Trespass. MARY YOUNG agt. GEORGE BUSSELL. The Pltf failing to prosecute she is nonsuited & ordered to pay the Deft's damages according to Law & Costs.

ADAM STEPHEN in open Court discharged his Servant THOMAS PAGE from his Service & the said Thomas also acknowledged that he had received full satisfaction for his freedom dues.

Suit on Petition. SAMUEL THORNBURY, junr. agt. WILLIAM DERHAM. Judgment is granted the Pltf for £3.8.9 & Costs.

Action of Debt. Messrs. STUART & ARMOUR agt. EDWARD TEMPLEMAN. The Deft confessed Judgment to the Pltfs for £40 & Costs. But this Judgment is to be discharged on payment of £20 with Interest thereon from the 20th day of December 1751 till the same is paid.

Action of Debt. Messrs. STUART & ARMOUR agt. VALENTINE HUDSON & DANIEL FRENCH. The Defts confessed Judgment to the Pltfs for 3,600 pounds of crop Tobacco & Costs. But this Judgment is to be discharged on payment of 1,800 pounds of like Tobacco with Interest from the 20th day of December 1751 till paid.

Action of Debt. Messrs. STUART & ARMOUR agt. WILLIAM SEBASTIAN & ANN ALLENTHORP. The Defts confessed Judgment to the Pltfs for 6,800 pounds of crop Tobacco & Costs.

[Page 246 Mar. 13, 1754]

March Court 1754

But this Judgment is to be discharged on payment of 3,400 pounds of like Tobacco with Interest thereon from the 20th day of December 1751 till paid. Endorsed on the Bond 28th April 1752. WILLIAM SEBASTIAN paid 934 lb. crop Tobo.
ANN ALLENTHORP paid 1504 nett.
      Do. paid me   __96__
               1600   Transfer in full for her part.

Action of Debt. Messrs. STUART & ARMOUR agt. ALEXANDER DOUGLASS. An Attachment is granted the Pltfs against his Estate for £15 & Costs.

Action of Debt. Messrs. STUART & ARMOUR agt. WILLIAM GREENLEASE. HAYWOOD TODD came into Court and undertook that if the Deft should be condemned in this action that he would pay the Condemnation for him or surrender his body to Prison, & the Deft prayed Oyer &c which is granted him.

Action of Debt. THOMAS CUNNINGHAME agt. JOHN THOMAS. The Deft not appearing Judgment is granted the Pltfs against him & WITHERS CONWAY his Security unless the Deft do appear at the next Court & answer the Pltf's Action.

Action of Debt. Messrs. STUART & ARMOUR agt. WILLIAM PATTEN & GEORGE RANDALL. The Defts confessed Judgment to the Pltfs for £18 & Costs. But this Judgment is to be discharged on payment of £9.6.4 with Interest from the first day of September 1751 till paid & upon JOHN PEYTON Gent. becoming security Pltfs agree to stay execution three Months.

In the Suit on Attachment obtained by WILLIAM ROWLEY Gent. against the Estate of JOHN WHITCOMB the said Rowley produced an Account against the said John for 739 pounds of Tobacco & 15 Shillings. And the Sheriff having returned the Attachment executed on some Corn fodder & hanging Tobacco, it's ordered that the Sheriff sell the same & satisfy the above Judgment & report to the next Court.

[Page 247 Mar. 13, 1754]

March Court 1754

Suit on Petition. WILLIAM THOMAS agt. LAWRENCE WASHINGTON. Judgment is granted the Pltf for £2.10 & one farthing & Costs.

Suit on Petition. WILLIAM ALLEN agt. THOMAS MATHENY. Judgment is granted the Pltf for 500 pounds of Tobacco & Costs.

Suit on Petition. ALEXANDER WHITMAN agt. HUMPHREY POPE. Judgment is granted the Pltf for £3.8 & Costs.

Suit on Petition. JOHN LEE & TRAVERSE COOKE, Gent. Churchwardens of Overwharton Parish agt. JOHN RAMY. Judgment is granted the Pltf for £2.3 & Costs.

249

Action of Trespass. GEORGE LONG agt. GEORGE PILCHER. The Pltf failing to prosecute his suit he is nonsuited and ordered to pay the Deft damages according to Law & Costs.

Ordered that WILLIAM ALLEN pay DANIEL MASON 75 pounds of Tobacco for three days attendance as an evidence for him against MATHENY.

Suit in Chancery. JOHN PEYTON, Gent. Guardian to LETTICE LYNTON, Orphan of JOHN LYNTON, decd. agt. JOHN RAMY. By Consent of the Parties all matters in difference between them are referred to the determination of the Reverend JOHN MONCURE & PETER HEDGMAN, Gent. & their award is to be made the Judgment of the Court.

HONOR GLASS being presented by the Grand jury for having a Bastard Child & failing to appear it's ordered that she pay to the Church wardens of Overwharton for the use of the Poor of the said Parish 50 Shillings current Money or 500 pounds of Tobacco & Cask with Costs & a Lawyer's Fee.

SARAH PESTRIDGE being presented by the grand jury for having a Bastard Child & failing to appear it's ordered that she pay to the Church wardens of Overwharton for the use of the Poor of the said Parish 50 Shillings current Money or 500 pounds of Tobacco & Cask with Costs & a Lawyer's Fee.

Suit on Petition. WILLIAM BLACKWELL, Gent. agt. JOHN PEYTON. Judgment is granted the Pltf for £2.3 & 360 pounds of Tobacco with Costs & a Lawyer's Fee.

Ordered that WILLIAM BLACKWELL pay THOMAS SEMAN 255 pounds of Tobacco for three days attendance as an evidence for him against Peyton & for coming & returning 30 Miles twice.

Suit on Petition. ANDREW EDWARDS agt. WILLIAM BARTLETT. Judgment is granted the Pltf for 528 pounds of Tobacco & Costs.

[Page 248 Mar. 13, 1754]

March Court 1754

Suit on Petition. JOHN READ agt. ABRAHAM FLETCHER. Judgment is granted the Pltf for £2.1.6 & Costs.

Suit on Petition. WILLIAM HORNBUCKLE agt. EDWARD GILL. Judgment is granted the Pltf for £3.2.6 & Costs.

Suit on Petition. ANDREW EDWARDS agt. WILLIAM PICKETT. Judgment is granted the Pltf for £2.10 & Costs.

Action of Trespass. JOHN CHAMP, Esqr. agt. RAWLEIGH CHINN. The Deft confessed Judgment to the Pltf for £40.13.3 & Costs. And by GEORGE RINGLESBY'S coming into Court & becoming Security for the Deft the Pltf by his Attorney agreed to stay Execution twelve Months for the same.

Action of Trespass. ROBERT WICKLIFF agt. WILLIAM PICKETT. The Deft not appearing Judgment is granted the Pltfs against him & ANDREW KENNY his Security unless the Deft do appear at the next Court & answer the Pltf's Action.

Action of Trespass Assault & Battery. WILLIAM SUDDOTH agt. JOHN PEYTON. The Pltf failing to prosecute his Suit he is nonsuited & ordered to pay the Deft damages according to Law & Costs.

In the Suit on Attachment obtained by JOHN PEYTON, Gent. against CHARLES HOPKINS, CHARLES HARDING the Garnishee declares he has nineteen pounds of Tobacco of the estate of the said Hopkins in his Hands.

In the Suit on the Attachment obtained by WILLIAM BLACK against the Estate of SOLOMON WAUGH, WILLIAM GARRARD, the Garnishee declared he had 273 pounds of Tobacco of the Estate of the said Solomon in his Hands.

Suit on Petition. JOHN PEYTON agt. ROBERT INGLISH. Judgment is granted the Pltf for 40 Shillings & Costs.

Suit on Petition. JOHN RAMY agt. JOHN PEYTON, Gent., Admr. of the Goods & Chattels, Rights & Credits of JOHN LYNTON decd. Judgment is granted the Pltf for £1.15.3.

[Page 249 Mar. 13, 1754]

March Court 1754

Suit on Petition. WILLIAM NORTHCUT agt. ARTHUR DUAS. Judgment is granted the Pltf for 450 pounds of Tobacco & Costs.

Action of Debt. WILLIAM CUNNINGHAM Admr. of THOMAS MCREADY agt. JOHN ARMSTRONG. The Deft not appearing Judgment is granted the Pltfs against him & JOHN MERCER, Gent. his Security unless the Deft do appear at the next Court & answer the Pltf's Action.

Suit of Trespass. THOMAS & ROBERT DUNLOPS agt. JOHN ARMSTRONG. The Deft not appearing Judgment is granted the Pltfs against him & JOHN MERCER, Gent. his Security unless the Deft do appear at the next Court & answer the Pltf's Action.

In the Suit on the Attachment obtained by HENRY PONTSON agt. RICHARD WEAVER, JOHN MURPHY & JAMES HILL two of the Garnishees appeared & declared that they had nothing of the Estate of the said Weaver in their Hands & an Attachment is ordered against the other Garnishee returnable to the next Court.

Action of Detinue. DAVID MCQUALTY agt. ELIZABETH MCABOY. A Jury to wit ROBERT WASHINGTON, JOHN FITZHUGH, GOWRY WAUGH, SAMUEL SELDEN, THOMAS BUNBURY, Junr., WILLIAM ETHERINGTON, ROBERT ASHBY, BENJAMIN MASSEY, JOHN WITHERS, WILLIAM HORTON, SAMUEL EARLE & ANDREW EDWARDS. The Jury finds for the Deft.

Action of Trespass. HARRY PIPER agt. JEREMIAH CARTER. JOSEPH CARTER Security for the Deft for Plea saith that the Deft did not assume. The Trial is referred till the next Court.

Action of Debt. HARRY PIPER, Assignee of JACKSON agt. JEREMIAH CARTER. JOSEPH CARTER Security for the Deft for Plea saith that the Deft did not assume. The Trial is referred till the next Court.

Ordered that DAVID MCQUALTY pay WILLIAM NORTHCUT 275 pounds of Tobacco for eleven days attendance as an Evidence for him against MCABOY.

[Page 250 Mar. 13, 1754]

March Court 1754

Ordered that DAVID MCQUALTY pay MARGARET NORTHCUT 275 pounds of Tobacco for eleven days attendance as an Evidence for him against MCABOY.

Ordered that DAVID MCQUALTY pay BENJAMIN ASBURY 150 pounds of Tobacco for 14 days attendance as an Evidence for him against MCABOY.

Ordered that ELIZABETH MCABOY pay ANN GRAY 350 pounds of Tobacco for 14 days attendance as an Evidence for her at Suit of MCQUALTY.

Ordered that ELIZABETH MCABOY pay WILLIAM CORBIN 250 pounds of Tobacco for ten days attendance as an Evidence for her at Suit of MCQUALTY.

Ordered that ELIZABETH MCABOY pay WILLIAM WALKER 430 pounds of Tobacco for ten days attendance as an Evidence for her at Suit of MCQUALTY & for coming & returning 30 Miles twice.

Action of Trespass. RICHARD BERNARD Gent. agt. JOHN SYLVIA. A Jury to wit ROBERT WASHINGTON, JOHN FITZHUGH, GOWRY WAUGH, SAMUEL SELDON, THOMAS BUNBURY, Junr., WILLIAM ETHERINGTON, ROBERT ASHBY, BENJAMIN MASSEY, JOHN WITHERS, WILLIAM HORTON, SAMUEL EARLE, & ANDREW EDWARDS. The Jury finds for the Pltf for 1,590 and half pounds of Tobacco & Costs.

Action of Debt. JOHN WEATHERS agt. MOURNING RICHARDS. The Deft for Plea saith that he hath paid the debt. The Trial is referred till the next Court.

The Suit on Attachment obtained by WILLIAM ROWLEY, Gent. against the estate of STEPHEN PILCHER is dismist the said Stephen paying Costs.

Action of Debt. WILLIAM BLACK agt. JAMES CHINN, JOSEPH CHINN & RAWLEIGH CHINN. The Defts confessed Judgment for £37.8.11 half penny & Costs. But this Judgment is to be discharged on payment of £18.14.5 with Interest thereon from the first day of June 1752 till the same is paid.

[Page 251 Mar. 13, 1754]

March Court 1754

Ordered that when any Suit shall be continued at either Party's Costs such Suit shall stand so continued at such Party's Costs till called again.

Then the Court adjourned till tomorrow morning 9 Oclock.
                                                    JOHN MERCER

At a Court continued and held for Stafford County 14th. March 1754.

Present   MOTT DONIPHAN   JOHN PEYTON
               HENRY FITZHUGH   THOMAS FITZHUGH
               JOHN STUART

Action of Debt. WILLIAM PICKETT agt. RICHARD BROOKS. The Pltf failing to prosecute his Suit he is nonsuited & ordered to pay the Deft damages according to Law & Costs.

Action of Trespass. WILLIAM PICKETT agt. MARK KENTON is dismist the Pltf paying Costs.

Action of Trespass. ROBERT MASSEY, Gent. agt. JACOB JOHNSON. The Errors filed in this Cause being argued are adjudged good. It's therefore considered by the Court that the Judgment be arrested and that the Deft recover of the Pltf his Costs.

Suit in Chancery. MICHAEL HALL agt. GRACE BERRY is dismist & the Complainant is ordered to pay the Deft her Costs.

Action of Trespass. WILLIAM MOUNTJOY agt. GEORGE GENT. The Errors filed in this Cause being argued are adjudged good. It's thereupon considered by the Court that the Judgment be arrested & that the Deft recover of the said Pltf his Costs.

Action of Debt. ANDREW COCHRANE & COMPANY agt. ADAM STEPHEN. The Demurrer joined in the Cause being argued is overruled and the Plea of the Deft adjudged good. It's thereupon considered by the Court that the Pltfs take nothing by their Bill & that the Deft recover of the said Pltfs his Costs.

[Page 252 Mar. 14, 1754]

March Court 1754

JANE WILLIAMS an insolvent debtor in Execution at the suit of DANIEL HANKINS gave into Court a Schedule of her Estate & took the Oath prescribed.

Upon Petition of ROSE CONNER late servant of JAMES CROP it's ordered that the said Crop pay her 15 bushels of Indian Corn & 30 Shillings in Money or Goods & Costs.

Ordered that JAMES CROP pay WILLIAM LUNSFORD 350 pounds of Tobacco for fourteen days attendance as an Evidence for him at Suit of CONNER.

Ordered that ROSE CONNER pay JAMES STUART 275 pounds of Tobacco for eleven days attendance as an Evidence for her against CROP.

Ordered that ROSE CONNER pay MARY STUART 275 pounds of Tobacco for eleven days attendance as an Evidence for her against CROP.

Ordered that ROSE CONNER pay ISBELL SUDDUTH 300 pounds of Tobacco for twelve days attendance as an Evidence for her against CROP.

Action of Debt. PETER ROSS agt. JEREMIAH CARTER. The Deft not appearing upon an Attachment ordered in this Suit it's considered by the Court that the Pltf recover of the said Deft 2060 pounds of crop Tobacco & his Costs. But this Judgment is to be discharged on Payment of 1030 pounds of crop Tobacco with Interest thereon from the 10th day of November 1750 till the same is paid. And the Sheriff having made return on the said Attachment that he had attached one narrow Ax, it's ordered that he sell the same & satisfy the said Peter his Judgment.

Action of Trespass Assault & Battery. JOHN RILEY agt. TRAVERSE COOKE. The Deft for Plea saith he is not guilty. The Tryall is referred till the next Court.

Action of Trespass. FRANCIS MADDEN agt. RICHARD RANDALL. The Deft for Plea saith he is not guilty and hath Time to give the special Matter in Evidence. The Tryal is referred till the next Court.

[Page 253 Mar. 14, 1754]

March Court 1754

Action of Debt. MARGARET PIPER agt. JAMES MAISES. The Deft not appearing Judgment is granted the Pltf against him & the Reverend JOHN MONCURE his Security unless the Deft do appear at the next Court & answer the Pltf's Action.

In the Suit on the Attachment obtained by BENJAMIN STROTHER, Gent. against the Estate of JOHN STACY, the said Benjamin produced an Account against the said John for 313 pounds of Tobacco. It's thereupon considered by the Court that the said Benjamin recover the same & his Costs. And the Sheriff having returned the said Attachment executed in the Hands of JOHN LEE Gent. who acknowledged to have in his Hands of the Estate of the said Stacy 30 Shillings & 7 pence, it's ordered that the Sheriff sell the same & satisfy the said Benjamin his Judgment.

Suit on Petition. JOHN HITE agt. SAMUEL EARLE, Admr. of HANNAH BAYLIS, decd. The Deft for Plea saith he hath fully administered. The Tryal is referred till the next Court.

Suit on Petition. WILLIAM CAMPBELL agt. ROBERT CARTER is dismist & the Pltf is ordered to pay the Deft his Costs.

255

Suit on Scire Facias. GEORGE JOHNSON agt. WILLIAM FITZHUGH, Esqr. & FRANCIS THORNTON, Gent., Exors. of GILSON BERRYMAN decd. The Said William & Francis having pleaded payment & fully administered the said George joined the Issue & the Trial is referred till the next Court.

Action of Debt. ROBERT INGLISH agt. MOURNING RICHARDS. GEORGE BRENT Security for the said Deft having pleaded Payment the Trial is referred till the next Court.

Administration on the Estate of RICHARD BERRY is granted SARAH BERRY, she having entered into Bond with WILLIAM GARRARD & JOHN PEYTON her Securities. HUSBANDFOOTE WHITECOTTON, NATHANIEL GRAY, WILLIAM LIMBRICK, & JAMES JONES Appraisers.

Action of Debt. MICHAEL WALLACE agt. ROBERT GARRARD. The Deft having pleaded payment the Tryal is referred till the next Court.

[Page 254 Mar. 14, 1754]

March Court 1754

Action of Trespass Assault & Battery & false Imprisonment. JOHN FITZPATRICK agt. CHARLES HARDING. The Deft for Plea saith he is not guilty. The Tryal is referred till the next Court.

Action of Trespass. JAMES STUART & MARY his Wife agt. ANN WILLIAMS. The Deft having pleaded not guilty the Trial is referred till the next Court.

Ejection Firma. John Seekright Assignee of MAXIMILLIAM ROBINSON agt. JOHN RALLS. The Deft having pleaded not guilty confessed Lease, Entry, & Ouster & agreed to insist only on the Title at Tryal, & the Trial is referred till the next Court.

Action of Trespass Assault & Battery. ANN BRUMLY agt. JAMES STUART & MARY his wife. The Defts having pleaded not guilty the trial is referred till the next Court.

Ejection Firma. John Seekright, Lessee of JOHN SMITH & JENNET his Wife, MARGARETT ORR, & BETHIA ORR agt. WILLIAM GREENLEESE by WILLIAM BERNARD his Attorney entered himself Deft in the Room of James Thrustout pleaded not guilty, confessed Lease, Entry, & Ouster & agreed to insist only on the Title at Tryal, & the Trial thereof is referred till the next Court.

Action of Trespass Assault & Battery. WILLIAM JONES agt. WILLIAM DAVIS. The Deft having pleaded not guilty the Trial thereof is referred till the next Court.

Suit on Petition. JOHN MCCULLOUGH agt. WILLIAM DAVIS is dismist & the Pltf his Costs by him about his defence in this behalf expended [*sic*].

Action of Trespass. ROBERT & EDWARD MAXWELLS agt. CUTHBERT BYRAM. The Deft not appearing the Judgment against him & PETER BYRAM his Security is confirmed & a Writ of Enquiry of damages is to be executed the next Court.

Ordered that WILLIAM DAVIS pay WILLIAM JONES 100 pounds of Tobacco

[Page 255 Mar. 14, 1754]

March Court 1754

for four days attendance as an Evidence for him at Suit of MCCULLOUGH.

Action of Trespass. WILLIAM HOWARD agt. RICHARD HEWITT. The Deft for Plea saith he is not guilty, & hath Leave to give the special Matter in Evidence. The Tryal is referred till the next Court.

Action of Trespass. WILLIAM HOWARD agt. ELIZABETH HARRIS. The Deft for Plea saith that she is not guilty & hath Leave to give the special Matter in Evidence. The Trial is referred till the next Court.

Action of Trespass Assault & Battery. FRANCIS BROOX agt. DARBY OCAIN. The Deft for Plea saith that he is not guilty. The Trial is referred till the next Court.

THOMAS GARNER being brought before this Court for Felony & examined with the Witnesses he is ordered to the Goal for an examining Court on Friday the 22d Instant.

BAILY WASHINGTON & MOSES LUNSFORD acknowledged themselves indebted to our Lord the King in the sum of £20 each in Case they fail to appear at the Courthouse of this County on the 22d of this Instant to give Evidence against THOMAS GARNER.

Ejection Firma. Thomas Turff agt. HENRY FITZHUGH for Lands & Appurtenances in the Parish of Overwharton which HENRY TYLER demised to the Pltf for a Term &c. It's ordered that the Surveyor go on the land in dispute & lay off the same as either Party would have it having regard to all Patents &

257

Evidences as shall be offered by either Party. And the Sheriff is to attend the Survey to remove force if any offered & the Surveyor is to return three fair Platts to the Clerk's Office in due Time before the Day of hearing.

Action of Debt. EDWARD CONNER agt. DARBY OCAIN. The Deft not appearing the Judgment against him & BENJAMIN STROTHER his Security is confirmed to the Pltf for 4000 pounds of Tobacco

[Page 256 Mar. 14, 1754]

March Court 1754

and Cash. It's thereupon considered by the Court that the Pltf recover same of the Deft & the said Benjamin & his Costs. But this Judgment is to be discharged on Payment of 2000 pounds of Tobacco & Cask with Interest thereon from the 15th day of April 1752 till the same is paid.

Action of Debt. GEORGE BUCHANAN & WILLIAM HAMILTON agt. RAWLEIGH CHINN Senr. The Deft not appearing the Judgment against him and LAURENCE SUDDUTH his Security is confirmed to the Pltf for £45.4.6 & Costs. But this Judgment is to be discharged on Payment of £22.12.3 with Interest thereon from the first day of August 1752 till the same is paid.

Action of Trespass. ABRAM BREDWELL agt. ROBERT ASHBY. The Deft for plea saith that he is not guilty & hath leave to give the special Matter in Evidence. The Trial is referred till the next Court.

Action of Trespass. WILLIAM BREDWELL agt. ROBERT ASHBY. The Deft for Plea saith that he is not guilty & hath leave to give the special Matter in Evidence. The Trial is referred till the next Court.

Action of Debt. EDWARD MUSE agt. JEREMIAH CARTER. The Deft not appearing Judgment is granted the Pltf against him & JOSEPH CARTER his Security unless the Deft do appear at the next Court & answer the Pltf's Action.

Action of Trespass. TRAVERSE COOKE agt. JOHN FARROW. The Deft for Plea saith that he is not guilty & the Trial is referred till the next Court.

Action of Debt. WILLIAM CUNNINGHAME agt. SOLOMON WAUGH. The Deft failing to appear Judgment is granted the Pltf against him for £27.4.4.

March Court 1754

It's therefore ordered that the Pltf recover the same of the said Deft & his Costs.

Ordered that STEPHEN LATHAM pay WILLIAM EATON 100 pounds of Tobacco for four days attendance as an evidence for him against SYLVIA.

Action of Trespass. THOMAS HORNBUCKLE agt. SAMUEL GRIGSBY. The Deft having filed his plea the Pltf hath time till the next Court to consider thereof.

Action of Trespass Assault & Battery. GERARD BANKS agt. SAMUEL GRIGSBY. The Deft having filed his plea the Pltf hath time till the next Court to consider thereof.

Then the Court adjourned till tomorrow Morning 9 Oclock.
JOHN MERCER

At a Court continued & held for Stafford County 15th. March 1754.

Present   JOHN MERCER   PETER DANIEL
             HENRY FITZHUGH   THOMAS FITZHUGH

Action of Debt. ROBERT WALKER agt. WILLIAM FITZHUGH & FRANCIS THORNTON Gent., Exors. of GILSON BERRYMAN decd. The Said William & Francis having pleaded payment & fully administered the said George joined the Issue & the Trial thereof is referred till the next Court.

Action of Trespass. ALEXANDER BROWN agt. WILLIAM FITZHUGH, Esqr. & FRANCIS THORNTON Gent., Exors. of GILSON BERRYMAN decd. The Defts for pleas saith the Testator did not assume. The Tryall is referred till the next Court.

Ejection Firma. Timothy Turff agt. Titus Twigg for Lands & Appurtenances in the Parish of Overwharton which JOHN MAUZY, junr. demised to the Pltf for a Term &c. LYNAUGH HOLMS being admitted Deft in the Room of the said Titus Twigg pleaded not guilty, confessed Lease, Entry & Ouster & agreed to insist only on the Title at Tryal & the Trial is referred till the next Court & thereupon the Pltf moving that the bounds of the said Land may be ascertained before the Trial it's ordered that the Surveyor of WESTMORELAND COUNTY in Company of an able Jury of Freeholders do go upon the said Land & lay off the same.

[Page 258 Mar. 15, 1754]

March Court 1754

Ejection Firma. Thomas Turff agt. THOMAS SEDDON for Lands & Appurtenances in the Parish of Overwharton which HENRY FITZHUGH, Esqr. demised to the Pltf for a Term &c. It's ordered that the Surveyor of the said County in Company of an able Jury of Freeholders go upon the said Lands & lay off the same.

Present MOTT DONIPHAN, JOHN PEYTON, Gent.

Action of Trespass Assault & Battery. ROBERT HILL agt. HUSBANDFOOTE WHITECOTTON is dismist the Pltf paying the Deft his Costs.

Ejection Firma. Solomon Saveall agt. THOMAS VIVION, Gent. for Lands & Appurtenance in the Parish of St. Paul's which BURDITT CLIFTON demised to the Pltf for a Term &c. It's ordered that the Surveyor of the said County in Company of an able Jury of Freeholders go upon the said Lands & survey & lay off the same.

[Page 259 Mar. 15, 1754]

March Court 1754

Action of Trespass. GEORGE WALLER agt. JOHN FITZPATRICK. The Deft having pleaded not guilty the Tryal thereof is referred till the next Court.

Action of Trespass. ANDREW EDWARDS agt. ADAM STEPHEN. The Deft for Plea saith he did not assume. The Tryal thereof is referred till the next Court.

Action of Trespass. CHARLES HARDING agt. SAMUEL EARLE. The Deft for Plea saith that he did not assume. The Tryal thereof is referred till the next Court.

JOHN FENTON MERCER, Gent. having applied to the Court to recommend him to his Honor the Governor for such a Commission in the Forces now listing in this colony as his Honor the Governor think him qualified for, the Court unanimously recommend him to his Honor being of Opinion that he will behave himself with diligence & resolution & that his Brothers serving in those Forces will be a Means of encouraging several Persons to inlist as they are very well respected in this & the adjoining Counties.

Action of Trespass. MATHEW BOGLE & COMPANY agt. JOHN HITCHING. The Deft not appearing the Judgment against him & WILLIAM SWETMAN, his Security is confirmed.

Action of Debt. WILLIAM ROWLEY, Gent. agt. JOHN JAMES. The Deft not appearing the Judgment against him & ROGER HILL & MARY MURRY his Securities is confirmed for 2274 pounds of crop Tobacco & Costs. But this Judgment is to be discharged on Payment of 1137 pounds of like Tobacco with Interest thereon from the 20th day of April 1752 till the same is paid.

Action of Trespass Assault & Battery. JOHN MATTHEWS agt. JOHN ENGLISH. The Deft for plea saith he is not guilty. The Trial thereof is referred till the next Court.

Action of Trespass Assault & Battery. JOHN CANADY agt. DANIEL CHAMBERS.

[Page 260 Mar. 15, 1754]

March Court 1754

The Deft for Plea saith he is not guilty. The Tryal is referred till the next Court.

Action of Trespass. GOWRY WAUGH agt. RAWLEIGH CHINN, junr. The Pltf failing to prosecute his Suit he is nonsuited & ordered to pay the Deft damages & Costs.

Action of Trespass Assault & Battery. MOSES GRIGSBY agt. DANIEL CHAMBERS. The Deft for Pleas saith he is not guilty. The Trial thereof is referred till the next Court.

Action of Trespass. PAUL SWENY agt. WILLIAM ROSE. The Demurrer in this Cause being joined is to be argued the next Court.

Action of Debt. CAIN WITHERS agt. PRESLY COX is dismist the Deft paying Costs.

Action of Trespass. CAIN WITHERS agt. PRESLY COX. The Deft having filed his Plea the Pltf hath time till the next Court to consider thereof.

Action of Trespass. ANTHONY STROTHER agt. BENJAMIN SELMAN. The Deft not appearing the Judgment against him & ROBERT ENGLISH,

THOMAS WEATHERS & WILLIAM GARRARD his Securities is confirmed & a Writ of Enquiry of damages is to be executed the next Court.

Action of Trespass Assault & Battery. JOHN FITZPATRICK agt. JOB SIMS. The Pltf failing to prosecute his Action he is nonsuited & ordered to pay the Deft damages & Costs.

Action of Trespass. MATTHEW BOGLE & COMPANY agt. JAMES CONWELL. The Deft not appearing the Judgment against him & THOMAS MADDOX his Security is confirmed & a Writ of Enquiry of damages is to be executed the next Court.

Action of Trespass. JOSEPH PORTER agt. CATHERINE WATERS. The Deft for Plea saith that she is not guilty with Leave to give the special Matter in Evidence. The Trial is referred till the next Court.

Suit on Petition. ANDREW EDWARDS & BETTY his Wife Admrs. of JAMES WAUGH, Gent. agt. PRESLY COX & ELIZABETH his Wife & WILLIAM DENT, Exors. of THOMAS DENT decd. Judgment is granted the Pltfs for £4.9 of the Goods & Chattels which were of the said Thomas in the hands of the said Defts

[Page 261 Mar. 15, 1754]

March Court 1754

In the Suit on Attachment obtained by ALEXANDER BROWN against the Estate of BENNETT ROSE, ordered that an Attachment issue against the Garnishees returnable to the next Court.

In the Suit on Attachment obtained by BENJAMIN MASSEY against the Estate of JOHN DUNBAR. JOHN THOMAS one of the Garnishees failing to appear it's ordered that an Attachment issue against him returnable to the next Court.

Action of Debt. JOHN PEYTON, Gent. Assignee of HENRY SUDDUTH agt. JEREMIAH CARTER. The Deft not appearing upon an Attachment in this Suit, Judgment is granted the Pltf against him for £10.19.2 & Costs. The Sheriff having made return that he has attached a Grind stone & iron pot, ordered that he sell the same & satisfy the above Judgment.

Action of Debt. MARY WISE agt. JOHN PEYTON. The Deft having pleaded not guilty the Trial is referred till the next Court.

Action of Trespass. JOSEPH PORTER agt. WILLIAM HOWARD. The Deft having pleaded not guilty the Trial thereof is referred till the next Court.

Action of Debt. GEORGE MASON, Esqr. agt. RANDALL JOHNSON. The Deft for his Securities having pleaded payment the Tryal thereof is referred till the next Court.

Action of Debt. JAMES BOYD agt. JOHN MURRY, JOHN MAUZY, WILLIAM HEDGMAN & SAMUEL EARLE. A Plurias Capias is ordered against the said Murray the other Defts having pleaded payment. The Tryal thereof is referred till the next Court.

Action of Debt. WILLIAM CUNNINGHAME & COMPANY agt. ELIAS ASHBY & LEONARD ALVEY. The Defts not appearing on Motion of the Pltf by their Attorney an Attachment is granted them against the Defts Estates for £23 with Interest from the 6th day of February 1752 & Costs.

Action of Detinue. JOHN PEYTON, Gent. agt. JEREMIAH CARTER.

[Page 262 Mar. 15, 1754]

March Court 1754

The Deft for Plea saith he don't detain. The Trial is referred till the next Court.

Action of Debt. WILLIAM HUNTER agt. JOHN HAMILTON, Gent. The Deft confessed Judgment to the Pltf for £28.16 & Costs. But this Judgment is to be discharged on Payment of £14.18.11 with Interest thereon from the 14th day of July 1752 till the same is paid.

In the Suit on the Attachment obtained by JOHN PEYTON, Gent. against the Estate of PETER STACY, the said John produced an Account against the said Peter for £3.19.10. It's thereupon considered by the Court that the said John recover the same & his Costs. And the Sheriff having returned the Attachment executed in the hands of WILLIAM HILL who declared he had two Shillings & six pence of the Estate of the said Peter which Sum he is ordered to pay to the said John in part Satisfaction of the above Judgment.

Action of Debt. JACOB WILLIAMS agt. WILLIAM SCAPLIN. The Deft for his Security having pleaded Payment the Trial is referred till the next Court.

Action of Trespass. ALEXANDER BROWN agt. MICHAEL BLACK is dismist the Deft paying Costs.

In the Suit on the Attachment obtained by ALEXANDER BROWN against the Estate of SOLOMON HARDWICK the conditional Order against JACOB

WILLIAMS one of the Garnishees of the said Solomon is confirmed to the said Alexander for what Estate of the said Solomon's he hath in his Hands.

Suit on Petition. CATHARINE ASHBY by ROBERT ASHBY her next Friend agt. SAMUEL BREDWELL. The Deft having pleaded not guilty the Trial is referred til the next Court.

Action of Debt. CHARLES STUART & COMPANY agt. FRANCIS BROOX.

[Page 263 Mar. 15, 1754]

March Court 1754

GEORGE RANDALL undertook that if the Deft should be condemned in this Action that he the said George would pay the Condemnation for him or surrender his Body to Prison & the Deft on his Motion hath a special Imparlance granted him till the next Court.

Action of Trespass. SAMUEL BREDWELL agt. CHARLES HARDING. The Deft for Plea saith he is not guilty. The Tryal is referred till the next Court.

Action of Debt. JOHN KNOX agt. THOMAS RIDDLE. BENJAMIN ROBINSON undertook that if the said Deft should be condemned in this Action that he would pay the Condemnation for him or surrender his Body to Prison & the said Deft having pleaded payment the Trial is referred till the next Court.

Action of Trespass Assault & Battery. WILLIAM HOWARD agt. DAVID MCQUALTY. The Deft having pleaded not guilty the Tryal is referred till the next Court.

Ejection Firma. Thomas Truman agt. Benjamin Bedright for Lands & Appurtenances in the Parish of Overwharton which JOHN ROUT demised to the Pltf for a Term &c. JOHN PEYTON & GEORGE WALLER acting Exors. of CHARLES WALLER decd. being admitted Defts in the Room of the said Benjamin pleaded not guilty & confessed Lease, Entry & Ouster & agreed to insist only on the Title at Tryal which Issue the Pltf joined & the trial is referred till the next Court. And thereupon the Pltf moving that the bounds of the said Land may be ascertained before the Trial it's ordered that the Surveyor in Company of an able Jury go upon the Lands & lay off the same having regard to all Patents & Evidences as shall be produced by either of the Parties. And the Surveyor is to return three fair Platts & Reports to the Clerk's Office in due time before the day of hearing.

Action of Debt. JOHN GRAHAM agt. HENRY WIGGINTON & ANN PORTER. ABRAHAM BREDWELL undertook that if the said Defts should be condemned in this Action that he the said Abraham would pay the Condemnatnion for them or surrender their Bodies to Prison.

Action of Debt. WILLIAM BLACK agt. BENJAMIN ASBURY. The Deft not appearing an Attachment is granted against the Deft's Estate for £7.19.7 with Interest from the first of June 1752 & Costs.

[Page 264 Mar. 15, 1754]

March Court 1754

Action of Debt. WILLIAM BLACK agt. SAMUEL WHITSON & JOSEPH CARTER. The Deft Whitson having pleaded Payment the Trial is referred till the next Court. And the Deft Carter failing to appear an Attachment is granted against the said Carter's Estate for £6.13 with Interest.

Action of Debt. WILLIAM PATTEN agt. DAVID ASHBY, ROBERT ASHBY junr., & ELIAS ASHBY. The Deft David not appearing an Alias is ordered against him returnable to the next Court & the other Defts having pleaded Payment the Trial is referred till the next Court.

Action of Trespass Assault & Battery. DAVID MCQUALTY agt. WILLIAM HOWARD. The Deft having pleaded not guilty the Trial is referred till the next Court.

Action of Trespass Assault & Battery. GRACE JACKSON agt. WILLIAM HOWARD. The Deft having pleaded not guilty the Trial is referred till the next Court.

Action of Trespass. DARBY OCAIN agt. ISAAC BRIDWELL. The Deft having pleaded not guilty the Trial is referred till the next Court.

Suit on Petition. WILLIAM SCAPELAND agt. BENJAMIN MASSEY. Judgment is granted the Pltf for £1.12.2 farthing & Costs.

Ordered that WILLIAM SCAPELAND pay JOHN HOLLAND 200 pounds of Tobacco for eight days attendance as an Evidence for him agsinst MASSEY.

Ordered that WILLIAM SCAPELAND pay THOMAS BUNBURY, Junr. 325 pounds of Tobacco for thirteen days attendance as an Evidence for him against MASSEY.

Ordered that BENJAMIN MASSEY pay BURGESS SULLIVANT 493 pounds of Tobacco for thirteen days attendance as an evidence for him at suit of SCAPELAND & for coming & returning eight Miles seven times.

Suit in Chancery. WILLIAM FITZHUGH an Infant under the Age of 21 years by CHARLES CARTER & LANDON CARTER Esqrs. his Guardians agt. ROBERT MASSEY. The Deft being dead Time is given the Complainants till the next Court to file their Bill of Revision.

Action of Debt. WILLIAM BLACK agt. MERRIMAN TILLER. The Deft not appearing Judgment against him & GERARD FOWKE, Gent. Sheriff of this County is Confirmed to the Pltf for £5.12.2.

March Court 1754

But this Judgment is to be discharged on Payment of £2.16.1 with Interest thereon from the first day of June 1752 till the same is paid.

Action of Trespass. ROBERT & EDWARD MAXWELLS agt. THOMAS HEATH. The Deft not appearing the Judgment against him & RICHARD HEWITT, his Security unless the Deft do appear at the next Court & answer the Pltf's Action.

Action of Trespass. ROBERT & EDWARD MAXWELLS agt. SAMUEL WHITSON. HENRY TYLER undertook that if the said Deft should be Condemned in this Action that he would pay the Condemnation or surrender his Body to Prison.

Action of Trespass. THOMAS & ROBERT DUNLOPS agt. SNOWDALL HORTON, Senr. The Deft confessed Judgment to the Pltf for _____ [*blank*].

Action of Trespass. THOMAS & ROBERT DUNLOPS agt. WILLIAM HORTON. The Deft for plea saith that he did not assume. The Trial is referred till the next Court.

Action of Debt. THOMAS & ROBERT DUNLOPS agt. AMOS & WILLIAM MATHENY. The Defts not appearing the Judgment against him & THOMAS MATHENY, his Security is confirmed to the Pltfs for £29.10.6 & Costs. But this Judgment is to be discharged on Payment of £14.15.3 with Interest from the first day of June 1752 till the same is paid. Received on the Bond for £6.18.

Action of Debt. THOMAS & ROBERT DUNLOPS agt. JAMES MATHENY. The Defts not appearing the Judgment against him & ROBERT DOOLING, his Security is confirmed to the Pltfs for £26.10.9 & Costs. But this Judgment is to be discharged on Payment of £13.5.4 half penny with Interest

March Court 1754

from the 14th day of December 1751 till the same is paid. Credit on the Bond for £6.5.4 half penny.

Action of Trespass. THOMAS & ROBERT DUNLOPS agt. JOB SIMS. The Deft confessed Judgment to the Pltfs for £17.4.11 & Costs.

Action of Debt. THOMAS & ROBERT DUNLOPS agt. RICHARD BROOX. The Deft not appearing Judgment is granted against him for £28.17.5 & Costs to be discharged on Payment of £14.4.8 half penny with Interest thereon from the first day of January 1752 till the same is paid. And the Sheriff having returned an Attachment said that he had attached two Beds, one green Rug, Counterpain & Sheets it's ordered that he sell the same & satisfy the Pltfs their Judgment. Indorsed on the Bill. Balance £9.1.5.

Action of Debt. CHARLES STUART & COMPANY agt. SNOWDALL HORTON junr. The Deft not appearing Judgment is granted against him & WILLIAM HORTON his Security for £31 & Costs. But this Judgment is to be discharged on Payment of £15.10 with Interest thereon from the 10th day of October 1752 till the same is paid.

JOHN MERCER Gent. is desired to send for Scales for BOYD'S HOLE WAREHOUSE.

Ordered that JOHN WASHINGTON, BAILY WASHINGTON, JOHN STITH, SAMUEL SELDEN, & GOWRY WAUGH be recommended to his Honor the Governor as fit Persons to be added to the Commission of the Peace for this County.

JOHN MERCER, Gent. is desired to wait on his Honor with the Recommendation of Justices & to acquaint his Honor with the state of the County.

Then the Court adjourned till Court in Course.
JOHN MERCER

April Court 1754

At a Court held for Stafford County April 9th. 1754.

Present	MOTT DONIPHAN	JOHN PEYTON
	PETER DANIEL	HENRY FITZHUGH
	THOMAS FITZHUGH	JOHN STUART

HARRY a negro boy belonging to JOHN INGLISH adjudged to be 14 years old.

Ordered that ROBERT CARTER pay CHARLES CARTER 300 pounds of Tobacco for twelve days attendance as an Evidence for him at suit of CAMPBELL.

Ordered that the Churchwardens of St. Paul's Parish bind MARY WARD according to Law.

Suit on Petition. JOHN HOOE Gent. agt. JOSEPH LANE. Judgment is granted the Pltf for £2.12 & Costs.

Action of Trespass. JOHN FILER agt. ELIZABETH STURDY. It's ordered that the Sheriff give the Deft Notice that she do not commit any further waste on the Land in Custody.

Action of Debt. WILLIAM CUNNINGHAM Merchant, Surviving Partner of THOMAS MCREADY agt. JOHN ARMSTRONG & JAMES STEVENS. The Defts not appearing Judgment is granted the Pltf against him & SAMUEL EARLE his Security unless the Deft appear at the next Court & answer the Pltf's Action.

Action of Debt. ANDREW COCHRANE & COMPANY agt. ADAM STEPHEN. The Deft not appearing Judgment is granted against the Deft's Estate for £22.7.6 returnable to the next Court.

Suit on Information brought by MOSLEY BATTALEY, Gent. on behalf of our Sovereign Lord the King agt. WILLIAM KING. The said William having pleaded not guilty the Tryal is referred till the next Court.

Action of Debt. GOWRY WAUGH agt. RAWLEIGH CHINN, junr. WILLIAM GARRARD undertook that he would pay the Condemnation for him. A special Imparlance is granted till the next Court.

Action of Trespass. THOMAS DOUGLASS & COMPANY agt. ADAM STEPHEN. The Deft not appearing an Attachment is granted the Pltfs against the Deft's Estate for £35.4.5 half penny & Costs.

Suit on Petition. MOSELY BATTALEY Gent. agt. JAMES HUGHS.

April Court 1754

Judgment is granted the Pltf for £1.11.3 & Costs.

Suit on Petition. DUNCOMB GRAHAM agt. JOHN LEE, Gent. Judgment is granted the Pltf for £1.18.10 Farthing (by the award of JAMES SCOTT Clerk & ROBERT BURGESS to whom the Matter in difference between them was referred) with Costs & a Lawyer's Fee.

Suit on Petition. ELIZABETH MCABOY agt. GRACE JACKSON & DAVID MCQUALTY. Judgment is granted the Pltf for £3.17.7 half penny & Costs.

Suit on Petition. WILLIAM CUNNINGHAM agt. MARGARET CHAPMAN. Judgment is granted the Pltf for £1.15.3 with Costs & a Lawyer's Fee.

Suit on Petition. SAMUEL DUNAWAY agt. JOHN BENNETT. Judgment is granted the Pltf for £3 & Costs.

Ordered that FRANCIS JOHNSON pay WILLIAM WRIGHT 25 pounds of Tobacco for one days Attendance as an Evidence for him against EDWARDS.

Ordered that FRANCIS JOHNSON pay JOHN MCGOMERIE 25 pounds of Tobacco for one days Attendance as an Evidence for him against EDWARDS.

Ordered that FRANCIS JOHNSON pay NATHANIEL SMITH 25 pounds of Tobacco for one days Attendance as an Evidence for him against EDWARDS.

The suit on Attachment obtained by WILLIAM CARR against the Estate of RICHARD ROGERS. Carr is ordered to pay Rogers his Costs.

Ordered that DUNCOMB GRAHAM pay SIMON LITTERELL 85 pounds of Tobacco for one days attendance as an Evidence for him against LEE & coming & returning twenty Miles once.

The Suit on Attachment obtained by ALLEN MCREA against the Estate of RICHARD ROGERS is dismist & the said McRea ordered to pay the said Rogers his Costs.

Action of Trespass Assault & Battery. JOHN ALEXANDER agt. WILLIAM DAVIS is dismist & the Pltf ordered to pay the Deft his Costs.

May Court 1754

Action of Debt. CHARLES STUART & COMPANY agt. WILLIAM
HOWARD, CHARLES WELLS, & BENJAMIN ROBINSON. The Defts
confessed Judgment for £42.18.8 & Costs. But this Judgment is to be
discharged on payment of £21.18.8 with Interest from the 13th day of March
1753 till the same is paid.

Then the Court adjourned till Court in Course.
MOTT DONIPHAN

At a Court held for Stafford County May 14th. 1754.

Present   MOTT DONIPHAN   JOHN PEYTON
                 PETER DANIEL   HENRY FITZHUGH
                 JOHN STUART

Administration on the Estate of ROBERT MASSEY decd. is granted
WINIFRED MASSEY she having entered into bond with WILLIAM
FITZHUGH & JOHN WASHINGTON, Gent. Securities. CADR. DADE,
ROBERT YATES, ROBERT WASHINGTON, JOHN SHORT, Appraisers.

Suit on Petition. THOMAS & ROBERT DUNLOPS agt. JOHN CUBBAGE.
The Deft confessed Judgment to the Pltfs for £1.13.10 with Costs & a Lawyer's
Fee.

JOHN PEYTON & PETER DANIEL Gent. are ordered to take a List of the
Tithables in the upper Parish & JOHN STUART, Gent. in the lower Parish for
the ensuing Year.

The Grand jury for the Body of this County gave their Presentments. It's
ordered that the Offenders be summoned.

Administration on the Estate of HENRY DADE is granted HOWSON HOOE
having entered into bond with HOWSON HOOE, Senr. & RICHARD HEWITT
his Securities. THOMAS MASSEY, JOHN WASHINGTON, LAWRENCE
WASHINGTON & WILLIAM ROGERS Appraisers.

THOMAS GARNER who was bound over to this Grand jury appeared & the
Evidences against him being heard the said Garner is discharged.

Action of Trespass. ANDREW COCHRANE & COMPANY agt. JOHN GRIGSBY. The Deft confessed Judgment to the Pltf for £14.10.

[Page 270 May 14, 1754]

May Court 1754

Suit on Petition. WILLIAM BLACK agt. EDWARD GROVES. Judgment is granted the Pltf for £2.4.7 three farthings & Costs.

Suit on Petition. WILLIAM BLACK agt. THOMAS STRIBLING. Judgment is granted the Pltf for £1.17 & Costs.

Suit on Petition. WILLIAM BLACK agt. CHARLES WELLS. Judgment is granted the Pltf for £1.11.8 & Costs.

Suit on Petition. MESSRS. PRELLE & STETTE agt. MARY OVERALL. Judgment is granted the Pltfs for £4.18.7 with Costs & a Lawyer's Fee.

Suit on Petition. JOHN JOHNSON agt. SAMUEL EARLE, Admr. of SAMUEL EARLE, junr., decd. Judgment is granted the Pltf for £2.17.6 & 73 pounds of Tobacco & Costs.

Suit on Petition. ANDREW MONROE, Gent. agt. JOHN THOMAS. Judgment is granted the Pltf for £2.17.9 with Costs & a Lawyer's Fee.

Action of Debt. WILLIAM BLACK agt. RICHARD PILCHER. The Deft confessed Judgment to the Pltf for £6 & Costs.

Action of Debt. WILLIAM BLACK agt. RICHARD PILCHER. The Deft confessed Judgment to the Pltf for £7.5.10 & Costs.

[Page 271 May 14, 1754]

May Court 1754

But this Judgment is to be discharged on payment of £3.12.11 with Interest from the first day of June 1752 till the same is paid.

Action of Trespass. THOMAS DOUGLASS & COMPANY agt. RAWLEIGH CHINN. An Alias Capias is ordered returnable to the next Court.

Action of Debt. ANDREW MONROE, Gent. agt. JOHN MURDOCK. The Deft not appearing Judgment is granted the Pltf against him & JOHN RALLS,

Senr. his Security unless the Deft do appear at the next Court & answer the Pltf's Action.

Action of Debt. MOORE FANTLEROY, Gent. agt. HUMPHREY POPE. The Deft not appearing Judgment is granted the Pltf against him & SETH BOTTS. his Security unless the Deft do appear at the next Court & answer the Pltf's Action.

Action of Trespass. ELIZABETH WITHERS agt. ANTHONY HANEY. An alias Capias is ordered returnable to the next Court.

Action of Debt. WILLIAM BLACK agt. JOHN ANGLE. The Deft not appearing Judgment is granted the Pltf against him & GERARD FOWKE, Gent. Sheriff of this unless the Deft do appear at the next Court & answer the Pltf's Action.

Action of Debt. WILLIAM BLACK agt. WILLIAM BURTON & JAMES HANSBROUGH. The Defts confessed Judgment to the Pltf for £11.2.8 & 350 pounds ot Tobacco & Costs. But this Judgment is to be discharged on payment of £5.11.4 & 175 pounds of Tobacco with Interest from the first day of June 1752 till the same is paid. Memorandum. This is to be paid in Crop Tobacco a 12/6 P hundred or Transfer deducting 6 pCent.

Action of Debt. RICE HOOE agt. JOHN THOMAS. The Deft confessed Judgment to the Pltf for 1864 pounds of Tobacco & £5.7.2 & Costs. But this Judgment is to be discharged on payment of 932 pounds of Tobacco & £2.13.7 with Interest from the first day of July 1754

[Page 272 May 14, 1754]

May Court 1754

till the same is paid.

Action of Debt. ALEXANDER GRANT agt. JOHN THOMAS. WITHERS CONWAY, THOMAS BUNBURY, junr., & COLCLOUGH STRIBLING undertook that if the Deft should be condemned in this action that they would pay the Condemnation for him or surrender his Body to Prison. On the Deft's Motion a special Imparlance is granted him till the next Court.

Ejection Firma. Thomas Turff agt. HENRY FITZHUGH, Esqr. for Lands and Appurtenances in the Parish of Overwharton which HENRY TYLER demised to the Pltf for a Term &c. It's ordered that the Surveyor go on the Lands in controversy & lay off the same as either Party would have it, having regard to all Pattents & Evidences as shall be produced by either Party.

Ejection Firma. Solomon Saveall agt. THOMAS VIVION for Lands and Appurtenances in the Parish of St. Paul's which BURDITT CLIFTON demised to the Pltf for a Term &c. The Surveyor in company of an able Jury is to lay off the Lands as either of the said Parties would have it. By Consent of the said Parties all Matters in difference between them are referred to the said Jury & agreed that their Award should be made the Judgment of the Court. The Jury agrees that the land is the Property of Capt. Burdett Clifton by a Purchase made from JOHN SOWELL for fifty Acres of Land. The Jury ordered each man to pay his own costs.

[Page 273 May 14, 1754]

June Court 1754

Ordered that the Churchwardens of Overwharton Parish bind JOHN FITZGERALD according to Law.

Then the Court adjourned till tomorrow morning 9 Oclock.
MOTT DONIPHAN

At a Court continued & held for Stafford County 15th. May 1754.

Present   PETER DANIEL   HENRY FITZHUGH
               FRANCIS THORNTON   THOMAS FITZHUGH

WILLIAM GARRARD made Oath to an Account against his Servant RACHAEL WHITAKER for 13 days runaway Time & £2.13 expended in taking her up. Ordered that the said Rachael serve him for the same.

WILLIAM FOSTER an insolvent debtor in Execution at the Suit of MAXWELL & COMPANY gave in a Schedule of his Estate whereupon he is discharged out of Custody.

A Bond from HENRY DADE to ROBERT YATES being proved by the Witnesses thereto is admitted to Record.

Then the Court adjourned till Court in course.
PETER DANIEL

At a Court held for Stafford County the 11th. of June 1754.

Present   JOHN MERCER   MOTT DONIPHAN
               JOHN PEYTON   PETER DANIEL

WILLIAM BUSSELL is appointed Constable in the Room of SAMUEL MITCHELL.

Action of Debt. HARRY PIPER Assignee of RICHARD JACKSON agt. JEREMIAH CARTER. The Deft confessed Judgment to the Pltf for £10.9.8. It's thereupon considered by the Court that the Pltf recover of the said Deft & JOSEPH CARTER his Security the Sum of £10.9.8 with Interest from the 19th day of August 1751 till the same is paid.

[Page 274 June 11, 1754]

June Court 1754

Action of Debt. JOHN WEATHERS agt. MOURNING RICHARDS. The Deft confessed Judgment to the Pltf for £8.12 & Costs.

Action of Debt. ROBERT INGLISH agt. MOURNING RICHARDS. The Deft confessed Judgment to the Pltf for £8.12. It's thereupon considered by the Court that the Pltf recover of the said Deft & GEORGE BRENT his Security the said £8.12 & Costs.

Action of Trespass. JOHN CHAMPE, Esqr. agt. GEORGE RINGLESBY. The Deft confessed Judgment to the Pltf for £12.10 & Costs.

Action of Trespass Assault & Battery. JOHN RILEY agt. TRAVERSE COOKE. A Jury to wit ROBERT INGLISH, GEORGE BELL, JOHN WITHERS, FRANCIS JOHNSON, WILLIAM NORTHCUT, JOHN RAMEY, CHARLES HARDING, BENJAMIN SELMAN, THOMAS NORMAN, WILLIAM HORTON, ROBERT ASHBY, & ANDREW EDWARDS. The Jury finds for the Pltf one shilling damage & Costs.

Ordered that MARY FRAZIER serve her Mistress MARY SUDDUTH according to Law for having a Bastard Child.

ISABELL SMITH agreed to quit her Mistress MARY SUDDUTH her Freedom dues for buying of her, & other services done her.

Action of Trespass. FRANCIS MADDIN

June Court 1754

agt. RICHARD RANDALL. A Jury to wit THOMAS ASHBY, JOSEPH CARTER, THOMAS CRAFFORD, HENRY WIGGINGTON, JOHN MURPHY, FRANKLYN LATHAM, THOMAS WITHERS, JOHN ANGEL, WILLIAM JORDAN, JESSE BAILS, DANIEL CHAMBERS, & EDWARD PILCHER. The Jury finds for the Pltf forty Shillings damage & Costs.

Suit on Scire Facias. GEORGE JOHNSON agt. WILLIAM FITZHUGH, Esqr. & FRANCIS THORNTON, Gent. acting Exors. of GILSON BERRYMAN decd. The said William & Francis confessed Judgment to the said George for £7.10 & 105 pounds of nett Tobacco.

Action of Debt. MICHAEL WALLACE agt. ROBERT GARRET. A Jury to wit ROBERT INGLISH, GEORGE BELL, JOHN WITHERS, JACOB JOHNSON, WILLIAM NORTHCUT, JOHN RAMAY, CHARLES HARDING, BENJAMIN SELMAN, WILLIAM HORTON, ROBERT ASHBY, ANDREW EDWARDS, & ANDREW KENNY were sworn to try the Issue joined & retired.

Ordered that FRANCIS MADDIN pay JOHN PAYTON 100 pounds of Tobacco for four days attendance for him as an Evidence against RANDALL.

Ordered that FRANCIS MADDIN pay URITH PAYTON 100 pounds of Tobacco for four days attendance for him as an Evidence against RANDALL.

Ordered that FRANCIS MADDIN pay ANDREW KENNY 100 pounds of Tobacco for four days attendance for him as an Evidence against RANDALL.

Ordered that FRANCIS MADDIN pay ANDREW DRUMMOND 111 pounds of Tobacco for three days attendance for him as an Evidence against RANDALL & for coming & returning six Miles thrice.

Ordered that ROBERT GARRETT pay SAMUEL EARL 25 pounds of Tobacco for one days Attendance as an Evidence for him at suit of

June Court 1754

WALLACE.

Ordered that ROBERT GARRETT pay CUTHBERT HARRISON 109 pounds of Tobacco for one days Attendance as an Evidence for him at Suit of WALLACE & for coming & returning 28 Miles.

Ordered that JOHN RILEY pay CHARLES WELLS 280 pounds of Tobacco for four days Attendance for him as an Evidence against COOKE & for coming & returning twenty Miles three Times.

Ordered that THOMAS KING be summoned to appear at the next Court to shew Cause why he did not attend as an Evidence for RILEY against COOKE.

JOHN CHAMP, Esqr. made Oath to his Account against WILLIAM SEBASTIAN which is ordered to be certified.

Then the Court adjourned till tomorrow morning 9 Oclock.
JOHN MERCER

At a Court continued & held for Stafford County 12th June 1754.

Present	JOHN MERCER	MOTT DONIPHAN
	JOHN PEYTON	PETER DANIEL
	HENRY FITZHUGH	THOMAS FITZHUGH

Suit on Petition. JOHN CHAMP, Esqr. agt. WILLIAM SEBASTIAN. Judgment is granted the Pltf for £4.17.11 & Costs.

Suit on Petition. ALEXANDER WOODROW & COMPANY agt. JOHN RAMAY. Judgment is granted the Pltf for £3.12.10 with Costs & a Lawyer's Fee.

Suit on Petition. ELIZABETH MCABOY agt. JAMES YELTON. Judgment is granted the Pltf for 45 Shillings & Costs.

Suit on Petition. ELIZABETH MCABOY agt. BENJAMIN ASBURY. Judgment is granted the Pltf for £1.15.7 & Costs.

Suit on Petition. ELIZABETH MCABOY agt. BENJAMIN ASBURY. Judgment is granted the Pltf for 212 pounds of Tobacco & Costs.

Ordered that ALEXANDER WOODROW & COMPANY pay SAMUEL MCKEY 50 pounds of Tobacco for two days Attendance as an Evidence for them against RAMAY.

Ordered that ELIZABETH MCABOY pay WILLIAM NORTHCUT 50 pounds of Tobacco for two days Attendance as an Evidence for her against YELTON.

Ordered that ELIZABETH MCABOY pay STEPHEN DURRAM 50 pounds of Tobacco for two days Attendance as an Evidence for her against YELTON.

[Page 277 June 12, 1754]

June Court 1754

Suit on Petition. JOHN SUTHERLAND agt. WILLIAM HORTON. Judgment is granted the Pltf for £2.7.11 with Costs & a Lawyer's Fee.

Absent JOHN PEYTON, Gent.

Suit on Petition. JOHN PEYTON, Gent. agt. JOHN GEORGE. Judgment is granted the Pltf for £4.8.3 & Costs.

Suit on Petition. JOHN PEYTON, Gent. agt. MARY PATTISON. Judgment is granted the Pltf for £1.6.8 half penny & Costs.

Suit on Petition. JOHN PEYTON, Gent. agt. JOHN HITE. Judgment is granted the Pltf for £1.11.1 & Costs.

Suit on Petition. JOHN PEYTON, Gent. agt. JOHN ANDERSON. Judgment is granted the Pltf for £1.13.7 half penny & Costs.

Present JOHN PEYTON, Gent.

Suit on Petition. THOMAS CRAFFORD agt. SAMUEL WHITSON. Judgment is granted the Pltf for £2.3 & Costs.

Suit on Petition. JOHN LEE & TRAVERSE COOKE, Gent. Churchwardens of Overwharton Parish agt. ANN DILLON. Judgment is granted the Pltfs for fifty Shillings or 500 pounds of Tobacco & Cask with Costs & a Lawyer's Fee.

Suit on Petition. JOHN LEE & TRAVERSE COOKE, Gent. Churchwardens of Overwharton Parish agt. ANN GRAY. Judgment is granted the Pltfs for fifty Shillings or 500 pounds of Tobacco & Cask with Costs & a Lawyer's Fee.

ANN DILLON being presented by the Grand jury for having a bastard Child failed to appear whereupon it's ordered that she pay to the Churchwardens of Overwharton Parish fifty Shillings or 500 pounds of Tobacco & Cask (for the Use of the poor of the said Parish) & Costs.

ANN LOWRY being presented by the Grand jury for having a bastard Child failed to appear whereupon it's ordered that she pay to the Churchwardens of

Overwharton Parish fifty Shillings or 500 pounds of Tobacco & Cask (for the Use of the poor of the said Parish) & Costs.

DARBY DISKIN being presented by the Grand jury for swearing three Oaths, it's ordered that he pay to the Churchwardens of Overwharton Parish 15 Shillings or 150 pounds of Tobacco & Costs.

Action of Debt. ANDREW COCHRANE & COMPANY agt. WILLIAM BUSSELL. The Deft confessed Judgment to the Pltfs for £5.9.2.

[Page 278 June 12, 1754]

June Court 1754

Action of Debt. HARRY PIPER agt. SAMUEL GARNER. The Deft confessed Judgment to the Pltf for £12.12.10 & 100 pounds of Tobacco & Costs.

Action of Trespass. RICHARD BERNARD, Gent. agt. THOMAS EVANS alias PESTRIDGE. The Deft confessed Judgment to the Pltf for £5.3 & Costs.

Action of Debt. WILLIAM CUNNINGHAM & COMPANY agt. JOHN THOMAS. The Deft not appearing Judgment is granted the Pltf against him & JACOB JOHNSON his Security unless the Deft do appear at the next Court & answer the Pltf's Action.

Action of Debt. ALEXANDER ABERDEEN & COMPANY agt. PETER MURPHY. The Deft not appearing Judgment is granted the Pltf against him & WITHERS CONWAY his Security unless the Deft do appear at the next Court & answer the Pltf's Action.

Action of Trespass. JOHN WASHINGTON, Gent. agt. WINIFRED MASSEY, Admx. of ROBERT MASSEY decd. The Deft not appearing Judgment is granted the Pltf against her & WITHERS CONWAY her Security unless the Deft do appear at the next Court & answer the Pltf's Action.

Action of Trespass. JOHN FITZHUGH agt. WINIFRED MASSEY, Admx. of ROBERT MASSEY decd. The Deft not appearing Judgment is granted the Pltf against her & WITHERS CONWAY her Security unless the Deft do appear at the next Court & answer the Pltf's Action.

June Court 1754

Action of Trespass. WILLIAM FITZHUGH, Gent. agt. WINIFRED MASSEY, Admx. of ROBERT MASSEY decd. The Deft not appearing Judgment is granted the Pltf against her & WITHERS CONWAY her Security unless the Deft do appear at the next Court & answer the Pltf's Action.

Action of Trespass. WILLIAM FITZHUGH, Esqr. & FRANCIS THORNTON, Gent. acting Exors. of GILSON BERRYMAN, decd. agt. WINIFRED MASSEY, Admx. of ROBERT MASSEY decd. The Deft not appearing Judgment is granted the Pltfs unless the Deft do appear at the next Court & answer the Pltf's Action.

Action of Trespass. JOHN STUART agt. WINIFRED MASSEY, Admx. of ROBERT MASSEY decd. The Deft not appearing Judgment is granted the Pltf against her & WITHERS CONWAY her Security unless the Deft do appear at the next Court & answer the Pltf's Action.

Suit on Scire Facias. JAMES HUNTER, WILLIAM TALIAFERRO, CHARLES DICK & FIELDING LEWIS Exors. of WILLIAM HUNTER, decd. agt. JOHN HAMILTON, Gent. The said John confessed Judgment for £28.16 & 104 pounds of Tobacco & fifteen Shillings or 150 pounds of Tobacco & Costs.

Suit on Petition. JOHN TAYLOE, Esqr. agt. GEORGE KNIGHT. Judgment is granted the Pltf for 500 pounds of Tobacco & 18 Shillings & 6 pence with Costs & a Lawyer's Fee.

Suit on Petition. BARTRAM EWELL, gent. agt. GEORGE KNIGHT. Judgment is granted the Pltf for £4.1.3 half penny & Costs & a Lawyer's Fee.

Ordered that BARTRAM EWELL pay WILLIAM CARR 280 pounds of Tobacco for four days Attendance as an Evidence for him against KNIGHT & for

June Court 1754

coming & returning 20 Miles three Times.

Ordered that GEORGE KNIGHT pay GEORGE HARPER 833 pounds of Tobacco for fourteen days attendance as an Evidence for him at Suit of EWELL & for coming & returning 23 Miles seven Times.

Ordered that JOHN TAYLOE, Esqr. pay BARTRAM EWELL 280 pounds of Tobacco for four days attendance as an Evidence for him against KNIGHT & for coming & returning 20 Miles three Times.

Action of Debt. MICHAEL WALLACE agt. ROBERT GARRAT. The Jury sworn yesterday in this Cause returned with the Verdict, "We of the Jury do find by an Order from the General Court against HANNAH BAYLIS for 1,005 pounds of Tobacco & four Shillings received by Wallace from Robert Garrat as pay by MR. HARRISON'S Evidence, & also 662 pounds of Tobacco by a Receipt of MR. STROTHER." And the Suit is continued till the next Court for the Matters of Law arising thereupon to be argued.

Action of Debt. WILLIAM BLACK agt. JOHN ENGLISH. The Deft confessed Judgment to the Pltf for 1708 pounds of crop Tobacco & £11.12 & Costs. But this Judgment is to be discharged on payment of 854 pounds of like Tobacco & £5.16 with Interest from the first day of June 1752 till the same is paid.

Action of Trespass. RICHARD BERNARD, Gent. agt. EDWARD HUMPSTON. The Deft for Plea saith that he did not assume. The Tryal is referred till the next Court.

Action of Debt. ARCHIBALD MCPHERSON, JAMES ALLEN & WILLIAM HUNTER, Exors. of JOHN ALLEN decd. agt. ADAM STEPHEN & CHARLES DICK. The Defts having pleaded payment the Trial is referred till the next Court.

Action of Debt. JOHN CLARK agt. DARBY OCAIN.

[Page 281 June 12, 1754]

June Court 1754

THOMAS CRAFFORD & WILLIAM PATTON undertook that if the Deft should be condemned in this Action that they would pay the Condemnation for him or surrender his Body to Prison. The Deft for Plea saith he owes nothing & the Trial is referred till the next Court.

Action of Debt. WILLIAM YOUNG agt. JOHN THOMAS is dismist the Deft paying Costs.

In the Suit on Attachment obtained by ALEXANDER BROWN against the Estate of JAMES WATSON. The said Alexander produced a Note of Hand of the said Watson's for £5.14.8. It's thereupon considered by the Court that the said Alexander recover the same of the said James & his Costs. And the Sheriff having returned the Attachment executed on two beds & furniture, one iron pot & hooks, & some other Trifles it's ordered that he sell the same & satisfy the above Judgment.

Suit on Petition. ROBERT BROWN agt. SIMON PERRY & THOMAS FLETCHER. Judgment is granted the Pltf for £1.15.6 & Costs.

Action of Trespass. GEORGE JOHNSON, Gent. agt. HENRY TYLER & GEORGE WALLER. The Pltf failing to prosecute his Suit he is nonsuited & ordered to pay the Defts damages & Costs.

Action of Trespass. PATRICK GRADY agt. SNOWDALL & WILLIAM HORTON. The Defts for plea say they did not assume. The Trial is referred till the next Court.

Action of Trespass. EDWARD HAMPTON agt. JOHN PEYTON. The Deft having pleaded not guilty the Trial is referred till the next Court.

Action of Debt. ALEXANDER BROWN agt. ADAM STEPHEN. The Deft having pleaded payment the Trial is referred till the next Court.

Action of Debt. ROBERT WICKLIFF agt. THOMAS FLETCHER &

[Page 282 June 12, 1754]

June Court 1754

SIMON PERRY. The Defts confessed Judgment to the Pltf for ninety pounds & Costs.

Suit on Petition. FRANCIS BROOX agt. JAMES MCDANIEL. Judgment is granted the Pltf for £2.17.7 half penny & Costs.

Action of Debt. MASON COMBS agt. SAMUEL EARLE Admr. of HANNAH BAYLIS decd. By Consent of the Parties SAMUEL SELDEN, Gent. one of the Jurors of the Jury is withdrawn & this Suit is continued till the next Court at the Deft's costs.

Action of Trespass. ROBERT & EDWARD MAXWELLS agt. CUTHBERT BYRAM is dismist the Deft paying Costs.

Action of Trespass. ABRAM BREDWELL agt. ROBERT ASHBY. A Jury to wit ANDREW EDWARDS, GEORGE BELL, JACOB JOHNSON, WILLIAM PICKETT, WILLIAM NORTHCUT, JOHN GRAVAT, THOMAS PRICE,

JOHN MAUZY, THOMAS MONROE, SAMUEL SELDEN, WILLIAM HORTON, & SAMUEL EARLE. The Jury finds for the Pltf forty Shillings damage & Costs. And the Deft filed Errors in Arrest of Judgment which are to be argued the next Court.

In the Suit on Attachment obtained by CATHERINE WATERS agasint the Estate of PHILIP SULIVAN the said Catherine produced an Account against the said Philip for £2.6. It's thereupon considered by the Court that the said Catherine recover the same & her Costs. And the Sheriff having returned the Attachment executed in the hands of GEORGE BRENT & he not appearing it's ordered that he be summoned to appear at the next Court to declare what of the Estate of the said Philips he hath in his Hands.

[Page 283 June 12, 1754]

June Court 1754

Ordered that CATHERINE WATERS pay WILLIAM CASH 135 pounds of Tobacco for three days attendance as an Evidence for her against SULLIVAN & for twice coming & returning ten miles.

Ordered that CATHERINE WATERS pay WILLIAM WATERS 135 pounds of Tobacco for three days attendance as an Evidence for her against SULLIVAN & for twice coming & returning ten miles.

Action of Debt. ROBERT WALKER agt. WILLIAM FITZHUGH, Esqr. & FRANCIS THORNTON, acting Exors. of GILSON BERRYMAN, decd. The Defts confessed Judgment to the Pltf for £16.16.5 half pence. Memorandum. The Pltf acknowledges to have received £10.19.4.

Action of Trespass. ANDREW EDWARDS agt. ADAM STEPHEN. The Deft confessed Judgment to the Pltf for £18.6 & Costs.

Action of Trespass. CHARLES HARDING agt. SAMUEL EARLE. A Jury to wit ANDREW EDWARDS, GEORGE BELL, JACOB JOHNSON, WILLIAM PICKETT, WILLIAM NORTHCUT, JOHN GRAVAT, THOMAS PRICE, JOHN MAUZY, THOMAS MONROE, SAMUEL SELDEN, WILLIAM HORTON, ROBERT ASHBY. The jury returned the Verdict, "We of the Jury find that the Deft promised to pay the Sum of Money & Tobacco…to the Pltf at three several Payments (to wit) at one thousand pounds of Tobacco & twenty Shillings P Year if the Deft obtained administration on the said HANNAH BAILIS' Estate. We find that the said Deft on the thirteenth day of November obtained Admr. on the said Estate." This suit is continued till the next Court for the Matters of Law arising thereupon to be argued.

Suit in Chancery. RICHARD FOOTE, Gent. agt. THOMAS ROSS & JOHN SHORT is dismist the Defts paying Costs.

[Page 284 June 12, 1754]

June Court 1754

Action of Trespass. PATRICK BOGLE & COMPANY agt. JOHN KITCHING. A Jury to wit ANDREW EDWARDS, GEORGE BELL, JACOB JOHNSON, WILLIAM PICKETT, WILLIAM NORTHCUT, JOHN GRAVATT, THOMAS PRICE, JOHN MAUZY, THOMAS MONROE, SAMUEL SELDEN, GEORGE WALLER, & WILLIAM HORTON. The Jury finds for the Pltf for £2.10.7 half penny. It's considered by the Court that the Pltf recover of the said Deft & WILLIAM SWETMAN his Security that amount.

Action of Trespass Assault & Battery. JOHN MATTHEWS agt. JOHN ENGLISH. The Jury finds for the Deft, the Pltf paying Costs.

Ordered that JOHN MATTHEWS pay ALEXANDER DONIPHAN 75 pounds of Tobacco for three days attendance as an evidence for him against INGLISH.

Ordered that JOHN ENGLISH pay ROBERT ENGLISH 125 pounds of Tobacco for five days attendance as an Evidence for him at suit of MATTHEWS.

Ordered that JOHN ENGLISH pay CAIN WITHERS 125 pounds of Tobacco for five days attendance as an Evidence for him at suit of MATTHEWS.

Action of Trespass. ROBERT & EDWARD MAXWELLS & COMPANY agt. SNODALL HORTON is dismist the Deft paying Costs.

Then the Court adjourned till tomorrow morning 9 Oclock.
                                                    JOHN MERCER

[Page 285 June 13, 1754]

June Court 1754

At a Court continued & held for Stafford County 13th. June 1754.

Present   JOHN MERCER   MOTT DONIPHAN
               JOHN PEYTON   PETER DANIEL
               THOMAS FITZHUGH

In the Suit on Attachment obtained by JOHN PEYTON, Gent. against the Estate of JAMES FERNSLEY the said John produced an Account against the said James for £3.12 half penny. It's considered by the Court that the said John recover the same from the Pltf & his Costs. And the Sheriff having returned the Attachment executed in the hands of JOHN CARTER who being summoned declared that he has eight Shillings in his Hands of the Estate of the said James which he is ordered to pay the said John in part satisfaction of the above Judgment.

Action of Trespass. JAMES BOYD agt. HENRY TYLER. By consent of the Parties all Matters in difference between them are referred to the determination of THOMAS FITZHUGH, DANIEL CAMPBELL, & WILLIAM CUNNINGHAM, Gent. & their award to be made the Judgment of the Court.

Action of Trespass. CHARLES HARDING agt. FRANCIS BROOX. The Deft for Plea saith he is not guilty with leave to give the special Matter in evidence. The Trial is referred till the next Court.

Upon Complaint of the Churchwardens of Overwharton Parish against GRACE JACKSON & ELIZABETH HACKNEY it appears to the Court that the said Jackson & Hackney are unable to maintain & Educate their Children. It's ordered that the Churchwardens bind HENRY JACKSON & MARY JACKSON & DANIEL, HANNAH, & SARAH HACKNEY according to Law.

Action of Trespass. SAMUEL BREDWELL agt. CHARLES HARDING. A Jury to wit THOMAS PRICE, JEREMIAH STARK, JOHN GRAVET, WILLIAM BUTLER, WILLIAM PICKETT, JOSEPH CARTER, WILLIAM HORTON, THOMAS NORMAN, JOHN PEYTON, SAMUEL EARLE, WILLIAM PATTEN, & HUMPHREY POPE. The Jury finds for the Pltf forty shillings damage & Costs.

Ordered that CHARLES HARDING pay GEORGE WALLER 75 pounds of

[Page 286 June 13, 1754]

June Court 1754

Tobacco for three days attendance as an Evidence for him at suit of BREDWELL.

Action of Trespass. JOSEPH PORTER agt. CATHERINE WATERS. A Jury to wit ANDREW EDWARDS, ELIAS ASHBY, JOHN MURPHY, JOHN DAVIS, THOMAS ASHBY, SAMUEL SELDEN, ALEXANDER STEPHENS, ANDREW KENNY, SNODALL HORTON, ROBERT ASHBY, HENRY WIGGINGTON, & CHARLES HARDING was sworn and retired.

284

Action of Debt. MARY WISE agt. JOHN PEYTON. A Jury to wit CAIN WITHERS, JAMES STARK, JOHN GRAVAT, WILLIAM BUTLER, WILLIAM PICKETT, JOHN CARTER, THOMAS NORMAN, SAMUEL EARLE, WILLIAM PATTEN, HUMPHREY POPE, THOMAS PORTER, & WILLIAM NORTHCUT. "We the Jury find that the Deft as a Constable did serve one Warrant & summon one Evidence for the Pltf & serve one Execution on the estate of JOHN POTTER for 24 shillings & 11 pence. We find that the Deft recd. half a Pistole for his Fees & for Extraordinary services upon the same Case. If upon the whole the Law be for the Pltf we find her 200 pounds of Tobacco." And this Suit is continued till the next Court for the Matters of Law arising thereupon to be argued.

Action of Debt. CHARLES STUART & COMPANY agt. ALEXANDER DOUGLASS. The Deft not appearing an Attachment is awarded the Pltfs for £15 & Costs returnable to the next Court.

Action of Debt. CHARLES STUART & COMPANY agt. WILLIAM GREENLEES. The Deft having pleaded Payment the Trial is referred till the next Court.

Action of Trespass. Messrs. GRANT & BROWN agt. ALEXANDER MURPHY. The Deft not appearing judgment is granted the Pltf against him & JOHN ADDISON his Security unless the Deft do appear at the next Court & answer the Pltf's Action.

Action of Debt. ROBERT BROWN agt. JOHN THOMAS. The Deft having pleaded payment the Trial is referred till the next Court.

[Page 287 June 13, 1754]

June Court 1754

Action of Debt. THOMAS CUMMINS agt. JOHN THOMAS. WITHERS CONWAY undertook that if the Deft should be condemned in this Action that he would pay the Condemnation for him or surrender his Body to Prison. The Deft having pleaded payment the Trial is referred till the next Court.

Action of Trespass. NATHANIEL GRAY agt. JOHN LEEWRIGHT & MARY his Wife Admrs. of ANTHONY KITCHING decd having pleaded nonassumpsit & fully administered. The Trial is referred till the next Court.

Suit on Scire Facias. CHARLES DICK, Gent. agt. PHILEMON WATERS. The Sheriff having twice returned that the said Philemon was not to be found, it's considered by the Court that the said Charles have Execution against the said

Philemon for five shillings & 118 pounds of nett Tobacco & fifteen shillings or 150 pounds of Tobacco & Costs.

Action of Trespass. ROBERT JACKSON, Gent. agt. CAIN WITHERS. The Deft confessed Judgment to the Pltf for £11.6.3 & Costs.

Action of Debt. WILLIAM BLACK agt. JACOB WILLIAMS & NATHANIEL HARRISON Esqr. The Defts not appearing judgment is granted the Pltf against them & WITHERS CONWAY their Security unless the Defts do appear at the next Court & answer the Pltf's Action.

Action of Trespass. ISAAC FOWLER & REBECCA his wife agt. WILLIAM HOLDBROOK. The Deft for Plea saith he is not guilty, with leave to give the special Matter in Evidence. The Trial is referred till the next Court.

Action of Trespass. CHARLES STUART & COMPANY agt. SAMUEL EARLE Admr. &c of SAMUEL EARLE decd. The Deft for Plea

[Page 288 June 13, 1754]

June Court 1754

saith the Intestate did not assume. The Trial is referred till the next Court.

Action of Trespass. CHARLES DICK, Gent. agt. WILLIAM LYNN. The Plea & Replication being joined the Trial is referred till the next Court.

Action of Trespass. WILLIAM ANDERSON agt. JOHN HAMILTON, Gent. The Deft having pleaded nonassumpsit the Pltf joined the Issue. The Trial is referred till the next Court.

Suit on Petition. WITHERS CONWAY agt. MICHAEL RYAN. Judgment is granted the Pltf for 559 ¼ pounds of Tobacco & 17 shilling & 3 pence half penny & Costs.

Action of Debt. WILLIAM CUNNINGHAME Admr. of THOMAS MACREDIE decd. agt. JOHN ARMSTRONG. The Deft not appearing the Judgment against him & JOHN MERCER, Gent. his Security is confirmed to the Pltf for £28 & Costs. But this Judgment is to be discharged on payment of £14 with Interest from the first day of June 1753 till the same is paid.

Action of Trespass. THOMAS & ROBERT DUNLOPS agt. JOHN ARMSTRONG. The Deft not appearing the Judgment against him & JOHN MERCER, Gent., his Security is confirmed, & Writ of Enquiry of damages is to be executed the next Court.

Ordered that SAMUEL BREDWELL pay ANDREW DRUMMOND 68 of Tobacco for two days Attendance as an evidence for him against HARDING & for coming & returning six Miles once.

Ordered that WITHERS CONWAY pay THOMAS PRICE 150 pounds of Tobacco for six days attendance as an Evidence for him against RYAN.

Action of Trespass. RICHARD BERNARD, Gent. agt. WILLIAM ROSE. The plea & Replication being joined the Trial is referred

[Page 289 June 13, 1754]

June Court 1754

till the next Court.

Suit in Chancery. The Minister & Church Wardens of St. Paul's Parish agt. WILLIAM FTIZHUGH, Gent. is dismist and the Complainant ordered to pay Costs.

Suit in Chancery. RICHARD BERNARD Admr. &c of THOMAS SHARP, decd. agt. NATHANIEL GRAY. The Pltf having put in his Replication this suit is set for Trial at the next Court.

Action of Debt. HUGH MITCHELL Assignee of BAYN SMALLWOOD agt. WILLIAM DAVIS. The Pltf hath leave to amend his declaration & the Deft hath a special Imparlance granted him till the next Court.

WILLIAM BLACK being Summoned as a Juror & failing to appear when called it's ordered that he be fined 400 pounds of Tobacco.

JOHN MURDOCK being Summoned as a Juror & failing to appear when called it's ordered that he be fined 400 pounds of Tobacco.

Ordered that JOHN PEYTON pay ARTHUR DUAS 475 pounds of Tobacco for 19 days attendance as an Evidence for him at Suit of WISE.

Action of Debt. RICHARD FRISTOE, senr. agt. JOHN KIRK. The Pltf having put in his Replication the Deft hath Time till the next Court to consider thereof.

Action of Trespass. MARGARET PIPER agt. JOHN MAYSIE. ALEXANDER ROSE, Gent. undertook that if the Deft should be condemned in this Action that he would pay the Condemnation for him or surrender his Body to Prison. The Deft pleaded nonassumpsit & the trial is referred till the next Court.

Ejection Firma. John Seekright agt. WILLIAM GREENLEES for Land & Appurtenances in the Parish of Overwharton which JOHN SMITH & JANET his Wife, MARGARET ORR, & BETHIA ORR demised to the Pltf for a Term &c. It's ordered that the Surveyor go upon the Lands in dispute & lay off the same.

Ejection Firma. Thomas Turff agt. HENRY FITZHUGH, Esqr. for Lands & Appurtenances in the Parish of Overwharton which HENRY TYLER demised to the Pltf for a Term &c.

[Page 290 June 13, 1754]

June Court 1754

It's ordered that the Surveyor go upon the Lands in Controversy & lay off the same as either Party would have it, having regard to all Pattents & Evidences as shall be produced by either of the Parties.

Action of Debt. EDWARD MUSE agt. JEREMIAH CARTER. The Deft not appearing the Judgment against him & JOSEPH CARTER his Security is confirmed to the Pltf for £5.7.6 & Costs.

Action of Trespass. WILLIAM FITZHUGH, Esqr. & FRANCIS THORNTON, Gent. acting Exors. of GILSON BERRYMAN, decd. agt. MARGARET FRENCH Admx. of MASON FRENCH, decd. The Deft having pleaded nonassumsit & fully administered, the Trial is referred till the next Court.

Action of Trespass. THOMAS HORNBUCKLE agt. SAMUEL GRIGSBY. The Pltf having put in his Demurer the Deft hath time till the next Court to consider thereof.

Action of Trespass Assault & Battery. GERRARD BANKS agt. SAMUEL GRIGSBY. The Pltf having put in his Demurer the Deft hath time till the next Court to consider thereof.

Ejection Firma. Timothy Turff agt. LYNAUGH HELMS for Lands & Appurtenances in the Parish of Overwharton which JOHN MAUZY demised to the Pltf for a Term &c. It's ordered that the surveyor of WESTMORELAND go upon the Lands in Controversy & lay off the same as either Party would have it having regard to all Pattents & Evidences as shall be produced by either Party.

June Court 1754

Action of Trespass. JOHN ADDISON agt. WILLIAM THOMAS. The Deft having pleaded not guilty the Trial is referred till the next Court.

Action of Trespass. JAMES YELTON agt. JOHN PEYTON. The Deft having pleaded not guilty with Leave to give the special Matter in Evidence. The Trial is referred till the next Court.

Action of Debt. Our King agt. ISAAC KNIGHT. The said Isaac having pleaded that he owes nothing MOSELY BATTELEY, Gent., Attorney for the King joined the Issue & the trial is referred till the next Court.

Action of Trespass. JAMES WRENN agt. NATHANIEL HARRISON, Esqr. acting Exor. for WILLIAM WALKER, Gent., decd. The Deft having pleaded nonassumpsit the Trial is referred till the next Court.

Action of Trespass. PAUL SWENY agt. WILLIAM ROSE. The Deft for plea saith he did not assume. The Trial is referred till the next Court.

Action of Trespass. PATRICK & WILLIAM BOGLE & COMPANY agt. JAMES CONNELL. A Jury to wit CAIN WITHERS, JAMES STARK, JOHN GRAVATT, WILLIAM BUTLER, WILLIAM PICKETT, JOHN CARTER, THOMAS NORMAN, SAMUEL EARLE, WILLIAM PATTEN, HUMPHREY POPE, THOMAS PORTER, & WILLIAM NORTHCUT. The Jury finds for the Pltfs £15.7.9 & 93 ½ pounds of Tobacco damages & Costs.

Action of Debt. GEORGE MASON, Esqr. agt. RANDALL JOHNSON. The Jury finds for

June Court 1754

The Pltf £7.19.4 half penny with Interest from the tenth day of November 1752. It's considered by the Court that the Pltf recover the same of the said Deft & JOHN RALLS, junr. & MOSES LUNSFORD his Securities.

Action of Debt. WILLIAM CUNNINGHAME & COMPANY agt. ELIAS ASHBY & LEONARD ALVEY. The Defts not appearing an Attachment is ordered. It's considered by the Court that the Pltfs recover of the Defts the sum of £47 & their Costs. But this Judgment is to be discharged on payment of £23.10 with Interest from the first day of August 1752 till the same is paid. And the Sheriff having returned the Attachment executed on a Bed & some furniture, two pots & some small quantity of pewter & of the Estate of LEONARD ASHBY [*sic*] one small Horse, it's ordered that he sell the same & satisfy the above Judgment.

Action of Trespass. GEORGE BELL agt. ELIZABETH WITHERS. The Deft having pleaded not guilty with Leave to give the special Matter in evidence the Trial is referred till the next Court.

Action of Debt. ROGER DREGHORN & COMPANY agt. JEREMIAH CARTER. The Deft having pleaded payment the Trial is referred till the next Court.

Action of Trespass. GRACE JACKSON agt. SAMUEL EARLE, Gent. The Deft having pleaded nonassumpsit the Trial is referred till the next Court.

Action of Trespass. SARAH MCCULLOUGH agt. SAMUEL BREDWELL. The Deft having pleaded not

[Page 293 June 13, 1754]

June Court 1754

guilty the Trial is referred till the next Court.

Action of Debt. ROBERT ASHBY agt. SAMUEL BREDWELL. The Deft for plea saith he owes nothing. The Trial is referred till the next Court.

Action of Debt. CHARLES STUART & COMPANY agt. FRANCIS BROOX. The Deft having pleaded the Trial is referred till the next Court.

Action of Trespass. JOHN TAYLOE, Esqr. agt. WILLIAM DAVIS. The Deft having pleaded not guilty the Trial is referred till the next Court.

Action of Trespass. JAMES YELTON agt. THOMAS SPALDING. The Deft having pleaded not guilty the Trial is referred till the next Court.

Ejection Firma. Thomas Trueman agt. JOHN PEYTON & GEORGE WALLER, Exors. of CHARLES WALLER, decd. for Lands & Appurtenances in the Parish of Overwharton which JOHN ROUT demised the Pltf for a Term &c. It's ordered that the Surveyor go upon the Lands in dispute & lay off the same as either Party would have it, having regard to all Patents & Evidences as shall be produced by either of the Parties.

Action of Trespass. MERRIMOND TILLER agt. HUSBANDFOOTE
WHITECOTTON. The Deft for plea saith he is not guilty. The Trial is referred
till the next Court.

Action of Debt. JOHN KNOX agt. THOMAS RIDDLE.

[Page 294 June 13, 1754]

June Court 1754

The Jury finds for the Pltf £6.11 & Costs.

Then the Court adjourned till tomorrow morning 9 Oclock.
JOHN MERCER

At a Court continued & held for Stafford County, 14th. June 1754.

Present JOHN MERCER   MOTT DONIPHAN
     JOHN PEYTON   PETER DANIEL

Action of Trespass. JOHN CHAMPE, Esqr. agt. SOLOMON WAUGH. The
Deft having pleaded nonassumpsit the Trial is referred till the next Court.

Action of Trespass. ROBERT & EDWARD MAXWELLS & COMPANY agt.
JOHN HONEY is dismist the Deft paying Costs.

Action of Trespass. ROBERT & EDWARD MAXWELLS & COMPANY agt.
THOMAS HEATH. The Deft not appearing the Judgment against him &
RICHARD HEWITT his Security is confirmed & a Writ of Enquiry of damages
is to be executed the next Court.

Action of Debt. JAMES BOYD agt. JOHN MAUZY, JOHN MURRY,
WILLIAM HEDGMAN & SAMUEL EARL. The Defts Mauzy, Hedgman &
Earle confessed Judgment to the Pltf for £49.10 & costs. But this Judgment is to
be discharged on payment of £24.15

[Page 295 June 13, 1754]

June Court 1754

with Interest from the 16th day of July 1752 till the same is paid.

Action of Debt. JACOB WILLIAMS agt. WILLIAM SCAPLEHORN. The
Deft confessed judgment to the Pltf for £28. It's considered by the Court that

291

the Pltf recover the same from the Deft & JOHN OLIVER his Security & his Costs.

Action of Debt. WILLIAM PATTEN agt. DAVID ASHBY, ROBERT ASHBY, Junr., & THOMAS ASHBY. The Jury finds for the Pltf 2100 pounds of Tobacco & Casks with Interest. Memorandum. The Bond is dated the 19th of August 1751. The first payment was to be made in June 1752, the other in June 1753 to be paid at ACQUIA or at the FALLS OF RAPPAHANNOCK.

Action of Trespass. JAMES STUART & MARY his wife agt. WILLIAM ROSS, Senr. The Deft having pleaded not guilty the Tryal is referred till the next Court.

Action of Trespass. JAMES STUART & MARY his wife agt. WILLIAM ROSS, Junr. The Deft having pleaded not

June Court 1754

guilty the Tryal is referred till the next Court.

Action of Trespass. JAMES STUART & MARY his wife agt. ELIZABETH RAPIER. The Deft having pleaded not guilty the Tryal is referred till the next Court.

Action of Trespass. ELIZABETH RAPIER agt. JAMES STUART & MARY his Wife. The Defts having pleaded not guilty the Tryal is referred till the next Court.

Action of Trespass. JOHN PEYTON agt. WILLIAM SWETMAN. The Deft having pleaded not guilty with leave to give the special matter in Evidence the Trial is referred till the next Court.

Action of Debt. JOHN THORNTON, Gent. agt. ANDREW CRAFFORD, ANDREW KENNY, & JOHN MINOR. The Defts for plea say they have performed the Covenants by them entered into. The Trial is referred till the next Court.

Suit on Petition. JOHN HARDIN agt. JOSEPH BLACK. Judgment is granted the Pltf for £4.4.3 & Costs.

Ordered that JOHN HARDING pay CHRISTIAN VELAND 100 pounds of Tobacco for four days attendance as an Evidence for him against BLACK.

Ordered that JOHN HARDING pay JOHN MURPHY 175 pounds of Tobacco for seven days attendance as an Evidence for him against BLACK.

Ordered that JOHN HARDING pay ELIZABETH MURPHY 125 pounds of Tobacco for five days attendance as an Evidence for him against BLACK.

Ordered that JOSEPH BLACK pay THOMAS PORTER 225 pounds of Tobacco for nine days attendance as an Evidence for him at Suit of HARDING.

Present THOMAS FITZHUGH, Gent.

Action of Trespass. CATHERINE ASHBY by ROBERT ASHBY her nearest Friend agt. SAMUEL BREDWELL. A Jury to wit

June Court 1754

JOHN GRAVATT, JOHN ANGELL, WILLIAM PICKETT, JOHN PAYTON, HUMPHREY POPE, SAMUEL EARLE, WILLIAM PORTER, FRANCIS BROOX, THOMAS NORMAN, JOHN HONEY, FRANKLYN LATHAM, & JOHN HARDING. The Jury finds for the Pltf £5 damage & Costs. And the Deft by his Attorney moved for a new Trial which is granted him.

Suit on Information. MOSLEY BATTALEY, Gent. on behalf of our Lord the King against WILLIAM JONES. The said Jones having pleaded not guilty the said Mosley joined the Issue & the Trial is referred till the next Court.

Suit on Information. MOSLEY BATTALEY, Gent. on behalf of our Lord the King against WILLIAM HOWARD. The said Howard having pleaded not guilty the said Mosley joined the Issue & the Trial is referred till the next Court.

Action of Trespass Assault & Battery. ROBERT WICKLIFF agt. ANDREW KENNY. The Deft having pleaded not guilty the Trial is referred till the next Court.

Suit on Information. MOSLEY BATTALEY, Gent. on behalf of our Lord the King against WILLIAM SCAPLIN. The said Scaplin having pleaded not guilty the said Mosley joined the Issue & the Trial is referred till the next Court.

Action of Debt. ANDREW COCHRANE & COMPANY agt. ADAM STEPHEN. The Deft not appearing an Attachment is ordered in this suit. It's considered by the Court that the Pltfs recover of the said Deft the sum of £22.17.5 & their Costs. But the Judgment is to be discharged on payment of £11.8.8 with Interest from the first day of March 1750 till the same is paid. And the Sheriff having returned the Attachment executed on a Washing Tub, & Cow or Steer, it's ordered that he sell the same & satisfy the above Judgment.

Action of Debt. JAMES WIGGINGTON agt. JOHN HIWARDEN. The Deft having pleaded that he owes nothing the Trial is referred till the next Court.

Action of Debt. GOWRY WAUGH agt. RAWLEIGH CHINN, Junr. The Deft having pleaded that he owes nothing, the Trial is referred till the next Court.

[Page 298 June 14, 1754]

June Court 1754

Action of Debt. RANDALL HOLDBROOK agt. EDWARD PAYNE. The Deft having pleaded that he owes nothing the Trial is referred till the next Court.

Action of Debt. ROBERT WICKLIFF agt. WILLIAM PICKETT. The Deft having pleaded that he owes nothing the Trial is referred till the next Court.

In the Suit on Attachment obtained by JOHN PEYTON, Gent. against the Estate of ALEXANDER BAXTER, the said John produced an Account against the said Alexander for £2.3.9. It's considered by the Court that the said John recover the same. And the Sheriff having returned the judgment executed in the hands of CHARLES HARDING & ANN MASON and there appearing to be Corn in the Hands of the said Ann, it's ordered that the Sheriff sell the same & satisfy the above Judgment.

In the Suit on Attachment obtained by ARTHUR MORSON against the Estate of RICHARD GAMBLE, ANDREW KENNY, & ANDREW EDWARDS who were summoned as Garnishees. The said Andrew Kenny had in his Hands fifteen Shillings, & the said Edwards six Shillings, & this Suit is continued till the next Court.

Action of Debt. THOMAS DOUGLASS & COMPANY agt. RAWLEIGH CHINN, Senr. & RAWLEIGH CHINN, Junr. ALEXANDER ROSE, Gent. undertook that if the said Defts should be condemned in this Action he would pay the Condemnation for them or surrender their Bodies to Prison.

Action of Debt. ANDREW MONROE agt. JOHN MURDOCK. The Deft not appearing the Judgment against him & JOHN RALLS Senr. his Security is confirmed for £26.6.6. But this Judgment is to be discharged on Payment of

294

June Court 1754

£13.3.3 with Interest from the first day of February 1754 till the same is paid.

Action of Debt. MOORE FANTLEROY, Gent. agt. HUMPHREY POPE. WILLIAM HORTON & THOMAS ASHBY undertook that if the Deft should be condemned in this Action that they would pay the Condemnation for him or surrender his body to prison.

Action of Trespass. JOSEPH PORTER agt. CATHERINE WATERS is dismist & each Party agrees to pay their own Costs.

Ordered that CATHERINE ASHBY pay CHARLES HARDING 175 pounds of Tobacco for seven days attendance as an Evidence for her against BREDWELL.

Ordered that CATHERINE ASHBY pay ELIZABETH COTTER 100 pounds of Tobacco for four days attendance as an Evidence for her against BREDWELL.

Ordered that CATHERINE ASHBY pay WILLIAM HORTON 125 pounds of Tobacco for five days attendance as an Evidence for her against BREDWELL.

Action of Trespass. JOHN TYLER agt. ELIZABETH STURDY for £100 damage by means of the Deft breaking & entering the Close of the Pltf at the Parish of Overwharton. It's ordered that the Surveyor in Company of an able Jury go upon the Lands in Controversy & lay off the same as either party would have it, and as the Jury shall think fit. And whereas some of the Lands in dispute lie in the County of KING GEORGE the Parties agree that the Surveyor of this County shall survey the whole.

Absent JOHN PEYTON, Gent.

Action of Detinue. JOHN PEYTON, Gent. agt. JEREMIAH CARTER.

June Court 1754

The Jury finds for the Pltf the within mentioned Negro Boy named HARRY, or £40 & £5 damage.

Present JOHN PEYTON, Gent.

Ordered that JOHN PEYTON, Gent. pay THOMAS NORMAN 100 pounds of Tobacco for four days attendance as an Evidence for him against CARTER.

Action of Debt. WILLIAM BLACK agt. SAMUEL WHITSON & JOSEPH CARTER. JOHN PEYTON, Gent. undertook that if the Deft Carter should be condemned in this Action that he would pay the Condemnation for him and the said Carter having pleaded payment the Pltf joined the Issue & the Trial is referred till the next Court & this Suit as to the Deft Whitson is continued.

Action of Debt. WILLIAM BLACK agt. JOHN ANGELL is dismist the Deft paying Costs.

Action of Trespass. ELEANOR HOGG agt. JOHN KNOX is dismist the Deft paying Costs.

Action of Debt. WILLIAM BLACK agt. WILLIAM BURTON & JAMES HANSBROUGH. The Defts confessed Judgment to the Pltf for £11.2.2 & 350 pounds of Tobacco. But this Judgment is to be discharged on payment of £5.11.4 & 175 pounds of Tobacco with Interest from the first day of June 1752 till the same is paid. Memorandum. To be paid in crop Tobacco at 12/6 P Cent, or transfer deducting six P Cent.

Action of Trespass. JOHN ALEXANDER agt. WILLIAM DAVIS. The Deft having pleaded not guilty the Pltf joined the Issue

[Page 301 June 14, 1754]

June Court 1754

& the Trial is referred till the next Court.

Action of Debt. ANDREW GRANT agt. JOHN THOMAS. The Deft having pleaded payment the Trial is referred till the next Court.

Suit on Scire Facias. JAMES HUNTER and others agt. WILLIAM FITZHUGH, Esqr. & FRANCIS THORNTON, Gent. acting Exors. of GILSON BERRYMAN, decd. The said William & Francis having pleaded payment the Trial is referred till the next Court.

Suit on Petition. JOHN KITE agt. SAMUEL EARLE, Gent., Admr. of HANNAH BAYLIS, decd. Judgment is granted the Pltf for 465 pounds of Tobacco & four Shillings & Costs.

Absent JOHN MERCER, Gent.

Suit on Petition. JOHN MERCER, Gent. agt. SAMUEL EARLE, Admr. of HANNAH BAYLIS, decd. Judgment is granted the Pltf for £2.10 & Costs.

Present JOHN MERCER, Gent.

Action of Trespass Assault & Battery. WILLIAM HOWARD agt. DAVID MCQUALTY. The Jury finds for the Pltf forty Shillings damage & Costs.

Action of Trespass Assault & Battery. DAVID MCQUALTY agt. WILLIAM HOWARD.

[Page 302 June 14, 1754]

June Court 1754

The Jury finds for the Deft HUMPHREY POPE.

Action of Trespass Assault & Battery. GRACE JACKSON agt. WILLIAM HOWARD. The Jury finds for the Pltf forty Shillings damage & Costs.

Action of Debt. JOHN GRAHAM, Gent. agt. HENRY WIGGINGTON & ANN PORTER. The Jury finds for the Pltf 159 pounds of Tobacco with Interest from the first day of June 1749.

Action of Debt. THOMAS & ROBERT DUNLOPS agt. FRANCIS

[Page 303 June 14, 1754]

July Court 1754

BROOX. The Deft confessed Judgment to the Pltf for £20.8 & Costs.

Ordered that WILLIAM HOWARD pay BARTON JACKSON 50 pounds of Tobacco for two days attendance as an Evidence for him against MCQUALTY.

Ordered that WILLIAM HOWARD pay LETTICE JACKSON 50 pounds of Tobacco for two days attendance as an Evidence for him against MCQUALTY.

In the Suit on Attachment obtained by JOHN FOUSHEE, Gent. against the Estate of WILLIAM WALKER is dismist & the said Walker paying Costs.

Absent THOMAS FITZHUGH

Ordered that the Clerk of this County send his Honor the Governor a Scheme held for this twelve Months past, of the Justices holding the same with the

297

Names of the several Persons recommended & such as have not sworn to the last Commission.

Then the Court adjourned till Court in Course.

JOHN MERCER

At a Court held for Stafford County July 9th. 1754.

Present   JOHN MERCER   MOTT DONIPHAN
                JOHN PEYTON   PETER DANIEL
                THOMAS FITZHUGH

JAMES MILLS produced his Account amounting to £29.6 for Scales & Weights for BOYD'S HOLE & CAVES WAREHOUSES. Therefore it's ordered to be certified to JOHN ROBINSON Treasurer who is desired to pay the same.

A new Commission of the Peace for this County together with a dedimus for administering the Oaths. MOTT DONIPHAN & JOHN PEYTON administered the Oaths to JOHN MERCER who administered the same to the said Mott Doniphan

[Page 304 July 9, 1754]

July Court 1754

& JOHN PEYTON, PETER DANIEL, THOMAS FITZHUGH, JOHN STUART, JOHN STITH, JOHN WASHINGTON, & BAILY WASHINGTON, Gent. subscribed the Test & abjuration Oath.

Present the above Justices.

THOMAS FITZHUGH, JOHN STUART, & JOHN STITH, Gent. are ordered to be recommended to his Honor the Governor for his Honor to make Choice of a Sheriff the ensuing year. FRANCIS THORNTON & WILLIAM FITZHUGH, Gent. refusing to swear in the Commission of the Peace is ordered to be certified.

Action of Debt. ARCHIBALD MCPHERSON, JAMES ALLEN, & WILLIAM & JAMES HUNTERS Esqrs., Exors. of JOHN ALLEN, decd. agt. ADAM STEPHEN & CHARLES DICK. The Defts confessed Judgment to the Pltfs for £86 & Costs. But this Judgment is to be discharged on payment of £43 with Interest from the first day of April 1751 till the same is paid.

298

Action of Debt. JOHN CLARK agt. DARBY OCAIN. A Jury to wit WILLIAM WRIGHT, RICE HOOE, WILLIAM FOOTE, RICHARD FOOTE, HUMPHREY GAINES, ROBERT WASHINGTON, CARTY WELLS, JOHN WALLER, JOHN FITZHUGH, ROBERT YATES, & JAMES KENNY. The Jury finds for the Pltf £5.7.6 & Costs & the Deft moved for a new Trial which is granted him.

Suit on Petition. ALEXANDER BROWN agt. THOMAS BUNBURY, Admr. of WILLIAM WORLY dect. Judgment is granted the Pltf for £2.11.10 of the Goods & Chattles of the said Intestate.

[Page 305 July 9, 1754]

July Court 1754

WILLIAM FOOTE garnishee of JAMES WATSON at the Suit of ALEXANDER BROWN declared that he had in his hands of the estate of the said Watson one Shilling & nine Pence, which he is ordered to pay the said Brown in part satisfaction of his debt.

Action of Trespass. EDWARD HUMPSTON agt. JOHN PEYTON. The Jury finds for the Pltf forty Shillings & Costs.

Action of Debt. ALEXANDER BROWN Assignee of JOHN BOYD agt. ADAM STEPHEN. The Deft confessed Judgment to the Pltf for £84 & Costs. But this Judgment is to be discharged on payment of £42 like Money with Interest from the 25th day of January 1753 till the same is paid.

GEORGE BRENT Garnishee of PHILIP SULIVANT at the suit of CATHERINE WATERS confessed that he had in his hands sufficient to satisfy the said Catherine her debt & costs against the said Philip and it's considered that he pay the same.

Action of Debt. CHARLES STUART & COMPANY agt. WILLIAM GREENLEES. A Jury to wit SETH BOTTS, GEORGE RINGLESBY, JOHN CHANCELLOR, GEORGE BOTTS, ROBERT ENGLISH, MOSES LUNSFORD, WILLIAM GEORGE, JOHN WITHERS, WILLIAM KENDALL, WILLIAM DYE

July Court 1754

WILLIAM HORTON, & PETER MURPHY. The Jury finds for the Pltf £46 & Costs. But this Judgment is to be discharged on payment of £23 with Interest from the first day of June 1752 till the same is paid.

Action of Trespass. MESSRS. GRANT & BROWN agt. ALEXANDER MURPHY. The Deft not appearing the Judgment against him & JOHN ADDISON his Security is confirmed & a Writ of Enquiry of damages is to be executed the next Court.

Action of Debt. THOMAS CUMMINGS agt. JOHN THOMAS. It's considered by the Court that the Pltf recover of the Deft 818 pounds of Tobacco & Cask & his Costs.

Action of Debt. WILLIAM BLACK agt. JACOB WILLIAMS & NATHANIEL HARRISON, Esqr. The Defts not appearing the Judgment against them & WITHERS CONWAY their Security is confirmed to the Pltf for £80 & Costs.

Suit on Petition. ALLEN MCRAE agt. SAMUEL ANGEL is dismist the Pltf paying Costs.

Action of Trespass. CHARLES DICK Gent. agt. WILLIAM LYNN.

July Court 1754

The Jury finds for the Pltf £12.5.4 & Costs.

Ordered that SAMUEL ANGELL pay JOHN BALANDINE 650 pounds of Tobacco for five days attendance as an Evidence for him at Suit of MCRAE & for coming & returning 35 Miles five Times.

Ordered that CHARLES DICK pay DANIEL FITZHUGH 46 pounds of Tobacco & one Shilling for one days attendance as an Evidence for him against LYNN & for coming & returning seven miles once together with his Ferriages at FREDERICKSBURGH.

Ordered that WILLIAM LYNN pay JOHN FOREMAN 46 pounds of Tobacco & one Shilling for one days attendance as an Evidence for him at suit of DICK & for coming & returning seven Miles once, together with his Ferriages at FREDERICKSBURGH.

Administration on the Estate of JOHN HARDIE is granted MARGARET HARDIE she having entered into Bond with BENJAMIN MASSEY & JOHN STONE her Securities. WITHERS CONWAY, BALDWIN DADE, THOMAS BUNBURY, & JOHN THOMAS, Appraisers.

Then the Court adjourned till tomorrow morning 9 Oclock.
JOHN MERCER

At a Court continued & held for Stafford County 10th July 1754.

Present   MOTT DONIPHAN   PETER DANIEL
                 JOHN STUART   JOHN STITH
                 JOHN WASHINGTON   BAILY WASHINGTON

Action of Trespass. THOMAS & ROBERT DUNLOPS agt. JOHN ARMSTRONG. A Jury to wit SAMUEL EARL, JOHN MAUZY, JOHN LEECH, SETH BOTTS, MERRIMOND TILLER, BENJAMIN ROBINSON, RICHARD PILCHER, WILLIAM ROSE, SAMUEL BREDWELL, ROBERT ASHBY, Junr., JOHN WITHERS, & THOMAS CRAWFORD. The Jury finds for the Pltf £12.5.7 half penny & Costs.

In the Suit on Attachment obtained by ARTHUR MORSON against the Estate of RICHARD

[Page 308 July 10, 1754]

July Court 1754

GAMBLE. The said Arthur produced a Bond of the said Richard for £14. It's considered by the Court that the said Arthur recover the same & his Costs. And the Sheriff returned the Attachment executed in the hands of ANDREW EDWARDS, ANDREW KENNY, & JOHN MERCER, Gent. who declared that the said Kenny had in his hands fifteen Shillings, Edwards six Shillings which they are ordered to pay the said Arthur in part satisfaction of the above Judgment & the said Mercer declared that he had no Estate of the said Gamble's in his Hands.

Ejection Firma. James Turff & John Twigg for Lands & Appurtenances in the Parish of Overwharton which WILLIAM FITZHUGH, Esqr. demised to the Pltf for a Term &c. On return of the Sheriff NATHANIEL MOORE Tenant in Possession of the Premises hath been served with a Copy of the said Declaration & he not appearing it's ordered that unless the said Tenant do appear at the next

Court, plead the general Issue, confess Lease Entry & Ouster, Judgment shall be granted the Pltf.

Ejection Firma. James Turff & John Twigg for Lands & Appurtenances in the Parish of Overwharton which MARQUIS CALMESE, Gent. demised to the Pltf for a Term &c. It appearing that WILLIAM THOMAS Tenant in Possession of the Premises hath been served with a Copy of the said Declaration & he not appearing it's ordered that unless the said Tenant do appear at the next Court, plead the general Issue, confess Lease Entry & Ouster, Judgment shall be granted the Pltf.

Action of Debt. MARGARET FRENCH Admx. of MASON FRENCH decd. agt. JOSEPH CHRISMOND & JOHN ADDISON. The Defts not appearing Judgment is granted the Pltf against them &

July Court 1754

GERARD FOWKE, Gent. Sheriff unless the Deft do appear at the next Court and answer the Pltf's Action.

Action of Debt. ROBERT MANNON agt. JOHN BROWN & JOHN THOMAS. WILLIAM ROSE undertook that if the Defts should be condemned in this Action that he would pay the Condemnation for them or surrender his Body to Prison. The Defts prayed Oyer &c which is granted them.

Action of Trespass. Revd. JOHN MONCURE agt. THOMAS LEMASTER & WILLIAM POTTER is dismist the Defts paying Costs.

Action of Debt. WILLIAM CUNNINGHAME agt. JAMES STUART. STEPHEN DURHAM & ELIZABETH MCABOY undertook that if the Deft should be condemned in this Action that they would pay the Condemnation for him or surrender his Body to Prison. The Deft prayed Oyer &c which is granted him.

Present JOHN MERCER, Gent.

Suit on Petition. ALLEN MCRAE agt. JAMES YELTON. Judgment is granted the Pltf for £2.16 with Interest from the tenth day of September 1753 till the same is paid & Costs & a Lawyer's Fee.

In the Suit on Attachment obtained by WILLIAM BLACK against the Estate of SOLOMON WAUGH, the said William produced a Bond from the hand of the said Solomon for £14.8.8. half penny. It's considered by the Court that the said

William recover the same from the said Solomon & his Costs. And the Sheriff having returned an Attachment executed in the hands of WILLIAM GARRARD who declared that he had 273 pounds of Tobacco of the said Solomon's in his Hands. It's thereupon ordered that the Sheriff sell the same & satisfy the said William his Judgment.

July Court 1754

Action of Trespass. JOHN TYLER agt. ELIZABETH STURDY for £100 by means of the Deft's breaking & entering the Close of the Pltf in the Parish of Overwharton. It's ordered that the Surveyor in Company of an able Jury go upon the Lands in Controversy & lay off the same as the Jury shall think fit, having regard to all Patents & Evidences as shall be produced by either of the Parties. And whereas some of the Lands in dispute lye in the County of King George, the Parties agree that the Surveyor of this County shall survey the whole.

Suit on Petition. WITHERS CONWAY agt. JOHN BROWN Admr. of STOCKETT decd. Judgment is granted the Pltf for £4.1.4 of the said Goods & Chattles of the said Intestate.

Ordered that WILLIAM HOLDBROOK pay ELIZABETH MCABOY 25 pounds of Tobacco for one days attendance as an Evidence for him at suit of FOWLER.

Ordered that WILLIAM HOLDBROOK pay JENNET HOLDBROOK 25 pounds of Tobacco for one days attendance as an Evidence for him at suit of FOWLER.

In the Suit on Attachment obtained by WILLIAM ROWLEY, Gent. against the Estate of CHARLES HARRISON for £9.13.7 it's considered by the Court that the said Pltf recover the same of the said Deft & his Costs. And the Sheriff having returned the Attachment executed in

July Court 1754

the Hands of JOHN SMITH who declared that he had in his hands 429 ½ pounds of Tobacco of the said Charles it's ordered that the Sheriff sell the same to satisfy the Judgment.

Action of Debt. JOHN LEECH agt. JOHN HAMILTON, Gent. A Jury to wit JOHN MAUZY, SETH BOTTS, WILLIAM TILLER, BENJAMIN ROBINSON, SAMUEL EARLE, RICHARD PILCHER, WILLIAM ROSE, ISAAC BREDWELL, ROBERT ASHBY, junr., JOHN WITHERS, THOMAS CRAWFORD, & CHARLES HARDING. The Jury finds that the Deft gave his Note of Hand to the Pltf in these words I will be security for MR. GOWERS paying you six Pistoles in a Month. After the Deft gave his said Note the Pltf took a Note from the said Gowers for the said debt. One month after the date I promise to pay to Mr. John Leech on his Order the Sum of six pounds nine Shillings Virginia currency for value received. The Jury finds for the Pltf for £6.9. The suit is continued till the next Court for the Matters of Law arising thereupon to be argued.

Action of Trespass. JAMES YELTON agt. JOHN PEYTON. The Jury finds for the Deft the Pltf paying his Costs.

Ordered that JAMES YELTON pay STEPHEN DURHAM 50 pounds of Tobacco for two days attendance for him against PEYTON.

Ordered that JAMES YELTON pay ROBERT DULIN 50 pounds of Tobacco for two days attendance for him against PEYTON.

Action of Trespass. RICHARD BERNARD, Gent. agt. WILLIAM ROSE.

[Page 312 July 10, 1754]

July Court 1754

The Jury finds for the Pltf 616 pounds of Tobo. damage & Costs.

Ordered that JOHN HAMILTON pay ELIZABETH KITCHEN 96 pounds of Tobacco & one Shilling for three days attendance as an Evidence for him at Suit of LEECH & for coming & returning seven Miles together with her Ferriages at FREDERICKSBURGH.

Ordered that JOHN LEECH pay GEORGE PILCHER 350 pounds of Tobacco for fourteen days attendance as an Evidence for him against HAMILTON.

Absent JOHN MERCER, MOTT DONIPHAN,
JOHN WASHINGTON, BAILY WASHINGTON

Action of Trespass. FRANCIS DADE agt. ROBERT MASSEY for £100 damages by means of the Defts breaking & entering the Close of the said Pltf in the Parish of St. Paul's. It's ordered that the Surveyor in Company of an able Jury go upon the Lands in controversy & lay off the same as either Party would

304

have it & having regard to all Patents & Evidences as shall be produced by either of the Parties. And it's further ordered that the Surveyor of WESTMORELAND attend & survey for the Pltf if required at the Pltf's Costs.

Ordered that RICHARD BARNARD, Gent. pay RICHARD FOOTE 100 pounds of Tobacco for four days attendance as an Evidence for him against ROSE.

Present MOTT DONIPHAN, JOHN WASHINGTON, BAILY WASHINGTON.
Absent JOHN PEYTON and PETER DANIEL, Gent.

[Page 313 July 10, 1754]

July Court 1754

Suit in Chancery. CHARLES WELLS & BENJAMIN ROBINSON agt. THOMAS VIVION & PETER DANIEL, Gent. It's ordered, decreed, & adjudged that a perpetual Injunction be granted the Complainants and that the Complainants recover of the said Defts their Costs.

Present JOHN MERCER, Gent.

Then the Court adjourned till tomorrow morning 9 Oclock.

At a Court continued & held for Stafford County 11th. July 1754.

Present   JOHN MERCER   JOHN PEYTON
            JOHN STITH   BAILY WASHINGTON

Action of Debt. HUGH MITCHEL agt. WILLIAM DAVIS. The Deft having pleaded that he owes nothing, the Trial is referred till the next Court.

Action of Debt. RICHARD BERNARD, Gent. agt. THOMAS FLEEMAN, Exor. of HENRY RYNOLDS decd. The Deft not appearing Judgment is confirmed to the Pltf against him for £42.8.9 with Interest from the second day of March 1747/8 till paid.

Ordered that JOHN PEYTON pay THOMAS SPALDING 71 pounds of Tobacco for two days attendance as an Evidence for him at suit of Yelton & for coming & returning seven Miles once.

Action of Debt. MICHAEL WALLACE agt. ROBERT GARRAT. The Special Verdict in this Cause being insufficient, a new Venire is ordered at the next Court.

305

July Court 1754

The Attachment obtained by JOHN NELSON against DANIEL MATHENY is dismist & the said Daniel is ordered to pay costs.

Present THOMAS FITZHUGH, Gent.

Action of Trespass. ABRAHAM BREDWELL agt. ROBERT ASHBY, Junr. The Errors filed in this Cause are adjudged good. It's thereupon considered by the Court that the Pltf take nothing by his Bill and that the Deft recover of the said Pltf his Costs.

Action of Trespass. THOMAS HORNBUCKLE agt. SAMUEL GRIGSBY. The Deft having pleaded not guilty the Trial is referred till the next Court.

Action of Trespass Assault & Battery. GERARD BANKS agt. SAMUEL GRIGSBY is to be argued next Court.

Action of Trespass. CHARLES HARDING agt. SAMUEL EARL, Gent. The Matters of Law arising from the special Verdict in this Cause being argued the Court are of Opinion that the Law is for the Deft.

Action of Debt. MOSLEY BATTALEY, Gent. on behalf of our Lord the King agt. ISAAC KNIGHT. A Jury to wit WILLIAM FITZHUGH, GOWRY WAUGH, MERRIMOND TILLER, HENRY WIGGINGTON, WILLIAM KENDALL, THOMAS JOHNSON, DARBY OCAIN, PETER MURPHY, JOHN KIRK, JOHN THOMAS, SETH BOTTS, & JOHN FITZHUGH. The Jury finds for our Sovereign Lord the King £50 & Costs.

July Court 1754

Action of Trespass. CAIN WITHERS agt. PRESLY COX. The Pltf having filed his Replication the Deft hath time till the next Court to consider thereof.

Action of Trespass. GEORGE BELL agt. ELIZABETH WITHERS. The Jury finds for the Pltf £10 damage & Costs.

Ordered that GEORGE BELL pay HUMPHRY GAINES 75 pounds of Tobacco for three days attendance as an Evidence for him against WITHERS.

Ordered that GEORGE BELL pay THOMAS SPALDING 46 pounds of Tobacco for one days attendance as an Evidence for him against WITHERS & for coming & returning seven Miles once.

Ordered that GEORGE BELL pay JOHN TYLER 74 pounds of Tobacco for two days attendance as an Evidence for him against WITHERS & for coming & returning eight miles once.

Ordered that GEORGE BELL pay JESSE BAILS 75 pounds of Tobacco for three days attendance as an Evidence for him against WITHERS.

Ordered that ELIZABETH WITHERS pay JOHN MAUZY 50 pounds of Tobacco for two days attendance as an Evidence for her at suit of BELL.

Ordered that GEORGE BELL pay JOHN FITZHUGH, Gent. 50 pounds of Tobacco for two days attendance as an Evidence for him against WITHERS.

Action of Trespass. DARBY OCAIN agt. ISAAC BREDWELL. By consent of the Parties SEB the Wife of SETH BOTTS her Deposition is to be taken before a Justice.

Then the Court adjourned till tomorrow morning 9 Oclock.

JOHN MERCER

[Page 316 July 11, 1754]

July Court 1754

At a Court continued & held for Stafford County 12th. July 1754.

Present MOTT DONIPHAN   PETER DANIEL
      THOMAS FITZHUGH JOHN WASHINGTON

Then the Court adjourned till tomorrow Morning 9 Oclock.

MOTT DONIPHAN

At a Court continued & held for Stafford County 13th. July 1754.

Present MOTT DONIPHAN   PETER DANIEL
      THOMAS FITZHUGH JOHN WASHINGTON

Then the Court adjourned till tomorrow Morning 9 Oclock.

MOTT DONIPHAN

At a Court continued & held for Stafford County August 13th. 1754.

Present   JOHN MERCER   JOHN PEYTON
                      JOHN STUART   JOHN WASHINGTON
                      BAILY WASHINGTON

At a Court held for Stafford County 10th. September 1754.

Present   JOHN MERCER   MOTT DONIPHAN
                      JOHN PEYTON   PETER DANIEL
                      THOMAS FITZHUGH   JOHN STITH
                      JOHN WASHINGTON   BAILY WASHINGTON

JOHN STUART, Gent. produced a Commission under the hand of the Honbl. ROBERT DINWIDDIE, Esqr. to be Sheriff of this County. WITHERS CONWAY, WILLIAM GARRARD, & ANTHONY GERRARD Sub Sheriffs.

Ordered that the Sheriff summon 24 of the most able Freeholders in this County to appear at Novr. Court to be of the Grandjury for the Body of this County.

HENRY FITZHUGH, GERARD FOWKE, Gent. took the several Oaths & subscribed

[Page 317 Sept. 10, 1754]

September Court 1754

the Test & Abjuration Oath, ordered to be Certified.

Present HENRY FITZHUGH &
GERARD FOWKE, Gentlemen.

Inspectors nominated, for BOYD'S HOLE, BALDWYN DADE, THOMAS BUNBURY, Junr., WITHERS CONWAY, & WILLIAM BUNBURY.

For CAVES, THOMAS MONROE, THOMAS HAY, WILLIAM MOUNTJOY & CAIN WITHERS.

For AQUIA, RICHARD HEWETT, BENJAMIN STROTHER, WILLIAM WRIGHT, & JOSEPH CARTER.

FRANCES DADE Orphan of HENRY DADE made Choice of BALDWYN DADE for her Guardian.

FRANCES PRICE Servant to PATRICK GRADY agreed to quit her Master her Freedom dues for the Time she hath to serve.

Ordered that JANE ELLIOTT serve her Master ANDREW KENNY for 21 days runaway Time & 540 pounds of Tobacco, & five Shillings expended in taking her up.

Ordered that RICHARD CONDRON be examined on Monday the 16th Instant.

WILLIAM SHUMATE acknowledges himself indebted to our Lord the King in the Sum of £20 for the Appearance of ANN his Wife at the Courthouse of this County on the 16th Instant to give Evidence against RICHARD CONDRON.

Action of Trespass. FRANCIS DADE agt. THOMAS MASSEY for £100 damage by Means of breaking & entering the Close of the Pltf in the Parish of St. Paul's. It's ordered that the Surveyor in Company of an able Jury go upon the Lands in Controversy & lay off the same as either party would have it, having regard to all Patents & Evidences as shall be produced by either of the Parties.

[Page 318 Sept. 10, 1754]

September Court 1754

And it's further ordered that the Sheriff of WESTMORELAND attend & survey for the Pltf (if required) at his Costs.

Suit in Chancery. LETTICE LYNTON by JOHN PEYTON, Gent. her Guardian & next Friend agt. JOHN RAMAY. All Matters in difference between them are referred to the determination of the Revd. JOHN MONCURE, PETER HEDGMAN, & JOHN MERCER, Gent. It's ordered that John Ramy & MARY his Wife deliver to the said John Peyton for the use of the said Lettice on the 21st of January next the Mulatto Slave JAMES, late ANTHONY LYNTON'S, & the Negroes PETER & JAMES received from WILLIAM LYNTON'S Estate cloathed as Negroes ought to be. That the said Deft pay to the said Peyton for the Use aforesaid £5.11.4 half penny a Moiety of the Estate of the Complainant's Brother JOHN LYNTON, decd. It's further decreed that if it shall appear hereafter that the said JOHN RAMY or MARY his Wife shall have received any thing more of the said WILLIAM LYNTON'S Estate than charged the said LETTICE LYNTON is not to be barred from such Part of it as she is intitled to, & that each Party pay their own Costs.

Then the Court adjourned till Court in Course.
JOHN MERCER

At a called Court held for Stafford County 16th day of Sepr. 1754.

Present   JOHN MERCER   MOTT DONIPHAN
                 JOHN PEYTON   PETER DANIEL
                 THOMAS FITZHUGH   JOHN STITH
                 JOHN WASHINGTON   BAILY WASHINGTON

RICHARD CONDRON, who was bound over by this County Court for his Examination for Felony was brought to the Barr, and having heard the Evidences well for as agasint him it's the Opinion of the Court that the said Condron be sent to the General Court for a further Trial.

The Deposition of ANNE SHUMATE, Wife of WILLIAM SHUMATE deposeth that on Saturday the 16th of July about the Hours of eleven or

[Page 319 Sept. 16, 1754]

September Court 1754

twelve of the Clock in the day, RICHARD CONDRON came to the said Shumate's house & after being a short time in the house asked the Deponent for Breakfast which she readily gave him & after eating his Breakfast the said Condron asked the Deponent for Money, to which the Deponent answered she had no Money to which he replied there was Money in the house & Money he would have & swore he would shoot her thro' the Body if she did not give him Money, & thereupon took her husband's Gun which was Sedon [*sic*] in the Chimney & cocked it & presented it at the Deponent's Breast, making a further demand for Money & finding he could get none the said Condron carried the said Gun out of the house & throw'd it in the Yard, & afterwards returned into the house & attempted to ravish the Deponent swearing he would lie with her & endeavour'd to pull up her Cloaths which she endeavoured to keep down, & after some struggle she told him that if he did not forbear, she would cry out to a Man who was not far off, altho' at the same time she knew not of any Person to come to her Assistance there not being any body but herself & a young Child in the house, or on the Plantation, her husband being gone from home two days before, & that upon the Deponent's speaking these words, the said Condron left her & carried her Child away with him about two or three hundred Yards from the house, & there left the Child in the Woods, & that she well knows the said Condron now Prisoner at the Bar to be the Person that committed the Offences aforementioned, & that after he was apprehended for the same she knew him as far as she could see him, & that when he came to the said Shumate's house & committed the said Offences he was cloathed with a brown Linen Shirt & pair of Trousers, & that she was very much affrighted at the Usage she received of the said Condron. And further this Deponent saith not.

her
ANN   X   SHUMATE
mark

The Deposition of WILLIAM SHUMATE aged about 23 Years deposeth that when this Deponent came home from Prince William on Sunday the 14th of July last he found his Wife very much frighted being then big with Child told him that a low thick squat man drest with a brown Linen Shirt & pair of trousers came to the Deponents house in his Absence the day before & behaved in the Manner mentioned in her Deposition & the Deponent enquiring about the Neighbourhood he was told it was RICHARD CONDRON by several of the Neighbours they having seen him drest in that Manner that same day & said that he looked as if he

[Page 320 Sept. 16, 1754]

September Court 1754

had been doing Mischief, & very much like an Hangman, & this Deponent further saith, That WILLIAM KENDALL, Junr. one of his Neighbours told him that as he went home from JOHN GREEN'S Reaping he said to his Wife that he thought RICHARD CONDRON looked more like a Rogue that day than he ever saw him altho' he always looked like one & that he looked as if he had been doing Mischief & that this discussion passed between him & his Wife the thirteenth before he had ever heard that he had been doing the Mischief mentioned in ANN SHUMATE'S Deposition, & this Deponent said that he had received some Money before the Time aforesaid but that he lent it out, & further saith not.

WILLIAM SHUMATE

The Deposition of ARTHUR DENT aged about 34 Years & the Deposition of JAMES PHILIPS aged about 54 Years. That on Saturday the thirteenth of July last they saw RICHARD CONDRON at JOHN GREEN'S Reaping about three or four OClock in the Afternoon & was then cloathed in a brown Linen Shirt & Trousers & that he appeared to these Deponents to be in a pretty deal of Confusion & that the rest of the Company at the Reaping took notice of it & talked of it & that at that time these Deponents did not know, or hear of the Mischief done at WILLIAM SHUMATE'S that day & further these Deponents say not.

his
ARTHUR   X   DENT
mark

his
JAMES PHILLIPS

311

mark

WILLIAM SHUMATE for himself, and ANN his Wife, ARTHUR DENT & JAMES PHILLIPS acknowledged themselves indebted in the Sum of £20 each for their Personal Appearance at the next General Court, on the sixth day thereof to give Evidence against RICHARD CONDRON.

JOHN MERCER

[Page 321 Oct. 8, 1754]

October Court 1754

At a Court held for Stafford County 8th October 1754.

Present MOTT DONIPHAN   PETER DANIEL
     THOMAS FITZHUGH JOHN WASHINGTON

JAMES KENNY in open Court discharged his Servant DANIEL HARVEY from any further Service the said Harvy agreeing to discharge his said Master from paying him any freedom dues.

Ordered that JAMES CAMPBELL serve his Master ADAM STEVEN for eight days runaway time & £4.6.6 expended in taking him up.

Ordered that MARDEN OWENS serve his Master ALEXANDER STEPHEN for eight days runaway time & £4.6.6 expended in taking him up.

The Inspectors at BOYDS HOLE made Oath that they had in their Hands 3,963 pounds of Tobacco, sold for eight Shillings & five pence P Cent.

AQUIA Inspectors made Oath that they had in their hands 7,637 pounds of Tobacco sold for eight Shillings & seven pence P Cent.

CAVES Inspectors made Oath that they had in their Hands 2,750 pounds of Tobacco, sold for seven Shillings & one penny P Cent.

On Motion of WILLIAM GARRARD his Licence for keeping Ordinary is renewed.

Action of Trespass. JOHN TYLER agt. ELIZABETH STURDY for £100 damage by means of the Deft's breaking & entering the Close of the Pltf in the Parish of Overwharton. It's ordered that the Surveyor in Company of an able Jury go upon the Lands in Controversy & lay off the same as either party would have it, having regard to all Patents & Evidences as shall be produced by either

312

of the Parties. And whereas some of the Lands in dispute lye in the County of KING GEORGE it's agreed by the Parties that the Surveyor of Stafford

[Page 321 [*sic*] Oct. 8, 1754]

October Court 1754

survey the Whole.

Suit on Petition. CHARLES JONES agt. WILLIAM FITZHUGH, Esqr. & FRANCIS THORNTON, Gent., acting Exors. of GILSON BERRYMAN, decd. Judgment is granted the Pltf for £4.13.3 & Costs.

Action of Trespass. TRAVERSE COOKE agt. JOHN FARROW. On the Motion of the Pltf it's ordered that the Deposition of JOHN JOHNSON be taken.

Ordered that TRAVERSE COOKE pay JOHN JOHNSON 575 pounds of Tobacco & three shillings for three says attendance as an Evidence for him against FARROW & for coming & returning 55 Miles three Times together with his Ferriages at OCCOQUAN.

Then the Court adjourned till tomorrow morning 9 Oclock.
MOTT DONIPHAN

At a Court continued & held for Stafford County 9th. Octor. 1754.

Present PETER DANIEL   GERARD FOWKE
     THOMAS FITZHUGH BAILY WASHINGTON

JOHN RALLS on his Motion hath his Ordinary Licence renewed.

Present JOHN PEYTON

Ordered that CATHERINE ASHBY pay HENRY WIGGINGTON 175 pounds of Tobacco for seven days attendance as an evidence for her against ASHBY.

Suit on Petition. GEORGE WALLER & WILLIAM ALLEN Exors. of EDWARD WALLER decd. agt. CHARLES HARDING. Judgment is granted the Pltfs for £3.4 & Costs.

Ordered that GEORGE WALLER & WILLIAM ALLEN pay SAMUEL EARLE 50 pounds of Tobo. for two days attendance for them against HARDING.

October Court 1754

Ordered that GEORGE WALLER & WILLIAM ALLEN pay GEORGE RANDALL 25 pounds of Tobo. for five days attendance for them against HARDING.

Suit on Petition. MOSELY BATTALEY, Gent. agt. ANDREW KENNY. Judgment is granted the Pltf for £2.6.1 half penny & Costs.

Suit on Petition. JACOB WILLIAMS agt. JOHN BROWN Admr. of JOHN HACKELL, decd. Judgment is granted the Pltf for £4.13.10 of the Goods & Chattles of the said Intestate & Costs.

Suit on Petition. JOHN EVANS, Junr. agt. STEPHEN DURRAM. Judgment is granted the Pltf for £2.17.9 & Costs.

Suit on Petition. ROBERT & EDWARD MAXWELLS & COMPANY agt. THOMAS WILSON. Judgment is granted the Pltfs for 365 pounds of Tobacco & Costs.

Suit on Petition. MARGARET FRENCH Admx. of MASON FRENCH agt. ALEXANDER DOUGLASS & JOHN LINIMETT. Judgment is granted the Pltf for £2.2 & Costs. But this Judgment is to be discharged on payment of £1.1 with Interest from the first day of April 1752 till the same is paid.

Suit on Petition. MARGARET FRENCH Admx. of MASON FRENCH agt. SAMUEL WHITSON & JOHN ADDISON. Judgment is granted the Pltf for £3.13.6 & Costs. But this judgment is to be discharged on payment of £1.16.9 with Interest from the first day of April 1752 till the same is paid.

Suit on Petition. WILLIAM OFFIT agt. LONG WHARTON. Judgment is granted the Pltf for £3.4.6 & Costs & a Lawyer's Fee.

Suit on Petition. MARY JAMES agt. THOMAS BELL. Judgment is granted the Pltf for £1.15.3 with Costs & a Lawyer's Fee.

Suit on Petition. WILLIAM KELLY agt. NATHANIEL PRICE. Judgment is granted the Pltf for £1.9.7 & Costs.

Suit on Petition. WILLIAM KELLY & PHILLIS his Wife agt. ALEXANDER DOUGLASS & JOHN CHRISTIE. Judgment is granted the Pltfs for £4.9 & Costs.

October Court 1754

Suit on Petition. WILLIAM KELLY & PHILLIS his Wife agt. SAMUEL WHITSON & NATHANIEL PRICE. Judgment is granted the Pltf for £1.10 & Costs.

Ejection Firma. John Seekright agt. JOHN RALLS, Senr. for Lands & Appurtenances in the Parish of Overwharton which MAXAMILLION ROBINSON, Gent. demised to the Pltf for a Term &c. It's ordered that the Surveyor go upon the Lands in Controversy & lay off the same as either Party would have it having regard to all Pattents & Evidences as shall be produced by either Party.

Suit on Petition. JOHN THOMAS agt. ROBERT STUART. Judgment is granted the Pltf for £1.16.2 farthing & Costs.

Suit on Petition. WILLIAM GARRARD agt. THOMAS JOHNSON. Judgment is granted the Pltf for seven Shillings & ten pence & 306 pounds of Tobacco & Costs.

Suit on Petition. WILLIAM HOWARD admr. of HUGH MCLANE decd. agt. JOHN HAMILTON, Gent. judgment is granted the Pltf for £1.19 with Costs & a Lawyer's Fee.

Suit on Petition. THOMAS HOARD admr. of HUGH MCLANE agt. GEORGE PILCHER. Judgment is granted the Pltf for £1.7.6 with Costs & a Lawyer's Fee.

Action of Trespass Assault & Battery. JOHN HURLEY agt. THOMAS PRATT. The Deft not appearing Judgment

October Court 1754

is granted the Pltf against him & WITHERS CONWAY his Security unless the Deft do appear at the next Court and answer the Pltf's Action.

Action of Debt. WILLIAM GARRARD agt. HUMPHREY POPE. The Deft not appearing an Attachment is ordered against the Deft's Estate for £13 & Costs returnable to the next Court.

Action of Debt. WILLIAM GARRARD agt. SAMUEL ANGEL. The Deft not appearing an Attachment is ordered against the Deft's Estate for £6.10.3 & 470 pounds of Tobo. & Costs returnable to the next Court.

Action of Debt. ALEXANDER HAY agt. THOMAS MONROE & THOMAS HAY Inspectors at CAVES WAREHOUSE. The Defts not appearing Judgment is granted the Pltf against them & JOHN STUART, Gent. Sheriff unless the Defts do appear at the next Court & answer the Pltfs Action.

Action of Debt. THOMAS TURNER Esqr. agt. ROBERT ENGLISH. WILLIAM GARRARD undertook that if the Deft should be condemned in this Action that he would pay the Condemnation for him or surrender his Body to Prison.

Action of Trespass. WILLIAM ALLEN agt. JOHN MURDOCK. The Deft confessed Judgment to the Pltf for £5.9.5 half penny & Costs.

Action of Trespass. WILLIAM ALLEN agt. JOSEPH BLACK. The Deft not appearing Judgment is granted the Pltf against him & ELIAS HORE his Security unless the Deft do appear at the next Court & answer the Pltf's Action.

Action of Debt. ALEXANDER WOODROE & COMPANY agt. JOSEPH WINLOCK. Judgment is granted the Pltf against him & WILLIAM LUNSFORD his Security unless the Deft do appear at the next Court & answer the Pltf's Action.

[Page 325 Oct. 9, 1754]

October Court 1754

Action of Debt. ALEXANDER WOODROE & COMPANY agt. JOHN HAMILTON, Gent. The Deft confessed Judgment to the Pltfs for £22 & Costs. But this Judgment is to be discharged on payment of £11 with Interest from the first day of May 1753 till the same is paid.

Action of Debt. ANDREW COCHRANE & COMPANY agt. WILLIAM HORTON. The Deft confessed Judgment to the Pltf for £60 & Costs. But this Judgment is to be discharged on payment of £30.6 half penny with Interest from the first day of August 1753 till the same is paid.

Action of Trespass. ANDREW COCHRANE & COMPANY agt. WILLIAM HORTON. The Deft confessed Judgment to the Pltf for £6.2.8 & Costs.

In the Suit on Attachment obtained by WILLIAM ALLEN against the Estate of FRANCIS BROOX. JOHN TOBY & WILLIAM KING Garnishees of the said

Francis being called it's ordered that an Attachment issue against them returnable to the next Court.

Ejection Firma. James Turff agt. John Twigg for Lands & Appurtenances in the Parish of Overwharton which WILLIAM FITZHUGH Esqr. demised to the Pltf for a Term &c. JOHN PEYTON, Gent. being admitted Deft in the room of the said Twigg pleaded not guilty, confesses Lease Entry & Ouster & agreed to insist only on the Title at Trial. The Trial is referred till the next Court.

[Page 326 Oct. 9, 1754]

October Court 1754

Ejection Firma. William Thrustout agt. Thomas Holdfast for Lands & Appurtenances in the Parish of Overwharton which ROBERT BRENT demised to the Pltf for a Term &c. It appearing that WILLIAM THOMAS Tenant in Possession of the Premises hath been duly served with a Copy of the Declaration & he not appearing it's ordered that unless the said Tenant do appear at the next Court, Judgment will be granted the Pltf and possession awarded the Pltf to put him in Possession thereof.

In the Suit on Attachment obtained by CHARLES WELLS against the Estate of FRANCIS BROOX the said Charles produced an Account against the said Francis for £10. It's considered by the Court that the said Charles recover the same of the said Francis & his Costs. And the Constable having made return that he had attached one Cornfield to the Value of nine Barrels, one oval Table, one Pot & hooks, & four & a half dozen Bottles & sundry other Lumber it's ordered that the Sheriff sell the same & satisfy the above Judgment.

JOHN THOMAS on his Motion hath his Ordinary Licence renewed.

ELIZABETH WALLER agreed in Court to serve her Master WILLIAM DAVIS one year for salivating.

Then the Court adjourned till tomorrow morning 9 Oclock.
JOHN PEYTON

[Page 327 Oct. 10, 1754]

October Court 1754

At a Court continued & held for Stafford County 10th. October 1754.

Present   MOTT DONIPHAN   JOHN PEYTON
             PETER DANIEL   GERARD FOWKE

317

Ordered that the Sheriff agree with Workmen to mend the PRISON.

Suit in Chancery. WILLIAM FITZHUGH an Infant under the Age of twenty one Years by CHARLES CARTER, Esqr. his Guardian agt. WINIFRED MASSEY Admx. of ROBERT MASSEY. The Deft not appearing an Attachment is granted him against her returnable to the next Court.

Action of Trespass. ROBERT BROWN agt. JOHN ADAMS is dismist the Pltf failing to give Security for his Costs.

Suit in Chancery. CADWALLER DADE & _____ [name not given] his Wife agt. WILLIAM FITZHUGH, Esqr. & FRANCIS THORNTON, Gent. Exors. of GILSON BERRYMAN. The Defts having filed their Demurrer time is given the Complainants till the next Court to consider thereof.

Action of Trespass. HUMPHREY POPE agt. CAIN WITHERS. The Deft for Plea saith he is not guilty & the Trial is referred till the next Court.

Action of Trespass. THOMAS DOUGLASS & COMPANY agt. ADAM STEPHEN. The Deft not appearing it's considered by the Court that the Pltf recover of the Deft £35.4.5 half penny & their Costs. And the Sheriff having returned the said Attachment executed on a pair of Cart Wheels, it's ordered that he sell the same & satisfy the above Judgment.

Action of Debt. MOORE FANTLEROY, Gent. agt. HUMPHREY POPE. The Deft for plea saith he has paid the debt.

[Page 328 Oct. 10, 1754]

October Court 1754

The Trial is referred till the next Court.

Suit on Scire Facias. JAMES HUNTER, WILLIAM TALIAFERRO, FIELDING LEWIS, & CHARLES DICK Exors. of WILLIAM HUNTER, decd. agt. WILLIAM FITZHUGH Esqr. & FRANCIS THORNTON, Gent. acting Exors. of GILSON BERRYMAN decd. The said William & Francis confessed Judgment to the Pltfs for £6.2.1 & 104 pounds of Tobo. & Costs.

Action of Debt. CHARLES STUART & COMPANY agt. FRANCIS BROOX. The Deft confessed Judgment to the Pltf for £42.18.8 & Costs. But this Judgment is to be discharged on payment of £21.9.4 with Interest from the first day of April 1753 till the same is paid.

Ordered that CHARLES HINSON be allowed £3.10 out of the Estate of CHARLES BIRCHELL decd. for attending WILLIAM BIRCHELL, son of the said Charles in his Sickness & for burying him.

Action of Trespass. JOHN TAYLOE, Esqr. agt. WILLIAM DAVIS. The Pltf failing to prosecute his Suit he is nonsuited & the Pltf is ordered to pay the Deft damages & Costs.

Action of Trespass. JAMES WREN agt. NATHANIEL HARRISON, Esqr. acting Exor. of WILLIAM WALKER, decd. The Court are of Opinion that the Pltf recover £13.5 of the Goods & Chattles of the said Testator.

[Page 329 Oct. 10, 1754]

October Court 1754

Ordered that ISAAC BREDWELL pay CHARLES HARDING 200 pounds of Tobacco for eight days attendance as an Evidence for him at Suit of OCAIN.

Ordered that WILLIAM DAVIS pay ANN GRAY 175 pounds of Tobacco for seven days attendance as an Evidence for him at Suit of TAYLOE.

Suit in Chancery. WILLIAM WALKER & ELIZABETH his Wife, JOHN THOMAS, & PRISCILLA MONKS agt. ANDREW EDWARDS & BETTY his Wife Admrs. of JAMES WAUGH, Gent., decd. The Defts having filed their answer time is given the Complainants till the next Court to consider thereof.

Action of Trespass. JAMES STUART & MARY his Wife agt. ELIZABETH RAPIER. A Jury to wit JOHN RALLS, JOHN CLARK, THOMAS CRAWFORD, WILLIAM SWETMAN, JOHN PEYTON, WILLIAM BUSSELL, EDWARD PILCHER, JACOB JOHNSON, DARBY OCAIN, THOMAS SUDDEN, RICHARD RANDALL, & WILLIAM HORTON. The Jury finds for the Deft and the Pltfs are ordered to pay her Costs.

Action of Trespass. ELIZABETH RAPIER agt. JAMES STUART & MARY his Wife. The Jury finds for the Pltf forty Shillings damage & Costs.

Ordered that JAMES WRENN pay WILLIAM WRENN 403 pounds of Tobacco for seven days attendance as an Evidence for him against WALKER.

Ordered that JOHN TAYLOE Esqr. pay WILLIAM JONES 150 pounds of Tobacco for six days attendance for him as an Evidence against DAVIS.

October Court 1754

Ordered that JOHN TAYLOE, Esqr. pay WILLIAM LONG 175 pounds of Tobacco for seven days attendance as an Evidence for him against DAVIS.

Ordered that JOHN TAYLOE, Esqr. pay THOMAS FLETCHER 100 pounds of Tobacco for four days attendance as an Evidence for him against DAVIS.

Ordered that JOHN TAYLOE, Esqr. pay ELIZABETH SHAW 150 pounds of Tobacco for six days attendance as an Evidence for him against DAVIS.

Ordered that ELIZABETH RAPIER pay SAMUEL MITCHEL 75 pounds of Tobacco for three days attendance as an evidence for her against STEWART & his Wife.

Ordered that WILLIAM ROSS pay JOSEPH WINLOCK 75 pounds of Tobacco for three days attendance as an Evidence for him against STUART & others.

Ordered that ELIZABETH RAPIER pay WILLIAM ROSS 75 pounds of Tobacco for three Days attendance as an evidence for her against STEWART & others.

Action of Trespass. JOHN PEYTON agt. WILLIAM SWETMAN. A Jury to wit JOHN KIRK, JOHN CLARK, THOMAS CRAFFORD, CHARLES HARDING, WILLIAM BUSSELL, EDWARD PILCHER, DARBY OCAIN, RICHARD RANDALL, WILLIAM JORDAN, HUMPHREY POPE, WILLIAM DYE, & TIMOTHY DULANY. The Jury finds for the Pltf for damage & Costs.

Ordered that JOHN PEYTON pay WILLIAM GARRARD 25 pounds of Tobacco for one days attendance as an evidence for him against SWETMAN.

Ordered that JOHN PEYTON pay THOMAS SPALDING 200 pounds of Tobacco for eight days attendance as an evidence for him against SWETMAN.

Ordered that WILLIAM SWETMAN pay GEORGE HINSON 75 pounds of Tobacco for three days attendance as an evidence for him at suit of PEYTON.

Ordered that WILLIAM SWETMAN pay ANDREW KENNY 75 pounds of Tobacco for three days attendance as an evidence for him at suit of PEYTON.

Action of Trespass Assault & Battery. ROBERT WICKLIFF agt. ANDREW KENNY. The Jury finds for the

October Court 1754

Pltf forty Shillings damage & Costs.

Ordered that ROBERT WICKLIFF pay GEORGE BRETT 445 pounds of Tobacco for seven days attendance as an evidence for him against KENNY & for coming & returning thirty Miles three Times.

Ordered that ROBERT WICKLIFF pay JOHN LYNTON 445 pounds of Tobacco for seven days attendance as an evidence for him against KENNY & for coming & returning thirty Miles three Times.

Suit in Chancery. HONOUR MCKEY agt. SAMUEL MCKEY. The Deft not appearing an Attachment is granted her against him returnable to the next Court.

Action of Trespass. JAMES STUART & MARY his Wife agt. WILLIAM ROSS junr. The Jury finds for the Deft & the Pltfs tho solemnly called came not but made default whereupon they are nonsuited & ordered to pay the Deft's damages & Costs & a Lawyer's Fee.

Action of Trespass. JAMES STUART & MARY his Wife agt. WILLIAM ROSS, Senr. The Jury finds for the Deft & the Pltfs tho solemnly called came not but made default whereupon they are nonsuited & ordered to pay the Deft's damages & Costs & a Lawyer's Fee.

Suit on Petition. WILLIAM PICKETT agt. JOHN HONEY. Judgment is granted the Pltf for £3.7 with Costs & a Lawyer's Fee.

Then the Court adjourned till Court in Course.
MOTT DONIPHAN

October Court 1754

At a Court held for Stafford County for proof public Claims Propositions, & Grievances, October 8th. day 1754.

Present	MOTT DONIPHAN	JOHN PEYTON
	PETER DANIEL	THOMAS FITZHUGH
	JOHN WASHINGTON	

ROBERT YATES produced a Certificate under the Hand of HENRY FITZHUGH, Esqr. for taking up a runaway Servant Man named JOSEPH JEFFERSON belonging to JAMES SEBURN of AUGUSTA COUNTY which is ordered to be certified.

EDWARD BETHELL produced a Certificate under the hand of JOHN PEYTON, Gent. for taking up a runaway servant Boy named JOHN WILLIAMS belonging to THOMAS HAMPTON of FAIRFAX COUNTY which is ordered to be certified.

THOMAS JOHNSON produced a Certificate under the hand of MOTT DONIPHAN, Gent. for taking up a runaway servant boy named JOSEPH BASSET belonging to HENRY ASHTON of WESTMORELAND COUNTY which is ordered to be certified.

WILLIAM DIE produced a Certificate under the hand of FRANCIS THORNTON, Gent. for taking up two runaway negro Men named JACOB & DICK belonging to WILLIAM ROBINSON of KING & QUEEN COUNTY which is ordered to be certified.

GEORGE WHITE produced a certificate under the hand of THOMAS FITZHUGH, Gent. for taking up a runaway Negro Woman named FLORA belonging to JOHN SKINKER of KING GEORGE COUNTY which is ordered to be certified.

[Page 333 Oct. 8, 1754]

November Court 1754

JOHN SYLY produced a certificate under the hand of JOHN PEYTON, Gent. for taking up a runaway Servant Man named WILLIAM COO belonging to DARBY OCAIN of this County which is ordered to be certified.

WILLIAM BURTON & DERRICK MANNON produced a certificate under the hand of MOTT DONIPHAN, Gent. for taking up a runaway Servant Man named JOHN BROWN belonging to JOHN BROWN of this County which is ordered to be certified.

A Proposition under the Hand of LAWRENCE WASHINGTON, Gent. & others the Inhabitants of this County to have a public Ferry from the said Washington's Land in this County to ANDREW MONROE'S Land in Maryland at upper CEDAR POINT which is ordered to be certified.

MOTT DONIPHAN

At a Court held for Stafford County 12ᵗʰ. Novr. 1754.

Present   MOTT DONIPHAN   JOHN PEYTON
                PETER DANIEL   HENRY FITZHUGH
                JOHN WASHINGTON

Weights to be tried at CAVES WAREHOUSE by MOTT DONIPHAN & PETER DANIEL. At BOYDS HOLE by HENRY FITZHUGH & JOHN WASHINGTON. At AQUIA by JOHN PEYTON & BAILY WASHINGTON.

A Grandjury for the Body of this County having received their Charge retired. And returning into Court with their Presentment it's ordered that the Offenders be summoned.

Ejection Firma. Thomas Turff agt. THOMAS SEDDON for Lands & Appurtenances in the Parish of Overwharton which HENRY FITZHUGH, Esqr. demised to the Pltf for a Term &c. On Motion of the said Henry it's ordered that a Dedimus issue to take the Deposition of JOHN MAUZY & ARTHUR DUAS at the Pltf's Costs.

[Page 334 Nov. 12, 1754]

November Court 1754

Then the Court proceded to lay the County Levy.

Stafford County	Dr.	lb. Tobacco
To Secretary NELSON by Account		207
To MOSELY BATTALEY King's Attorney		2000
To the Clerk by Law		1254
To ditto by Account		2335
To the Sheriff by Law		1254
To JAMES HANSBROUGH by Account		126
To JOHN MERCER, Gent. by Account		1026
To ALEXANDER STEPHEN by Account		891
To CHARLES HARDING by Account		200
To JAMES WAYTON Levy overpaid		16
To JOHN HOOE, Gent. for ditto		16
To GEORGE RINGLESBY for ditto		16
To CHARLES HARDING further by Account		540
To JOSEPH WHITE by Account		120
To EDWARD BETHEL by Account		200
To WILLIAM GEORGE by Account		80
To GEORGE RINGLESBY further by Account		224

To JOHN STONE by Account	325
To JACOB JOHNSON by ditto	367
To JOHN WITHERS for guarding the Prisoner Condron	300
To THOMAS WITHERS for ditto	870
To WILLIAM CORBIN for ditto	990
To ROBERT ENGLISH for ditto	360
To ANTHONY GARRARD for ditto	600
To WILLIAM GARRARD by Account	3523
	17840
To 6 P. Cent on 17840	1070
	18910
By 2028 Tithes at 10 P Poll & a Fraction in the Sheriff's Hands of 1370	18910

Ordered that the Sheriff collect for each Tithable person within this County ten pounds of Tobacco in order to discharge the County Levy.

The Order for summoning BIRKET PRATT, THOMAS PRATT, THOMAS PRICE, CHANDLER FOWKE, JOHN SHORT, SAMUEL THORNBURY, & EDWARD BURGESS for not appearing tho summoned as Jurors in the Suit between FRANCIS DADE Pltf & ROBERT MASSEY Deft

[Page 335 Nov. 13, 1754]

November Court 1754

is renewed.

Then the Court adjourned till tomorrow morning 9 Oclock.
                    MOTT DONIPHAN

At a Court continued & held for Stafford County 13th. November 1754.

Present   MOTT DONIPHAN   JOHN PEYTON
               PETER DANIEL   HENRY FITZHUGH
               JOHN WASHINGTON

Ordered that FRANCIS DADE be summoned to appear at the next Court to answer to such Things as shall then & there be objected against him.

Suit on Petition. CHARLES HARDING agt. GEORGE WALLER. By consent of the Parties all Matters in difference between them are referred to the determination of the Revd. JOHN MONCURE & JOHN PEYTON, Gent. & their award to be made the Judgment of the Court.

Suit on Petition. JAMES STUART agt. WILLIAM ROSS, junr. Judgment is granted the Pltf for 157 pounds of Tobo. & Costs.

Suit on Petition. ROBERT BOGGASS agt. RICHARD ROGERS. Judgment is granted the Pltf for £3.18.11 farthing with Costs & a Lawyer's Fee.

Present JOHN MERCER, Gent.

Action of Debt. DANIEL & ALEXANDER CAMPBELLS agt. FRANCIS MARTYN, JOHN CUBBAGE, & WILLIAM HEFFERNON. The Deft Cubbage not appearing Judgment is granted the Pltf against him & JOHN STUART, Gent. Sheriff of this County unless the Deft do appear at the next Court & answer the Pltf's Action. And it's ordered that alias issue against the said FRANCIS MARTYN & WILLIAM HEFFERNON returnable to the next Court.

Action of Trespass. JOHN CHAMP, Esqr. agt. SOLOMON WAUGH. The Deft confessed Judgment to the Pltf for £11.9.2 half penny. It's considered by the Court that the Pltf recover the same of the Deft & his Costs.

Ordered that the Sheriff pay GEORGE WALLER 49 pounds of Tobacco out of the Fraction in his hands.

[Page 336 Nov. 13, 1754]

November Court 1754

Ordered that JAMES STUART pay BARNABAS WILLIAMS 50 pounds of Tobacco for two days attendance as an Evidence for him against ROSS.

Ordered that JAMES STUART pay MARY WISE 50 pounds of Tobacco for two days attendance as an Evidence for him against ROSS.

Ordered that the Sheriff take WILLIAM DAVIS into his Custody till he enter into Bond in £20 with two Securities each in the Sum of £10 for his good Behavior & keeping the Peace. JOHN LEERIGHT & ALEXANDER DOUGLASS acknowledged themselves indebted to our Sovereign Lord the King in the Sum of £10 each as Security for the said William.

Ordered that the Sheriff take WILLIAM LONG into his Custody till he enter into Bond in £20 with two Securities each in the Sum of £10 for his good Behavior & keeping the Peace. WILLIAM JONES & ALEXANDER

DOUGLASS acknowledged themselves indebted to our Sovereign Lord the King in the Sum of £10 each as Security for the said William.

Present BAILY WASHINGTON, Gent.

Upon Petition of WILLIAM ASBURY it's ordered that SAMUEL GARNER & ISABEL his Wife be summoned to appear at the next Court to answer the said Petition.

Ordered that SARAH TODD be summoned to appear at the next Court to answer to such Things as shall be then & there objected against her concerning JAMES MARTYN an Orphan Child in her Possession.

Ordered that the Sheriff demand of THOMAS FITZHUGH, Gent. £20 his Fine for refusing the Sheriff's Commission & if he pays the same the Sheriff is ordered to receive it.

WILLIAM KING is appointed Overseer of the Road in the Room of CHARLES HARDING.

ISAAC ROSE is appointed Overseer of the Road from PASBITANZY BRIDGE to the farther part of the County by HOOE'S ORDINARY on the Ridge.

[Page 337 Nov. 13, 1754]

November Court 1754

Ordered that a Road be cleared from GREEN'S POST to BRENT TOWN ROAD & that the same be kept in repair by Collo. WILLIAM FITZHUGH'S Tithes, ROBERT FRISTOE'S, JOSEPH COMBS, WILLIAM MOORE'S, JOHN ABBIT'S, SNODAL LATHAM'S, & BAILY WASHINGTON'S Tithes & that they be exempt from other Roads. BAILY WASHINGTON, Junr. is appointed Overseer of the same Road.

Administration on the Estate of WILLIAM HOLDBROOK, decd. is granted JAMES CUMBERFORD who married the Widow of the said William. THOMAS MONROE, WILLIAM MILLS, WILLIAM MOUNTJOY, & SAMUEL EARLE Appraisers.

Action of Debt. GOWRY WAUGH agt. RAWLEIGH CHINN, Junr. The Deft confessed Judgment to the Pltf for 1260 pounds of Tobacco & Costs.

In the Suit on Attachment obtained by GEORGE RINGLESBY against the Estate of JOHN FINIGHAN the said George produced an Account against the said John for £5 payable the first of January next. It's considered by the Court that the said George recover the same of the said John & his Costs. And the Sheriff having returned the Attachment executed on some fother Corn & Tobacco, it's ordered that he sell the same & satisfy the above Judgment. Memorandum. The Pltf acknowledges to have received forty Shillings of ALEXANDER DONIPHAN.

Suit on Petition. ALEXANDER DOUGLASS agt. WILLIAM KELLY. Judgment is granted the Pltf for £2.1.10 half penny & Costs.

Suit on Petition. ANDREW ANDERSON agt. PAUL SWEENY. Judgment is granted the Pltf for £2.15.4 with Costs & a Lawyer's Fee.

Suit on Petition. ANDREW GRANT agt. ISAAC ROSE. Judgment is granted the Pltf for his Costs.

Action of Debt. MOSES GRIGSBY agt. ZACHARIAH UNDERWOOD is dismist, no Appearance.

Action of Debt. THOMAS FREEMAN agt. JOHN THOMAS,

[Page 338 Nov. 13, 1754]

November Court 1754

ALEXANDER DOUGLASS, NATHANIEL PRICE, & SAMUEL WHITING. The Defts prayed Oyer &c which is granted them.

Action of Trespass. ANDREW GRANT agt. JOHN LIMOTT. The Deft not appearing Judgment is granted the Pltf against him & JACOB JOHNSON his Security unless the Deft do appear at the next Court & answer the Pltf's Action.

Action of Trespass. ANDREW GRANT agt. WILLIAM THORNBURY. The Deft not appearing Judgment is granted the Pltf against him & WITHERS CONWAY his Security unless the Deft do appear at the next Court & answer the Pltf's Action.

Suit on Scire Facias. The Honorable WILLIAM FAIRFAX, Esqr., GEORGE WILLIAM FAIRFAX, GEORGE WASHINGTON, NATHANIEL CHAPMAN, & AUGUSTINE WASHINGTON, Exors. of the last Will & Testament of LAWRENCE WASHINGTON, decd. agt. WILLIAM FITZHUGH, Gent. The said William prayed Oyer &c which is granted him.

Action of Debt. WHIDDON WALLACE agt. SIMON PERRIE & THOMAS FLETCHER. THOMAS FLEEMAN & PETER SIDEBOTTOM undertook that if the Deft Fletcher should be condemned in this Action that they would pay the

327

Condemnation for him or surrender his Body to Prison & the said Fletcher prayed Oyer &c which is granted him & the Deft Perry not appearing it's ordered that an Alias Capias issue against him returnable to the next Court. WILLIAM DAVIS in open Court became security for the Pltf's Costs in this Suit.

Action of Debt. JOHN THORNTON, Gent. agt. ANDREW CRAWFORD, ANDREW KENNY, & JOHN MINOR. A Jury to wit JOHN CLARK, JOHN KIRK, GEORGE RANDALL, WILLIAM ALLEN, THOMAS SUDDON, EDWARD PILCHER, JAMES BERRY, CHARLES HARDING, THOMAS CRAWFORD, WILLIAM KING, WILLIAM BURTON, & GEORGE BELL. The Jury finds for the Pltf £19.13.9 & 344 pounds of Tobacco & Costs.

On Motion of JOHN LEWRIGHT his Ordinary Licence is renewed.

Ordered that JOHN THORNTON, Gent. pay EDWARD HERNDON, junr. 325 pounds of Tobacco & three Shillings for four days attendance

[Page 339 Nov. 13, 1754]

November Court 1754

as an Evidence for him against KENNY & others & for coming & returning 25 Miles three times as also for his Ferriages at FREDERICKSBURGH.

Then the Court adjourned till tomorrow morning 9 Oclock.
JOHN MERCER

At a Court continued & held for Stafford County November 14th. 1754.

Present   JOHN MERCER   MOTT DONIPHAN
                 HENRY FITZHUGH   GERARD FOWKE
                 JOHN WASHINGTON   BAILY WASHINGTON

Action of Debt. JOHN THORNTON, Gent. agt. ANDREW KENNY & others. JOHN PEYTON & others special Bail for the said Andrew Kenny brought the said Kenny into Court for their discharge which MOSELY BATTALEY Gent. Attorney for the Pltf refused to take there being no Execution issued against his Body.

Action of Trespass. SARAH MCCULLOUGH agt. SAMUEL BREDWELL. A Jury to wit EDWARD PILCHER, JOHN CLARK, WILLIAM PORCH, JOHN TOBY, WILLIAM KING, JOHN PEYTON, THOMAS CRAWFORD, THOMAS SPALDING, BENJAMIN ROBINSON, GEORGE

328

RANDALL, JOHN KIRK, & MERRIMOND TILLER. The Jury finds for the Pltf forty Shillings damage & Costs.

Ordered that WILLIAM HORTON who failed to attend (tho summoned) as a Witness in the Suit depending between SARAH MCCULLOUGH agt. SAMUEL BREDWELL unless he appears at the next Court & shew Cause why he did not attend.

Action of Trespass. NATHANIEL GRAY, agt. WILLIAM FITZHUGH, Esqr. & FRANCIS THORNTON, Gent. acting Exors. of GILSON BERRYMAN decd. The Defts having pleaded non-Assumpsit & fully administered the Trial is referred till the next Court.

[Page 340 Nov. 14, 1754]

November Court 1754

Action of Trespass Assault & Battery. WILLIAM SUDDUTH agt. JOHN PAYTON. The Deft having pleaded not guilty the Trial is referred till the next Court.

Action of Debt. WILLIAM CUNNINGHAM & COMPANY agt. JOHN THOMAS. JACOB JOHNSON & WITHERS CONWAY undertook that if the Deft should be condemned in this Action that they would pay the Condemnation for him or surrender his Body to Prison & the Deft having pleaded that he owed nothing. The Trial is referred till the next Court.

Action of Debt. CHARLES CARTER, Esqr. agt. WINIFRED MASSEY Admx. of ROBERT MASSEY decd. The Deft having pleaded payment & fully administered, the Trial is referred till the next Court.

Action of Trespass. WILLIAM FITZHUGH, Gent. agt. WINIFRED MASSEY Admx. of ROBERT MASSEY, decd. The Deft having pleaded payment & fully administered, the Trial is referred till the next Court.

Action of Trespass. PATRICK GRADY agt. SNODALL & WILLIAM HORTON abates by the Pltf's Death.

Action of Trespass. JAMES BOYDIE agt. HENRY TYLER is dismist each Party paying their own Costs.

Action of Trespass. CATHERINE ASHBY agt. SAMUEL BREDWELL. A Jury to wit JOHN GRAVAT, JOHN ANGELL, WILLIAM PICKETT, JOHN PAYTON, HUMPHREY POPE, SAMUEL EARLE, WILLIAM POTTER, FRANCIS BROOX, THOMAS NORMAN, JOHN HONEY, FRANKLYN

LATHAM, & JOHN HARDING. The Jury finds that the Deft said the Pltf pull'd the Wool off his Sheep. If the Law be for the Pltf we find for her forty Shillings damage. This Suit is continued till the next Court for the Matters of Law arising thereupon to be argued.

Ordered that SARAH MCCULLOUGH pay CHARLES HARDING 275 pounds of Tobacco for eleven days Attendance as an Evidence for her against BREDWELL.

Ordered that SARAH MCCULLOUGH pay THOMAS ASHBY 200 pounds of Tobacco for eight days Attendance as an Evidence for her against BREDWELL.

Action of Debt. ROBERT ASHBY agt. SAMUEL BREDWELL.

[Page 341 Nov. 14, 1754]

November Court 1754

The Jury finds for the Deft. It's considered by the Court that the Deft recover his Costs from the Pltf.

Ordered that ROBERT ASHBY pay THOMAS SEDDON 275 pounds of Tobacco for eleven days attendance as an Evidence for him against BREDWELL.

Action of Trespass. CHARLES HARDING agt. FRANCIS BROOX being agreed is dismist.

Action of Debt. CHARLES STUART & ARMAUS agt. ALEXANDER DOUGLASS. The Deft not appearing an Attachment is granted them against his Estate for £15 with Interest & Costs returnable to the next Court.

Action of Trespass. ISAAC FOWLER & REBECCA his Wife agt. WILLIAM HOLDBROOK abates by the Deft's death.

Ejection Firma. James Turff agt. John Twigg for Lands & Appurtenances in the Parish of Overwharton which WILLIAM FITZHUGH, Esqr. demised to the Pltf for a Term &c. JOHN PEYTON, Gent. being admitted Deft in the room of the said Twigg pleaded not guilty, confessed Lease Entry & Ouster and agreed to insist only on the Title at Tryal. The Trial is referred till the next Court.

Ejection Firma. James Turff agt. John Twigg for Lands & Appurtenances in the Parish of Overwharton which MARQUIS CALMESE demised to the Pltf for a Term &c. WILLIAM THOMAS being admitted Deft in the room of the said

Twigg pleaded not guilty, confessed Lease Entry & Ouster and agreed to insist only on the Title at Tryal. The Trial is referred till the next Court.

Action of Trespass. ANDREW GRANT agt. HOWSON HOOE, junr. Admr. of HENRY DADE, decd. The Deft having filed his Plea, Time is given the Pltf till the next Court to consider thereof.

November Court 1754

Action of Debt. JAMES HUNTER agt. WINIFRED MASSEY Admx. of ROBERT MASSEY decd. The Deft having pleaded Payment & fully administered the Trial is referred till the next Court.

GERRARD FOWKE is appointed Feoffee of MARLBORO TOWN in the Room of TRAVERSE COOKE.

Action of Trespass. ANDREW GRANT agt. WILLIAM KELLY & PHILLIS his Wife Admrs. of JAMES MCINTOSH decd. The Defts having pleaded non-Assumpsit & fully Administered the Trial is referred till the next Court.

Action of Debt. MARGARET FRENCH Admx. &c of MASON FRENCH, decd. agt. JOSEPH CHRISMOND & JOHN ADDISON. The Defts not appearing the Judgment against them & GERARD FOWKE, Gent. late Sheriff of this County is confirmed to the Pltf for £6.17.10 & an pence & Costs.

Action of Debt. WILLIAM KELLY & PHILLIS his Wife agt. NATHANIEL PRICE & JOHN GORDON. The Defts say they owe nothing. The Trial is referred till the next Court.

Action of Debt. ROBERT MANNON agt. BENJAMIN MASSEY. The Deft says that he owes nothing. The Trial is referred till the next Court.

Action of Trespass. WILLIAM GARRARD agt. SAMUEL ANGELL. The Deft not appearing upon an Attachment ordered in this Suit Judgment is granted the Pltf for £6.10.3 & 470 pounds of Tobacco. And the Sheriff having returned the said Attachment executed on three Cows, one Calf, Corn, & a pair of Cart Wheels, & Grubbing Hoe, & Cow Hide it's ordered that he sell the same & satisfy the above Judgment.

December Court 1754

GERARD FOWKE Gent. took the Oath & Subscribed the Test & Abjuration Oath in respect to his Majesty's Commission.

The Court do accept the Terms mentioned in Memorial given into Court by JOHN MERCER, Gent. relating to the Lotts not taken up in MARLBORO TOWN & the said Mercer agreeing to give Bond in £10,000 to indemnify them. And the Feoffees are desired to make a Conveyance of the County's Right to the 26 Lotts mentioned in the said Memorial.

Ordered that JOHN KENADY pay JOHN CHAMBERS 150 pounds of Tobacco for six days attendance as an Evidence for him against CHAMBERS.

Ordered that PATRICK GRADY pay WILLIAM WOODWARD 145 pounds of Tobacco for six days attendance as an Evidence for him against HORTON & for three Times coming & returning five Miles.

Then the Court adjourned till Court in Course.

JOHN MERCER

At a called Court held for Stafford County 4th. Decr. 1754.

Present	JOHN MERCER	MOTT DONIPHAN
	JOHN PEYTON	PETER DANIEL
	GERARD FOWKE	THOMAS FITZHUGH

GEORGE CARTER being committed to the Goal of this County under the hand of JOHN PETYON Gent. dated the 29th day of Novr. last, for Felony, was brought to the Bar & having heard the Evidenced as well for as against him it's the unanimous Opinion of the Court that the said Carter is guilty of the Felony he stands charged with & that he be sent to WILLIAMSBURGH for a further Tryal.

WILLIAM WRIGHT of Stafford County aged 52 years or thereabouts deposeth that on Sunday the 29th of Sepr. last this Deponent's Stallion was turned out at his House & the Horse being missing next Morning he sent two or three times to look for him & not being to be found he concluded that he was stolen that he never heard anything about him till the Sunday after, when he heard a Horse was killed, & cut a sunder. On his going to see

December Court 1754

the Remains of the Horse a great part of which was eaten, he was satisfied it was his Horse & several Others who saw the said Remains declared they was of the same Opinion, & for further Proof this Deponent got the Hoof & Shoe off one his forelegs & carried it to JOHN NIXON the Smith who had shod him who on sight thereof said he would swear it was the Shoe he had put on the said Deponent's Horse.

WILLIAM WRIGHT

BETTY DULIN aged 19 years or thereabouts saith that on Monday the 30th September last about sunset she saw GEORGE CARTER the Prisoner at the Bar driving before him a large black Stallion & seemed to be much tired & the Horse attempted once or twice to take the Road that went towards WILLIAM WRIGHT'S but said Carter turned him another Way & she verily believes it was the same Horse she had seen the said Wright ride to Church some time before.

her
BETTY   B   DULIN
mark

ANGEL JACOBUS JORDAN aged 18 years or thereabouts saith that on Thursday the third of October last going home he saw a large black Stallion lying dead by the Road cut in two that this deponent turning up his Buttock to see his Brand it appeared to him that the brand was skinned off.

his
ANGEL JACOBUS   A   JORDAN
mark

ROBERT ASHBY, junr. aged 36 years or thereabouts saith that on Monday the 30th of Sepr. last sometime in the Morning he saw a Man ride by his House upon a Horse which this Deponent believed to be WILLIAM WRIGHT'S Horse, who this Deponent took to be VALENTINE PEYTON, & upon a dispute with his Wife who the Man was seeing the same Man returning some time later in the arfternoon upon the same Horse he walked out & discovered the Man to be GEORGE CARTER the Prisoner at the Bar.

ROBERT ASHBY

WILLIAM TOLSON aged 16 years or thereabouts saith that on Monday the 30th of September last early in the Morning he saw GEORGE CARTER riding up BRENT TOWN ROAD upon a large black Horse.

his
WILLIAM   X   TOLSON
mark

December Court 1754

SNODALL HORTON junr. aged 24 Years or thereabouts saith that on Monday I met a man early in the Morning riding up the road & in the Evening of the same day I met the same Man & Horse returning & I believe the man was GEORGE CARTER to whom I spoke & asked him if his Horse was tired & he said yes which vext him much & he said he had been at MR. FOOTES. This was about half a Mile from where I heard the Horse was killed & the Monday I saw him was that Monday before the following Sunday when I first heard of the horse being killed.

his
SNODAL   S   HORTON
mark

CHARLES HARDING aged 51 or thereabouts saith that on Monday the 30th day of Sepr. as he was standing by the Roadside he saw a man riding down the Road upon a large black Stallion, branded with an O on the near Buttock which was WILLIAM WRIGHT'S Horse, & the Man he does not positively know & on Friday following he saw the same Horse further down the same Road dead & his brand cut.

CHARLES HARDING

JOHN NIXON aged 47 Years or thereabouts saith that the Horse & Shoe of a foreleg of a horse that was dead & shewed to me by WILLIAM WRIGHT was the Hoof & Shoe of the said Wright's Horse that I had sometime before shod.

JOHN NICKSON

WILLIAM WRIGHT, NICHOLAS DULIN for BETTY his Wife, ANGEL JACOBUS JORDAN, ROBERT ASHBY, junr., WILLIAM TOALSON, SNODAL HORTON, junr., CHARLES HARDING, & JOHN NIXON acknowledged themselves indebted to our Sovereign Lord the King each in the Sum of £20 in case they fail to appear at the Capitol in WILLIAMSBURGH on the sixth day of the the next General Court to give Evidence against GEORGE CARTER.

JOHN MERCER

March Court 1755

At a called Court held for Stafford County March 8th. 1755.

Present	JOHN PEYTON	PETER DANIEL
	GERARD FOWKE	THOMAS FITZHUGH
	JOHN WASHINGTON	BAILY WASHINGTON

JOHN FRAZIER & WILLIAM THOMPSON being committed to the Goal of this County by a Mitimus under the hand of John Washington, Gent. dated the 28th of February last for Felony, & having heard the Evidences as well for as against them it's the Court's Opinion that they be sent to WILLIAMSBURGH for a farther Trial.

ANDREW GRANT the younger aged 18 years or thereabouts saith that the Goods here in Court produced are belonging to the Store kept by his Father & that he was present with WILLIAM STRIBLING when the same were taken out of the Possession of JOHN FRAZIER.

ANDREW GRANT, junr.

WILLIAM STRIBLING age 23 Years or thereabouts saith that upon being informed by one of his Servants that JOHN FRAZIER had some new Goods in his Possession searched & finding the same in his Box went & acquainted MR. GRANT upon which the said Grant got a Warrant & had him the said Frazier taken up & asking him how he came by the said Goods, said he brought them into the Country with him.

his
WILLIAM   X   STRIBLING
mark

JOHN FRAZIER saith that the Goods found upon him was given to him in the Night by WILLIAM THOMPSON between the Door & Door Post (the Door being locked) of Mr. Grants Store House.

his
JOHN   X   FRAZIER
mark

[Page 347 Mar. 8, 1755]

March Court 1755

WILLIAM THOMPSON saith that he gave the Goods produced in Court to JOHN FRAZIER in the Night between the Door & Doorpost of MR. GRANT'S STORE (the Door being locked) being overpersuaded by the said Frazier so to do.

WILLIAM THOMPSON

ANDREW GRANT & WILLIAM STRIBLING acknowledged themselves indebted to our Lord the King in the Sum of £20 in Case they fail to appear at the Capitol in WILLIAMSBURGH on the sixth day of the next General Court to give Evidence against JOHN FRAZIER & WILLIAM THOMPSON.

MOTT DONIPHAN

At a Court held for Stafford County 11th March 1755.

Present	MOTT DONIPHAN	JOHN PEYTON
	PETER DANIEL	HENRY FITZHUGH
	JOHN STITH	JOHN WASHINGTON
	THOMAS FITZHUGH	

Ordered that Liquors stand rated as before.

BURDITT CLIFTON on his Motion hath his Ordinary Licence renewed.

Ordered that SARAH PESTRIDGE appear at the next Court to answer the Petition of HENRY SMITH & JESSE MOSS.

Present JOHN PEYTON, BAILY WASHINGTON, Gent.

Ordered that the Church Wardens of Overwharton Parish bind JOHN RAPIER to WILLIAM ROSS, junr. according to Law.

Ordered that the Churchwardens of St. Paul's Parish bind EDWARD CONNER & WILLIAM SHEARER according to Law.

Ordered that AGNESS MCCOLLISTER serve her Master JOHN RALLS for six days runaway time & ten Shillings &

[Page 348 Mar. 11, 1755]

March Court 1755

180 pounds of Tobacco expended in taking her up.

RACHAEL LUNSFORD, Wife of MOSES LUNSFORD came into Court & being first privately examined, relinquishes her Right of, in, & to certain Lands conveyed by the said Husband to CHARLES HARDING which is ordered to be recorded.

Administration of the Estate of GEORGE PILCHER is granted JOHN NELSON he having entered into Bond with JAMES BUCHANAN his Security. CAIN WITHERS, WILLIAM GARRARD, GOWRY WAUGH, & THOMAS JONES Appraisers.

336

Ordered that WILLIAM KELLY & PHILLIS his Wife be summoned to appear at the next Court to answer the Petition of WILLIAM JOHNSON.

Present JOHN MERCER, Gent.

Ordered that the Sheriff summon 24 of the most able Freeholders of this County to appear at May Court next to be a Grandjury for the Body of this County.

In the Suit on Attachment obtained by JOHN NELSON & COMPANY against the Estate of WILLIAM COX the said John produced an Account against the said William for £4.18. It's considered by the Court that the said John & Company recover the same of the said William & their Costs. And the Sheriff having returned the Attachment executed in the hands of THOMAS TURNHAM & WILLIAM SMITH the said Smith declared that he had in his hands an Ax, a Gun, & old Kersey Coat. It's ordered that the Sheriff sell the same & satisfy the above Judgment.

In the Suit on Attachment obtained by JOHN ALEXANDER against the Estate of THOMAS BURN the said John produced an account against the said Thomas for £5. It's considered by the Court that the said John recover the same of the said Thomas & his Costs. And the Sheriff having returned the Attachment executed on one bed & furniture, one Chest, two Tables, one Bowl, one Iron Pot & Hooks, one Box Iron, one old Box, & some other Trifles. It's ordered that the Sheriff sell the same & satisfy the above Judgment.

Ordered that the Churchwardens of Overwharton Parish bind WILLIAM GROVES according to Law.

[Page 349 Mar. 11, 1755]

March Court 1755

Action of Debt. JOHN PEYTON, Gent. agt. SIMON STACY & PETER RUFFNER. The Defts not appearing Judgment is granted the Pltf unless the Defts appear at the next Court & answer the Pltf's Action.

In the Suit on Attachment obtained by GOWRY WAUGH against the Estate of ENOCH HENSLEY is dismist the said Enoch paying Costs.

In the Suit on Attachment obtained by ALEXANDER DONIPHAN against the Estate of JOHN FINIGAN, the said Alexander produced a penal Obligation for £12.8.8 & 18 pounds of Tobacco. It's considered by the Court that the said Alexander recover the same of the said John & his Costs. But this Judgment is to be discharged on payment of £6.4.4 & nine pounds of Tobacco with Interest from the 30th day of September 1754 till the same is paid. And the Sheriff having made return that he had attached four Bottles, one Cider Cask, some Lumber & 150 pounds of Tobacco in the hands of JOHN CANADAY & some Lumber in the hands of EDWARD RASPIN, it's ordered that he sell the same & satisfy the above Judgment.

Suit on Petition. JOHN SPRAYBRY agt. BENJAMIN ROBINSON & JESSE BAILS Exors. of HENRY ROBINSON decd. Judgment is granted the Pltf for six shillings & ten pence & 375 pounds of Tobacco.

Ordered that JOHN SPRABRY pay JOHN RAMAY 100 pounds of Tobacco for four days attendance as an Evidence for him against ROBINSON'S Executors.

Suit on Petition. JOHN BAILIE agt. JOSEPH CLIFT. Judgment is granted the Pltf for 268 pounds of crop Tobo. with Costs & a Lawyer's Fee.

Suit on Petition. RICHARD HOOE agt. JACOB WILLIAMS. Judgment

[Page 350 Mar. 11, 1755]

March Court 1755

is granted the Pltf for £2.7.1 & Costs.

Suit on Petition. JOHN SHORT agt. ANDREW EDWARDS. Judgment is granted the Pltf for £3.2.10 & Costs.

Action of Debt. JOHN SHORT agt. JOHN THOMAS. The Deft not appearing Judgment is granted the Pltf against him & WITHERS CONWAY his Security unless the Deft do appear at the next Court & answer the Pltf's Action.

Action of Debt. CHARLES ASHTON agt. JOHN FITZHUGH. WILLIAM FITZHUGH, Gent. undertook that if the Deft should be condemned in this Action that he would pay the Condemnation for him or surrender his Body to Prison whereupon the Deft prayed Oyer &c which is granted him.

Ordered that THOMAS FITZHUGH be prosecuted according to Law for not accepting the Sheriff's Commission.

JOHN STUART, JOHN STITH, & JOHN WASHINGTON, Gent. acknowledged their Bond to our Sovereign Lord the King which is ordered to be recorded.

Then the Court adjourned till tomorrow morning 9 Oclock.
                                                    JOHN MERCER

At a Court continued & held for Stafford County March 12ᵗʰ. 1755.

Present   MOTT DONIPHAN   HENRY FITZHUGH
                    JOHN STITH   JOHN WASHINGTON
                    BAILY WASHINGTON

Action of Trespass. ALEXANDER BROWN agt. ROBERT STUART. The Deft not appearing Judgment is granted the Pltf against him & BALDWYN DADE his Security unless the Deft do appear at the next Court & answer the Pltf's Action.

Action of Trespass. JOHN MUSCHET agt. WILLIAM BUTLER. The Deft not appearing Judgment is granted the Pltf against him & GEORGE BRENT his Security unless the Deft do appear at the next Court & answer the Pltf's Action.

[Page 351 Mar. 12, 1755]

March Court 1755

Action of Debt. JOHN PEYTON, Gent. agt. FRANCIS DAY. The Deft not appearing an Attachment is awarded him against the Deft's Estate for _____ [*left blank*] & Costs returnable to the next Court.

Action of Debt. JOHN PEYTON agt. ELIZABETH HACKNEY is dismist the Deft paying Costs.

Action of Trespass. JOHN PEYTON, Gent. agt. JOSEPH DUNAWAY. The Deft not appearing Judgment is granted the Pltf against him & NICHOLAS DULIN & JOHN NIXON his Securities unless the Deft do appear at the next Court & answer the Pltf's Action.

Action of Debt. JOHN PEYTON, Gent. agt. SAMUEL WHITSON. The Deft confessed Judgment to the Pltf for £6.4.2 & Costs.

Action of Debt. CHARLES ASHTON, Gent. Admr. of MARY ASHTON, decd. agt. JOHN THOMAS. The Deft not appearing Judgment is granted the Pltf against him & WITHERS CONWAY his Security unless the Deft do appear at the next Court & answer the Pltf's Action.

Suit on Petition. JOHN RAMAY agt. JOHN PEYTON, Gent. Admr. of JOHN LYNTON, decd. Judgment is granted the Pltf for £2.15.10.

                    Present JOHN PEYTON, PETER DANIEL, Gent.

In the Suit on Attachment obtained by JOHN RALLS against the Estate of JOHN STACY. The said John produced an

[Page 352 Mar. 12, 1755]

March Court 1755

Account against the said JOHN STACY for £3.1.4 farthing & Costs. And the Sheriff having returned the said Attachment executed in the hands of BENJAMIN STROTHER, Gent. who declared he had in his hands a Riple Gun of the Estate of the said Stacy. It's ordered that the Sheriff sell the same according to Law & that after satisfying the said Strother 390 pounds of Tobacco out of the Sale thereof that he pay the residue to the said Ralls.

Action of Debt. ALEXANDER DONIPHAN agt. WILLIAM LAMPTON. The Deft confessed Judgment to the Pltf for £17.2.2 & Costs.

Action of Trespass. ALEXANDER DONIPHAN agt. SAMUEL WHITSON. The Deft confessed Judgment to the Pltf for _____ [*left blank*]. It's considered by the Court that the Pltf recover the same & his Costs.

Absent JOHN PEYTON, Gent.

Action of Debt. JOHN PEYTON, Gent. agt. JAMES MCDANIEL. The Deft not appearing an Attachment is awarded him against the Deft's Estate for _____ [*left blank*] & Costs.

Suit on Petition. JOHN PEYTON, Gent. agt. HENRY WIGGINGTON. Judgment is granted the Pltf for £3.8.4 & Costs.

Suit on Petition. JOHN PEYTON, Gent. agt. JOSEPH DUNAWAY. Judgment is granted the Pltf for 804 pounds of crop Tobacco & Costs.

[Page 353 Mar. 12, 1755]

March Court 1755

Suit on Petition. JOHN PEYTON, Gent. agt. WILLIAM FOSTER. Judgment is granted the Pltf for £4.15 & Costs.

Present JOHN PEYTON, Gent.

Action of Trespass. BOGLE & COMPANY agt. WILLIAM THORNBURY. The Deft not appearing Judgment is granted the Pltf against him & WITHERS

CONWAY his Security unless the Deft do appear at the next Court & answer the Pltf's Action.

Present JOHN MERCER, Gent.

Action of Debt. JOHN ARMSTRONG agt. GEORGE WHITE. The Deft not appearing Judgment is granted the Pltf against him & WITHERS CONWAY his Security unless the Deft do appear at the next Court & answer the Pltf's Action.

Action of Trespass. RICHARD BERNARD, Gent. agt. EDWARD HUMSTON. A Jury to wit JOHN RALLS, ALEXANDER DONIPHAN, JOHN FITZHUGH, JOHN FITZHUGH, junr., WILLIAM ADIE, JOHN HOOE, JOSEPH CARTER, WILLIAM MILLS, JAMES HANSBROUGH, WILLIAM ALLEN, & CAIN WITHERS. The Deft's Demurrer to the Evidence being adjudged good the Jury is discharged & it's considered by the Court that the Pltf take nothing by his Bill & that the Pltf pay the Deft's Costs.

Action of Debt. JOHN CLARK agt. DARBY OCAIN. A Jury to wit ROBERT FRISTOE, ROBERT MANNON, HUSBANDFOOTE WHITECOTTON, JOHN PEYTON, CHARLES HARDING, HUMPHREY POPE, JOHN RAMAY, JAMES BERRY, JOHN SPRABIA, WILLIAM SUDDUTH, WILLIAM MATHENY, & SAMUEL MITCHELL. The Jury finds for the Deft, the Pltf paying the Deft's Costs.

[Page 354 Mar. 12, 1755]

March Court 1755

Present THOMAS FITZHUGH, Gent.

Action of Debt. CHARLES STUART & COMPANY agt. THOMAS DOUGLASS. JOHN WASHINGTON & WILLIAM BERNARD undertook that if the Deft should be condemned in this Action that they would pay the Condemnation for him or surrender his Body to Prison & the Deft prayed Oyer &c which is granted him.

Action of Trespass. CHARLES STUART & COMPANY agt. SAMUEL EARL Admr. of SAMUEL EARL, decd. The Deft confessed Judgment to the Pltf for £33.19.10 & Costs.

Ejection Firma. WILLIAM FITZHUGH, Esqr. agt. JOHN PEYTON, Gent. for Lands & Appurtenances in the Parish of Overwharton. It's ordered that the Surveyor go upon the Lands in Controversy & lay off the same as either Party would have it, having Regard to all Patents & Evidences as shall be produced by either of the Parties.

341

Action of Trespass. JOHN HOOE, Gent. agt. WINIFRED MASSEY Admx. of ROBERT MASSEY decd. The Deft for plea saith that the Testator did not assume & that she hath fully administered. The Trial is referred till the next Court.

Action of Trespass. JOHN BOGLE & COMPANY agt. WINIFRED MASSEY Admx. of ROBERT MASSEY decd. The Deft for plea saith that the Testator did not assume & that she hath fully administered. The Trial is referred till the next Court.

Action of Trespass. JAMES HUNTER surviving Partner of WILLIAM HUNTER decd. agt. WINIFRED MASSEY

[Page 355 Mar. 12, 1755]

March Court 1755

Admx. of ROBERT MASSEY decd. The Deft for plea saith that the Testator did not assume & that she hath fully administered. The Trial is referred till the next Court.

Action of Debt. CHARLES CARTER, Esqr. agt. WINIFRED MASSEY Admx. of ROBERT MASSEY decd. It's considered by the Court that the Pltf recover the Sum of £280 of the Goods & Chattles of the said Intestate. But this Judgment is to be discharged on payment of £140 with Interest from the 21st day of June 1751 till the same is paid. £7.11.10 paid in part of Interest to be allowed.

Action of Debt. WILLIAM FITZHUGH, Gent. agt. WINIFRED MASSEY Admx. of ROBERT MASSEY decd. It's considered by the Court that the Pltf recover the Sum of £108 of the Goods & Chattles of the said Intestate. But this Judgment is to be discharged on payment of £132.14.10 with Interest from the third day of February 1751 till the same is paid.

Action of Debt. JAMES HUNTER surviving Partner of WILLIAM HUNTER decd. agt. WINIFRED MASSEY Admx. of ROBERT MASSEY decd. It's considered by the Court that the Pltf recover the Sum of

March Court 1755

£1,096.3.3 of the Goods & Chattles of the said Intestate. But this Judgment is to be discharged on payment of £455.17.1 half penny with Interest from the third day of September 1751 till the same is paid.

Action of Trespass. MARGARET PIPER agt. JOHN MAISIE. The Pltf failing to prosecute her suit she is nonsuited & ordered to pay the Deft damages according to Law & Costs.

Action of Trespass. HARRY PIPER agt. JEREMIAH CARTER. The Pltf failing to prosecute his suit he is nonsuited & ordered to pay the Deft damages according to Law & Costs.

Action of Debt. ROBERT MANNON agt. BENJAMIN MASSEY. The Deft confessed Judgment to the Pltf for £59.2.4 & Costs. But this Judgment is to be discharged on payment of £29.11.2 farthing with Interest from the first day of June 1754 till the same is paid & the Pltf agreed to stay Execution two Weeks.

Action of Debt. ROBERT MANNON agt. JOHN BROWN & JOHN THOMAS. The Defts having pleaded payment the Trial is referred till the next Court.

Action of Debt. WILLIAM CUNNINGHAME, Merchant agt. JAMES STUART. The Deft having pleaded payment the Trial is referred till the next Court.

Absent MOTT DONIPHAN, PETER DANIEL, Gent.

Action of Trespass. TRAVERSE COOKE agt. JOHN FARROW. A Jury to wit ANDREW EDWARDS, JOHN FITZHUGH, JOHN FITZHUGH, JOSEPH CARTER, JOHN LEWRIGHT, WEEDON SMITH, JAMES CUMBERFORD, WILLIAM ALLEN, SAMUEL EARL, THOMAS SPALDING, DARBY OCAIN, & JOHN GREEN.

March Court 1755

The Jury finds for the Pltf £10 damage & Costs.

343

Ordered that JOHN FARROW pay WILLIAM TACKET 343 pounds of Tobacco for four days attendance as an Evidence for him at suit of COOKE & for coming & returning 27 Miles three times.

Ordered that JOHN FARROW pay JOHN NOVELL 536 pounds of Tobacco for four days attendance as an Evidence for him at suit of COOKE & for coming & returning 30 Miles once.

Ordered that JOHN FARROW pay WILLIAM FARROW 298 pounds of Tobacco for four days attendance as an Evidence for him at suit of COOKE & for coming & returning 22 Miles three times.

Ordered that WILLIAM MILLS, FRANCIS STROTHER, JAMES HANSBROUGH, & CAIN WITHERS be fined each of them 400 pounds of Tobacco for not attending as Jurors in the Suit between TRAVERSE COOKE & JOHN FARROW.

Then the Court adjourned till tomorrow morning 9 Oclock.

At a Court held for Stafford County by Virtue of a Commission or Oyer & Terminer, the 2nd day of April 1755.

A Commission of Oyer & Terminer for the Trial of JOSEPH a negro man slave belonging to GERARD FOWKE, Gent. together with a dedimus for administering the Oaths, JOHN WASHINGTON & BAILY WASHINGTON, Gent. administered the Oaths to MOTT DONIPHAN, Gent. who administered the said Oaths to JOHN WASHINGTON, BAILY WASHINGTON, JOHN PEYTON, & PETER DANIEL, Gent.

[Page 358 Apr. 2, 1755]

March Court 1755

JOSEPH a negro Man slave belonging to GERARD FOWKE was committed to the Goal of Stafford County by a Mittimus under the hand of MOTT DONIPHAN, Gent. for feloniously burning the House of the said Gerard was led to the Bar in Custody of the Sheriff & thereupon MOSELY BATTALEY, Gent. deputy Attorney of our Sovereign Lord the King brought an Indictment into Court against the said Joseph in these words, Be it remembered that on the second day of April 1755 Mosely Battaley comes into Court & gives the Court to understand that Joseph did on the 26th day of February 1755 at the Parish of St. Paul's with force & Arms feloniously, wickedly & maliciously burn & destroy the dwelling house of him the said GERARD FOWKE. And thereupon the said JOSEPH was publickly arraigned & pleaded not guilty & put himself upon the Court. The Witnesses were examined in open Court as well as what

344

the said Joseph could alledge in his defence, the Court do adjudge that the said Joseph be acquitted of the said Indictment.

MOTT DONIPHAN

At a Court held for Stafford County by virtue of a Commission of Oyer & Terminer the 2nd day of April 1755.

JOSEPH a negro man Slave belonging to GERARD FOWKE, Gent. who was committed to the Goal of this County by a Mittimus under the hand of MOTT DONIPHAN,

[Page 359 Apr. 2, 1755]

March Court 1755

Gent. was led to the Bar in Custody of the Sheriff & thereupon MOSELY BATTALEY, Gent., deputy Attorney for our Sovereign Lord the King brought into Court an Indictment against the said Joseph in these Words, Be it remembered that JOSEPH did on or about the 16th of January 1755 at the Parish of St. Paul's with force & arms in the Night did feloniously steal, take & carry away out of a Cart belonging to SAMUEL WASHINGTON one blue broad Cloath Coat to the Value of 20 Shillings the Property of the said Samuel. And thereupon the said Joseph was publickly arraingned & for plea said that he is guilty of the felony in the said Indictment mentioned. Therefore it is considered by the Court that the said Joseph be hanged by the neck until he is dead. And the Sheriff is ordered to make Execution of the said Joseph on Monday the fourteenth Instant between the hours of ten in the Morning & three in the afternoon & the said Joseph is valued by the Court to £50 current Money.

MOTT DONIPHAN

At a Court held for Stafford County 8th April 1755.

Present   MOTT DONIPHAN   JOHN PEYTON
                  PETER DANIEL   JOHN STITH
                  JOHN WASHINGTON

Administration on the Estate of WILLIAM SEBASTIAN decd. is granted JOHN SHORT, he having entered into bond with WILLIAM BERNARD, Gent. his Security. CHANDLER FOWKE, WILLIAM DYE, JOHN FITZHUGH, & WILLIAM BUNBURY Appraisers.

April Court 1755

Ordered that JOHN CHAMPE & COMPANY pay THOMAS MARKEN 170 pounds of Tobacco for two days attendance as an Evidence for them against SPINKS & for coming & returning 20 Miles twice.

Absent PETER DANIEL, Gent.

Administration on the Estate of MERRIMOND TILLER decd. is granted PETER DANIEL, Gent. having entered into Bond with JOHN SHORT his Security. RAWLEIGH CHINN, THOMAS MONROE, THOMAS HAY, & WILLIAM JORDAN, Appraisers.

Present PETER DANIEL, Gent.

Ordered that FRANCIS MCCARTY pay WILLIAM NAILOR 100 pounds of Tobacco for one days Attendance to prove the Will of CORNELIUS MCCARTY, decd. & for coming & returning 25 Miles.

Upon the Petition of HENRY BUSSEY he is set Levy free for the future.

Ordered that ABRAHAM BREDWELL pay SETH BOTTS 150 pounds of Tobacco for six days attendance as an Evidence for him against OCAIN.

Ordered that THOMAS HORNBUCKLE pay WILLIAM BURTON 150 pounds of Tobacco for six days attendance as an Evidence for him against GRIGSBY.

Ordered that JANE ENGLISH serve her Mistress CATHERINE OVERALL according to Law for having a bastard Child.

Then the Court adjourned till tomorrow morning 9 Oclock.
MOTT DONIPHAN

At a Court continued & held for Stafford County 9th of April 1755.

Present   MOTT DONIPHAN   JOHN PEYTON
                    HENRY FITZHUGH   THOMAS FITZHUGH
                    JOHN STITH

Suit on Petition. ANDREW GRANT agt. JOHN HOLLAND is dismist the Deft paying Costs.

Absent JOHN PEYTON, Gent.

Suit on Petition. JOHN PEYTON, Gent. agt. ROBERT EDWARDS. Judgment is granted the Pltf for £2.17.10 & Costs.

Suit on Petition. JOHN PEYTON, Gent. agt. JAMES MCDANIEL

[Page 361 Apr. 9, 1755]

April Court 1755

is dismist the Deft paying Costs.

Present JOHN PEYTON, Gent.

Suit on Petition. THOMAS CRAWFORD agt. JAMES MCDANIEL. Judgment is granted the Pltf for £1.12 & Costs.

Suit on Petition. ALEXANDER WOODROE & COMPANY agt. ANDREW KENNY. Judgment is granted the Pltfs for £3.14.9 with Costs & a Lawyer's Fee.

Action of Trespass. ANTHONY STROTHER agt. ANDREW EDWARDS. The Deft not appearing Judgment is granted the Pltf against him & WITHERS CONWAY his Security unless the Deft do appear at the next Court & answer the Pltf's Action.

Ordered that PATRICK GRADY pay RICHARD RANDALL 125 pounds of Tobacco for five days attendance as an Evidence for him against HORTON.

Action of Debt. BENJAMIN TYLER agt. RICHARD BROOX. The Deft not appearing an Attachment is granted against his Estate for 1,000 pounds of Tobacco & Cask & Costs returnable to the next Court.

Action of Debt. TRAVERSE COOKE agt. JAMES MCDANIEL. The Deft not appearing Judgment is granted the Pltf against him & JOHN STUART, Gent. his Security unless the Deft do appear at the next Court & answer the Pltf's Action.

Suit on Information. Our Lord the King against ELIZABETH MCABOY. The said Elizabeth pleaded not guilty & hath leave to give the special Matter in Evidence. MOSELY BATTALEY, Gent. Attorney for the King joined the Issue & the Trial is referred till the next Court.

Suit on Information. Our Lord the King against MARGARET DENNIS. The said Margaret pleaded not

April Court 1755

guilty with leave to give the special Matter in Evidence. MOSELY BATTALEY, Attorney for the King joined the Issue & the Trial is referred till the next Court.

Action of Trespass. CAIN WITHERS agt. WILLIAM LYNN. The Deft pleaded not guilty with leave to give the special Matter in Evidence. The Trial is referred till the next Court.

Absent HENRY FITZHUGH & THOMAS FITZHUGH, Gent.

Action of Trespass. WILLIAM ANDERSON agt. JOHN HAMILTON. The Deft confessed Judgment to the Pltf for £5.17 & Costs.

Action of Debt. JOHN LEECH agt. JOHN HAMILTON. The special Verdict in this Cause being argued the Court are of opinion that the Law is for the Pltf. It's thereupon considered that the Pltf recover of the Deft the Sum of £6.9 & his Costs.

Action of Debt. FRANCIS DADE agt. THOMAS MASSEY for £100 damage by Means of the Deft's breaking & entering the Close of the Pltf at the Parish of St. Paul's. The several Orders for a Survey in this Cause not being complied with, it's again ordered that the Surveyor in Company of an able Jury go upon the said Lands in Controversy & lay off the same as either Party would have it having regard to all Patents & Evidences as shall be produced by either of the Parties.

April Court 1755

Action of Debt. RICHARD FRISTOE, Senr. agt. JOHN KIRK. A Jury to wit WILLIAM NORTHCUT, WILLIAM ALLEN, JOHN PEYTON, WILLIAM BUSSELL, JAMES ONEAL, junr., JOHN TOBY, SPENCER BASHAW, MURDA MCCOY, SAMUEL MITCHELL, RICHARD RANDALL, WILLIAM MILLS, & JACOB JOHNSON. The Jury finds for the Pltf £9.6.6 & Costs.

Ejection Firma. MAXIMILLIAN ROBINSON, Gent. agt. JOHN RALLS for Lands & Appurtenances in the Parish of Overwharton. It's ordered that the Surveyor go upon the Lands in Controversy & lay off the same as either Party would have it having regard to all Patents & Evidences as shall be produced by either of the Parties.

Action of Trespass Assault & Battery. FRANCIS BROOX agt. DARBY OCAIN. A Jury to wit CAIN WITHERS, JOHN FITZHUGH, JAMES BERRY, JOHN SHORT, WILLIAM JOHNSON, JOHN WALLER, WILLIAM MATHENY, JOHN MASON, ALEXANDER DONIPHAN, HUSBANDFOOTE WHITECOTTON, ROBERT MANNON, & JOHN KIRK. The Jury finds for the Deft. The Deft is to recover of the Pltf his Costs.

Present HENRY FITZHUGH & THOMAS FITZHUGH, Gent.

Suit on Petition. ROBERT & EDWARD MAXWELLS agt. PETER BYRAM, junr. Judgment is granted the Pltfs for 631 pounds of Tobacco & Costs.

Action of Debt. PETER WIGGINGTON who as well for our Lord the King for the Use of the Church Wardens of Overwharton Parish as for himself prosecutors agt. JOHN HIWARDEN.

[Page 364 Apr. 9, 1755]

April Court 1755

The Jury finds for the Pltf 1,500 pounds of Tobacco & Costs.

Action of Trespass Assault & Battery. JOHN CANADY agt. DANIEL CHAMBERS. The Jury finds for the Deft. The Deft to recover his Costs from the Pltf.

Ordered that JOHN CANADAY pay WILLIAM BURTON 300 pounds of Tobacco for twelve days attendance as an Evidence for him against CHAMBERS.

Ordered that DANIEL CHAMBERS pay CATHERINE JEFFERICE 100 pounds of Tobacco for four days attendance as an Evidence for him at suit of CANADAY.

Ordered that DARBY OCAIN pay THOMAS CRAFFORD 475 pounds of Tobacco for nineteen days attendance as an Evidence for him against BROOX.

Ordered that DARBY OCAIN pay HENRY STUDDART 425 pounds of Tobacco for seventeen days attendance as an Evidence for him against BROOX.

Ordered that DARBY OCAIN pay RICHARD OCAIN 275 pounds of Tobacco for eleven days attendance as an Evidence for him against CLARK.

Suit on Petition. GUSTAVUS BROWN Esqr. agt. JACOB JOHNSON. Judgment is granted the Pltf against him for £4.19 with Costs & a Lawyer's Fee.

Ordered that GUSTAVUS BROWN, Esqr. pay JOHN SHORT 100 pounds of transfer Tobacco for four days attendance as an Evidence for him against JOHNSON.

[Page 365 Apr. 9, 1755]

April Court 1755

Action of Debt. ROBERT DREGHORN & COMPANY agt. JEREMIAH CARTER. It's considered by the Court that the Pltf recover of the Deft the Sum of £18.14 & their Costs.

Action of Debt. ROBERT WICKLIFF agt. WILLIAM PICKET. The Jury finds for the Pltf £9.15.9 debt & twenty Shillings & Costs.

Ordered that ROBERT WICKLIFF pay SAMUEL MITCHEL 375 pounds of Tobacco for fifteen days attendance as an Evidence for him against PICKETT.

Ordered that ROBERT WICKLIFF pay GEORGE WHITECOTTON 500 pounds of Tobacco for twenty days attendance as an Evidence for him against PICKETT.

Ordered that ROBERT WICKLIFF pay ANTHONY GARRARD 500 pounds of Tobacco for twenty days attendance as an Evidence for him against PICKETT.

Then the Court adjourned till tomorrow morning 9 Oclock.
MOTT DONIPHAN

[Page 366 Apr. 10, 1755]

April Court 1755

At a Court continued & held for Stafford County 10ᵗʰ. April 1755.

Present   MOTT DONIPHAN   JOHN PEYTON
                 JOHN WASHINGTON   BAILY WASHINGTON

Action of Trespass Assault & Battery. JOHN ADDISON agt. WILLIAM THOMAS. The Deft having pleaded not guilty the Trial is referred till the next Court.

350

Action of Trespass. CAIN WITHERS agt. PRESLY COX. The Replication in this Case is joined & the Trial is referred till the next Court.

Action of Debt. ROBERT ASHBY agt. HENRY WIGGINGTON. The Deft having pleaded that he owes nothing, the Trial is referred till the next Court.

Action of Debt. ROBERT ASHBY agt. ABRAHAM BREDWELL. The Deft having pleaded that he owes nothing, the Trial is referred till the next Court.

Action of Debt. MARY WISE agt. JOHN PEYTON. The special Verdict in this Cause being argued is adjudged for the Deft. It's farther considered by the Court that the Pltf take nothing by her Bill & that the Deft recover of the Pltf his Costs.

Action of Trespass. CATHERINE ASHBY by ROBERT ASHBY her next Friend agt. SAMUEL BREDWELL. The special Verdict in this Cause being argued is adjudged for the Deft. It's thereupon considered by the Court that the Pltf take nothing by her Bill & that the Pltf recover of the Deft his Costs.

Action of Trespass. SARAH MCCULLOUGH by JOSEPH MCCULLOUGH her next Friend agt. SAMUEL BREDWELL. The Errors in this Cause being argued are adjudged good. It's thereupon considered by the Court that the Judgment given in this suit be reversed and that the Deft recover of the Pltf his Costs.

Ejection Firma. JOHN ROUT agt. _____ [left blank] for Lands & Appurtenances in the Parish of Overwharton. JOHN WALLER, by JOHN PEYTON, Gent. is admitted Deft in the

[Page 367 Apr. 10, 1755]

April Court 1755

Room of the said _____ [left blank] pleaded not guilty and confessed Lease Entry & Ouster & agreed to insist only on the Title at Trial. The Trial is referred till the next Court.

Action of Trespass. JAMES YELTON agt. THOMAS SPALDING. A Jury to wit ANDREW EDWARDS, WILLIAM WREN, JOHN WHITING, JAMES WATSON, COLCLOUGH STRIBLING, HUMPHREY POPE, WILLIAM MILLS, WHARTON HOLLIDAY, WILLIAM RUSSELL, WILLIAM ALLEN, JOHN ARMSTRONG, & JOHN CANNON. The Jury finds for the Pltf £5 damage. The Deft moved for a new Trial which is granted him.

Ordered that JAMES YELTON pay JOHN PAYTON 425 pounds of Tobacco for 17 days attendance as an Evidence for him against SPALDING.

Ordered that THOMAS SPALDING pay PATIENCE MILLS 150 pounds of Tobacco for six days attendance as an Evidence for him at suit of YELTON.

Action of Debt. WILLIAM BLACK agt. SAMUEL WHITSON & JOSEPH CARTER. It's considered by the Court that the Pltf recover of the Deft the Sum of £13.1 with Interest from the 26th day of April 1752 till the same is paid & the Pltf agreed to stay Execution two Months.

Action of Trespass. ROBERT & EDWARD MAXWELLS agt. THOMAS HEATH. The Jury finds for the Pltf 1,410 pounds of crop Tobacco & Costs.

[Page 368 Apr. 10, 1755]

April Court 1755

Action of Trespass. ROBERT & EDWARD MAXWELLS agt. SAMUEL WHITSON. The Jury finds for the Pltf £7.11.10 & Costs. And HENRY TYLER who became special Bail for the Deft delivers him up in discharge of his Bail.

Action of Debt. WILLIAM CUNNINGHAME, ANDREW SLOWAN & COMPANY agt. JOHN THOMAS. The Deft confessed Judgment to the Pltfs for £20 & Costs. But this Judgment is to be discharged on payment of £10 with Interest from the sixth day of November 1753 till the same is paid.

Action of Trespass. JOHN WASHINGTON, Gent. agt. WINIFRED MASSEY Admx. of ROBERT MASSEY decd. The Deft having pleaded that the Intestate did not assume & that she hath fully administered. The Trial is referred till the next Court.

Action of Trespass. JOHN FITZHUGH agt. WINIFRED MASSEY Admx. of ROBERT MASSEY decd. The Deft having pleaded that the Intestate did not assume & that she hath fully administered. The Trial is referred till the next Court.

Action of Trespass. WILLIAM FITZHUGH & FRANCIS THORNTON Esqr. acting Exors. of GILSON BERRYMAN agt. WINIFRED MASSEY Admx. of ROBERT MASSEY decd. The Deft having pleaded that the Intestate did not assume & that she hath fully administered the Trial is referred till the next Court.

Action of Trespass. JOHN STORKE, Gent. agt. WINIFRED MASSEY Admx. of ROBERT MASSEY decd. The Deft having pleaded that the Intestate did not assume & that she hath fully administered the Trial is referred till the next Court.

Suit on Petition. JOHN BERRY agt. BENJAMIN CHANCY. Judgment

[Page 369 Apr. 10, 1755]

April Court 1755

is granted the Pltf for £4 & Costs.

Ordered that JAMES BERRY pay JOHN LEWRIGHT 200 pounds of Tobacco for eight days attendance as an evidence for him against CHANCY.

Action of Debt. THOMAS HOWARD agt. JOHN BLACK & GOWRY WAUGH. The Defts having pleaded payment the Trial is referred till the next Court.

Action of Trespass. RICHARD LEE Esqr. agt. CAIN WITHERS. The Deft for Plea saith that he did not assume. The Trial is referred till the next Court.

Action of Trespass. ANDREW GRANT agt. OSMOND CHRISMOND. The Deft confessed Judgment to the Pltf for _____ [left blank]. It's considered by the Court that the Pltf recover the same of the Deft & his Costs.

Action of Trespass. JANE RIGSBY Excx. of the last Will & Testament of ALEXANDER RIGSBY decd. agt. WINIFRED MASSEY Admx. of ROBERT MASSEY decd. The Deft having pleaded that the Intestate did not assume & that she hath fully administered, the Trial is referred till the next Court.

Action of Trespass Assault & Battery. JOHN HURLY agt. THOMAS PRATT. The Deft not appearing Judgment against him & WITHERS CONWAY is confirmed & a Writ of Enquiry of damages is to be executed the next Court.

Action of Debt. GEORGE WALLER & WILLIAM ALLEN acting Exors. of EDWARD WALLER decd. agt. JOHN MURDOCK. The Deft having filed his plea, the Pltfs have time till the next Court to consider thereof.

Action of Trespass. WILLIAM ALLEN agt. JOSEPH BLACK. The Deft not appearing the Judgment against him & ELIAS HORE his Security is confirmed & a Writ of Enquiry of damges is to be executed the next Court.

April Court 1755

Action of Trespass. ALEXANDER WOODROE & COMPANY agt. JOSEPH WINLOCK. The Deft not appearing the Judgment against him & WILLIAM LUNSFORD his Security is confirmed & a Writ of Enquiry of damges is to be executed the next Court.

Suit on Scire Facias. ELIZABETH MCABOY agt. JAMES YELTON. The said James having pleaded payment with Leave to give the special Matter in Evidence the Trial is referred till the next Court.

Suit on Scire Facias. HENRY WIGGINGTON agt. ALEXANDER GRANT. The Sheriff having twice returned that the said Alexander was not to be found. It's thereupon considered by the Court that the said Henry have Execution against the said Alexander for 482 pounds of Tobacco & 179 pounds of Tobacco & Costs.

Action of Debt. JACOB WILLIAMS agt. ANDREW KENNY. The Deft confessed Judgment to the Pltf for £8.12 & Costs. And the Pltf prayed that the Deft might be in Execution which is granted.

Action of Debt. ALEXANDER & DANIEL CAMPBELLS agt. FRANCIS MARTYN, JOHN CUBBAGE, JAMES HEFFERNON. The Defts confessed Judgment to the Pltf for £22 & Costs. But this Judgment is to be discharged on paymnent of £11 with Interest from the first day of September 1753 till the same is paid & 107 pounds of Tobacco & fifteen Shillings or 150 pounds of Tobacco the Costs of a Suit mentioned in the Bond. Endorsed on the Bond, paid 12th May 1754--£2.15.

Action of Trespass. ELIZABETH MCABOY agt. JOHN MAY. The Deft having pleaded not guilty the Trial is referred till the next Court.

Action of Trespass. ROBERT & EDWARD MAXWELLS agt. RICHARD ROGERS. A Plurias Capias is ordered returnable to the next Court.

April Court 1755

Suit on Petition. ROBERT & EDWARD MAXWELLS agt. WILLIAM MASON. Judgment is granted the Pltfs for 378 pounds of crop Tobacco & £1.9.11 & Costs.

Suit on Petition. ROBERT & EDWARD MAXWELLS agt. JAMES SUDDUTH. Judgment is granted the Pltfs for 282 pounds of crop Tobacco & Costs.

Action of Debt. THOMAS FLEEMAN agt. JOHN THOMAS & others. The Defts for Plea say they owe nothing. The Trial is referred till the next Court.

Action of Trespass. ANDREW GRANT agt. JOHN LIMMOT. The Deft not appearing the Judgment against him & JACOB JOHNSON is confirmed & a Writ of Enquiry of Damages is to be executed the next Court.

Action of Trespass. ANDREW GRANT agt. WILLIAM THORNBURY is dismist the Deft paying Costs.

Suit on Scire Facias. NATHANIEL CHAPMAN and others Exors. of LAWRENCE WASHINGTON, Gent. decd. agt. WILLIAM FITZHUGH, Gent. The said William having pleaded that he owes nothing the said Nathaniel & others joined the Issue & the Trial is referred till the next Court.

Action of Debt. WHIDDON WALLACE agt. SIMON PERRIE & THOMAS FLETCHER. The Defts having pleaded payment the Trial is referred till the next Court.

Action of Debt. JOHN PEYTON, Gent. agt. SIMON STACY & PETER RUFNER. The Defts not appearing Judgment is confirmed to the Pltf for £6.3 & 632 pounds of crop Tobacco & Costs.

Action of Trespass Assault & Battery. JOHN BAKER agt. WILLIAM SHUMATE. The Deft having pleaded not guilty the Trial is referred till the next Court.

Action of Debt. CHARLES STUART & COMPANY agt. ALEXANDER DOUGLASS. The Deft having pleaded Payment the Trial is referred til the next Court.

April Court 1755

Action of Trespass. ANDREW GRANT agt. ALEXANDER MURPHY. The Deft not appearing Judgment against him & JOHN ADDISON his Security is confirmed & a Writ of Enquiry of damages is to be executed the next Court.

Action of Debt. GUSTAVUS BROWN, Esqr. agt. ANDREW EDWARDS. The Deft having pleaded Payment the Trial is referred till the next Court.

Action of Debt. JOHN SHORT agt. JOHN THOMAS. The Deft confessed Judgment to the Pltf for £8.13.6 & Costs.

JOSEPH WHITE being presented by the Grandjury for swearing one Oath & summoned failed to appear, whereupon it is ordered that the said Joseph pay to the Churchwardens of Overwharton Parish (for the use of the Poor) five Shilllings or 50 pounds of Tobacco & Costs.

WHARTON HOLIDAY being presented by the Grandjury for swearing two Oaths it is ordered that he pay to the Churchwardens of Overwharton Parish (for the use of the Poor) ten Shilllings or 100 pounds of Tobacco & Costs.

Action of Trespass. JEOFFRY JOHNSON agt. DANIEL CHAMBERS Exor. of JOSEPH CHAMBERS, decd. The Deft for Plea saith the Testator did not assume & that he hath fully administered. The Trial is referred till the next Court.

Action of Debt. CHARLES ASHTON, Gent. agt. JOHN FITZHUGH. The Deft having pleaded payment the Trial is referred till next Court.

Action of Trespass. ALEXANDER BROWN & COMPANY agt. ROBERT STUART. The Deft not appearing the Judgment against him & BALDWYN DADE his Security is confirmed & a Writ of Enquiry of damages is to be executed next Court.

[Page 373 Apr. 10, 1755]

April Court 1755

Action of Trespass Assault & Battery. CHRISTOPHER THRELKELD, Junr. agt. JOHN PAYTON. The Deft having pleaded not guilty with leave to give the special Matter in Evidence the Trial is referred till the next Court.

Action of Trespass. CHRISTOPHER THRELKELD, Junr. agt. JOHN PAYTON. The Deft having pleaded not guilty with leave to give the special Matter in Evidence the Trial is referred till the next Court.

Action of Debt. JOHN PEYTON, Gent. agt. FRANCIS DAY. The Deft not appearing upon an Attachment in this Suit it's considered by the Court that the Pltf recover of the said Deft the Sum of £5.9 & 200 pounds of crop Tobacco & Costs. And the Sheriff having returned the Attachment executed on a Feather Bed, Horse & some Lumber, it's ordered that he sell the same & satisfy the above Judgment.

Action of Trespass. JOHN PEYTON, Gent. agt. JOSEPH DUNAWAY. The Deft not appearing the Judgment against him & NICHOLAS DULIN & JOHN NIXON his Securities is confirmed & a Writ of Enquiry of damages is to be executed the next Court.

Action of Debt. JOHN PEYTON, Gent. agt. THOMAS & WILLIAM JORDANS. The Deft Thomas not being taken, it's ordered that a plurias capias issue against him returnable to the next Court.

Action of Debt. CHARLES ASHTON Admr. &c. of MARY ASHTON decd. agt. JOHN THOMAS. WITHERS CONWAY undertook that if the Deft should be condemned in this Action he would pay the Condemnation for him or surrender his Body to Prison & the Deft having filed his plea the Trial is referred till the next Court.

Suit on Petition. JOHN STORK, Gent. agt. JOHN JONES. Judgment is granted the Pltf for £4.18.6

April Court 1755

with Costs & a Lawyer's Fee.

Suit on Petition. ROBERT & EDWARD MAXWELLS agt. WEEDON SMITH. Judgment is granted the Pltfs for 365 pounds of crop Tobacco & Costs.

Suit on Petition. JOHN ARMSTRONG agt. WILLIAM SWETMAN. Judgment is granted the Pltf for £1.12.5 half penny with Costs & a Lawyer's Fee.

Action of Debt. JOHN PEYTON, Gent. agt. JAMES MCDANIEL is dismist the Deft paying Costs.

Action of Trespass. WILLIAM ALLEN, Attorney of HOLDBROOK agt. JAMES CUMBERFORD is dismist & the Pltf is ordered to pay Costs.

Action of Trespass. PATRICK & WILLIAM BOGLES & COMPANY agt. WILLIAM THORNBURY. The Deft not appearing the Judgment against him & WITHERS CONWAY his Security is confirmed & a Writ of Enquiry of damages is to be executed the next Court.

In the Suit on Attachment obtained by ROBERT & EDWARD MAXWELLS against WILLIAM BUTLER. It's ordered that an Attachment issue against the Garnishee returnable to the next Court.

Then the Court adjourned till Court in Course.
MOTT DONIPHAN

www.ingramcontent.com/pod-product-compliance
Lightning Source LLC
Chambersburg PA
CBHW070542270326
41926CB00013B/2173